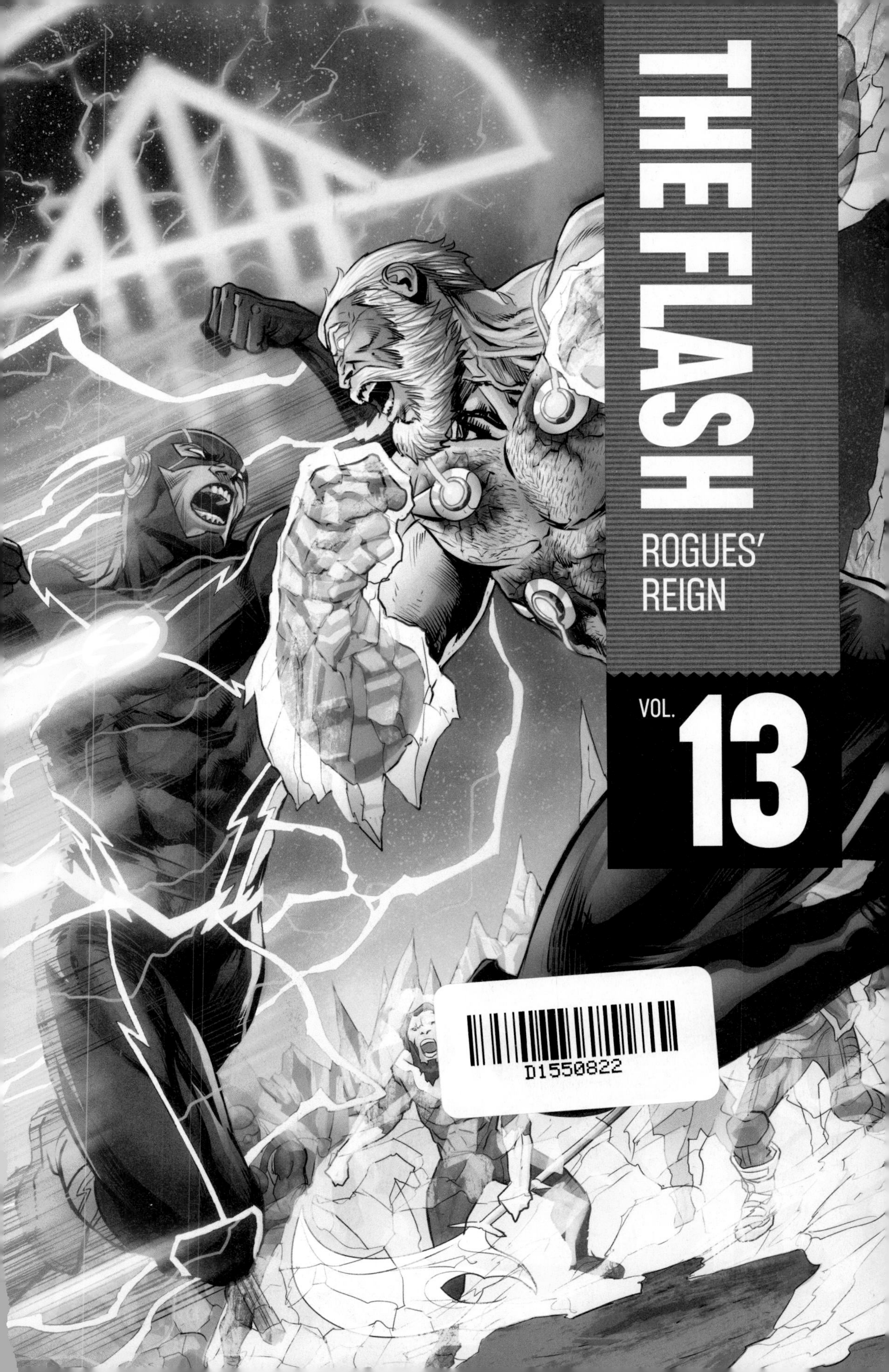
THE FLASH
ROGUES' REIGN
VOL. 13

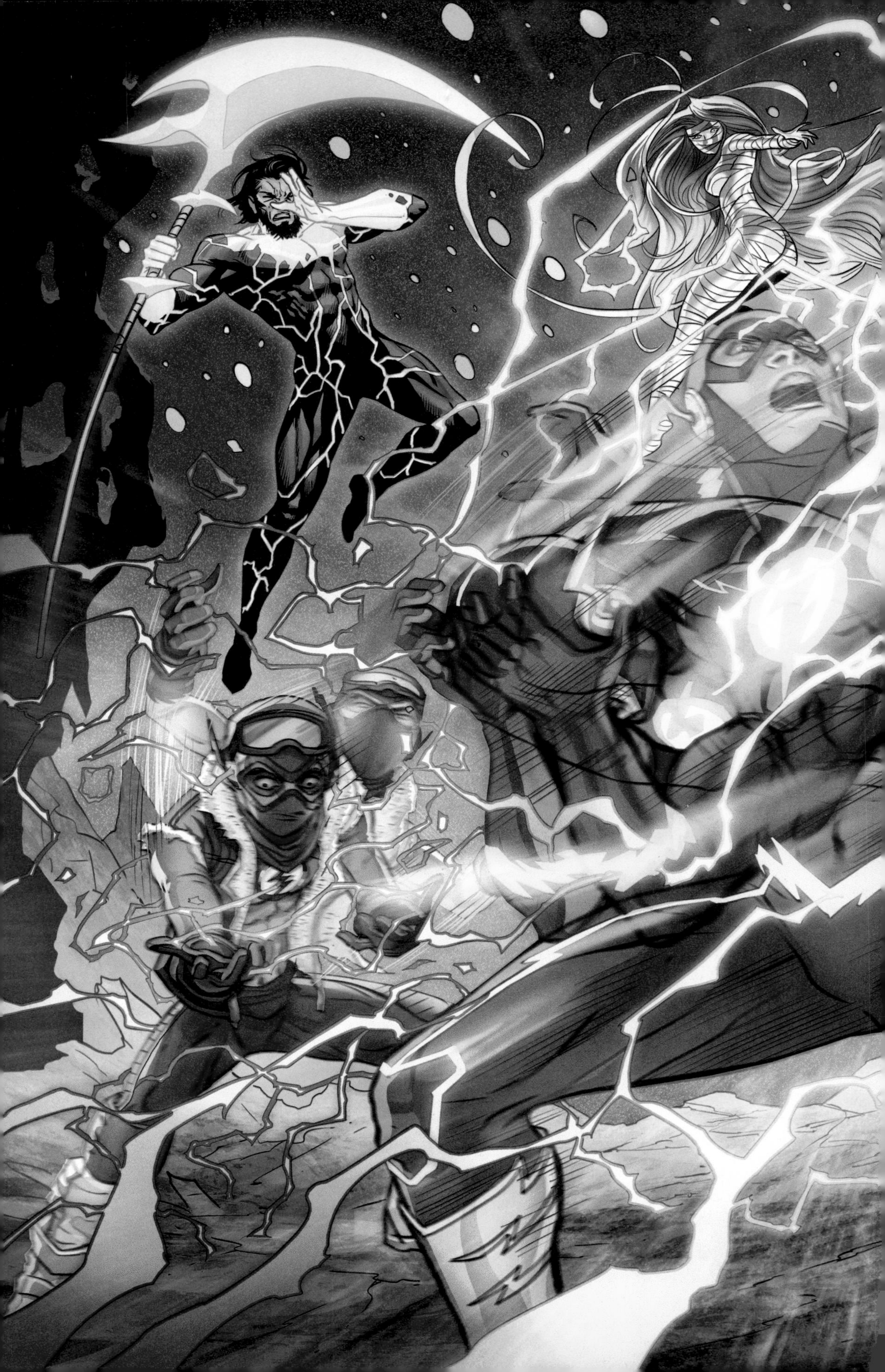

THE FLASH
ROGUES' REIGN

writer
JOSHUA WILLIAMSON

pencillers
RAFA SANDOVAL
CHRISTIAN DUCE

inkers
JORDI TARRAGONA
RAFA SANDOVAL
CHRISTIAN DUCE

colorists
ARIF PRIANTO
HI-FI
LUIS GUERRERO

letterer
STEVE WANDS

collection cover artists
RAFA SANDOVAL,
JORDI TARRAGONA,
and TOMEU MOREY

VOL. **13**

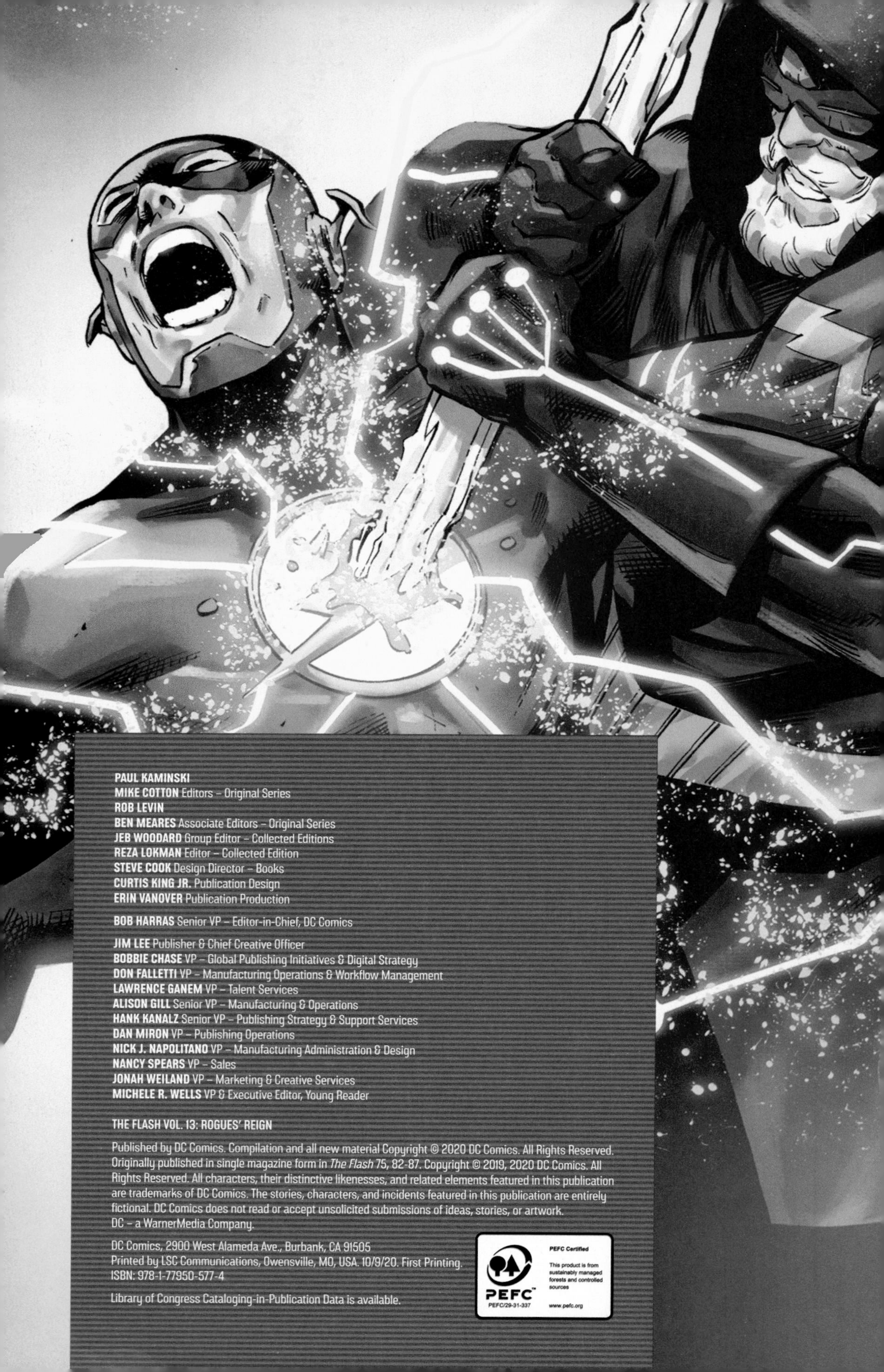

PAUL KAMINSKI
MIKE COTTON Editors – Original Series
ROB LEVIN
BEN MEARES Associate Editors – Original Series
JEB WOODARD Group Editor – Collected Editions
REZA LOKMAN Editor – Collected Edition
STEVE COOK Design Director – Books
CURTIS KING JR. Publication Design
ERIN VANOVER Publication Production

BOB HARRAS Senior VP – Editor-in-Chief, DC Comics

JIM LEE Publisher & Chief Creative Officer
BOBBIE CHASE VP – Global Publishing Initiatives & Digital Strategy
DON FALLETTI VP – Manufacturing Operations & Workflow Management
LAWRENCE GANEM VP – Talent Services
ALISON GILL Senior VP – Manufacturing & Operations
HANK KANALZ Senior VP – Publishing Strategy & Support Services
DAN MIRON VP – Publishing Operations
NICK J. NAPOLITANO VP – Manufacturing Administration & Design
NANCY SPEARS VP – Sales
JONAH WEILAND VP – Marketing & Creative Services
MICHELE R. WELLS VP & Executive Editor, Young Reader

THE FLASH VOL. 13: ROGUES' REIGN

DC Comics, 2900 West Alameda Ave., Burbank, CA 91505
Printed by LSC Communications, Owensville, MO, USA. 10/9/20. First Printing.
ISBN: 978-1-77950-577-4

Library of Congress Cataloging-in-Publication Data is available.

PEFC
PEFC/29-31-337
PEFC Certified
This product is from sustainably managed forests and controlled sources
www.pefc.org

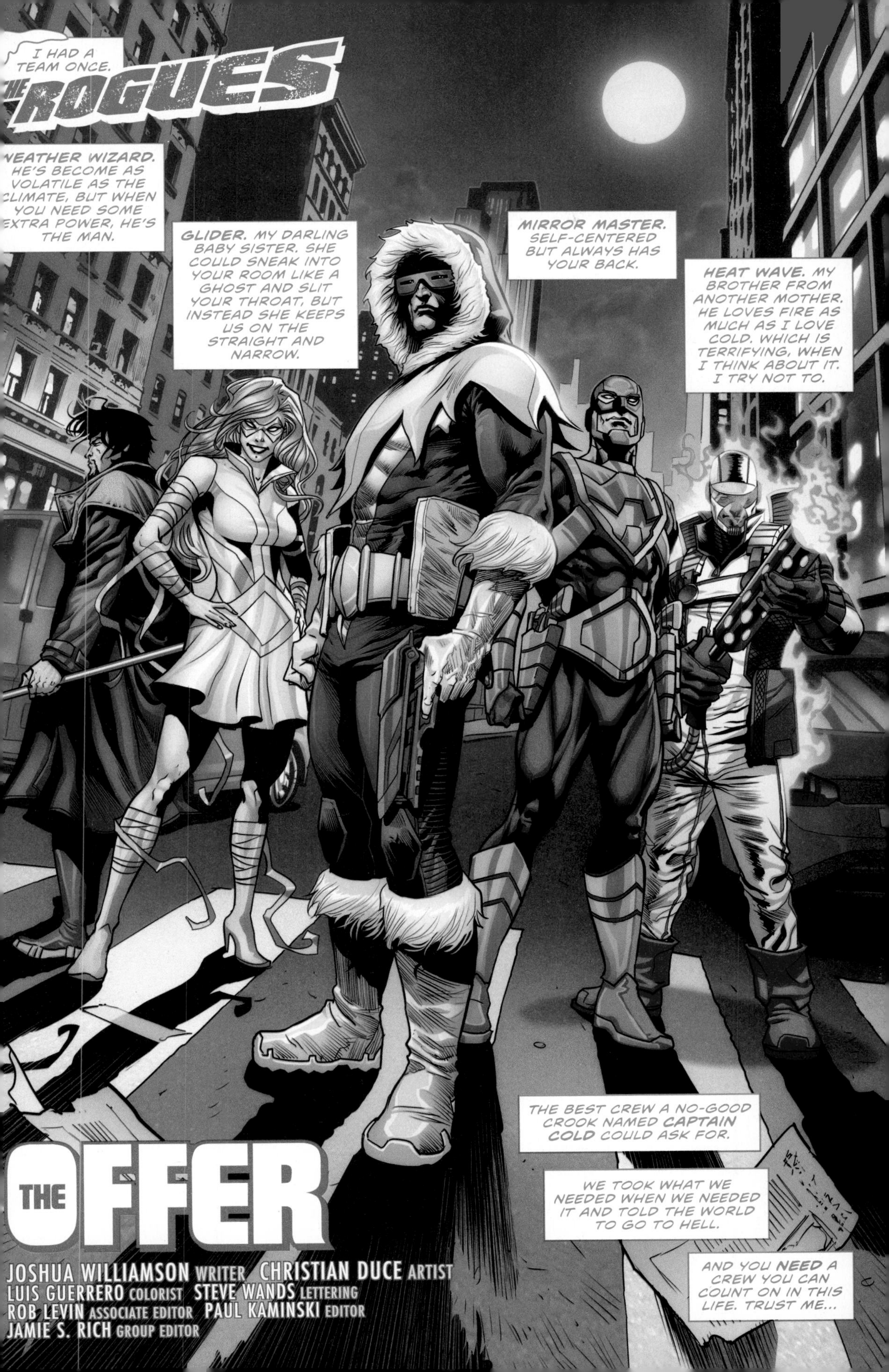
I HAD A TEAM ONCE.
THE ROGUES
WEATHER WIZARD. HE'S BECOME AS VOLATILE AS THE CLIMATE, BUT WHEN YOU NEED SOME EXTRA POWER, HE'S THE MAN.
GLIDER. MY DARLING BABY SISTER. SHE COULD SNEAK INTO YOUR ROOM LIKE A GHOST AND SLIT YOUR THROAT, BUT INSTEAD SHE KEEPS US ON THE STRAIGHT AND NARROW.
MIRROR MASTER. SELF-CENTERED BUT ALWAYS HAS YOUR BACK.
HEAT WAVE. MY BROTHER FROM ANOTHER MOTHER. HE LOVES FIRE AS MUCH AS I LOVE COLD. WHICH IS TERRIFYING, WHEN I THINK ABOUT IT. I TRY NOT TO.
THE BEST CREW A NO-GOOD CROOK NAMED CAPTAIN COLD COULD ASK FOR.
WE TOOK WHAT WE NEEDED WHEN WE NEEDED IT AND TOLD THE WORLD TO GO TO HELL.
AND YOU NEED A CREW YOU CAN COUNT ON IN THIS LIFE. TRUST ME...
THE OFFER
JOSHUA WILLIAMSON WRITER CHRISTIAN DUCE ARTIST
LUIS GUERRERO COLORIST STEVE WANDS LETTERING
ROB LEVIN ASSOCIATE EDITOR PAUL KAMINSKI EDITOR
JAMIE S. RICH GROUP EDITOR

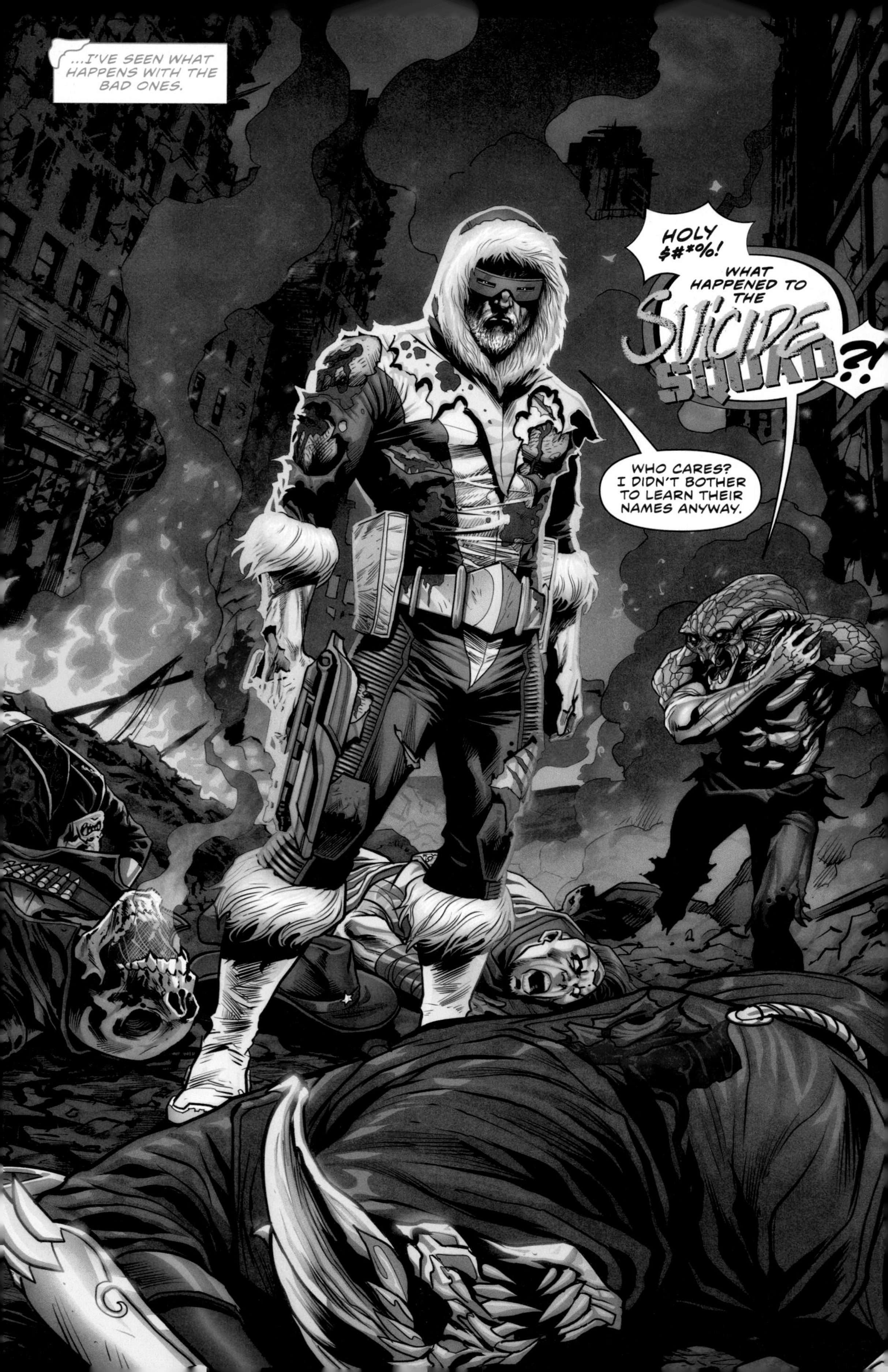
...I'VE SEEN WHAT HAPPENS WITH THE BAD ONES.
HOLY $#*%! WHAT HAPPENED TO THE SUICIDE SQUAD?!
WHO CARES? I DIDN'T BOTHER TO LEARN THEIR NAMES ANYWAY.

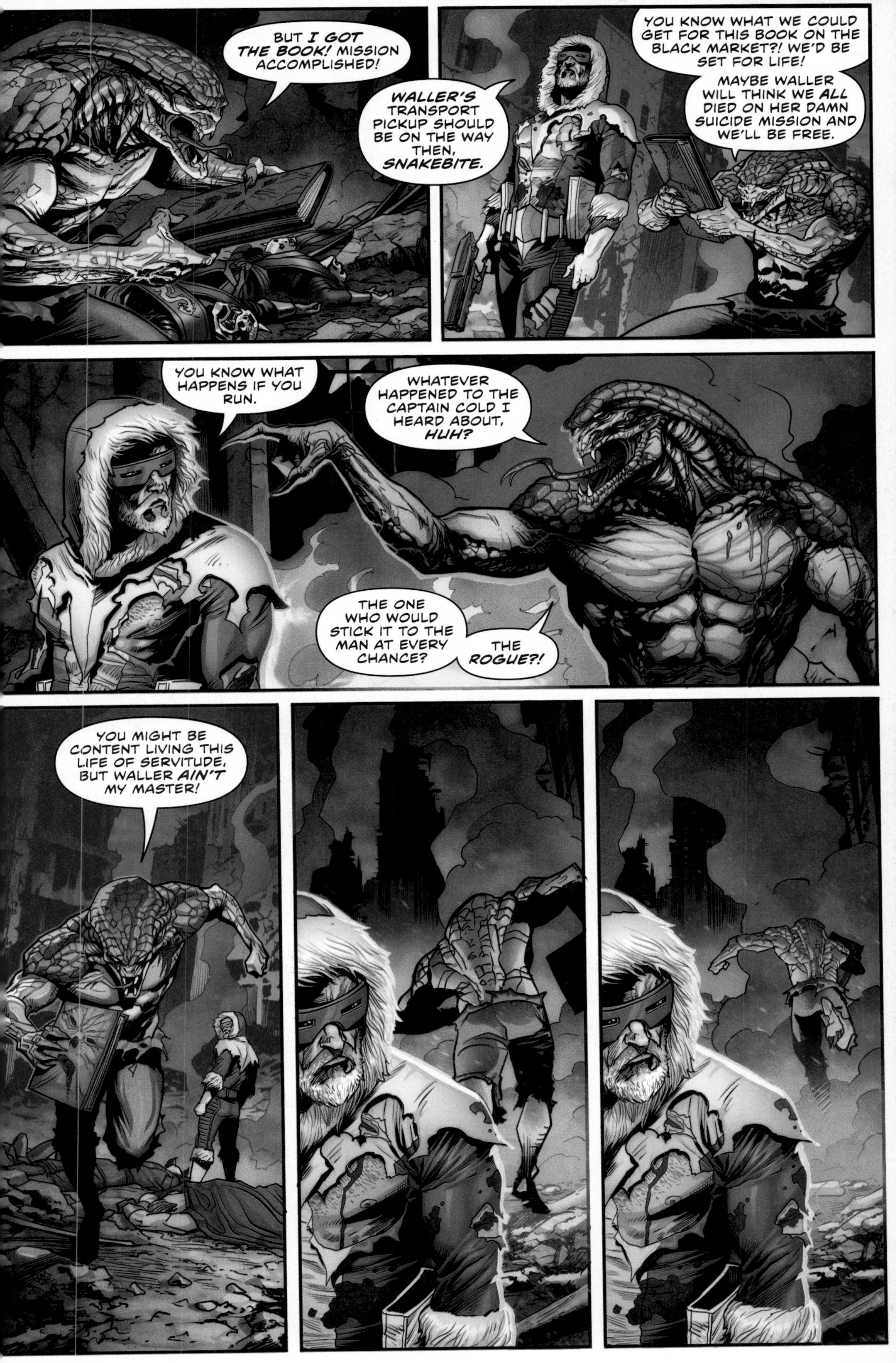
BUT I GOT THE BOOK! MISSION ACCOMPLISHED!
WALLER'S TRANSPORT PICKUP SHOULD BE ON THE WAY THEN, SNAKEBITE.
YOU KNOW WHAT WE COULD GET FOR THIS BOOK ON THE BLACK MARKET?! WE'D BE SET FOR LIFE!
MAYBE WALLER WILL THINK WE ALL DIED ON HER DAMN SUICIDE MISSION AND WE'LL BE FREE.
YOU KNOW WHAT HAPPENS IF YOU RUN.
WHATEVER HAPPENED TO THE CAPTAIN COLD I HEARD ABOUT, HUH?
THE ONE WHO WOULD STICK IT TO THE MAN AT EVERY CHANCE?
THE ROGUE?!
YOU MIGHT BE CONTENT LIVING THIS LIFE OF SERVITUDE, BUT WALLER AIN'T MY MASTER!

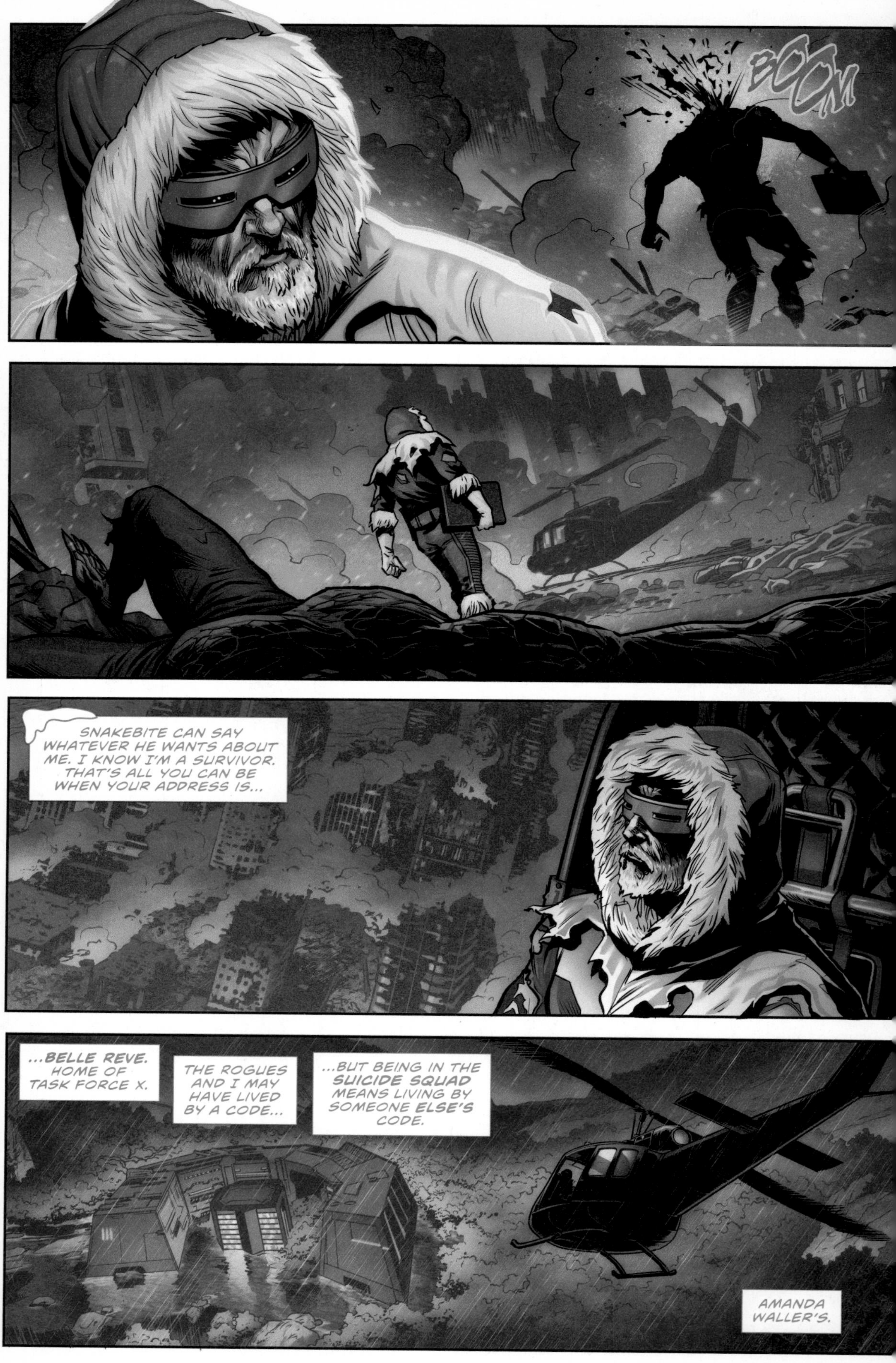
BOOM
SNAKEBITE CAN SAY WHATEVER HE WANTS ABOUT ME. I KNOW I'M A SURVIVOR. THAT'S ALL YOU CAN BE WHEN YOUR ADDRESS IS...
...BELLE REVE. HOME OF TASK FORCE X.
THE ROGUES AND I MAY HAVE LIVED BY A CODE...
...BUT BEING IN THE SUICIDE SQUAD MEANS LIVING BY SOMEONE ELSE'S CODE.
AMANDA WALLER'S.

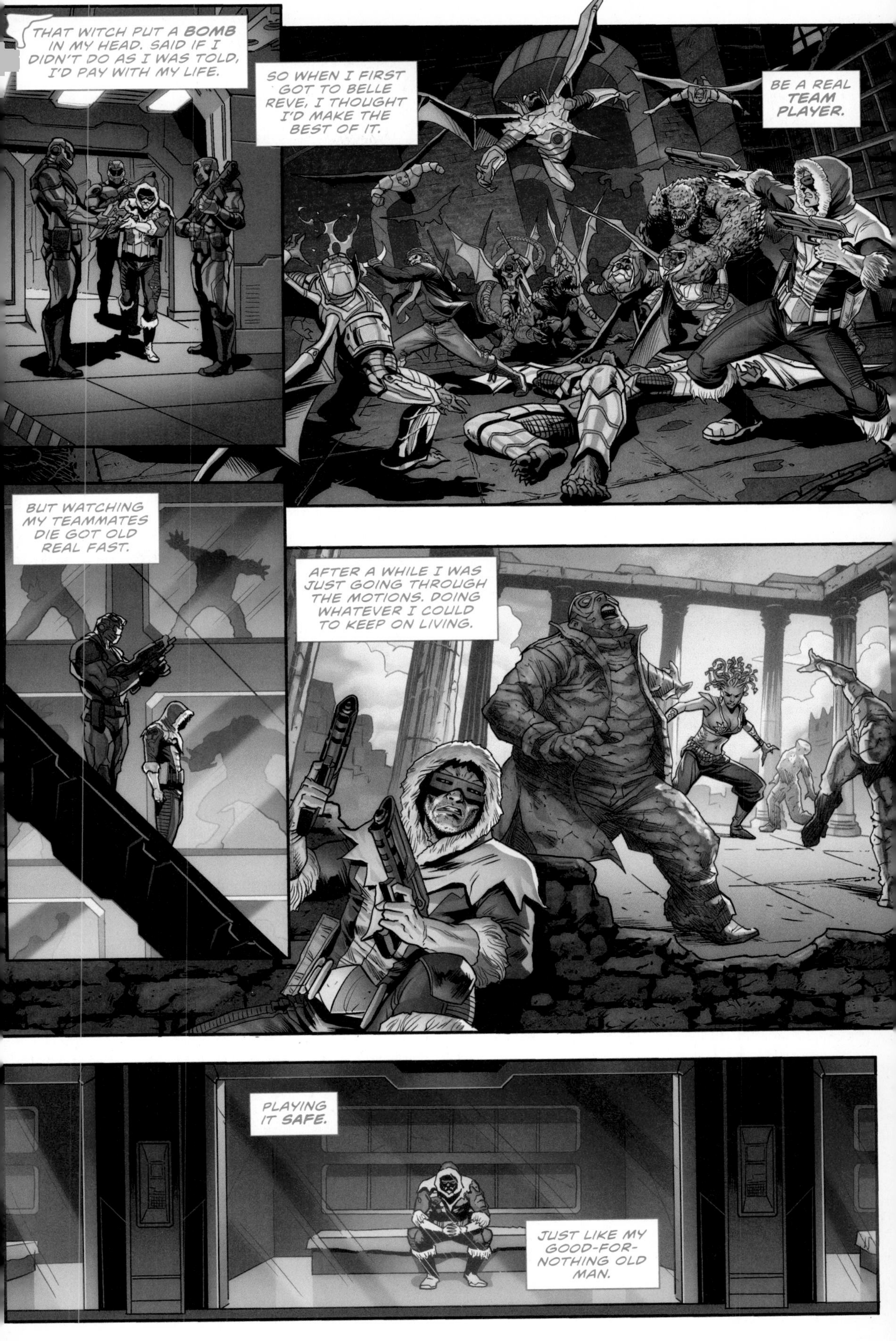
THAT WITCH PUT A BOMB IN MY HEAD. SAID IF I DIDN'T DO AS I WAS TOLD, I'D PAY WITH MY LIFE.
SO WHEN I FIRST GOT TO BELLE REVE, I THOUGHT I'D MAKE THE BEST OF IT.
BE A REAL TEAM PLAYER.
BUT WATCHING MY TEAMMATES DIE GOT OLD REAL FAST.
AFTER A WHILE I WAS JUST GOING THROUGH THE MOTIONS. DOING WHATEVER I COULD TO KEEP ON LIVING.
PLAYING IT SAFE.
JUST LIKE MY GOOD-FOR-NOTHING OLD MAN.

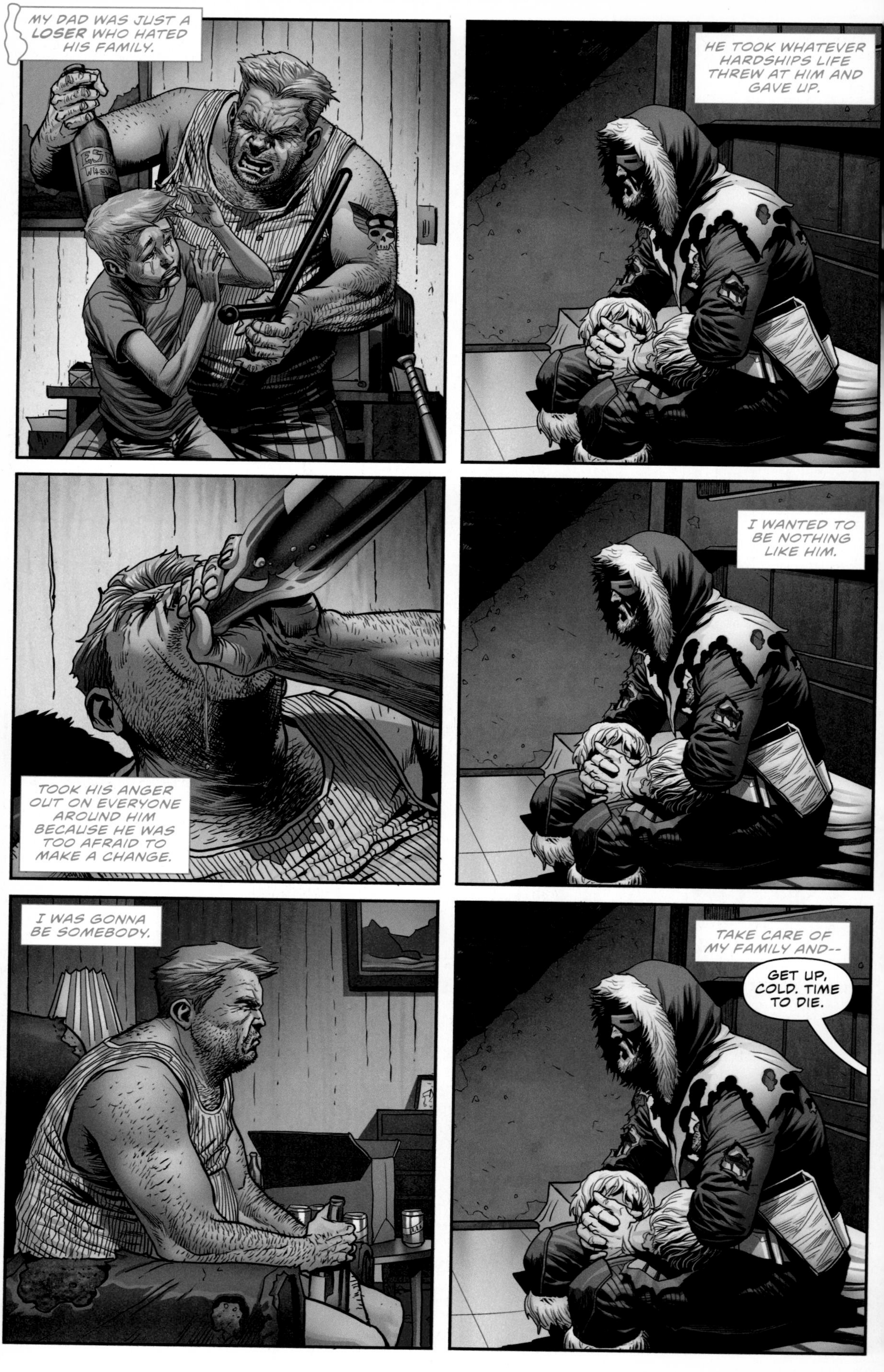
MY DAD WAS JUST A LOSER WHO HATED HIS FAMILY.
HE TOOK WHATEVER HARDSHIPS LIFE THREW AT HIM AND GAVE UP.
TOOK HIS ANGER OUT ON EVERYONE AROUND HIM BECAUSE HE WAS TOO AFRAID TO MAKE A CHANGE.
I WANTED TO BE NOTHING LIKE HIM.
I WAS GONNA BE SOMEBODY.
TAKE CARE OF MY FAMILY AND--
GET UP, COLD. TIME TO DIE.

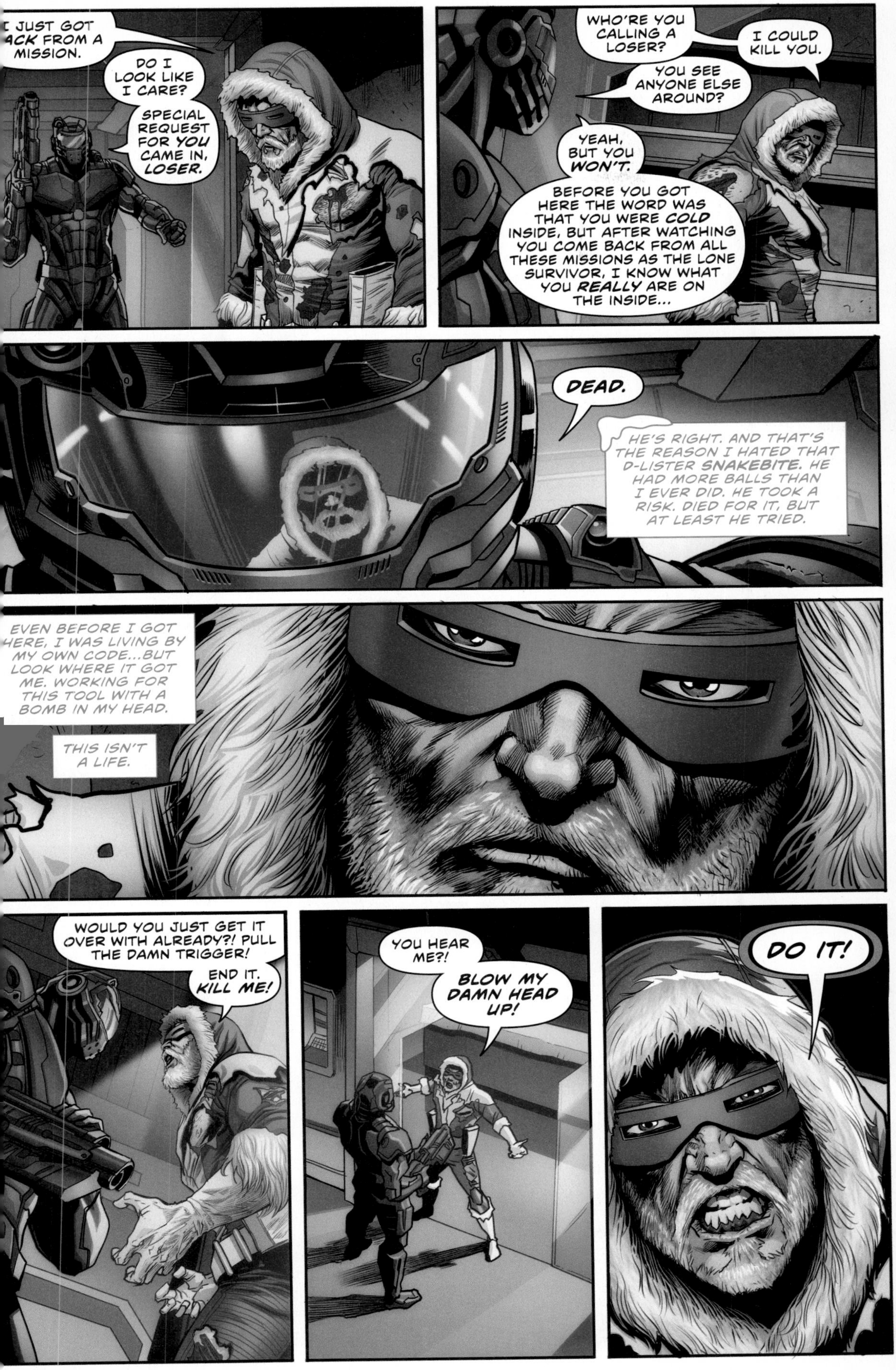
I JUST GOT BACK FROM A MISSION.
DO I LOOK LIKE I CARE?
SPECIAL REQUEST FOR YOU CAME IN, LOSER.
WHO'RE YOU CALLING A LOSER?
I COULD KILL YOU.
YOU SEE ANYONE ELSE AROUND?
YEAH, BUT YOU WON'T.
BEFORE YOU GOT HERE THE WORD WAS THAT YOU WERE COLD INSIDE, BUT AFTER WATCHING YOU COME BACK FROM ALL THESE MISSIONS AS THE LONE SURVIVOR, I KNOW WHAT YOU REALLY ARE ON THE INSIDE...
DEAD.
HE'S RIGHT. AND THAT'S THE REASON I HATED THAT D-LISTER SNAKEBITE. HE HAD MORE BALLS THAN I EVER DID. HE TOOK A RISK. DIED FOR IT, BUT AT LEAST HE TRIED.
EVEN BEFORE I GOT HERE, I WAS LIVING BY MY OWN CODE...BUT LOOK WHERE IT GOT ME. WORKING FOR THIS TOOL WITH A BOMB IN MY HEAD.
THIS ISN'T A LIFE.
WOULD YOU JUST GET IT OVER WITH ALREADY?! PULL THE DAMN TRIGGER!
END IT. KILL ME!
YOU HEAR ME?!
BLOW MY DAMN HEAD UP!
DO IT!

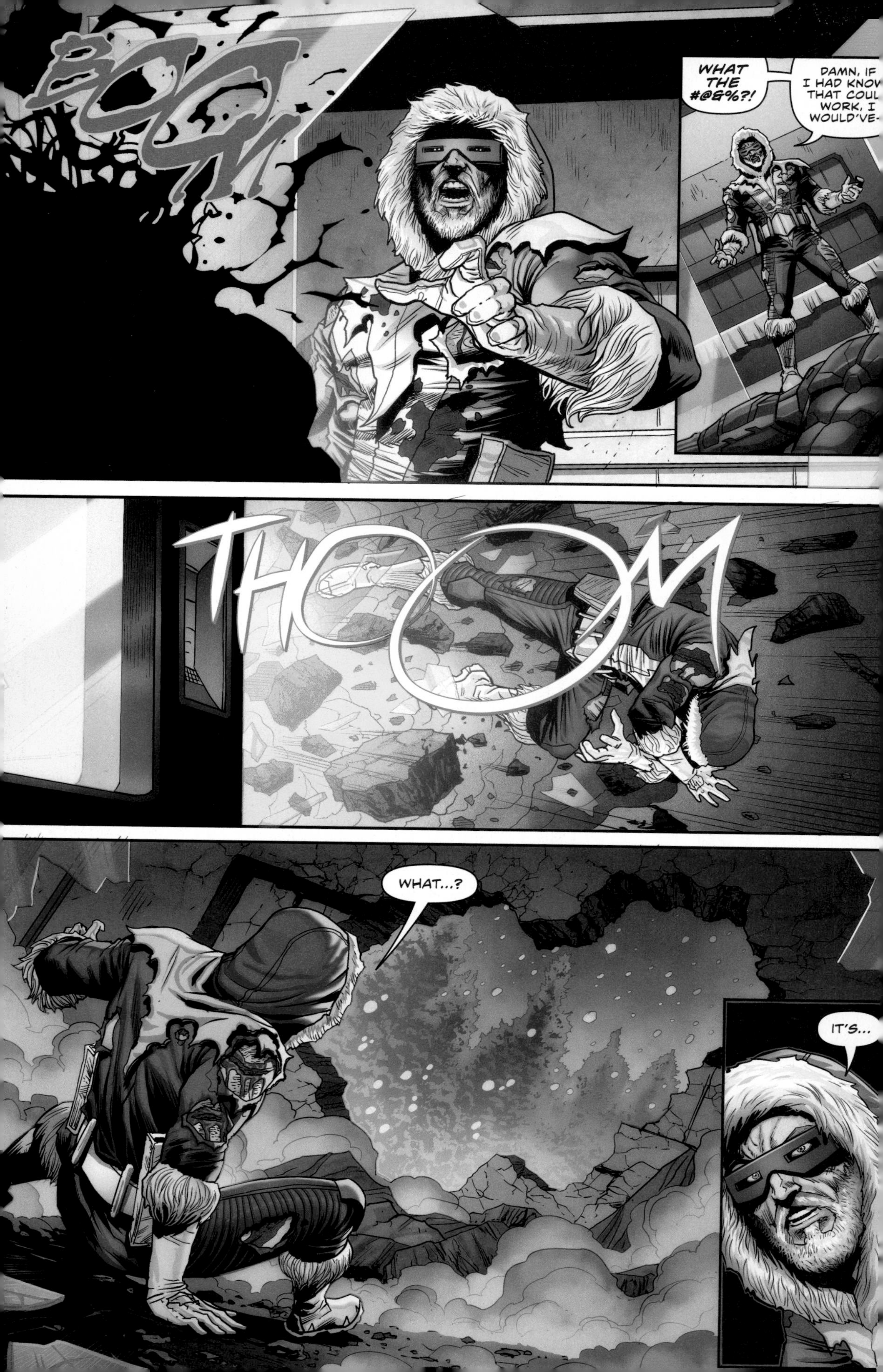
BOOM
WHAT THE #@&%?!
DAMN, IF I HAD KNOW THAT COUL WORK, I WOULD'VE-
THOOM
WHAT...?
IT'S...

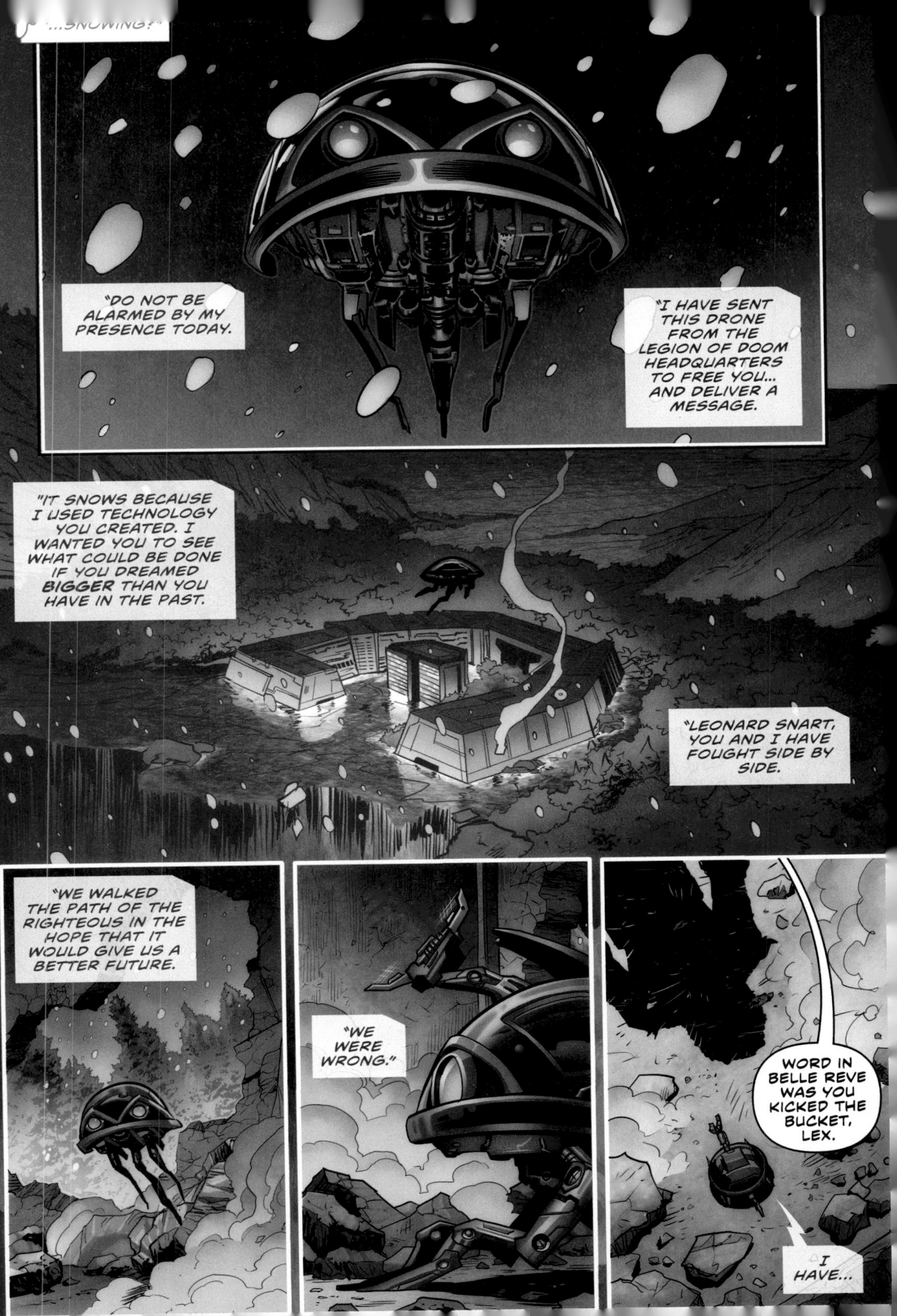
"...SNOWING?"
"DO NOT BE ALARMED BY MY PRESENCE TODAY.
"I HAVE SENT THIS DRONE FROM THE LEGION OF DOOM HEADQUARTERS TO FREE YOU... AND DELIVER A MESSAGE.
"IT SNOWS BECAUSE I USED TECHNOLOGY YOU CREATED. I WANTED YOU TO SEE WHAT COULD BE DONE IF YOU DREAMED BIGGER THAN YOU HAVE IN THE PAST.
"LEONARD SNART, YOU AND I HAVE FOUGHT SIDE BY SIDE.
"WE WALKED THE PATH OF THE RIGHTEOUS IN THE HOPE THAT IT WOULD GIVE US A BETTER FUTURE.
"WE WERE WRONG."
WORD IN BELLE REVE WAS YOU KICKED THE BUCKET, LEX.
I HAVE...

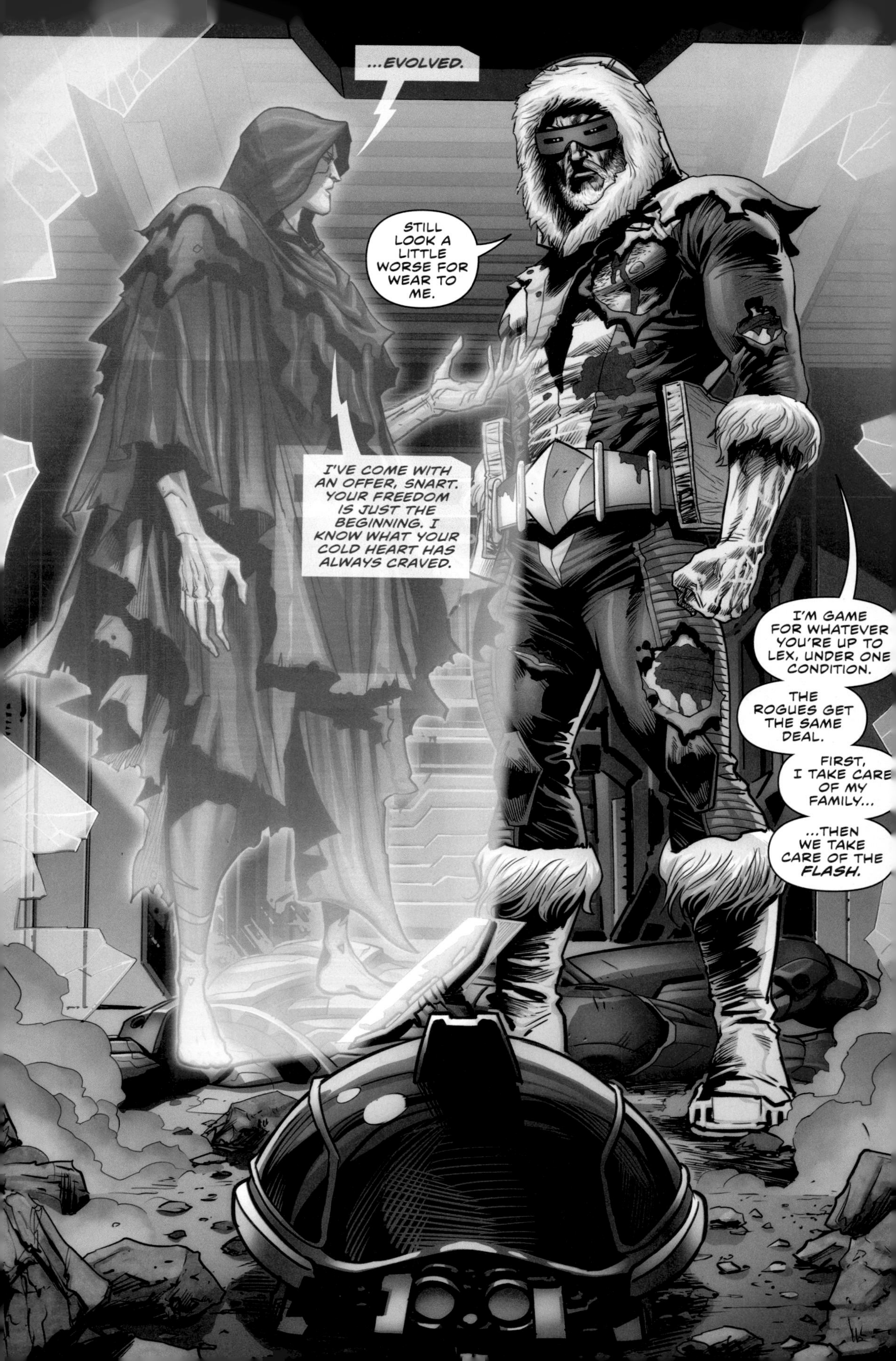
...EVOLVED.
STILL LOOK A LITTLE WORSE FOR WEAR TO ME.
I'VE COME WITH AN OFFER, SNART. YOUR FREEDOM IS JUST THE BEGINNING. I KNOW WHAT YOUR COLD HEART HAS ALWAYS CRAVED.
I'M GAME FOR WHATEVER YOU'RE UP TO LEX, UNDER ONE CONDITION.
THE ROGUES GET THE SAME DEAL.
FIRST, I TAKE CARE OF MY FAMILY...
...THEN WE TAKE CARE OF THE FLASH.

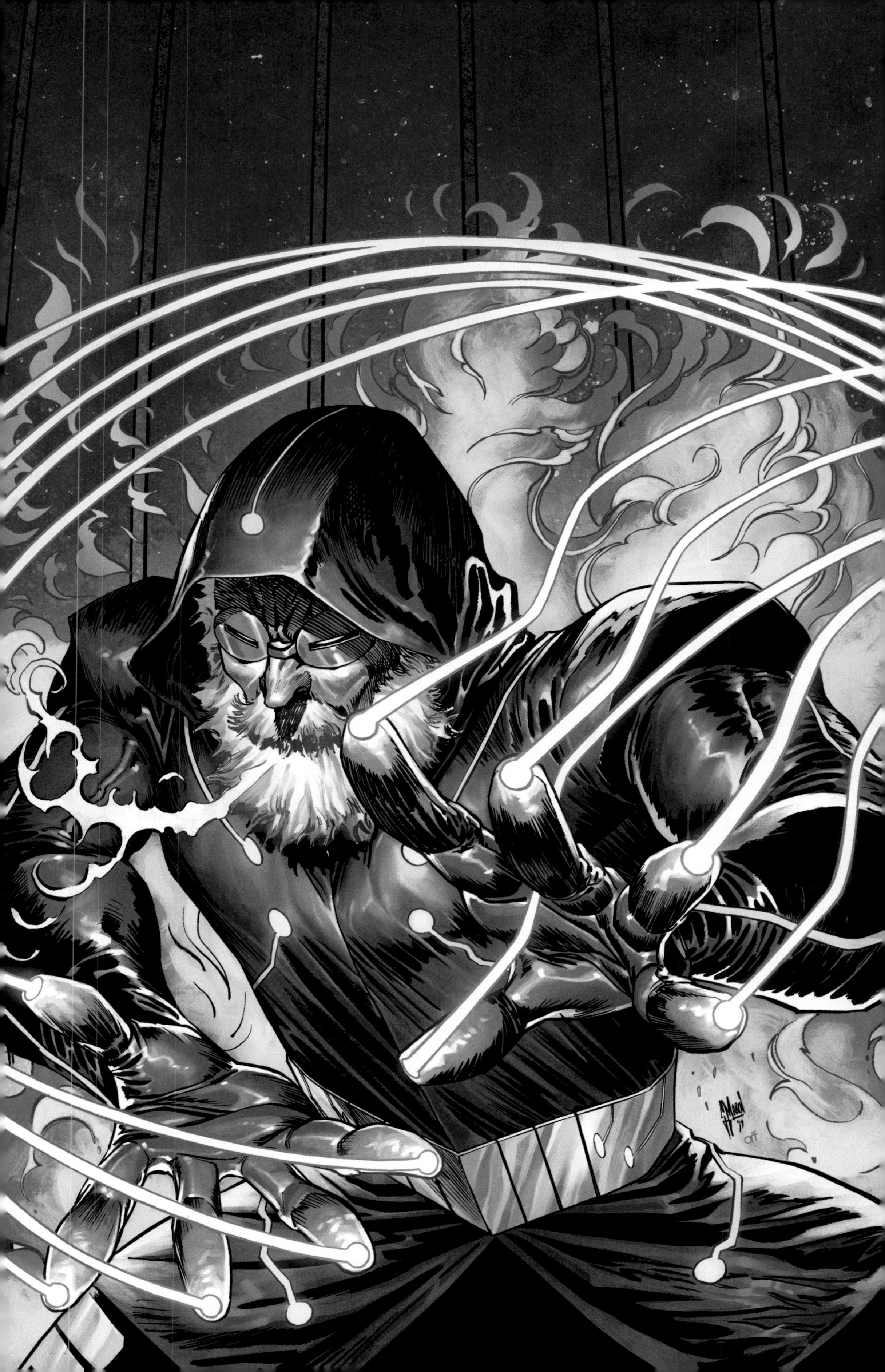

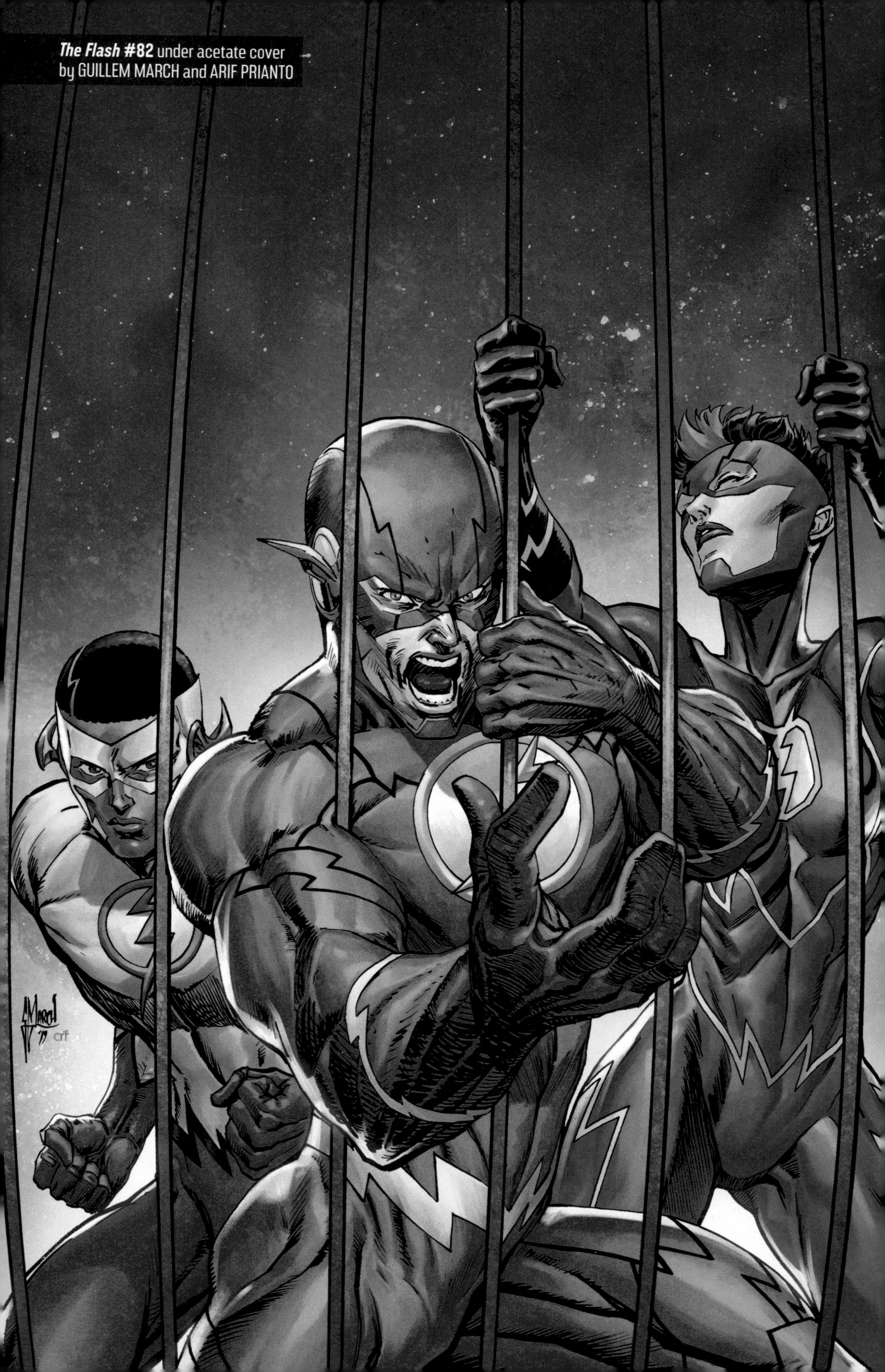

The Flash **#82** under acetate cover
by GUILLEM MARCH and ARIF PRIANTO

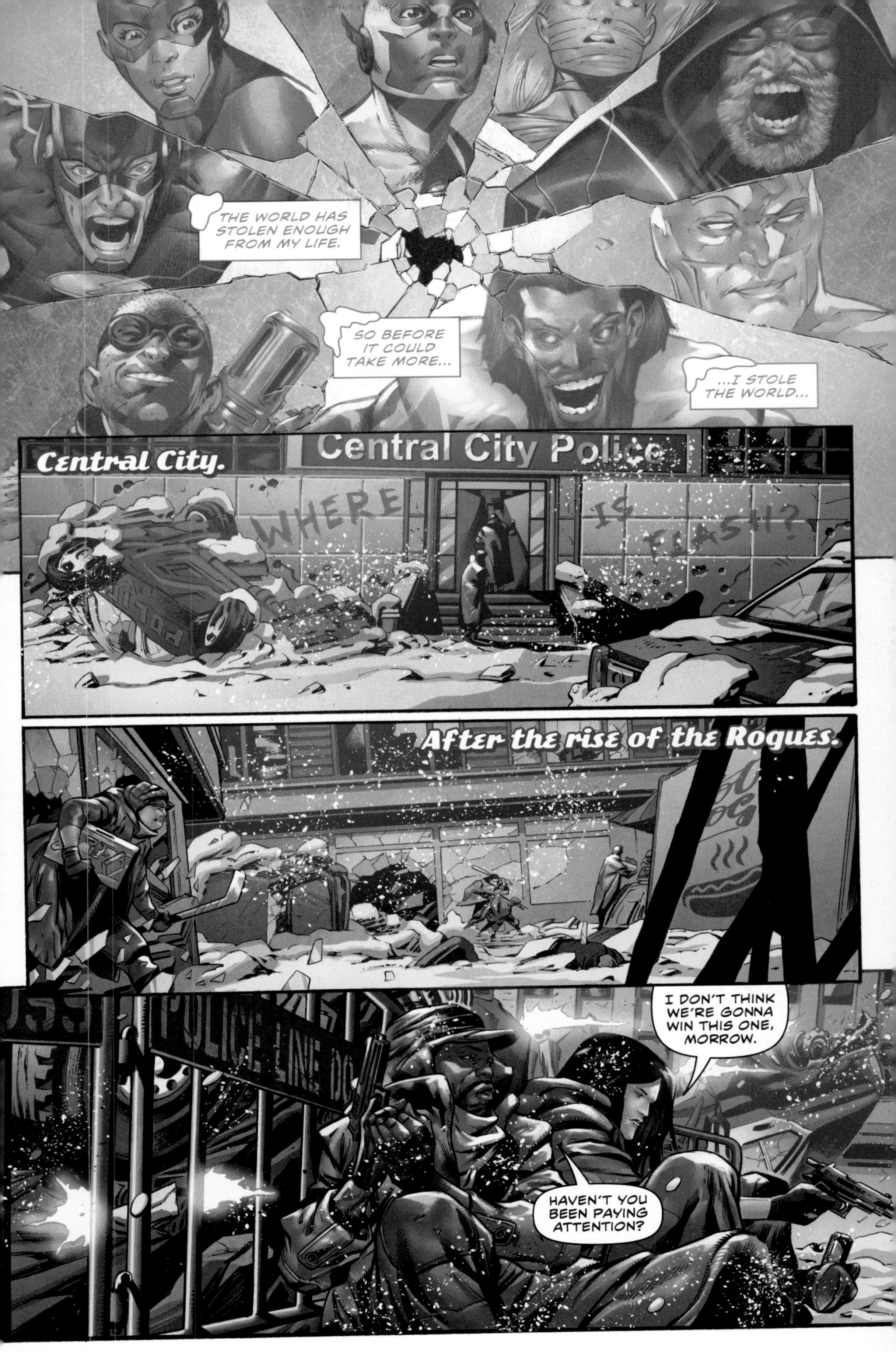
THE WORLD HAS STOLEN ENOUGH FROM MY LIFE.
SO BEFORE IT COULD TAKE MORE...
...I STOLE THE WORLD...
Central City.
Central City Police
WHERE IS FLASH?
After the rise of the Rogues.
POLICE LINE DO
I DON'T THINK WE'RE GONNA WIN THIS ONE, MORROW.
HAVEN'T YOU BEEN PAYING ATTENTION?

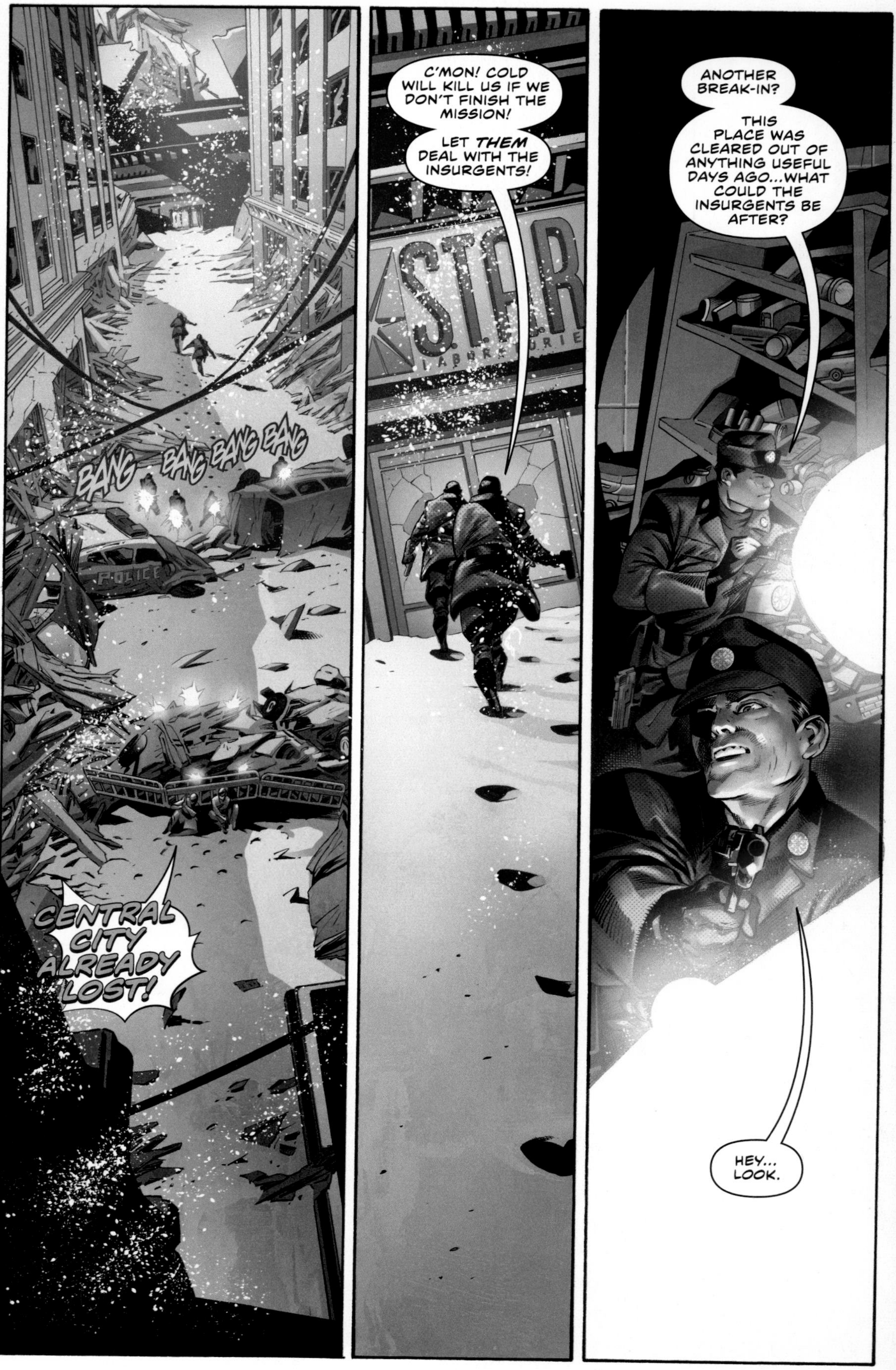
BANG BANG BANG BANG
POLICE
CENTRAL CITY ALREADY LOST!
C'MON! COLD WILL KILL US IF WE DON'T FINISH THE MISSION!
LET *THEM* DEAL WITH THE INSURGENTS!
S.T.A.R.
LABORATORIES
ANOTHER BREAK-IN?
THIS PLACE WAS CLEARED OUT OF ANYTHING USEFUL DAYS AGO...WHAT COULD THE INSURGENTS BE AFTER?
HEY... LOOK.

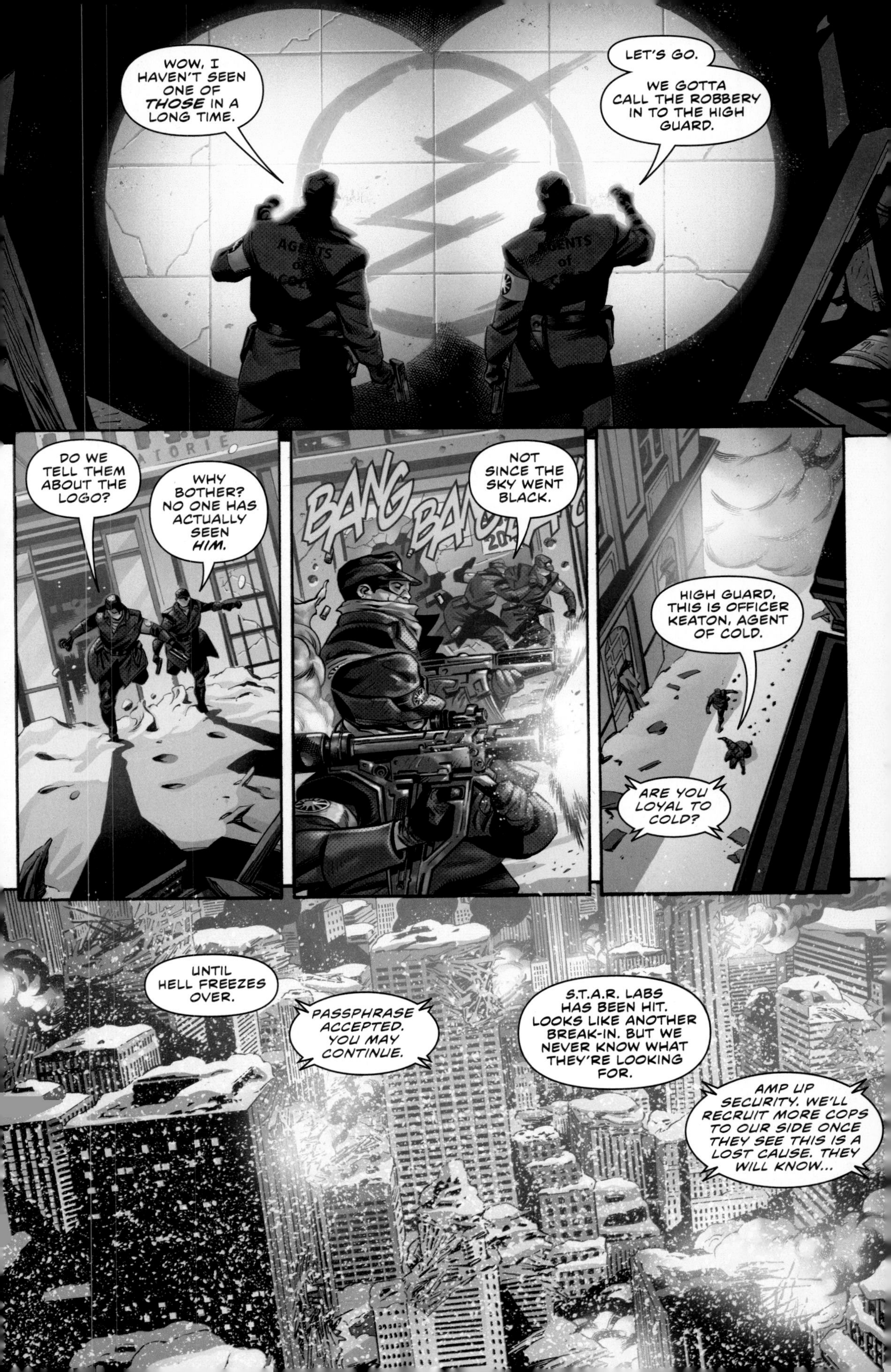
WOW, I HAVEN'T SEEN ONE OF *THOSE* IN A LONG TIME.
LET'S GO.
WE GOTTA CALL THE ROBBERY IN TO THE HIGH GUARD.
AGENTS of COLD
DO WE TELL THEM ABOUT THE LOGO?
WHY BOTHER? NO ONE HAS ACTUALLY SEEN *HIM*.
BANG BANG
NOT SINCE THE SKY WENT BLACK.
HIGH GUARD, THIS IS OFFICER KEATON, AGENT OF COLD.
ARE YOU LOYAL TO COLD?
UNTIL HELL FREEZES OVER.
PASSPHRASE ACCEPTED. YOU MAY CONTINUE.
S.T.A.R. LABS HAS BEEN HIT. LOOKS LIKE ANOTHER BREAK-IN. BUT WE NEVER KNOW WHAT THEY'RE LOOKING FOR.
AMP UP SECURITY. WE'LL RECRUIT MORE COPS TO OUR SIDE ONCE THEY SEE THIS IS A LOST CAUSE. THEY WILL KNOW...

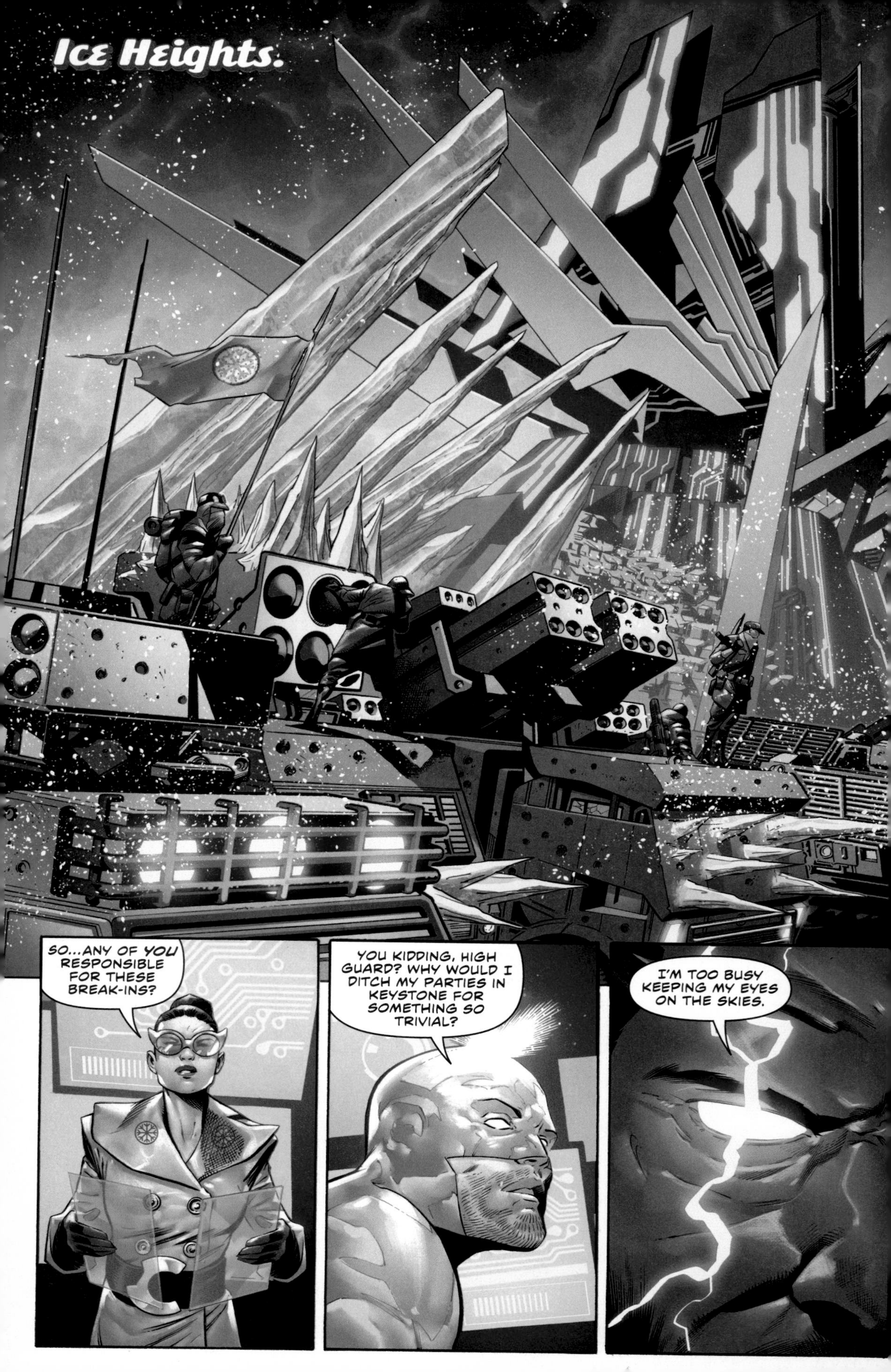
Ice Heights.
SO...ANY OF YOU RESPONSIBLE FOR THESE BREAK-INS?
YOU KIDDING, HIGH GUARD? WHY WOULD I DITCH MY PARTIES IN KEYSTONE FOR SOMETHING SO TRIVIAL?
I'M TOO BUSY KEEPING MY EYES ON THE SKIES.

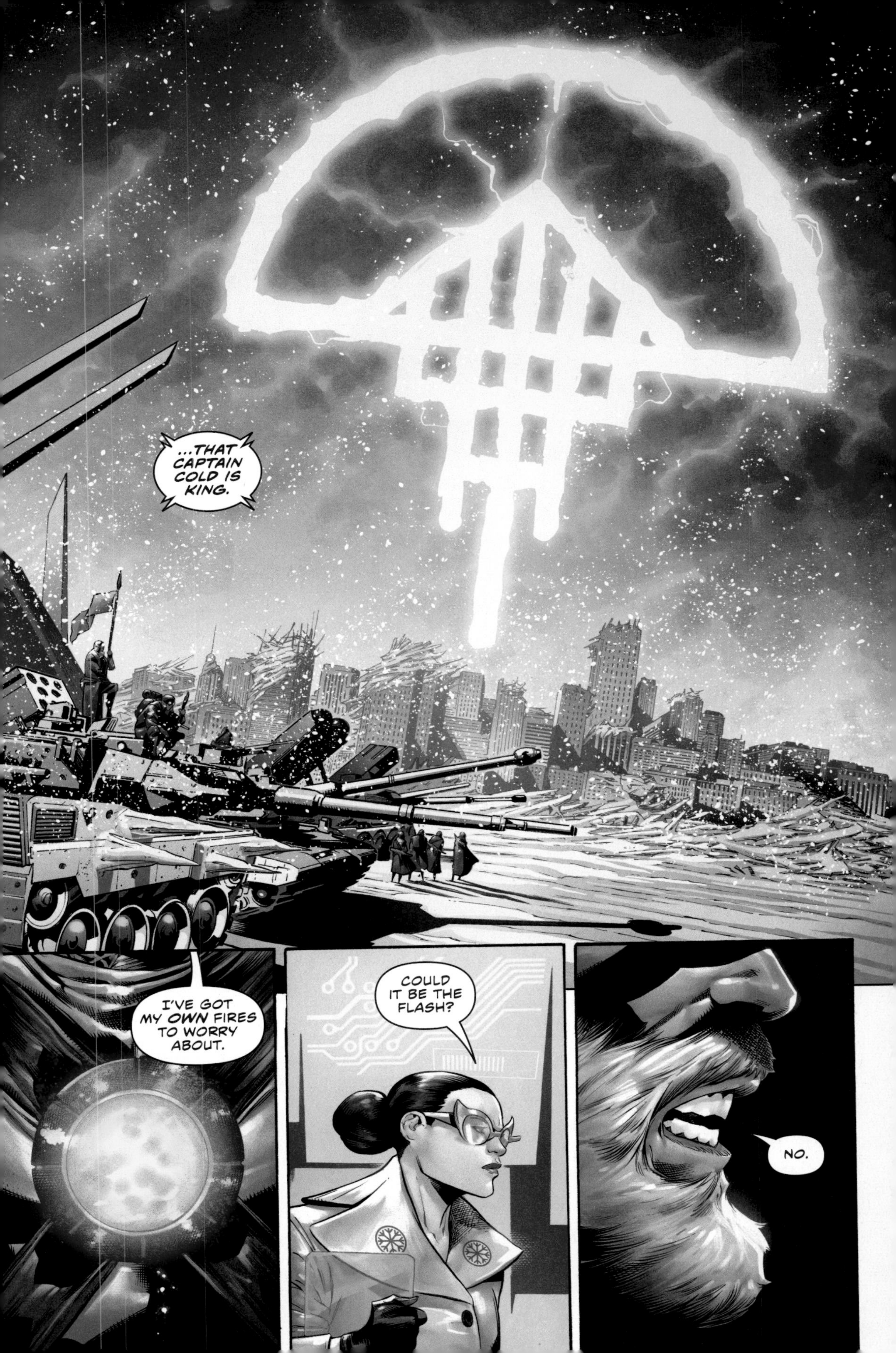
...THAT CAPTAIN COLD IS KING.
I'VE GOT MY OWN FIRES TO WORRY ABOUT.
COULD IT BE THE FLASH?
NO.

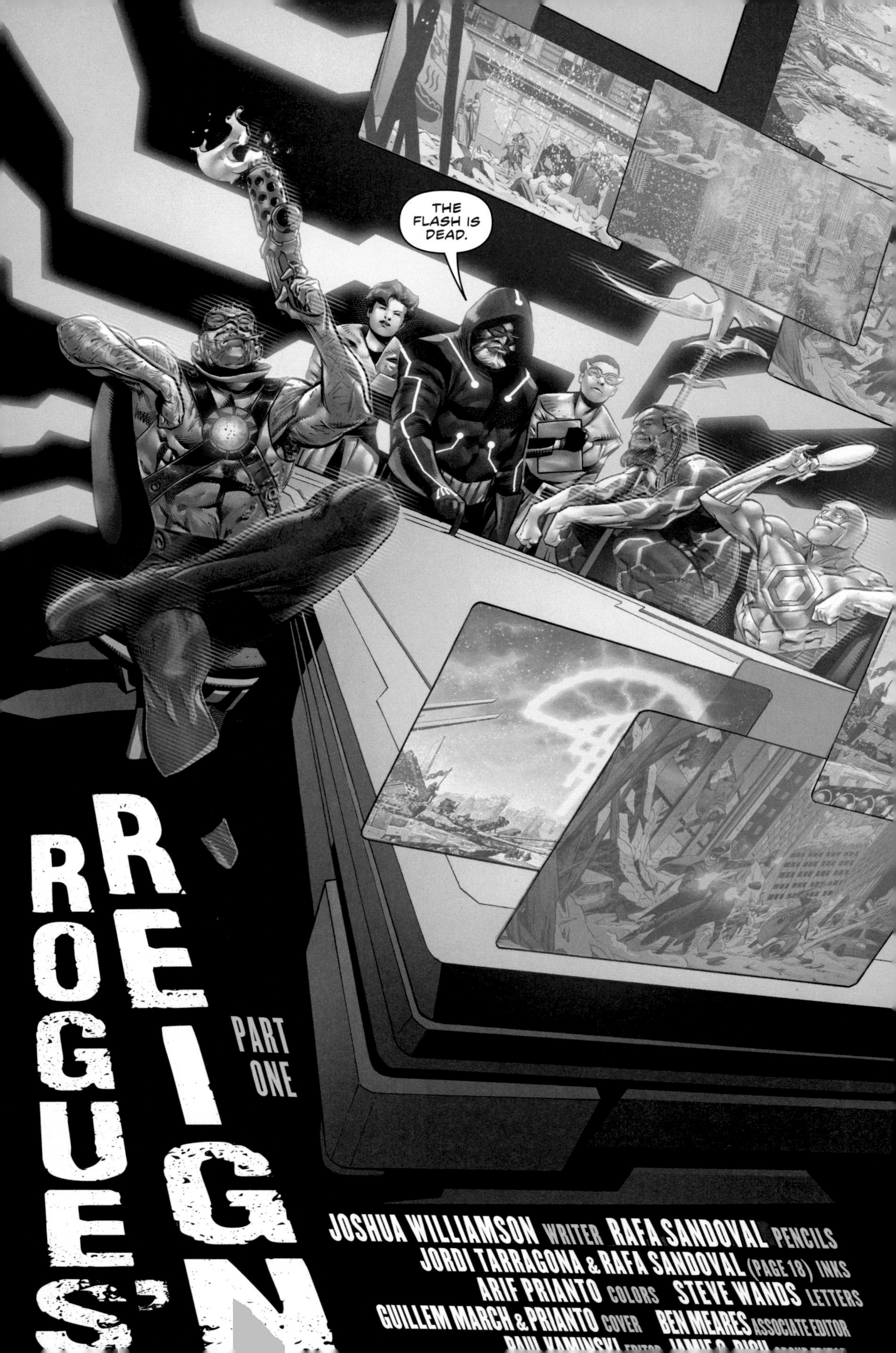
THE FLASH IS DEAD.
ROGUES' REIGN
PART ONE
JOSHUA WILLIAMSON WRITER RAFA SANDOVAL PENCILS
JORDI TARRAGONA & RAFA SANDOVAL (PAGE 18) INKS
ARIF PRIANTO COLORS STEVE WANDS LETTERS
GUILLEM MARCH & PRIANTO COVER BEN MEARES ASSOCIATE EDITOR

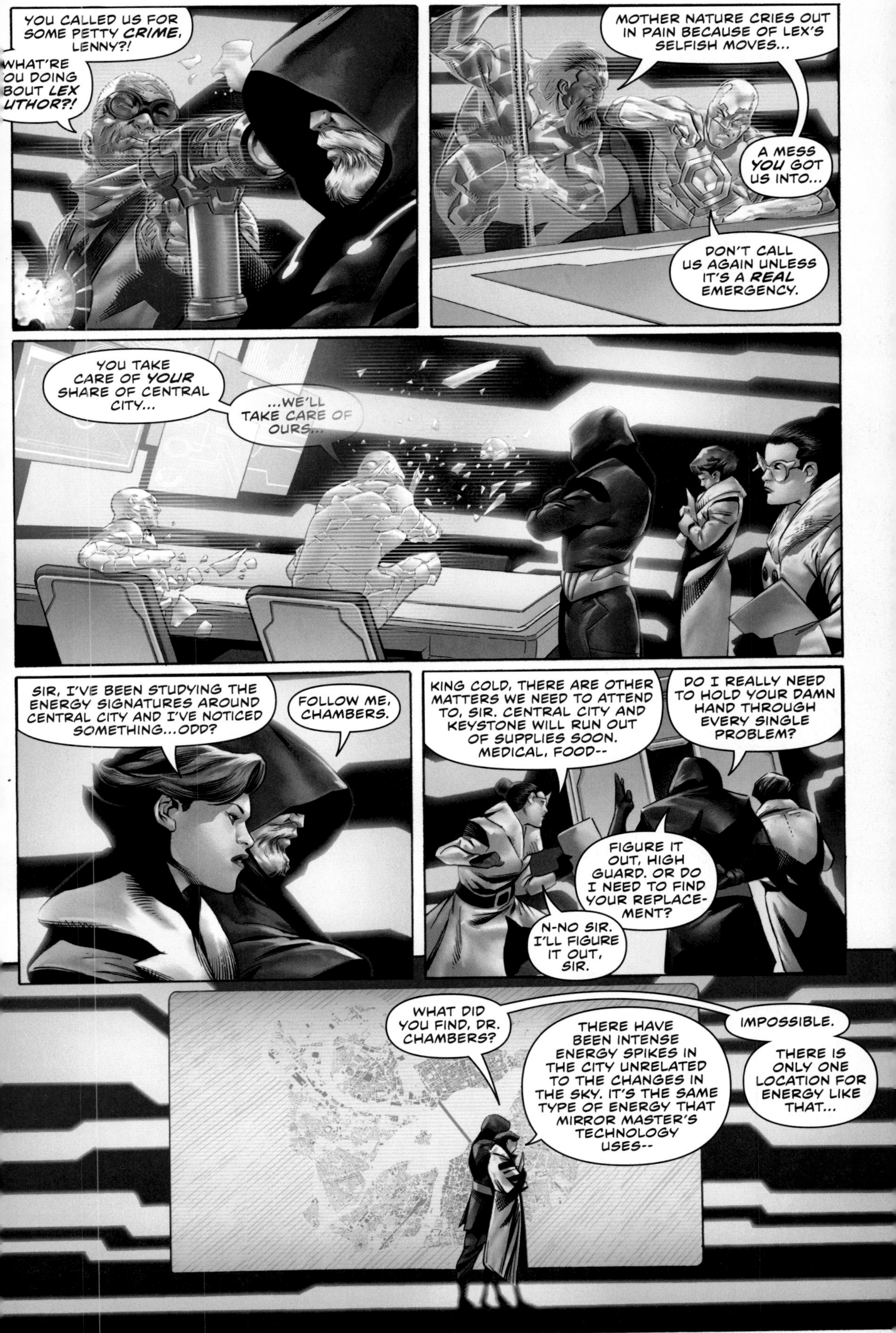
YOU CALLED US FOR SOME PETTY CRIME, LENNY?!
WHAT'RE OU DOING BOUT LEX UTHOR?!
MOTHER NATURE CRIES OUT IN PAIN BECAUSE OF LEX'S SELFISH MOVES...
A MESS YOU GOT US INTO...
DON'T CALL US AGAIN UNLESS IT'S A REAL EMERGENCY.
YOU TAKE CARE OF YOUR SHARE OF CENTRAL CITY...
...WE'LL TAKE CARE OF OURS...
SIR, I'VE BEEN STUDYING THE ENERGY SIGNATURES AROUND CENTRAL CITY AND I'VE NOTICED SOMETHING...ODD?
FOLLOW ME, CHAMBERS.
KING COLD, THERE ARE OTHER MATTERS WE NEED TO ATTEND TO, SIR. CENTRAL CITY AND KEYSTONE WILL RUN OUT OF SUPPLIES SOON. MEDICAL, FOOD--
DO I REALLY NEED TO HOLD YOUR DAMN HAND THROUGH EVERY SINGLE PROBLEM?
FIGURE IT OUT, HIGH GUARD. OR DO I NEED TO FIND YOUR REPLACE-MENT?
N-NO SIR. I'LL FIGURE IT OUT, SIR.
WHAT DID YOU FIND, DR. CHAMBERS?
THERE HAVE BEEN INTENSE ENERGY SPIKES IN THE CITY UNRELATED TO THE CHANGES IN THE SKY. IT'S THE SAME TYPE OF ENERGY THAT MIRROR MASTER'S TECHNOLOGY USES--
IMPOSSIBLE.
THERE IS ONLY ONE LOCATION FOR ENERGY LIKE THAT...

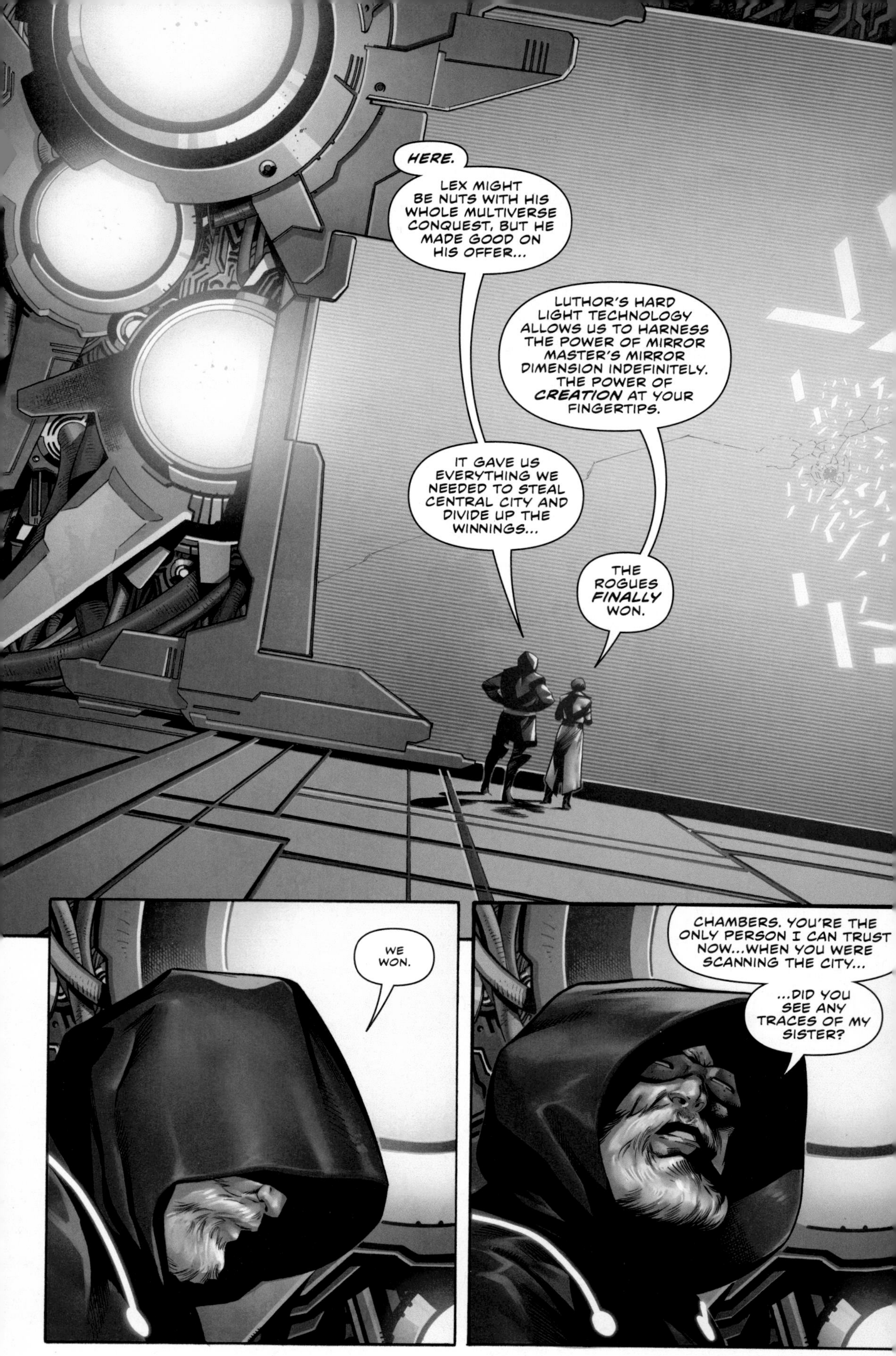
HERE.
LEX MIGHT BE NUTS WITH HIS WHOLE MULTIVERSE CONQUEST, BUT HE MADE GOOD ON HIS OFFER...
IT GAVE US EVERYTHING WE NEEDED TO STEAL CENTRAL CITY AND DIVIDE UP THE WINNINGS...
LUTHOR'S HARD LIGHT TECHNOLOGY ALLOWS US TO HARNESS THE POWER OF MIRROR MASTER'S MIRROR DIMENSION INDEFINITELY. THE POWER OF CREATION AT YOUR FINGERTIPS.
THE ROGUES FINALLY WON.
WE WON.
CHAMBERS. YOU'RE THE ONLY PERSON I CAN TRUST NOW...WHEN YOU WERE SCANNING THE CITY...
...DID YOU SEE ANY TRACES OF MY SISTER?

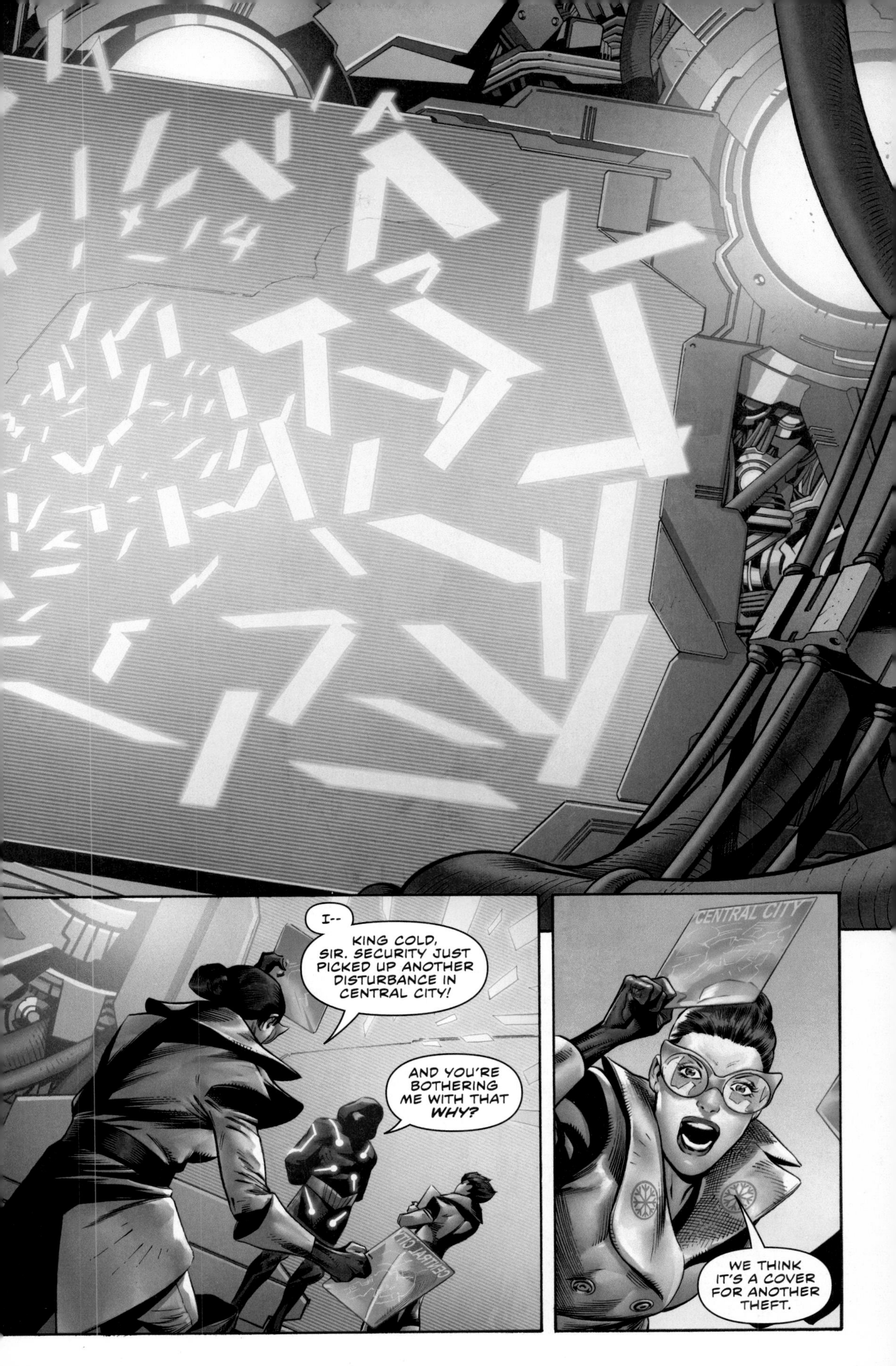
I--
KING COLD, SIR. SECURITY JUST PICKED UP ANOTHER DISTURBANCE IN CENTRAL CITY!
AND YOU'RE BOTHERING ME WITH THAT *WHY?*
CENTRAL CITY
CENTRAL CITY
WE THINK IT'S A COVER FOR ANOTHER THEFT.

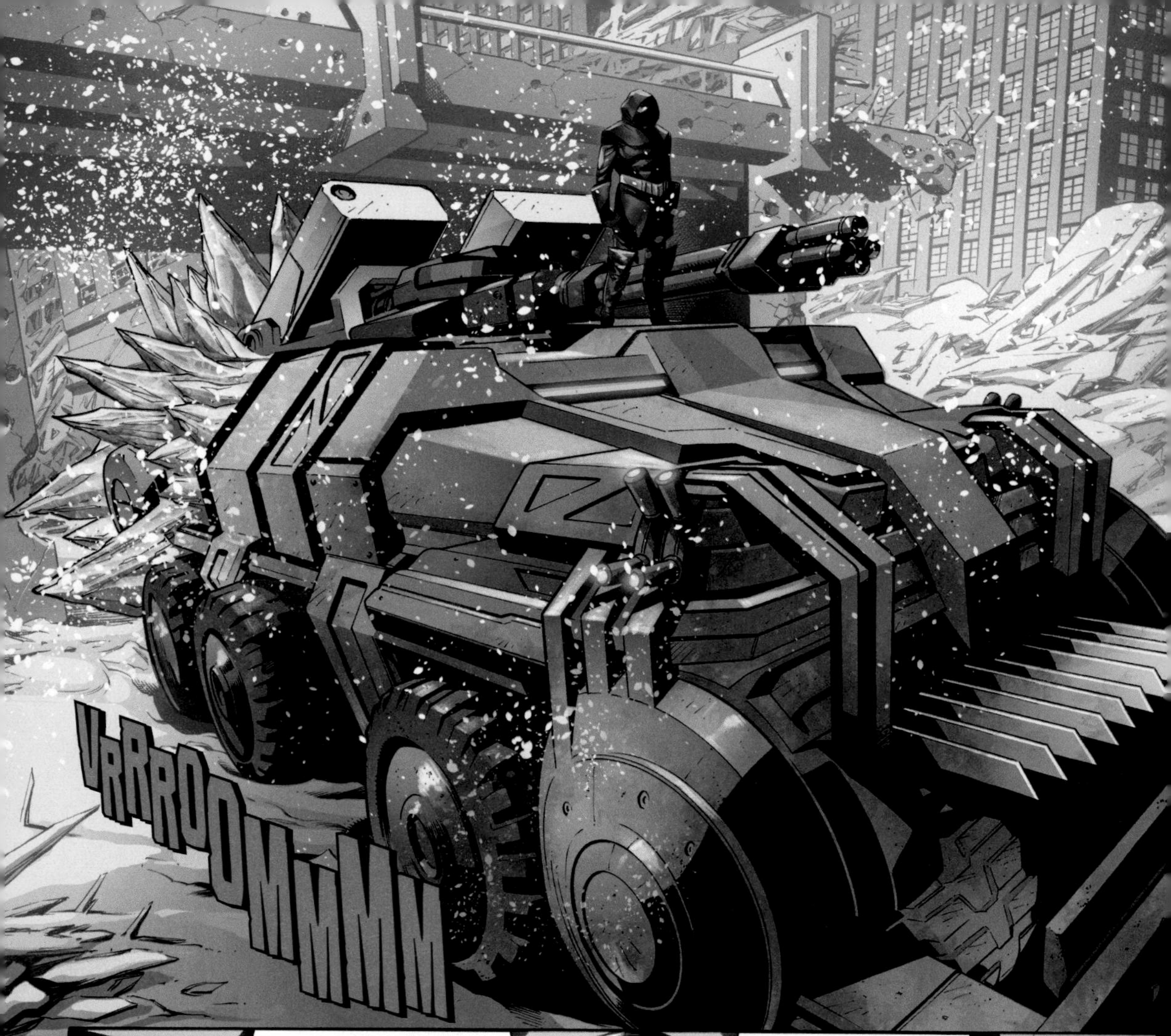
VRRROOMMMMM

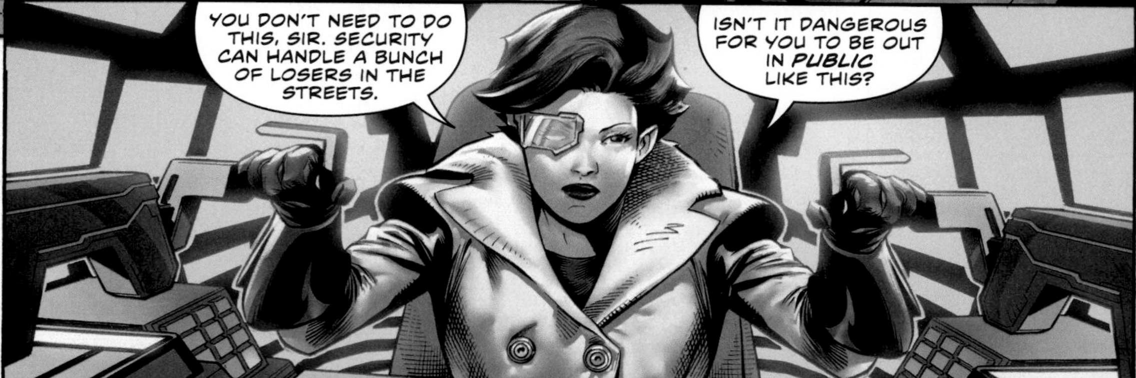
YOU DON'T NEED TO DO THIS, SIR. SECURITY CAN HANDLE A BUNCH OF LOSERS IN THE STREETS.
ISN'T IT DANGEROUS FOR YOU TO BE OUT IN *PUBLIC* LIKE THIS?

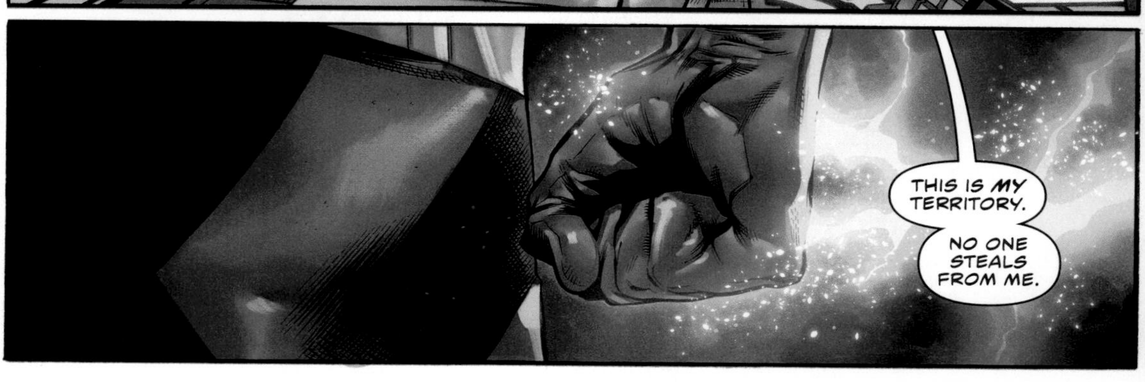
THIS IS *MY* TERRITORY.
NO ONE STEALS FROM ME.

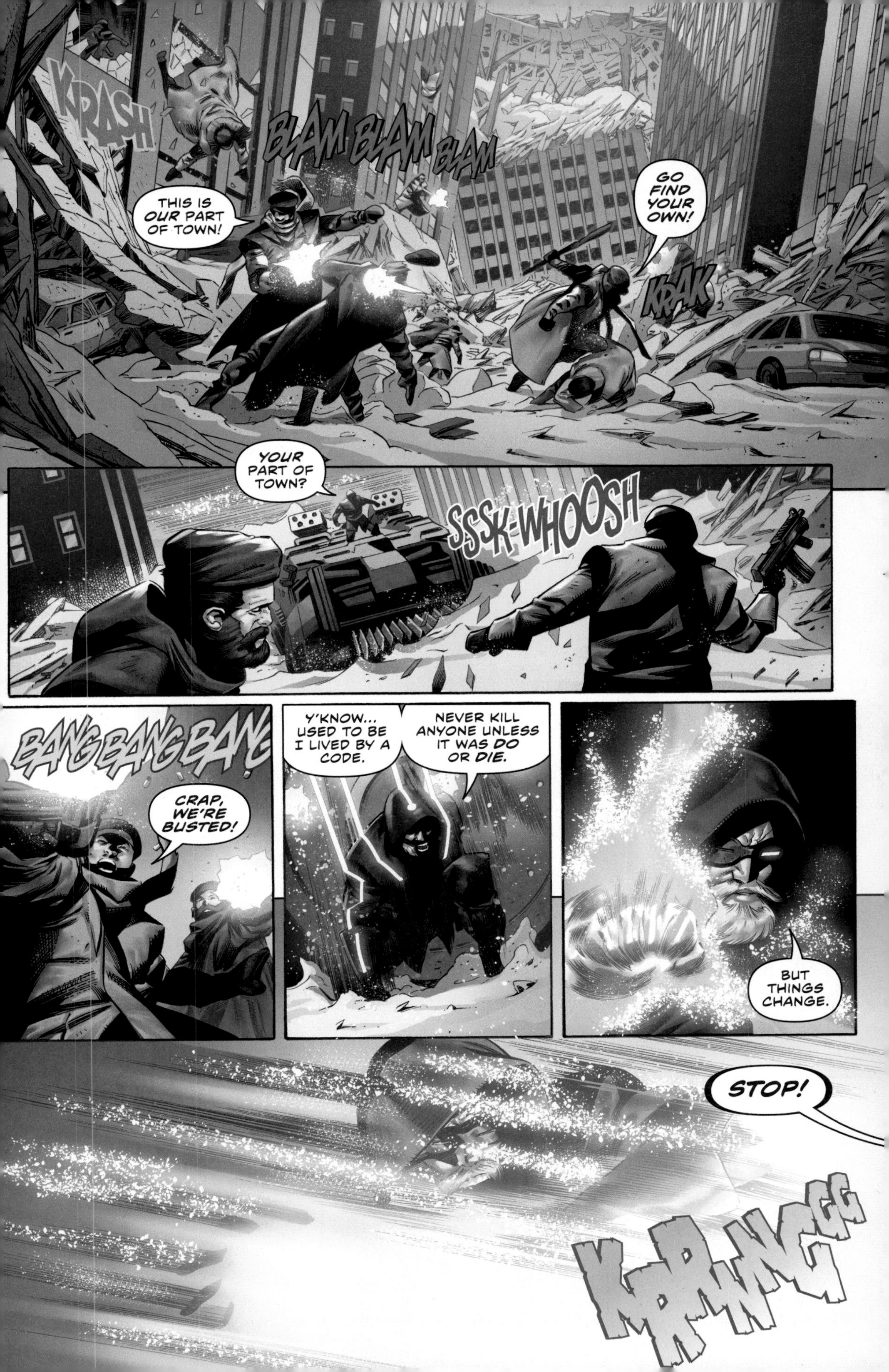
KRASH
BLAM BLAM BLAM
THIS IS OUR PART OF TOWN!
GO FIND YOUR OWN!
KRAK
YOUR PART OF TOWN?
SSSK-WHOOSH
BANG BANG BANG
CRAP, WE'RE BUSTED!
Y'KNOW... USED TO BE I LIVED BY A CODE.
NEVER KILL ANYONE UNLESS IT WAS DO OR DIE.
BUT THINGS CHANGE.
STOP!
KRANGG

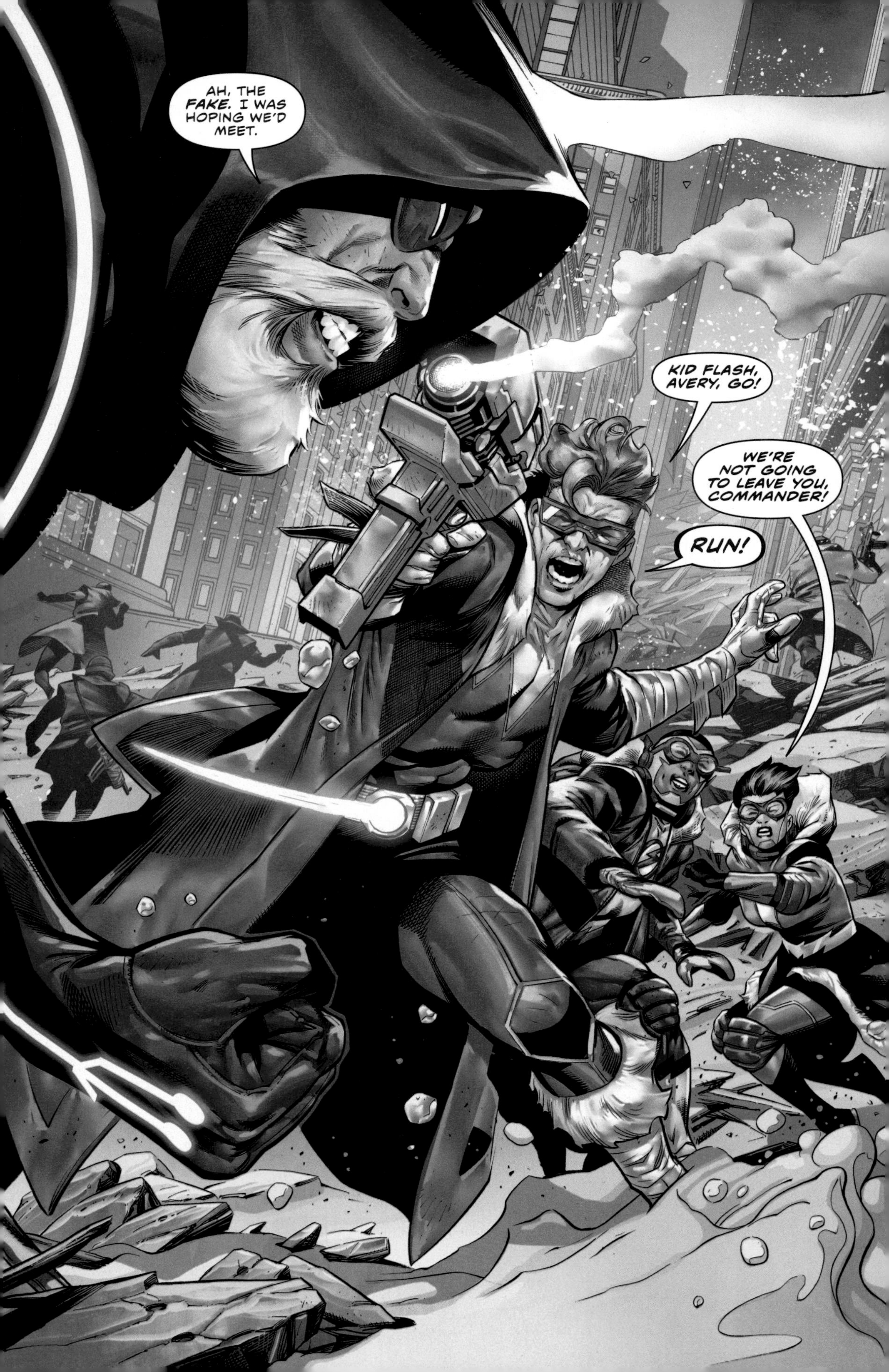

AH, THE FAKE. I WAS HOPING WE'D MEET.
KID FLASH, AVERY, GO!
WE'RE NOT GOING TO LEAVE YOU, COMMANDER!
RUN!

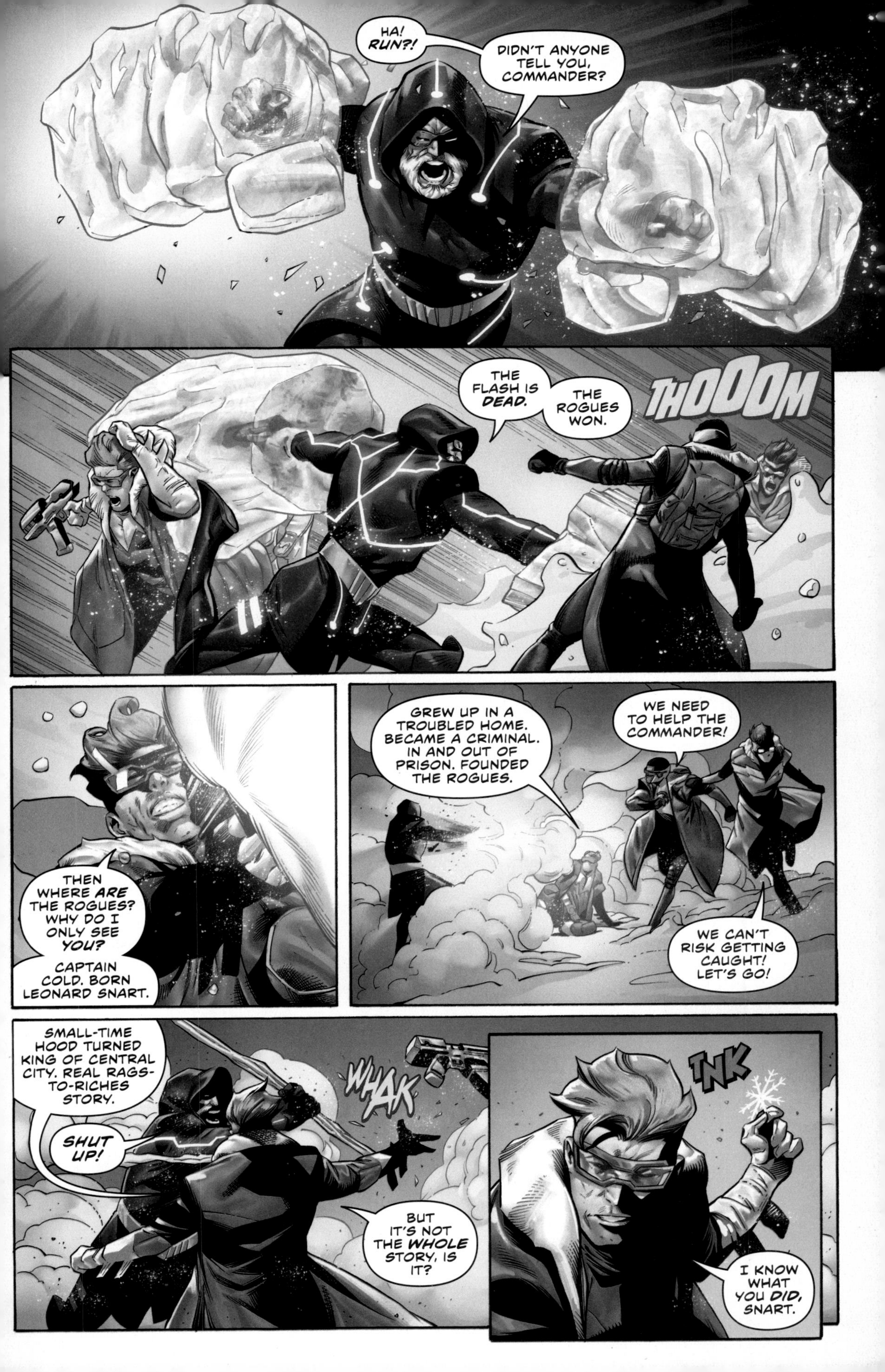
HA! RUN?!
DIDN'T ANYONE TELL YOU, COMMANDER?
THE FLASH IS DEAD.
THE ROGUES WON.
THOOOM
THEN WHERE ARE THE ROGUES? WHY DO I ONLY SEE YOU?
CAPTAIN COLD. BORN LEONARD SNART.
GREW UP IN A TROUBLED HOME. BECAME A CRIMINAL. IN AND OUT OF PRISON. FOUNDED THE ROGUES.
WE NEED TO HELP THE COMMANDER!
WE CAN'T RISK GETTING CAUGHT! LET'S GO!
SMALL-TIME HOOD TURNED KING OF CENTRAL CITY. REAL RAGS-TO-RICHES STORY.
SHUT UP!
WHAK
BUT IT'S NOT THE WHOLE STORY, IS IT?
TNK
I KNOW WHAT YOU DID, SNART.

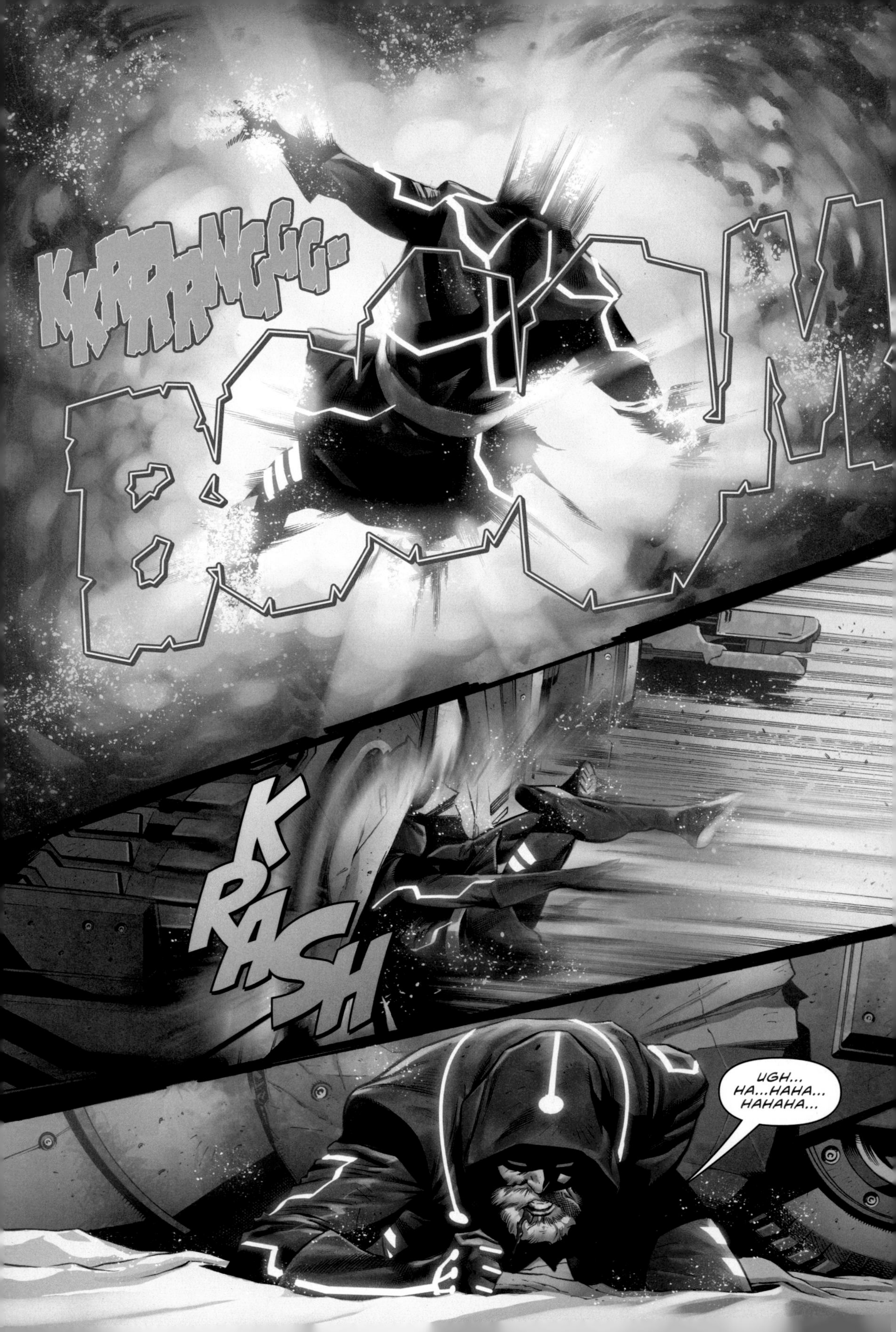
KKRRRANGGG-
BOOM
KRASH
UGH... HA...HAHA... HAHAHA...

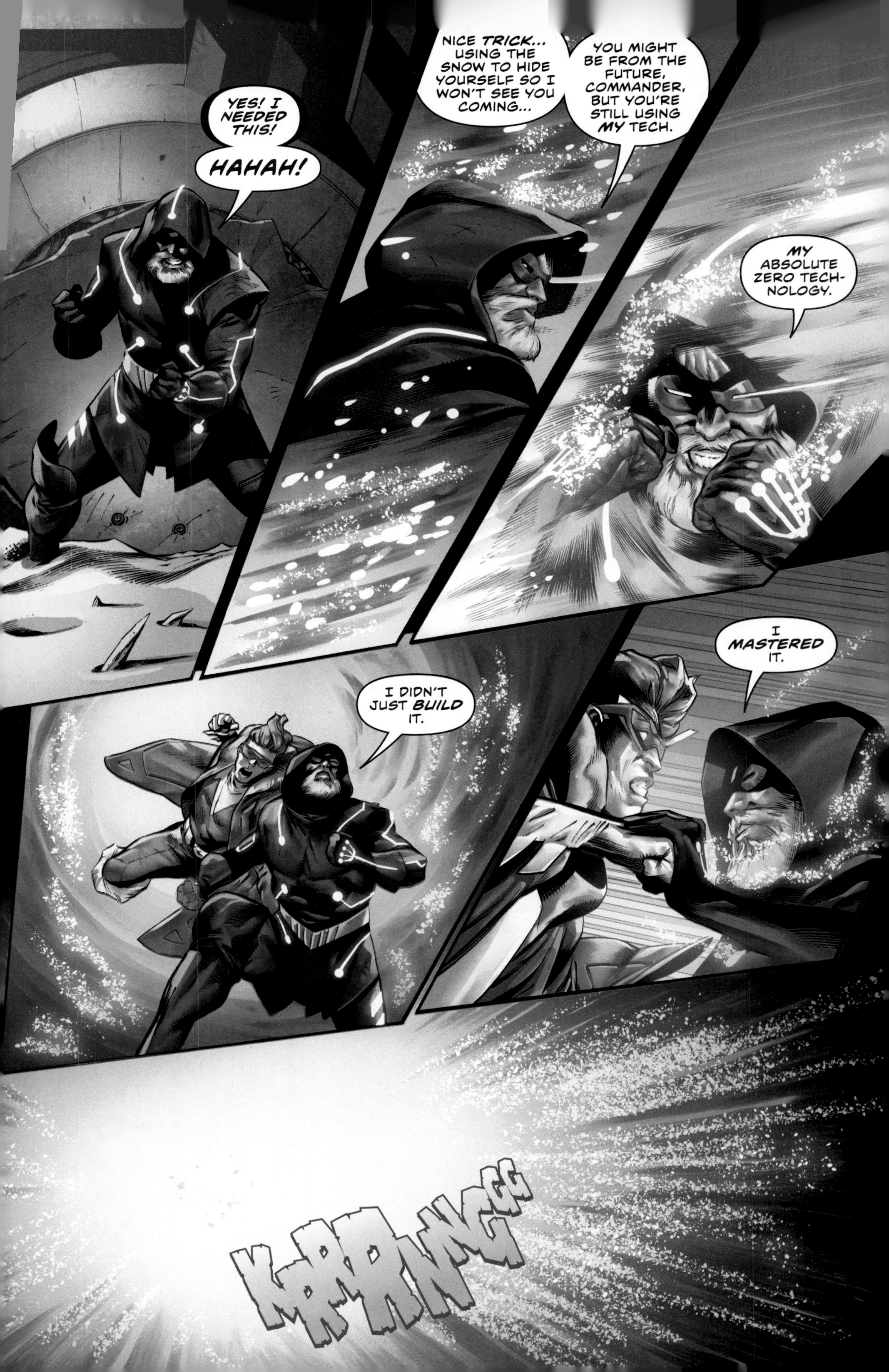

YES! I NEEDED THIS!
HAHAH!
NICE TRICK... USING THE SNOW TO HIDE YOURSELF SO I WON'T SEE YOU COMING...
YOU MIGHT BE FROM THE FUTURE, COMMANDER, BUT YOU'RE STILL USING MY TECH.
MY ABSOLUTE ZERO TECH-NOLOGY.
I DIDN'T JUST BUILD IT.
I MASTERED IT.
KRRANGG

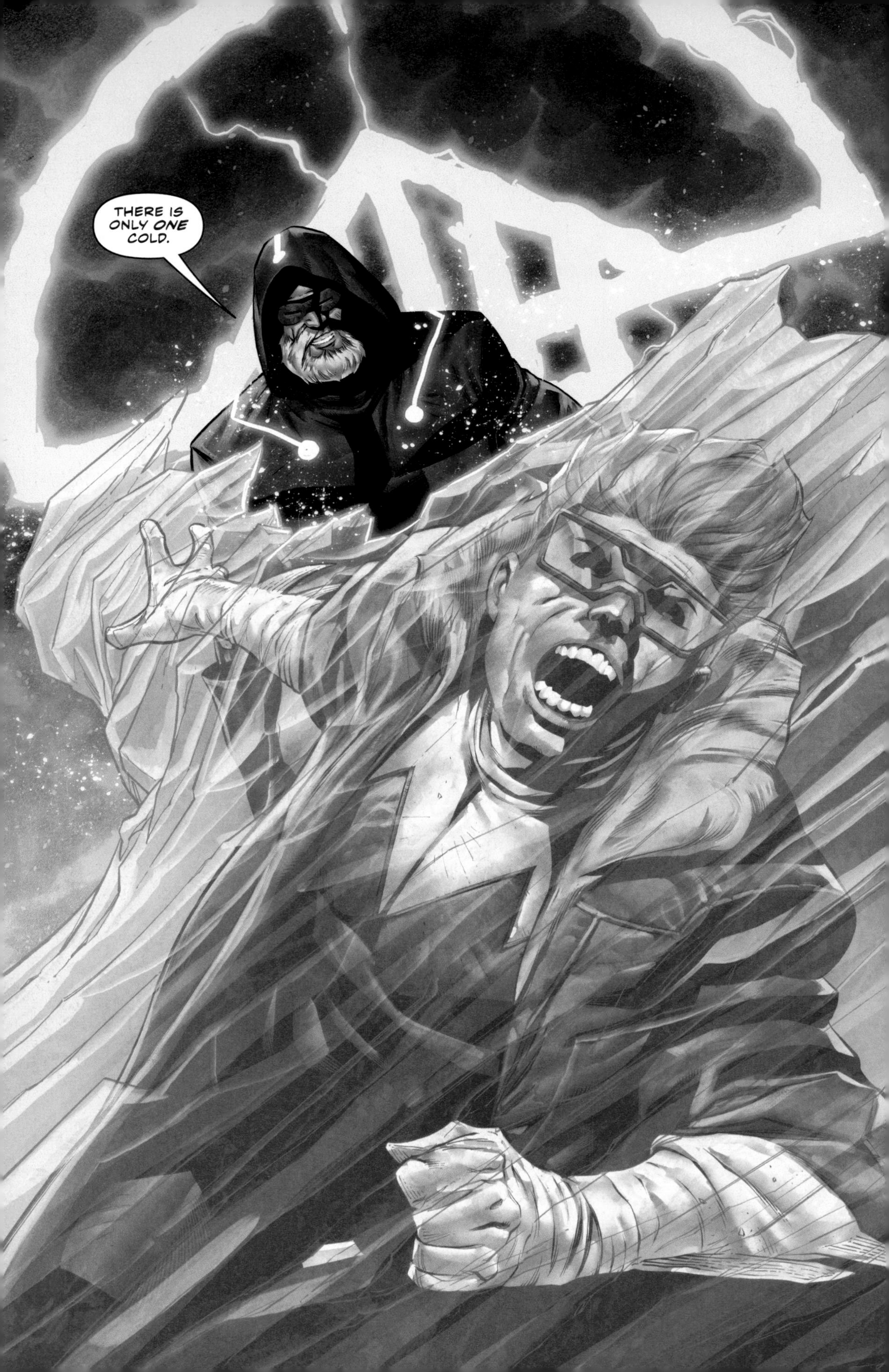
THERE IS ONLY *ONE* COLD.

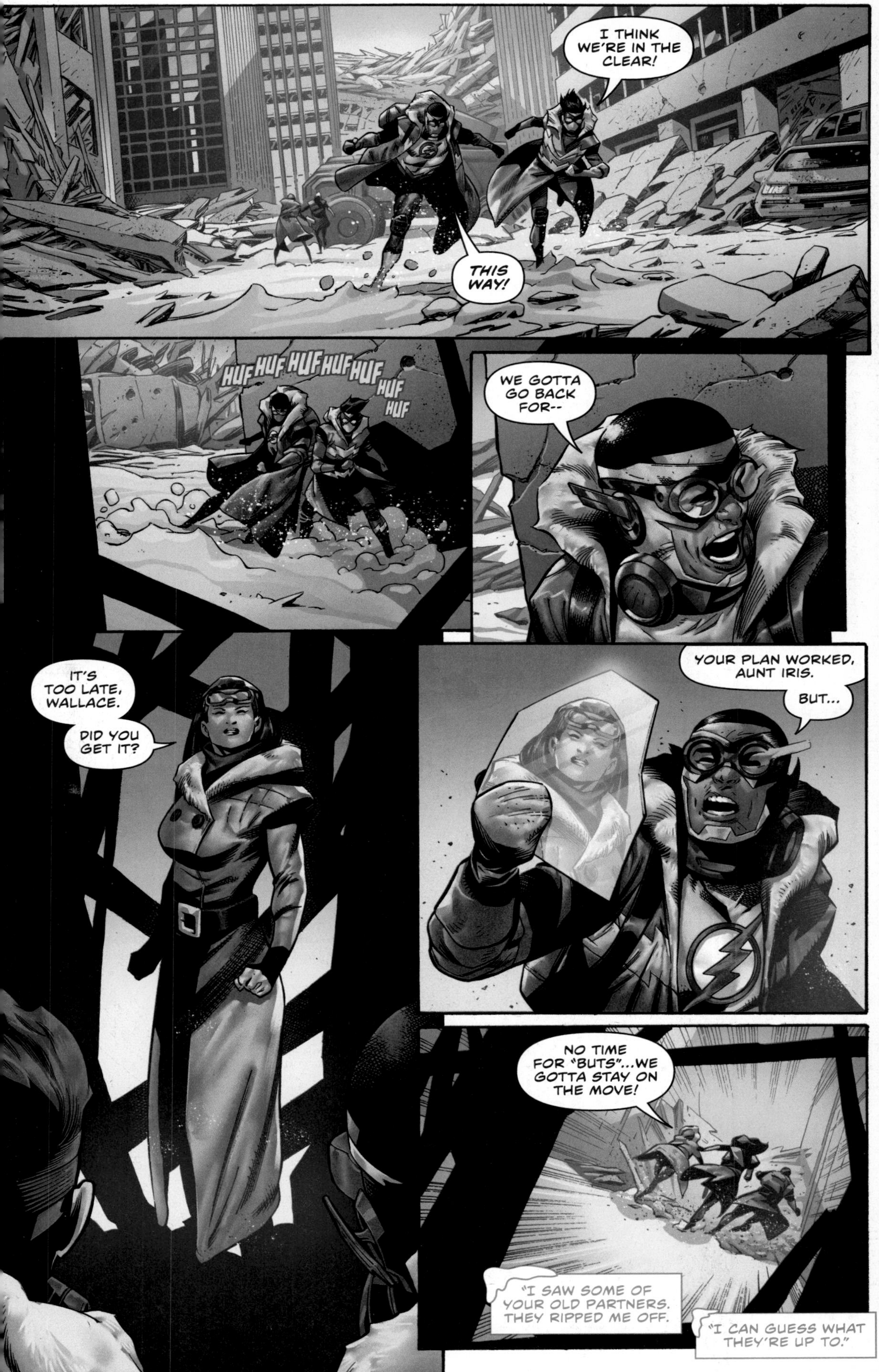
I THINK WE'RE IN THE CLEAR!
THIS WAY!
HUF HUF HUF HUF HUF HUF HUF
WE GOTTA GO BACK FOR--
IT'S TOO LATE, WALLACE.
DID YOU GET IT?
YOUR PLAN WORKED, AUNT IRIS.
BUT...
NO TIME FOR "BUTS"...WE GOTTA STAY ON THE MOVE!
"I SAW SOME OF YOUR OLD PARTNERS. THEY RIPPED ME OFF.
"I CAN GUESS WHAT THEY'RE UP TO."

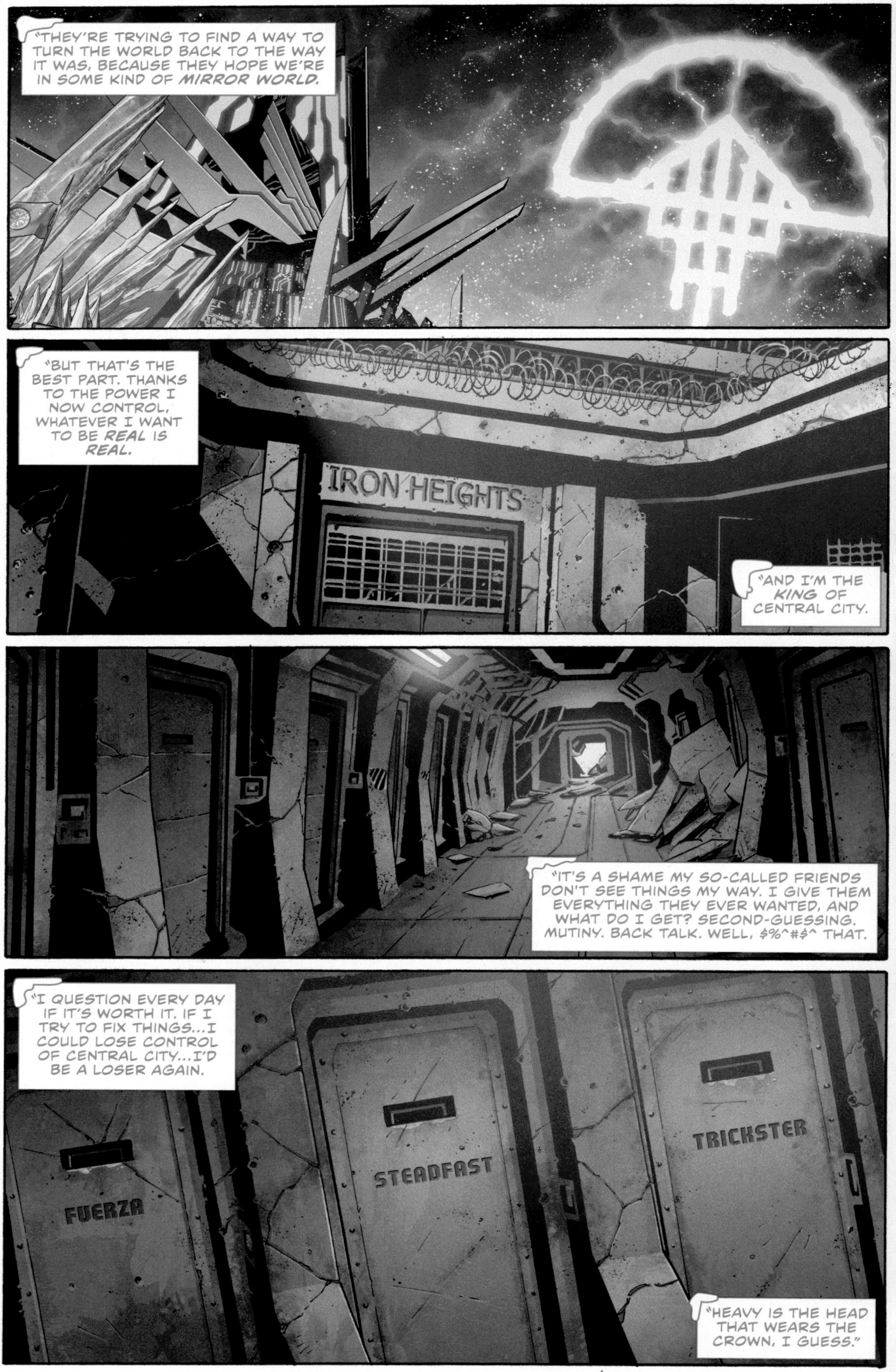
"THEY'RE TRYING TO FIND A WAY TO TURN THE WORLD BACK TO THE WAY IT WAS, BECAUSE THEY HOPE WE'RE IN SOME KIND OF MIRROR WORLD.
"BUT THAT'S THE BEST PART. THANKS TO THE POWER I NOW CONTROL, WHATEVER I WANT TO BE REAL IS REAL.
IRON HEIGHTS
"AND I'M THE KING OF CENTRAL CITY.
"IT'S A SHAME MY SO-CALLED FRIENDS DON'T SEE THINGS MY WAY. I GIVE THEM EVERYTHING THEY EVER WANTED, AND WHAT DO I GET? SECOND-GUESSING. MUTINY. BACK TALK. WELL, $%^#$^ THAT.
"I QUESTION EVERY DAY IF IT'S WORTH IT. IF I TRY TO FIX THINGS...I COULD LOSE CONTROL OF CENTRAL CITY...I'D BE A LOSER AGAIN.
FUERZA
STEADFAST
TRICKSTER
"HEAVY IS THE HEAD THAT WEARS THE CROWN, I GUESS."

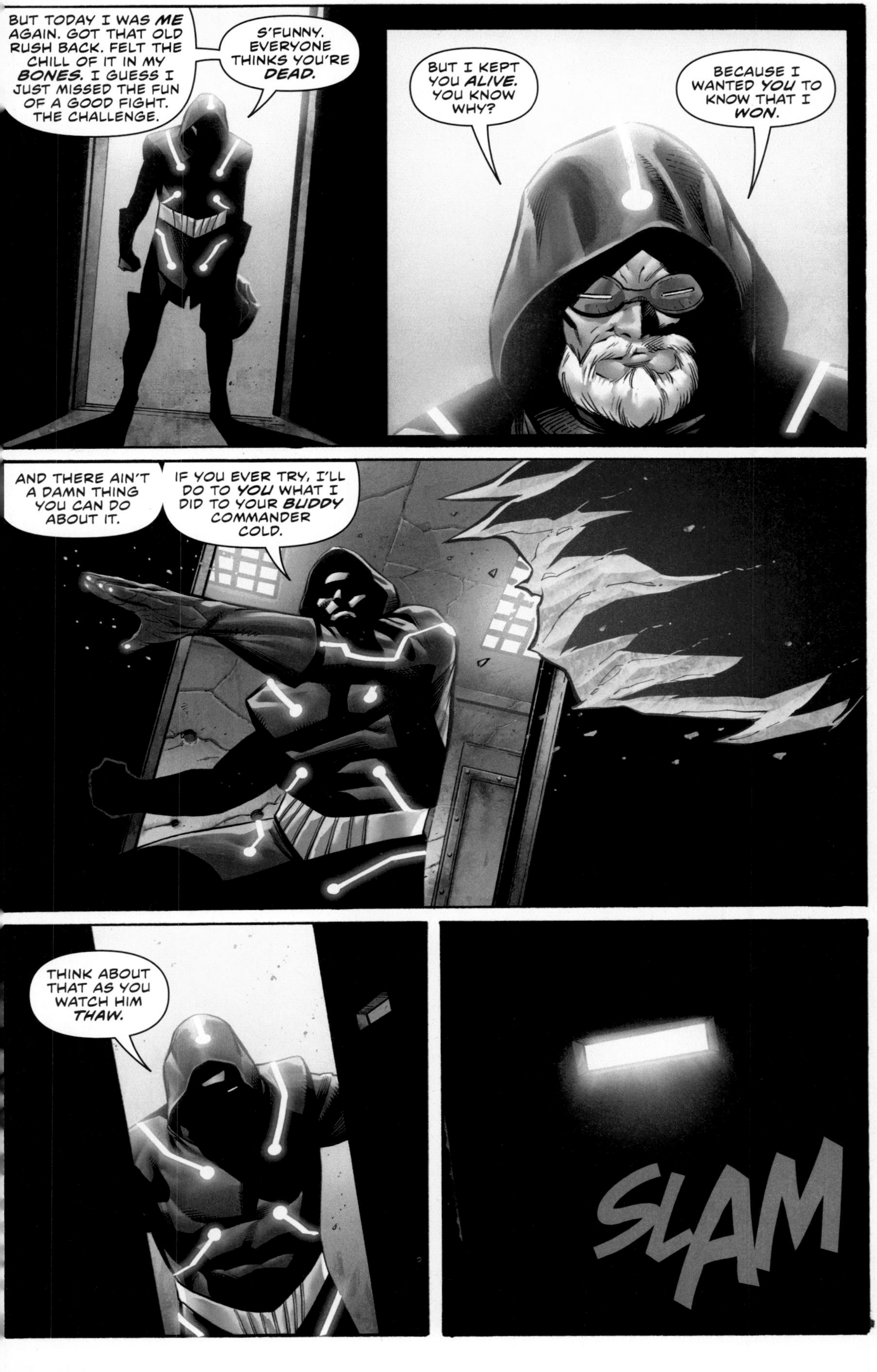
BUT TODAY I WAS ME AGAIN. GOT THAT OLD RUSH BACK. FELT THE CHILL OF IT IN MY BONES. I GUESS I JUST MISSED THE FUN OF A GOOD FIGHT. THE CHALLENGE.
S'FUNNY. EVERYONE THINKS YOU'RE DEAD.
BUT I KEPT YOU ALIVE. YOU KNOW WHY?
BECAUSE I WANTED YOU TO KNOW THAT I WON.
AND THERE AIN'T A DAMN THING YOU CAN DO ABOUT IT.
IF YOU EVER TRY, I'LL DO TO YOU WHAT I DID TO YOUR BUDDY COMMANDER COLD.
THINK ABOUT THAT AS YOU WATCH HIM THAW.
SLAM

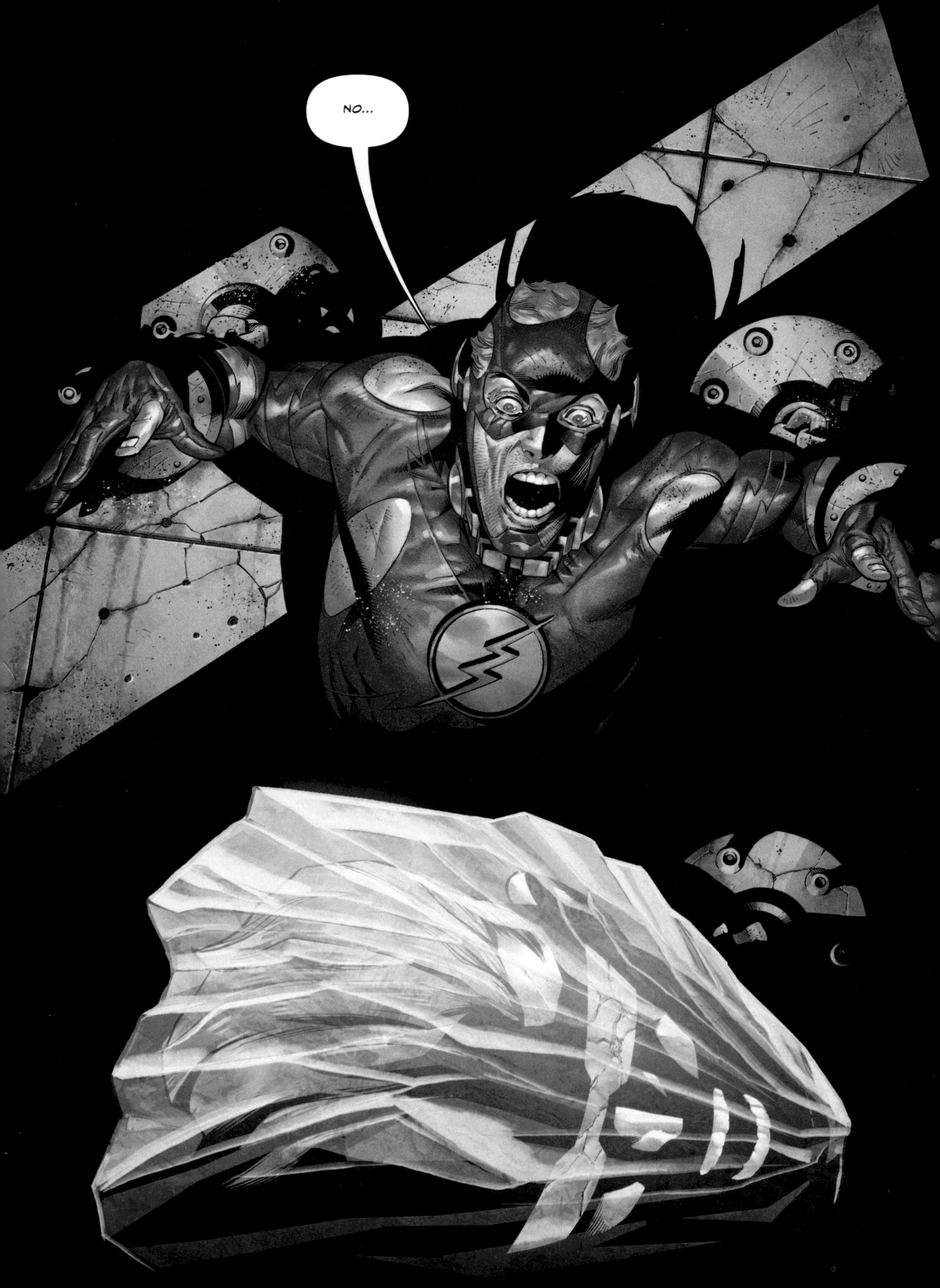
NO...

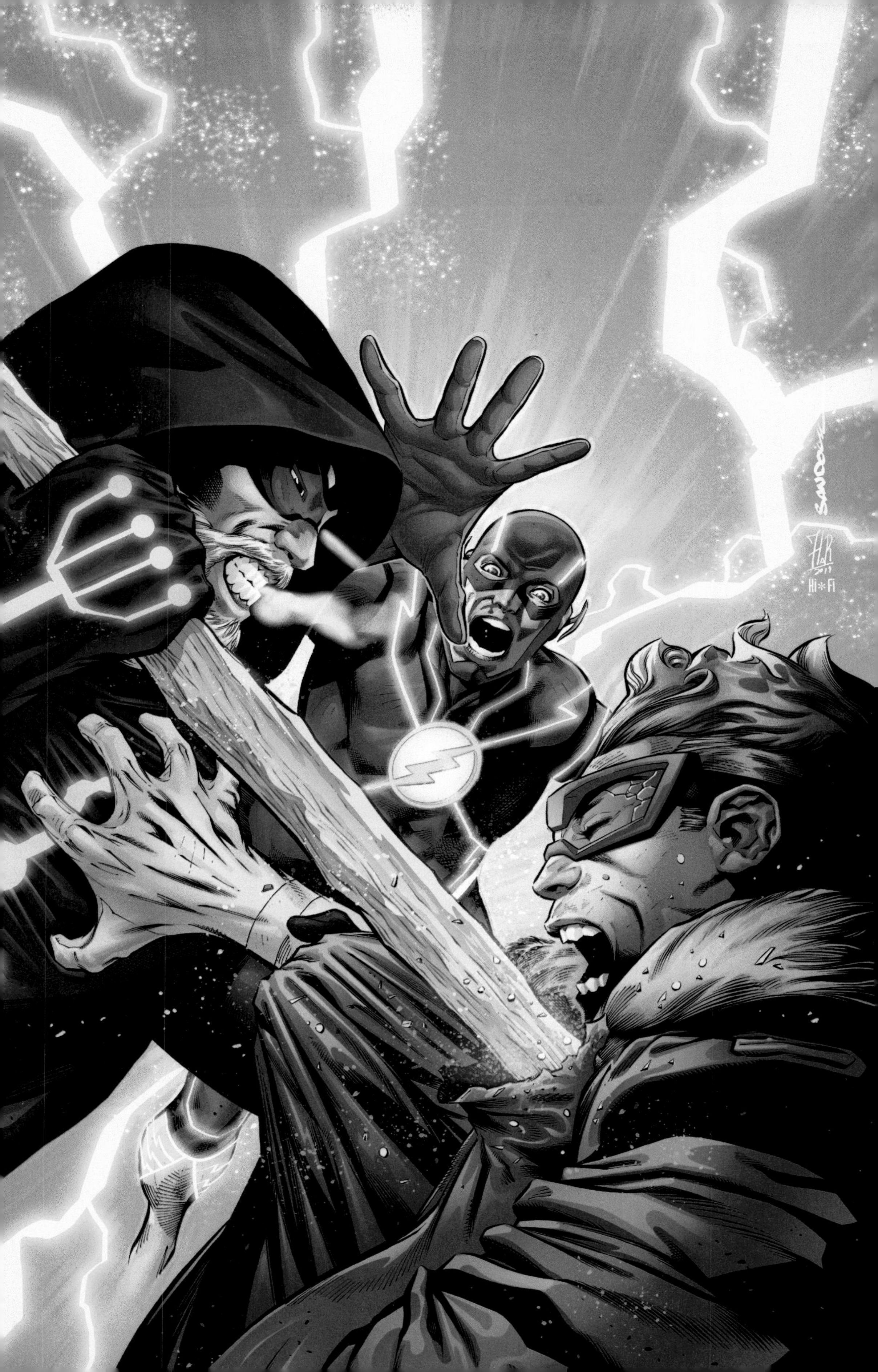

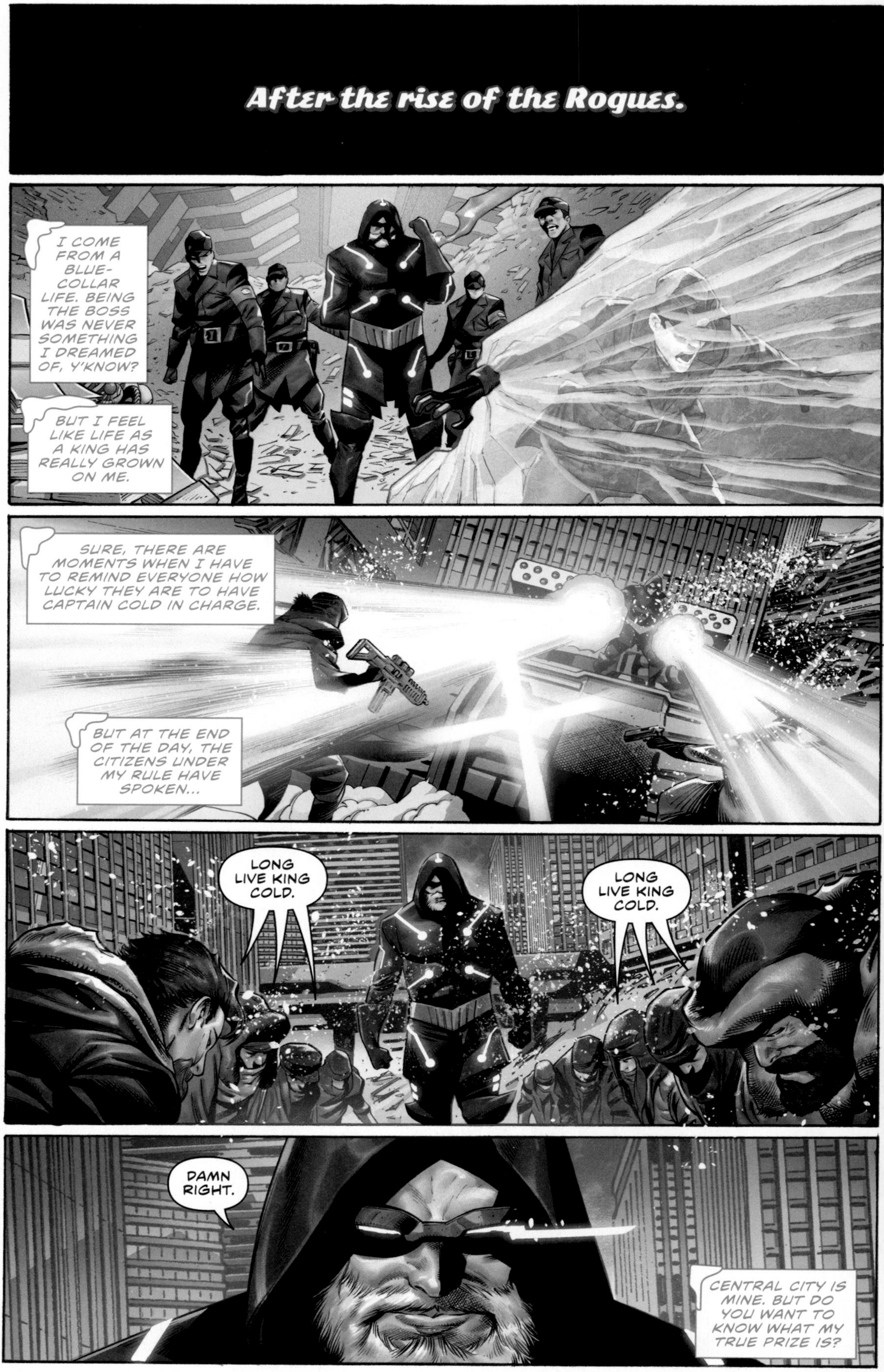
After the rise of the Rogues.
I COME FROM A BLUE-COLLAR LIFE. BEING THE BOSS WAS NEVER SOMETHING I DREAMED OF, Y'KNOW?
BUT I FEEL LIKE LIFE AS A KING HAS REALLY GROWN ON ME.
SURE, THERE ARE MOMENTS WHEN I HAVE TO REMIND EVERYONE HOW LUCKY THEY ARE TO HAVE CAPTAIN COLD IN CHARGE.
BUT AT THE END OF THE DAY, THE CITIZENS UNDER MY RULE HAVE SPOKEN...
LONG LIVE KING COLD.
LONG LIVE KING COLD.
DAMN RIGHT.
CENTRAL CITY IS MINE. BUT DO YOU WANT TO KNOW WHAT MY TRUE PRIZE IS?

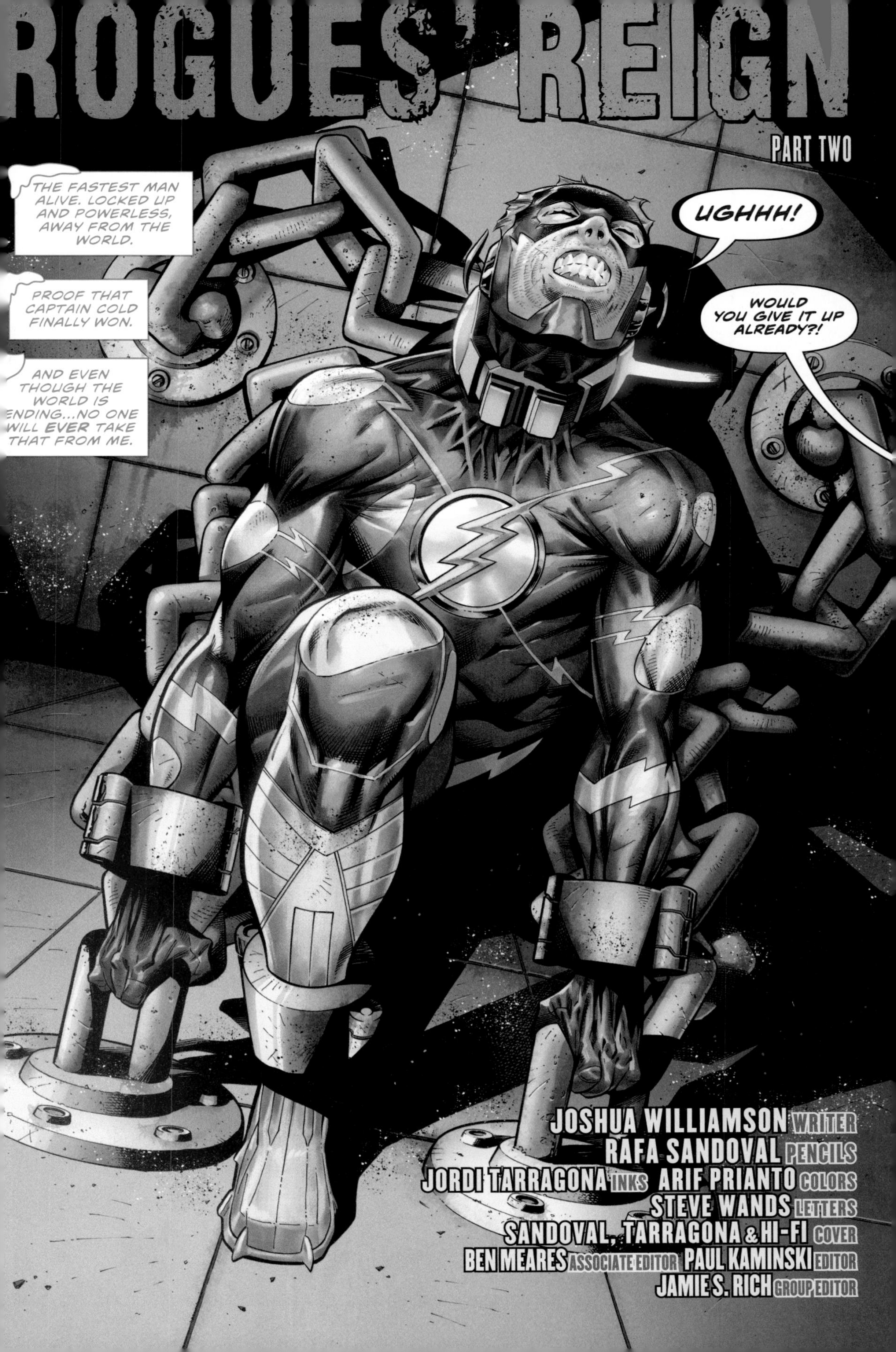
ROGUES' REIGN
PART TWO
THE FASTEST MAN ALIVE. LOCKED UP AND POWERLESS, AWAY FROM THE WORLD.
PROOF THAT CAPTAIN COLD FINALLY WON.
AND EVEN THOUGH THE WORLD IS ENDING...NO ONE WILL EVER TAKE THAT FROM ME.
UGHHH!
WOULD YOU GIVE IT UP ALREADY?!
JOSHUA WILLIAMSON WRITER
RAFA SANDOVAL PENCILS
JORDI TARRAGONA INKS ARIF PRIANTO COLORS
STEVE WANDS LETTERS
SANDOVAL, TARRAGONA & HI-FI COVER
BEN MEARES ASSOCIATE EDITOR PAUL KAMINSKI EDITOR
JAMIE S. RICH GROUP EDITOR

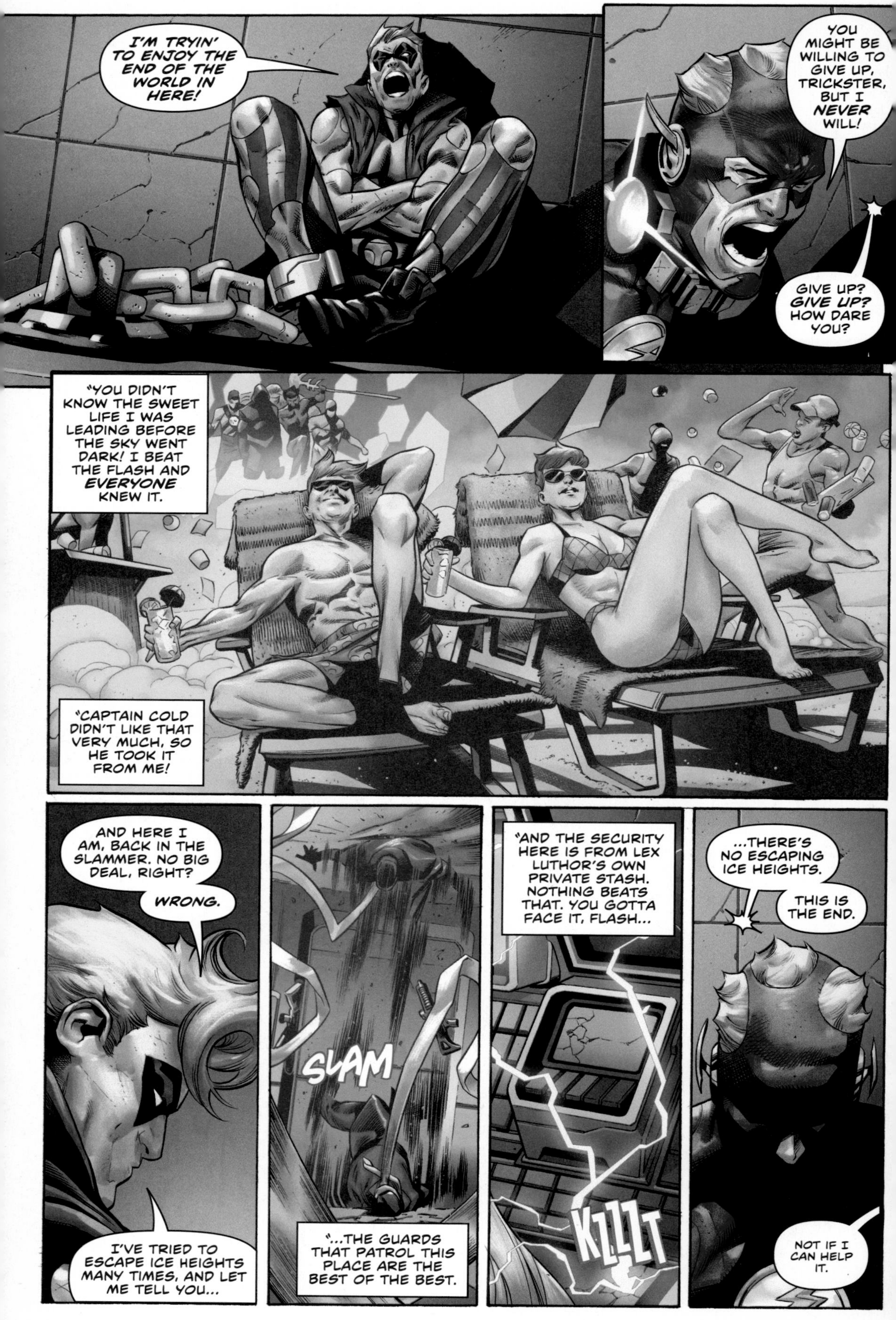
I'M TRYIN' TO ENJOY THE END OF THE WORLD IN HERE!
YOU MIGHT BE WILLING TO GIVE UP, TRICKSTER, BUT I NEVER WILL!
GIVE UP? GIVE UP? HOW DARE YOU?
"YOU DIDN'T KNOW THE SWEET LIFE I WAS LEADING BEFORE THE SKY WENT DARK! I BEAT THE FLASH AND EVERYONE KNEW IT.
"CAPTAIN COLD DIDN'T LIKE THAT VERY MUCH, SO HE TOOK IT FROM ME!
AND HERE I AM, BACK IN THE SLAMMER. NO BIG DEAL, RIGHT?
WRONG.
I'VE TRIED TO ESCAPE ICE HEIGHTS MANY TIMES, AND LET ME TELL YOU...
SLAM
"...THE GUARDS THAT PATROL THIS PLACE ARE THE BEST OF THE BEST.
"AND THE SECURITY HERE IS FROM LEX LUTHOR'S OWN PRIVATE STASH. NOTHING BEATS THAT. YOU GOTTA FACE IT, FLASH...
KZZZT
...THERE'S NO ESCAPING ICE HEIGHTS.
THIS IS THE END.
NOT IF I CAN HELP IT.

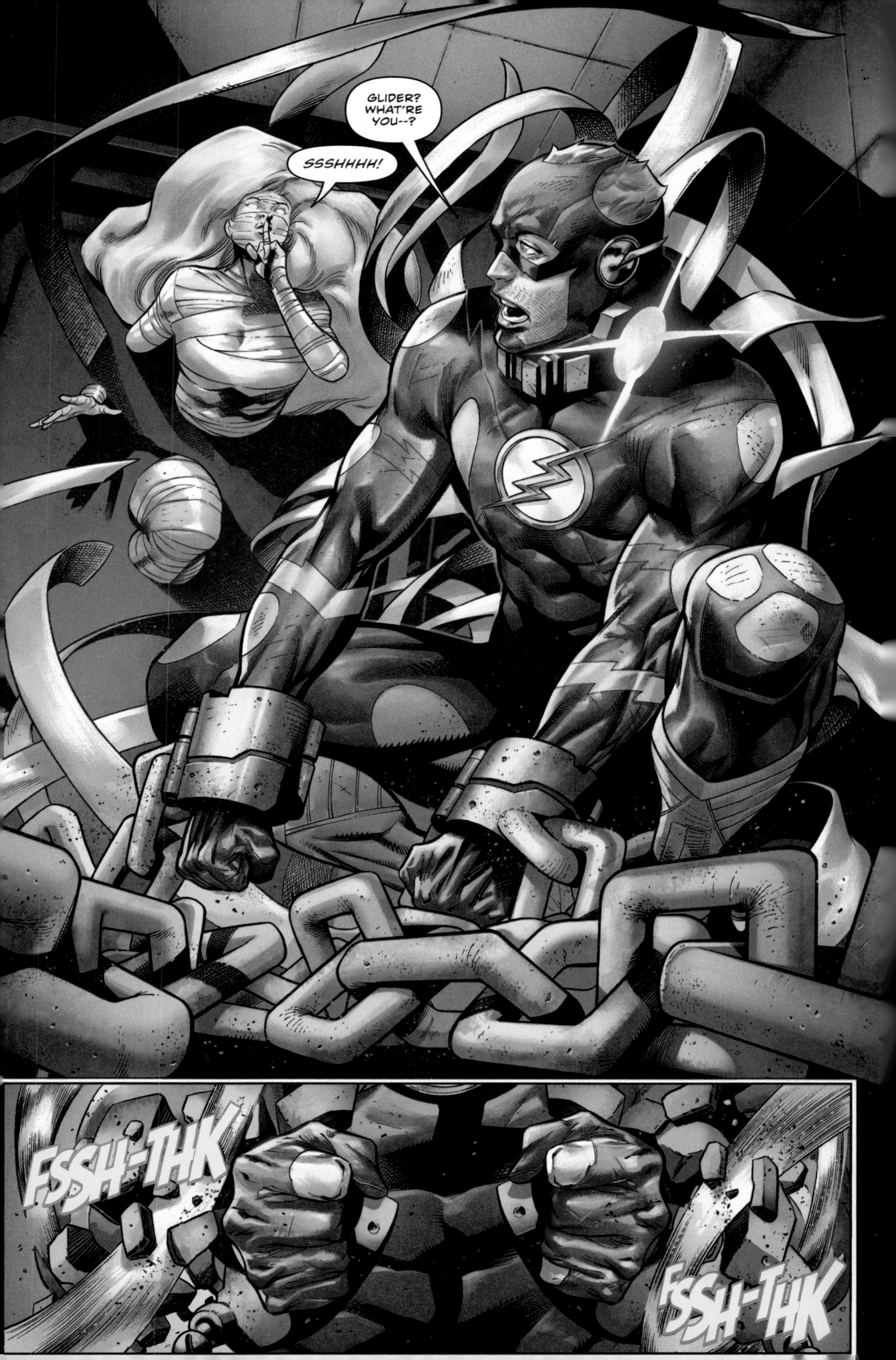
GLIDER? WHAT'RE YOU--?
SSSHHHH!
FSSH-THK
FSSH-THK

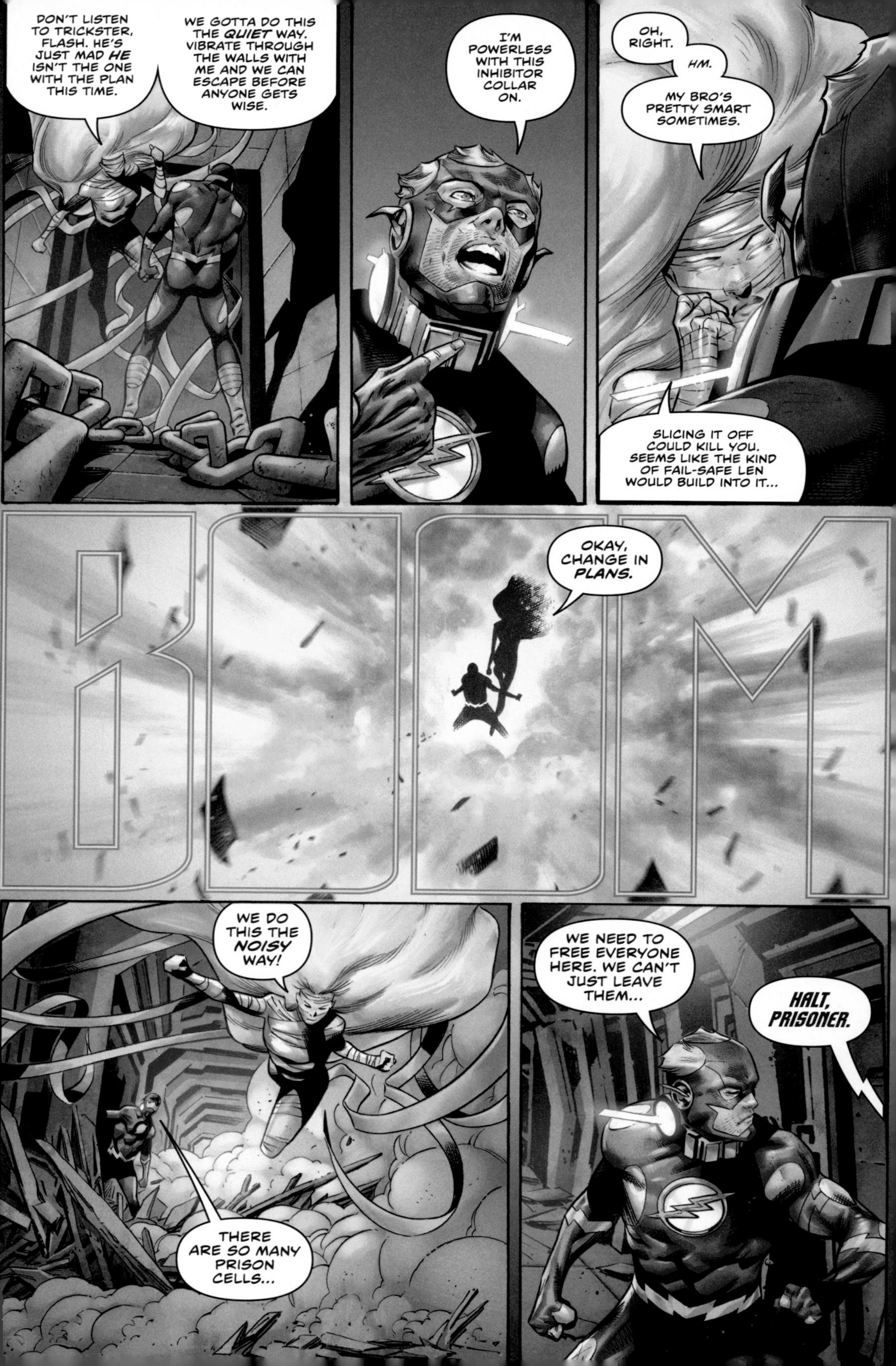
DON'T LISTEN TO TRICKSTER, FLASH. HE'S JUST MAD HE ISN'T THE ONE WITH THE PLAN THIS TIME.
WE GOTTA DO THIS THE QUIET WAY. VIBRATE THROUGH THE WALLS WITH ME AND WE CAN ESCAPE BEFORE ANYONE GETS WISE.
I'M POWERLESS WITH THIS INHIBITOR COLLAR ON.
OH, RIGHT.
HM.
MY BRO'S PRETTY SMART SOMETIMES.
SLICING IT OFF COULD KILL YOU. SEEMS LIKE THE KIND OF FAIL-SAFE LEN WOULD BUILD INTO IT...
BOOM
OKAY, CHANGE IN PLANS.
WE DO THIS THE NOISY WAY!
THERE ARE SO MANY PRISON CELLS...
WE NEED TO FREE EVERYONE HERE. WE CAN'T JUST LEAVE THEM...
HALT, PRISONER.

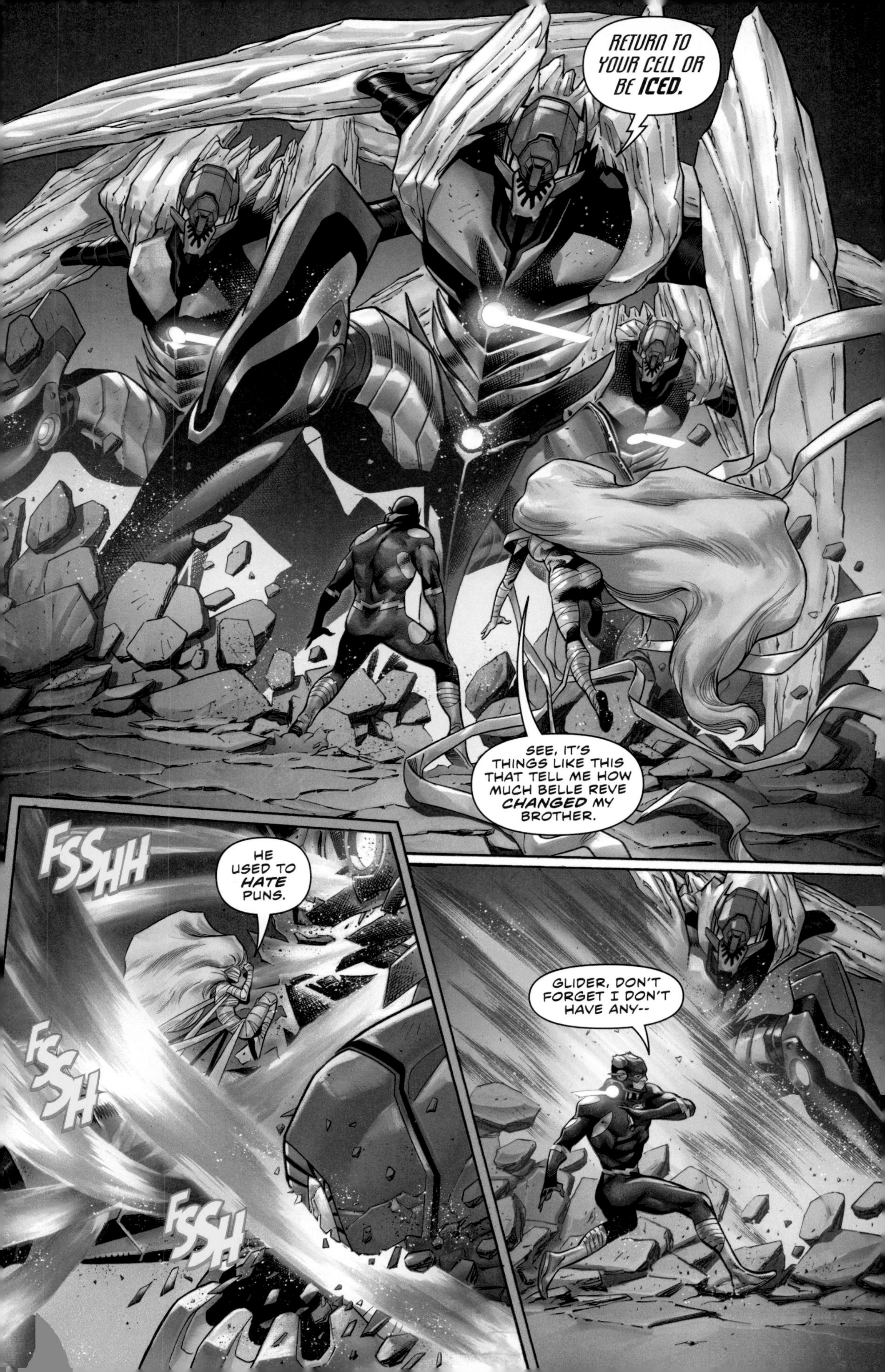
RETURN TO YOUR CELL OR BE ICED.
SEE, IT'S THINGS LIKE THIS THAT TELL ME HOW MUCH BELLE REVE CHANGED MY BROTHER.
FSSHH
HE USED TO HATE PUNS.
FSSH
FSSH
GLIDER, DON'T FORGET I DON'T HAVE ANY--

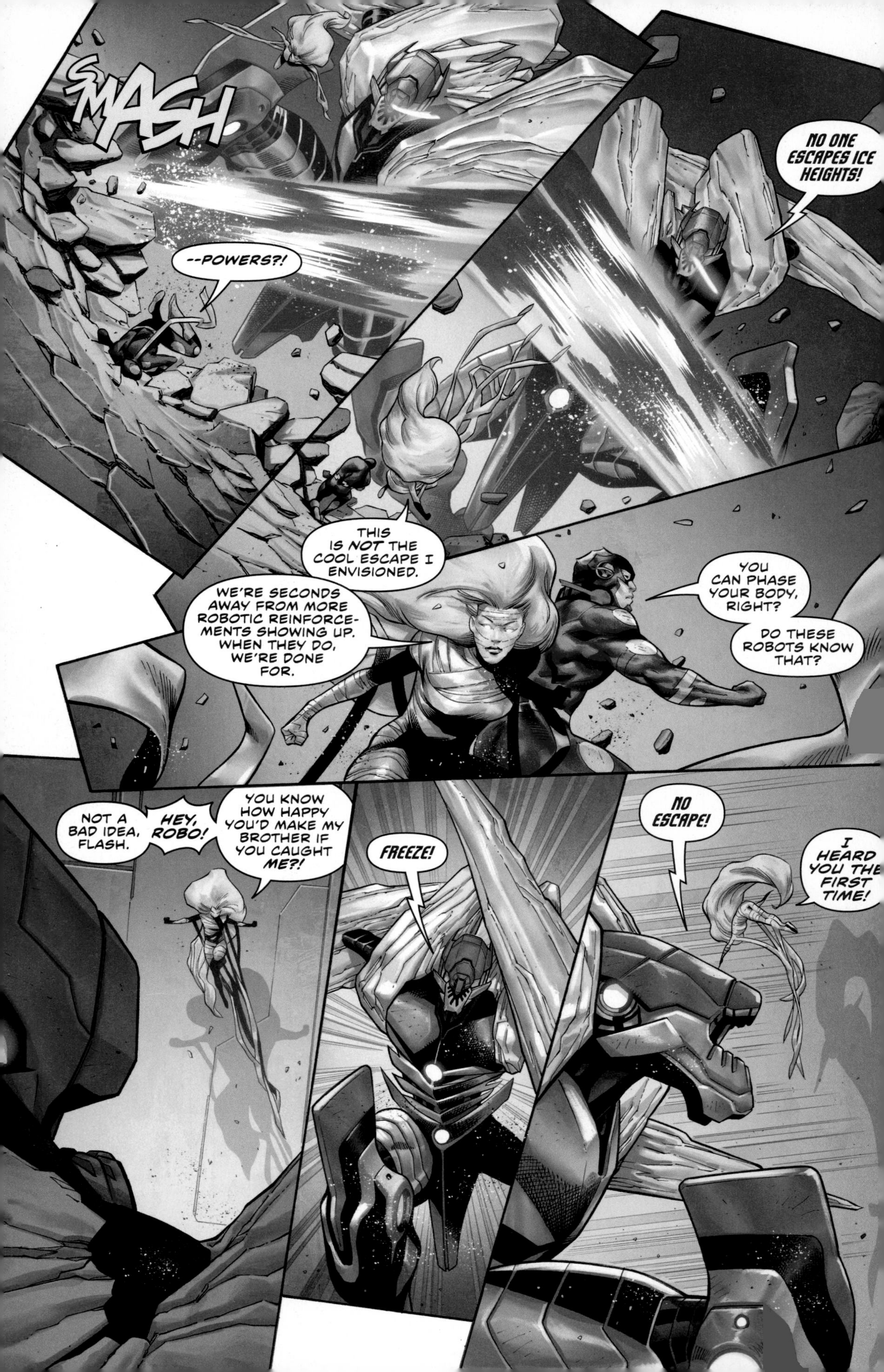
SMASH
--POWERS?!
NO ONE ESCAPES ICE HEIGHTS!
THIS IS NOT THE COOL ESCAPE I ENVISIONED.
WE'RE SECONDS AWAY FROM MORE ROBOTIC REINFORCEMENTS SHOWING UP. WHEN THEY DO, WE'RE DONE FOR.
YOU CAN PHASE YOUR BODY, RIGHT?
DO THESE ROBOTS KNOW THAT?
NOT A BAD IDEA, FLASH.
HEY, ROBO!
YOU KNOW HOW HAPPY YOU'D MAKE MY BROTHER IF YOU CAUGHT ME?!
FREEZE!
NO ESCAPE!
I HEARD YOU THE FIRST TIME!

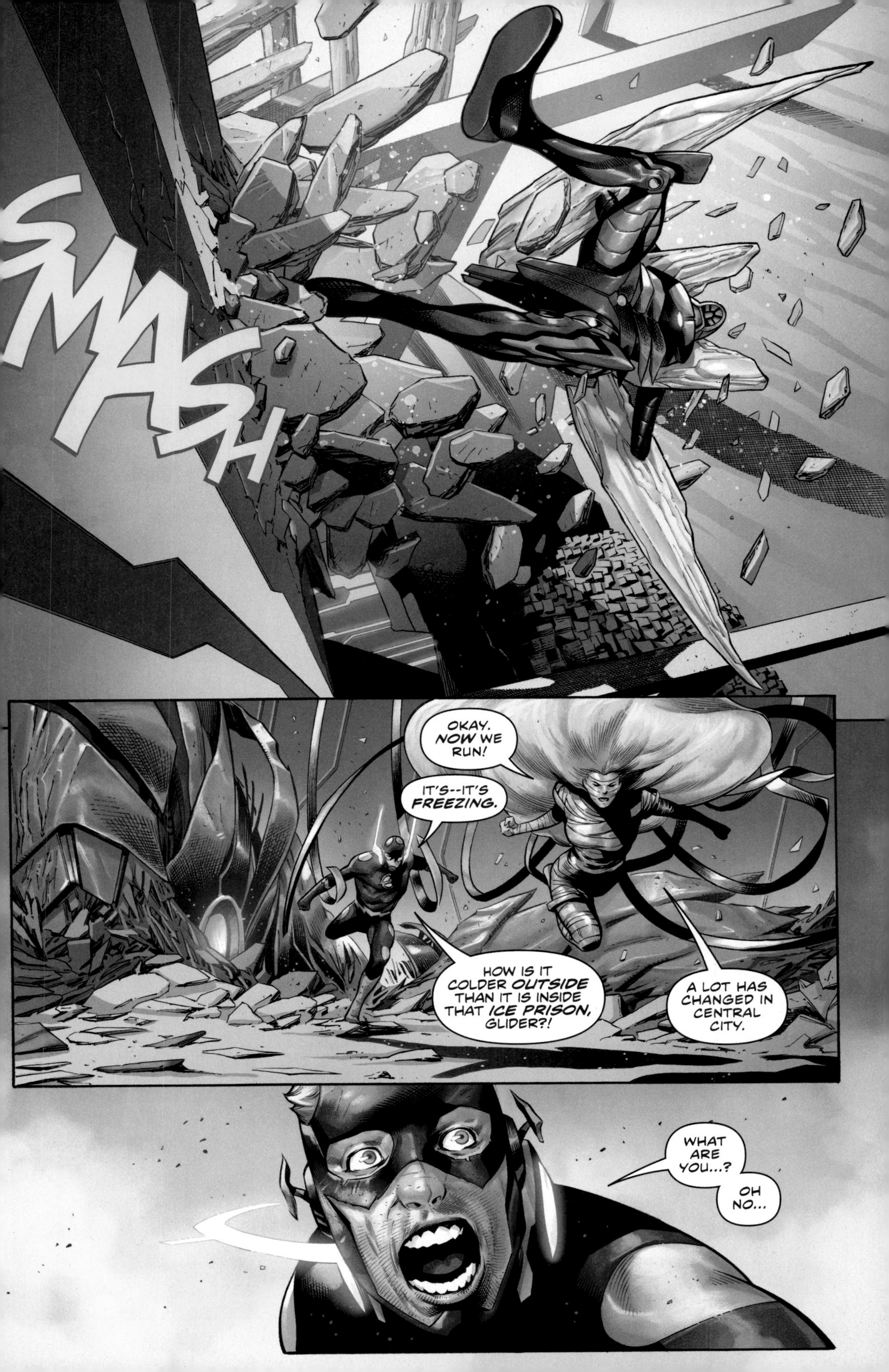
SMASH
OKAY. NOW WE RUN!
IT'S--IT'S FREEZING.
HOW IS IT COLDER OUTSIDE THAN IT IS INSIDE THAT ICE PRISON, GLIDER?!
A LOT HAS CHANGED IN CENTRAL CITY.
WHAT ARE YOU...?
OH NO...

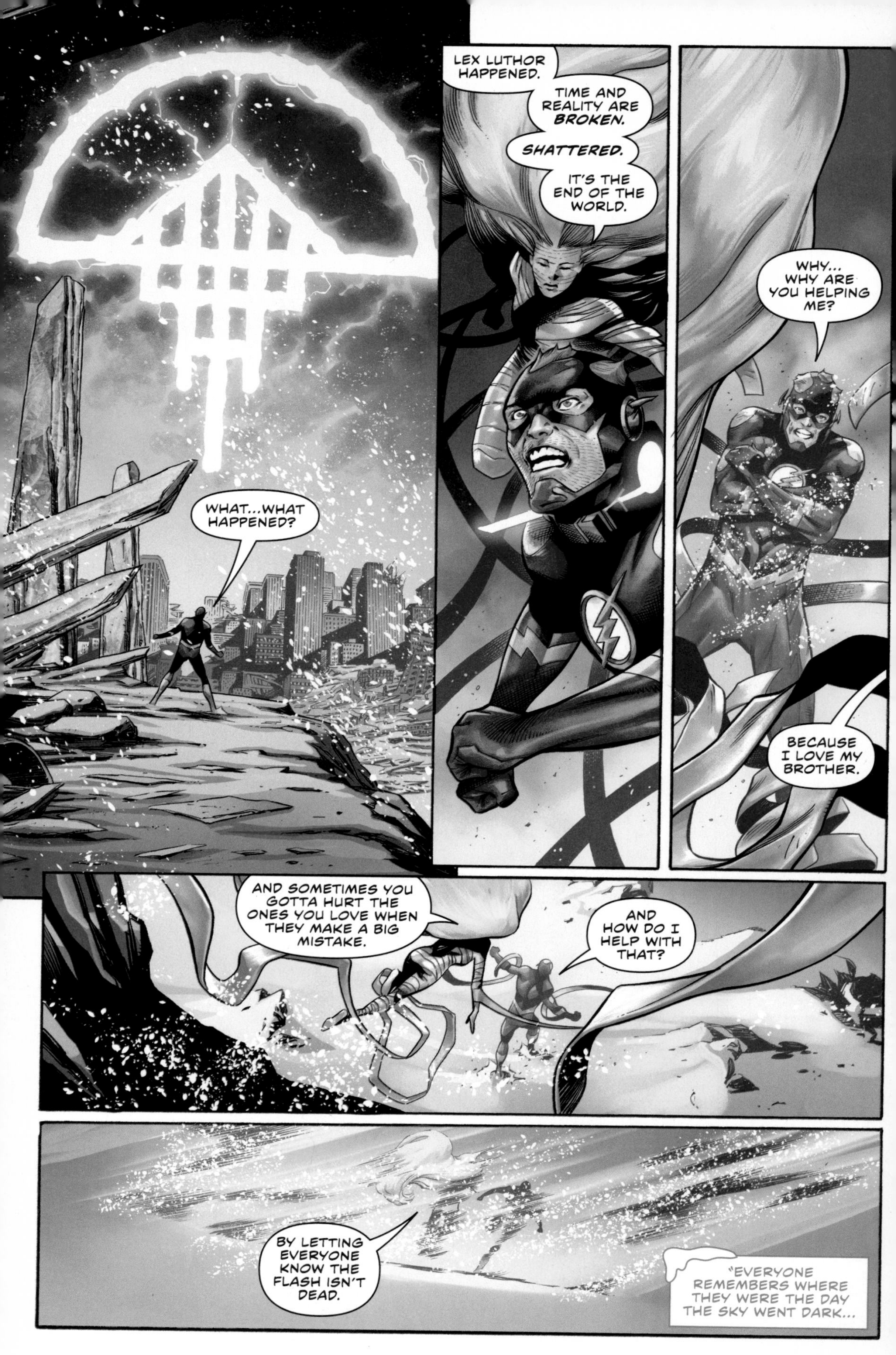
WHAT...WHAT HAPPENED?
LEX LUTHOR HAPPENED.
TIME AND REALITY ARE BROKEN.
SHATTERED.
IT'S THE END OF THE WORLD.
WHY... WHY ARE YOU HELPING ME?
BECAUSE I LOVE MY BROTHER.
AND SOMETIMES YOU GOTTA HURT THE ONES YOU LOVE WHEN THEY MAKE A BIG MISTAKE.
AND HOW DO I HELP WITH THAT?
BY LETTING EVERYONE KNOW THE FLASH ISN'T DEAD.
"EVERYONE REMEMBERS WHERE THEY WERE THE DAY THE SKY WENT DARK...

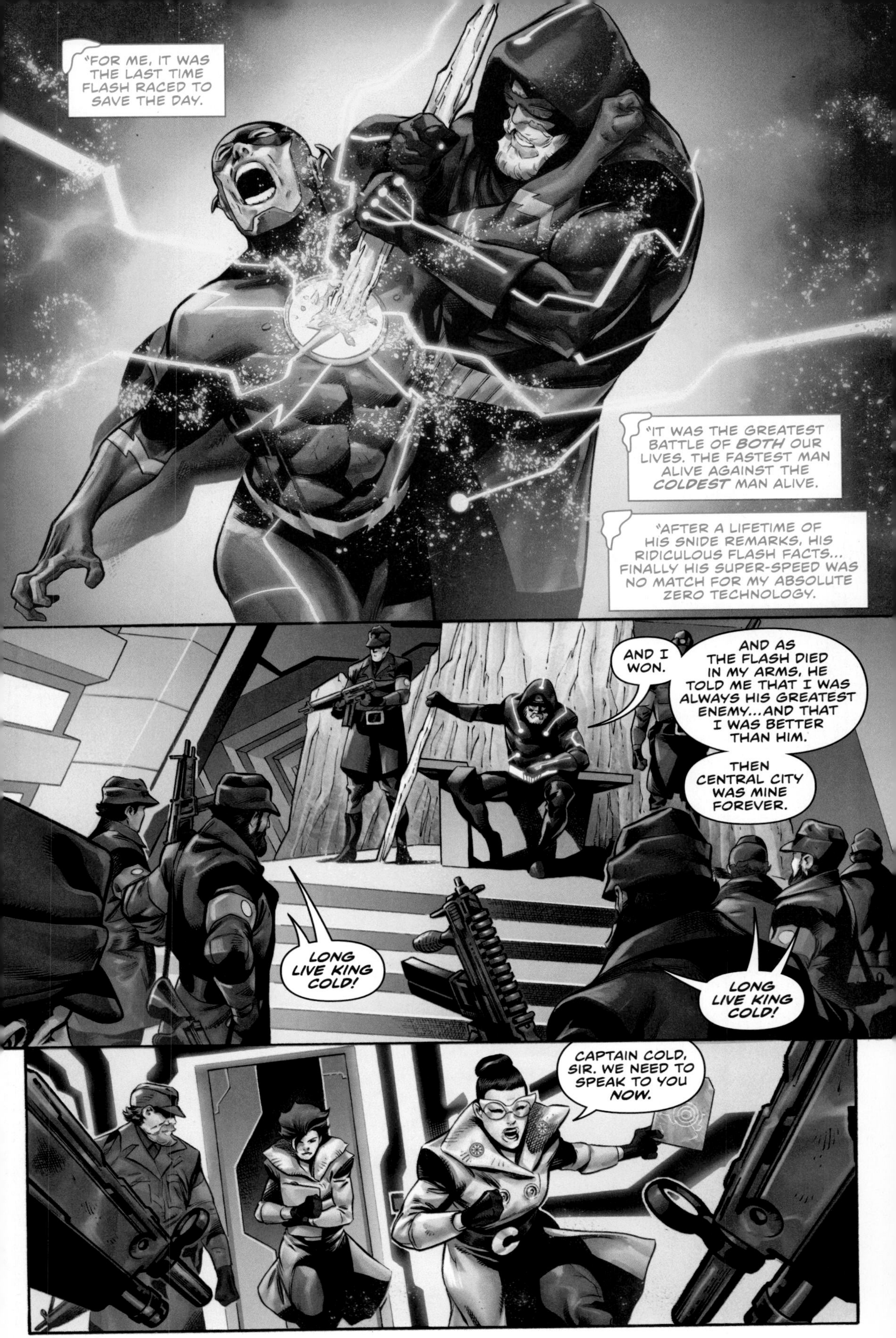
"FOR ME, IT WAS THE LAST TIME FLASH RACED TO SAVE THE DAY.
"IT WAS THE GREATEST BATTLE OF BOTH OUR LIVES. THE FASTEST MAN ALIVE AGAINST THE COLDEST MAN ALIVE.
"AFTER A LIFETIME OF HIS SNIDE REMARKS, HIS RIDICULOUS FLASH FACTS... FINALLY HIS SUPER-SPEED WAS NO MATCH FOR MY ABSOLUTE ZERO TECHNOLOGY.
AND I WON.
AND AS THE FLASH DIED IN MY ARMS, HE TOLD ME THAT I WAS ALWAYS HIS GREATEST ENEMY...AND THAT I WAS BETTER THAN HIM.
THEN CENTRAL CITY WAS MINE FOREVER.
LONG LIVE KING COLD!
LONG LIVE KING COLD!
CAPTAIN COLD, SIR. WE NEED TO SPEAK TO YOU NOW.

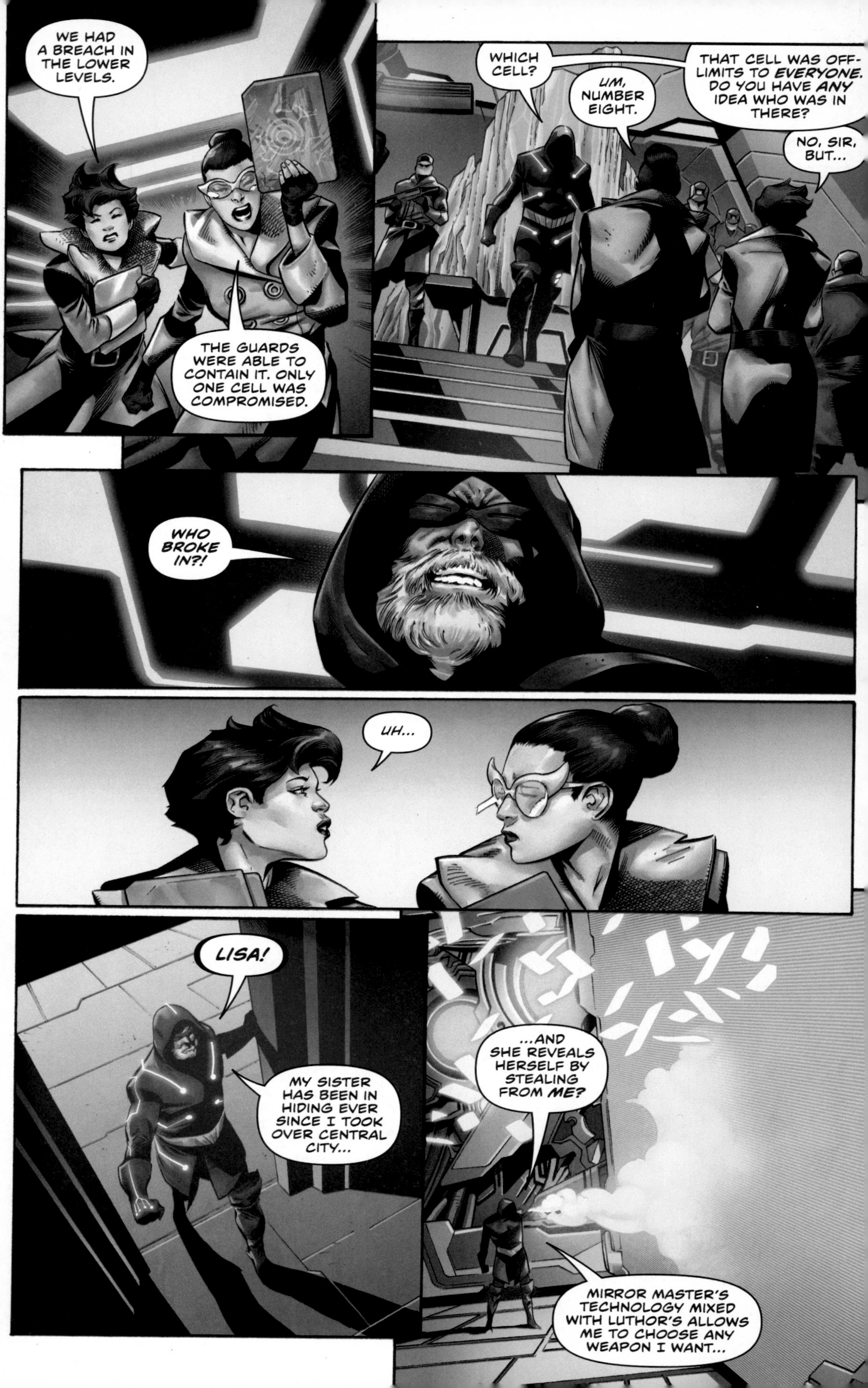
WE HAD A BREACH IN THE LOWER LEVELS.
THE GUARDS WERE ABLE TO CONTAIN IT. ONLY ONE CELL WAS COMPROMISED.
WHICH CELL?
UM, NUMBER EIGHT.
THAT CELL WAS OFF-LIMITS TO EVERYONE. DO YOU HAVE ANY IDEA WHO WAS IN THERE?
NO, SIR, BUT...
WHO BROKE IN?!
UH...
LISA!
MY SISTER HAS BEEN IN HIDING EVER SINCE I TOOK OVER CENTRAL CITY...
...AND SHE REVEALS HERSELF BY STEALING FROM ME?
MIRROR MASTER'S TECHNOLOGY MIXED WITH LUTHOR'S ALLOWS ME TO CHOOSE ANY WEAPON I WANT...

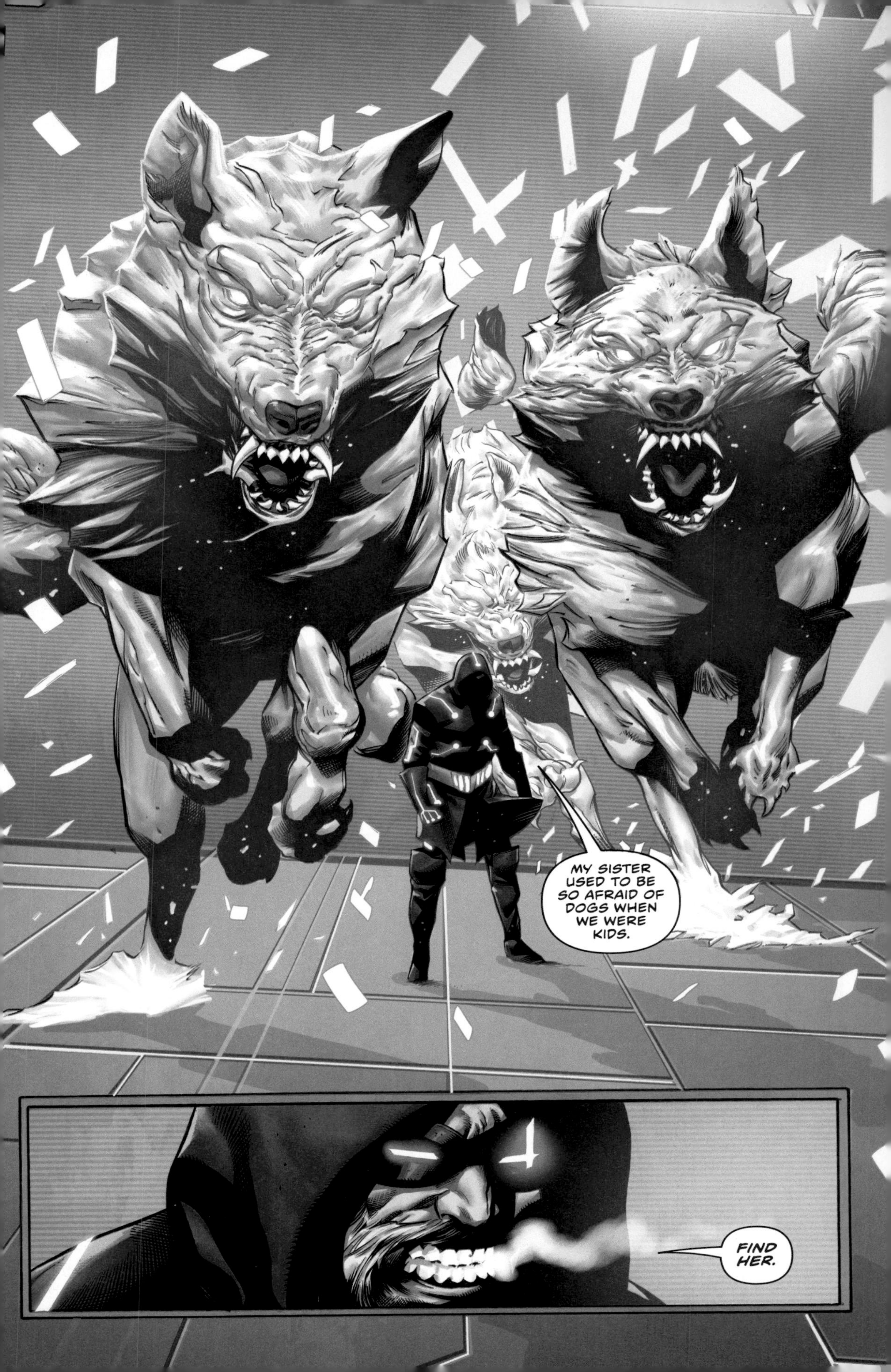
MY SISTER USED TO BE SO AFRAID OF DOGS WHEN WE WERE KIDS.
FIND HER.

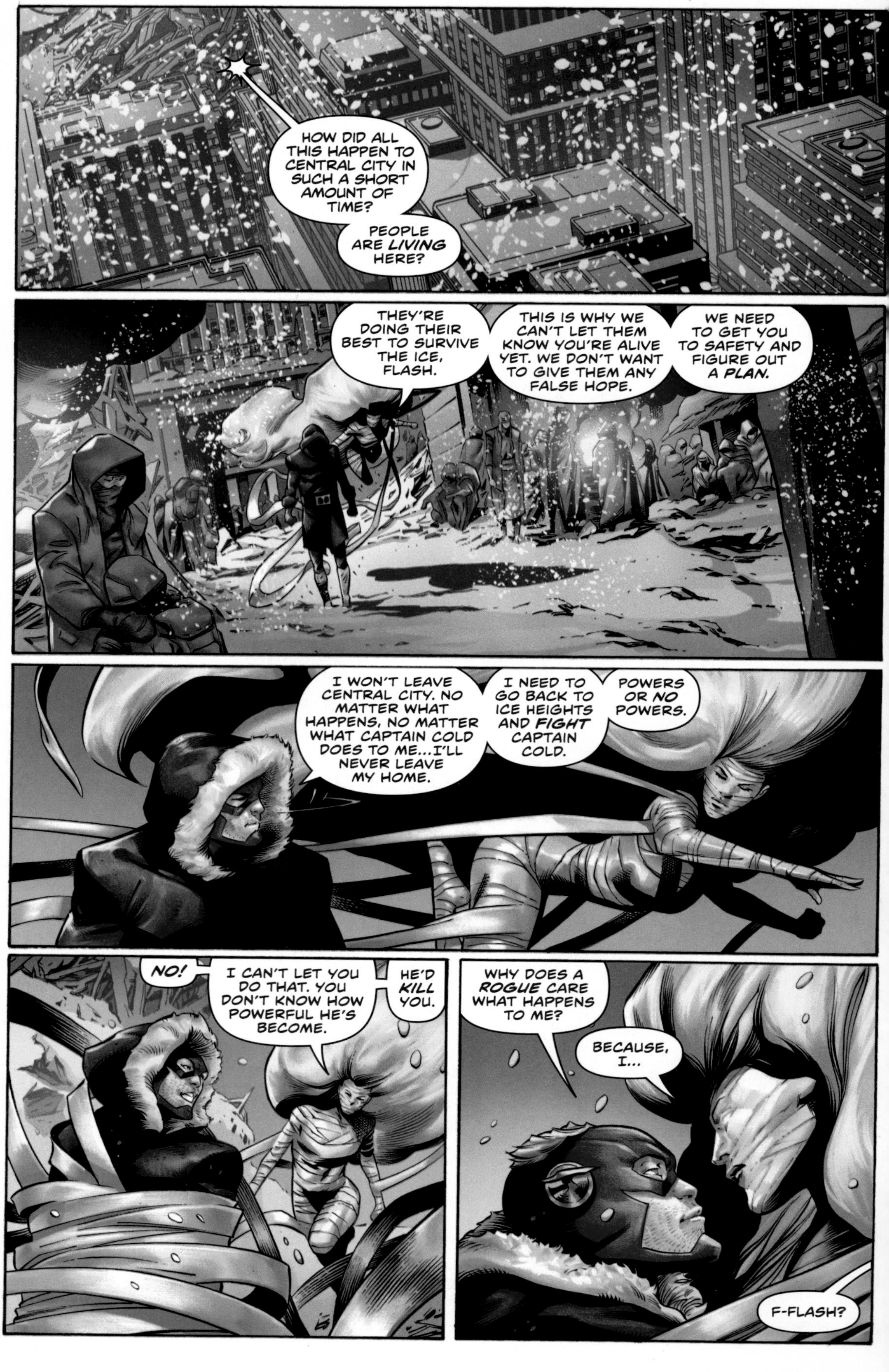
HOW DID ALL THIS HAPPEN TO CENTRAL CITY IN SUCH A SHORT AMOUNT OF TIME?
PEOPLE ARE *LIVING* HERE?
THEY'RE DOING THEIR BEST TO SURVIVE THE ICE, FLASH.
THIS IS WHY WE CAN'T LET THEM KNOW YOU'RE ALIVE YET. WE DON'T WANT TO GIVE THEM ANY FALSE HOPE.
WE NEED TO GET YOU TO SAFETY AND FIGURE OUT A *PLAN.*
I WON'T LEAVE CENTRAL CITY. NO MATTER WHAT HAPPENS, NO MATTER WHAT CAPTAIN COLD DOES TO ME...I'LL NEVER LEAVE MY HOME.
I NEED TO GO BACK TO ICE HEIGHTS AND *FIGHT* CAPTAIN COLD.
POWERS OR *NO* POWERS.
NO!
I CAN'T LET YOU DO THAT. YOU DON'T KNOW HOW POWERFUL HE'S BECOME.
HE'D *KILL* YOU.
WHY DOES A *ROGUE* CARE WHAT HAPPENS TO ME?
BECAUSE, I...
F-FLASH?

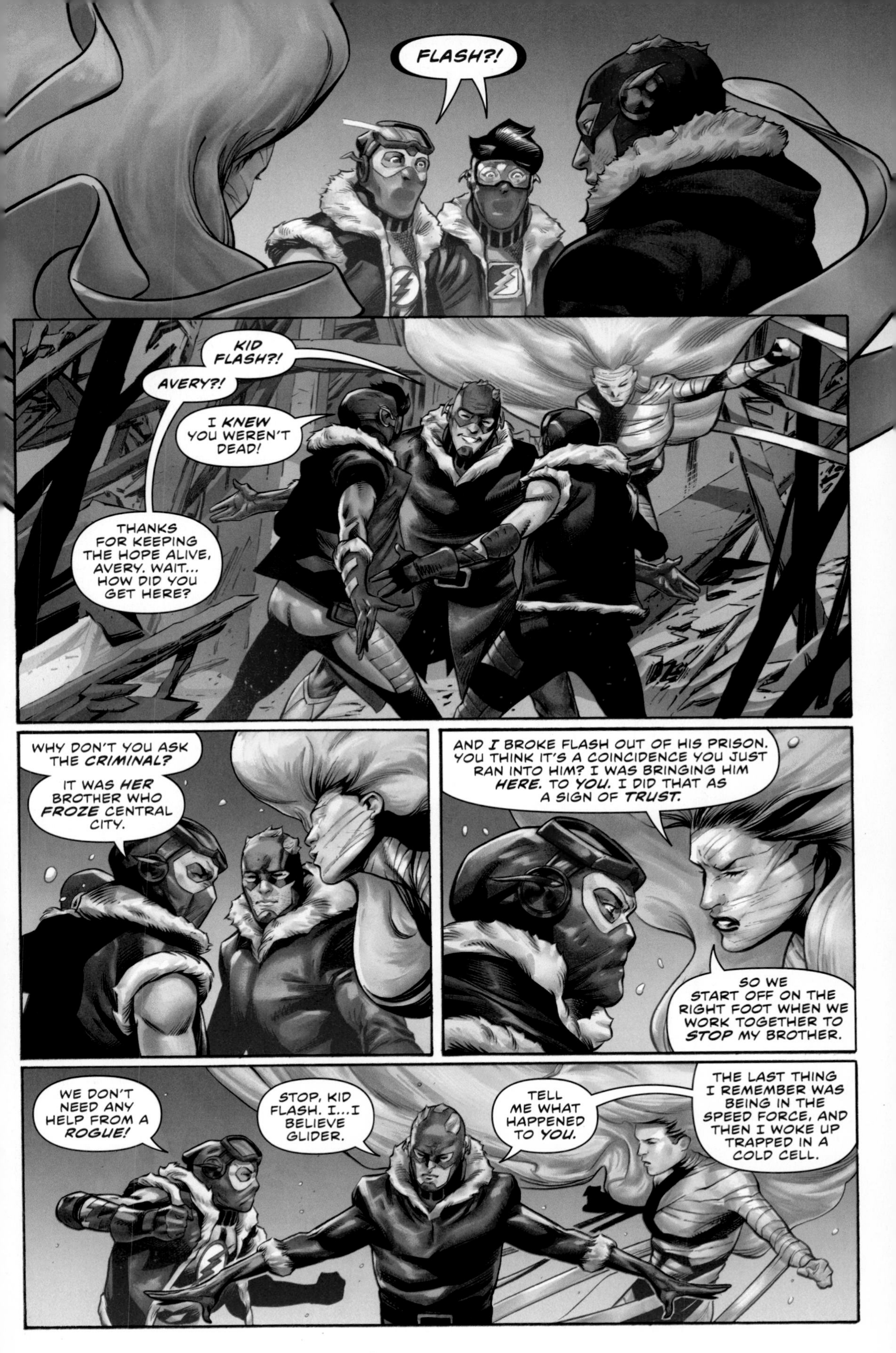
FLASH?!
KID FLASH?!
AVERY?!
I KNEW YOU WEREN'T DEAD!
THANKS FOR KEEPING THE HOPE ALIVE, AVERY. WAIT... HOW DID YOU GET HERE?
WHY DON'T YOU ASK THE CRIMINAL?
IT WAS HER BROTHER WHO FROZE CENTRAL CITY.
AND I BROKE FLASH OUT OF HIS PRISON. YOU THINK IT'S A COINCIDENCE YOU JUST RAN INTO HIM? I WAS BRINGING HIM HERE. TO YOU. I DID THAT AS A SIGN OF TRUST.
SO WE START OFF ON THE RIGHT FOOT WHEN WE WORK TOGETHER TO STOP MY BROTHER.
WE DON'T NEED ANY HELP FROM A ROGUE!
STOP, KID FLASH. I...I BELIEVE GLIDER.
TELL ME WHAT HAPPENED TO YOU.
THE LAST THING I REMEMBER WAS BEING IN THE SPEED FORCE, AND THEN I WOKE UP TRAPPED IN A COLD CELL.

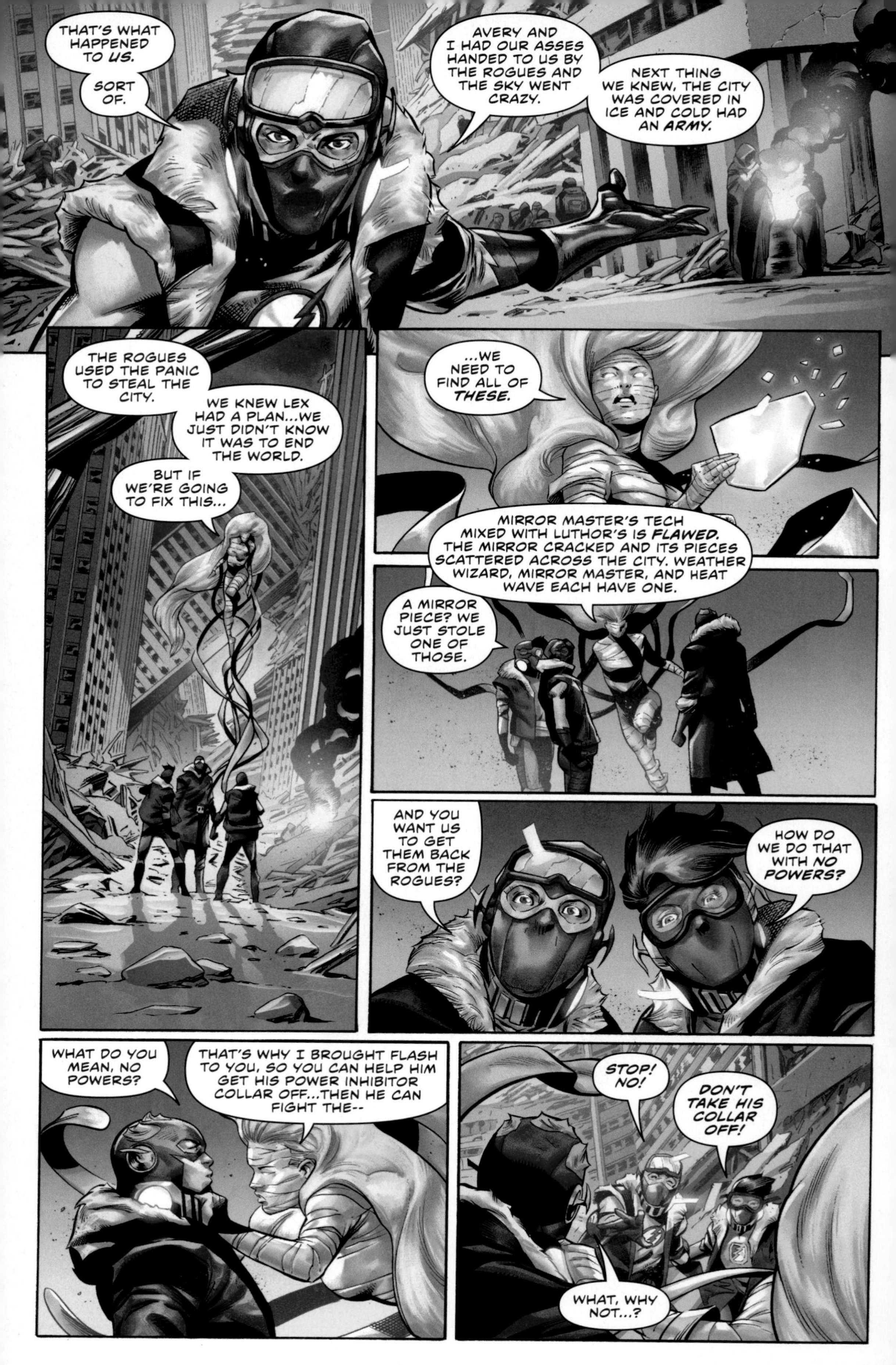
THAT'S WHAT HAPPENED TO *US.*
SORT OF.
AVERY AND I HAD OUR ASSES HANDED TO US BY THE ROGUES AND THE SKY WENT CRAZY.
NEXT THING WE KNEW, THE CITY WAS COVERED IN ICE AND COLD HAD AN *ARMY.*
THE ROGUES USED THE PANIC TO STEAL THE CITY.
WE KNEW LEX HAD A PLAN...WE JUST DIDN'T KNOW IT WAS TO END THE WORLD.
BUT IF WE'RE GOING TO FIX THIS...
...WE NEED TO FIND ALL OF *THESE.*
MIRROR MASTER'S TECH MIXED WITH LUTHOR'S IS *FLAWED.* THE MIRROR CRACKED AND ITS PIECES SCATTERED ACROSS THE CITY. WEATHER WIZARD, MIRROR MASTER, AND HEAT WAVE EACH HAVE ONE.
A MIRROR PIECE? WE JUST STOLE ONE OF THOSE.
AND YOU WANT US TO GET THEM BACK FROM THE ROGUES?
HOW DO WE DO THAT WITH *NO POWERS?*
WHAT DO YOU MEAN, NO POWERS?
THAT'S WHY I BROUGHT FLASH TO YOU, SO YOU CAN HELP HIM GET HIS POWER INHIBITOR COLLAR OFF...THEN HE CAN FIGHT THE--
STOP! NO!
DON'T TAKE HIS COLLAR OFF!
WHAT, WHY NOT...?

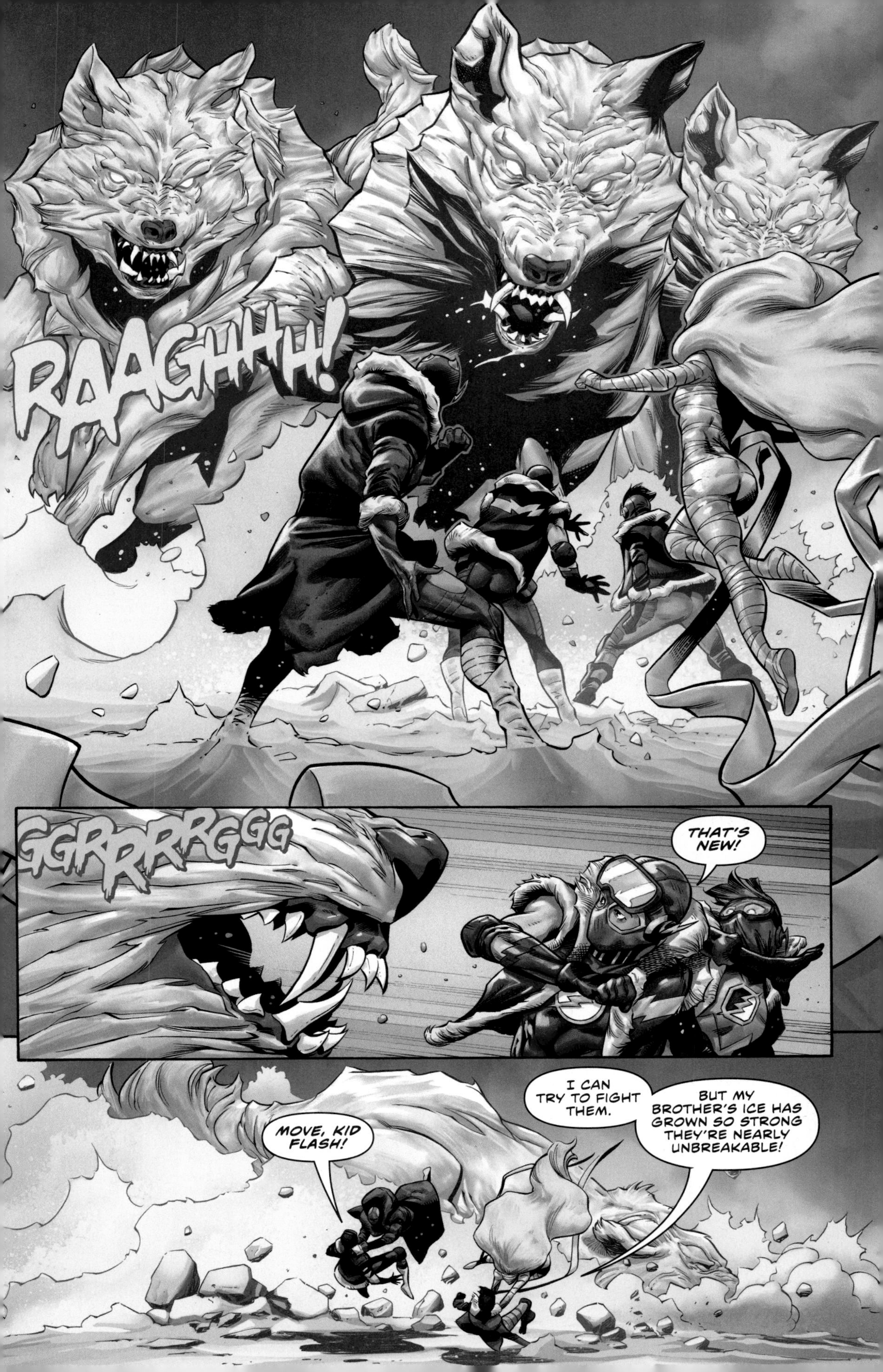
RAAGHHH!
GGRRRRGGG
THAT'S NEW!
MOVE, KID FLASH!
I CAN TRY TO FIGHT THEM.
BUT MY BROTHER'S ICE HAS GROWN SO STRONG THEY'RE NEARLY UNBREAKABLE!

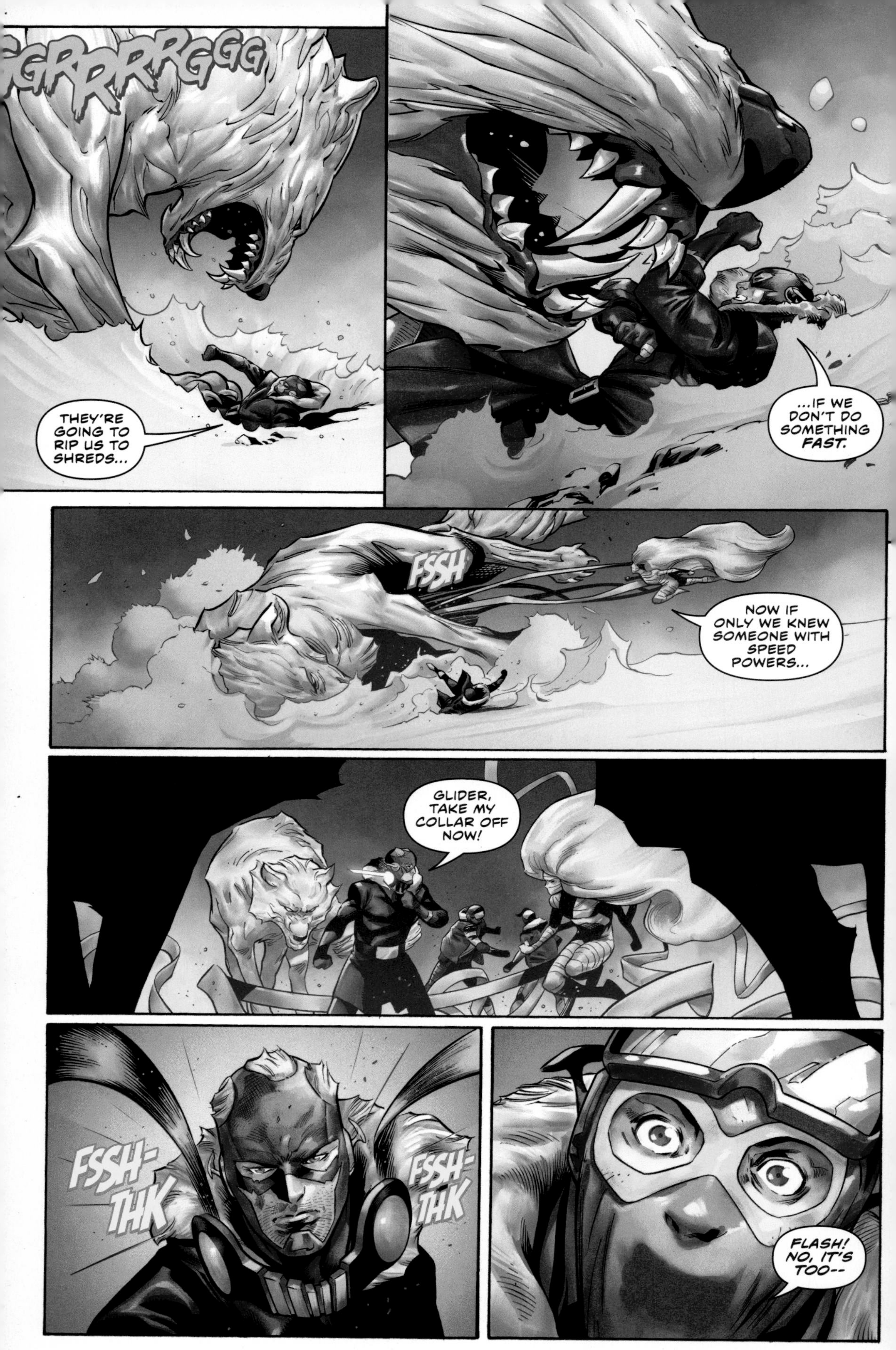
GRRRRGGG
THEY'RE GOING TO RIP US TO SHREDS...
...IF WE DON'T DO SOMETHING FAST.
FSSH
NOW IF ONLY WE KNEW SOMEONE WITH SPEED POWERS...
GLIDER, TAKE MY COLLAR OFF NOW!
FSSH-THK
FSSH-THK
FLASH! NO, IT'S TOO--

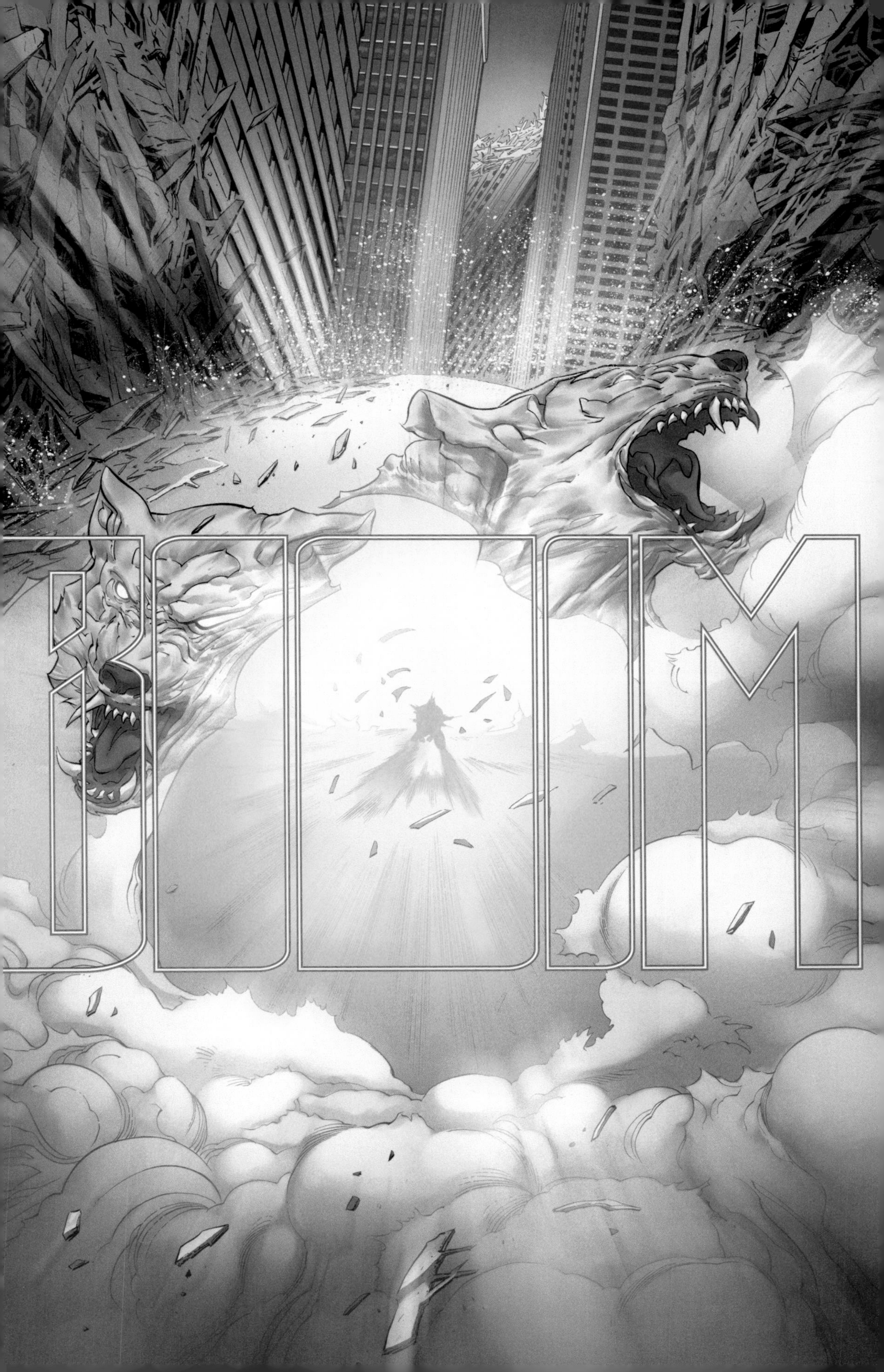
BOOM

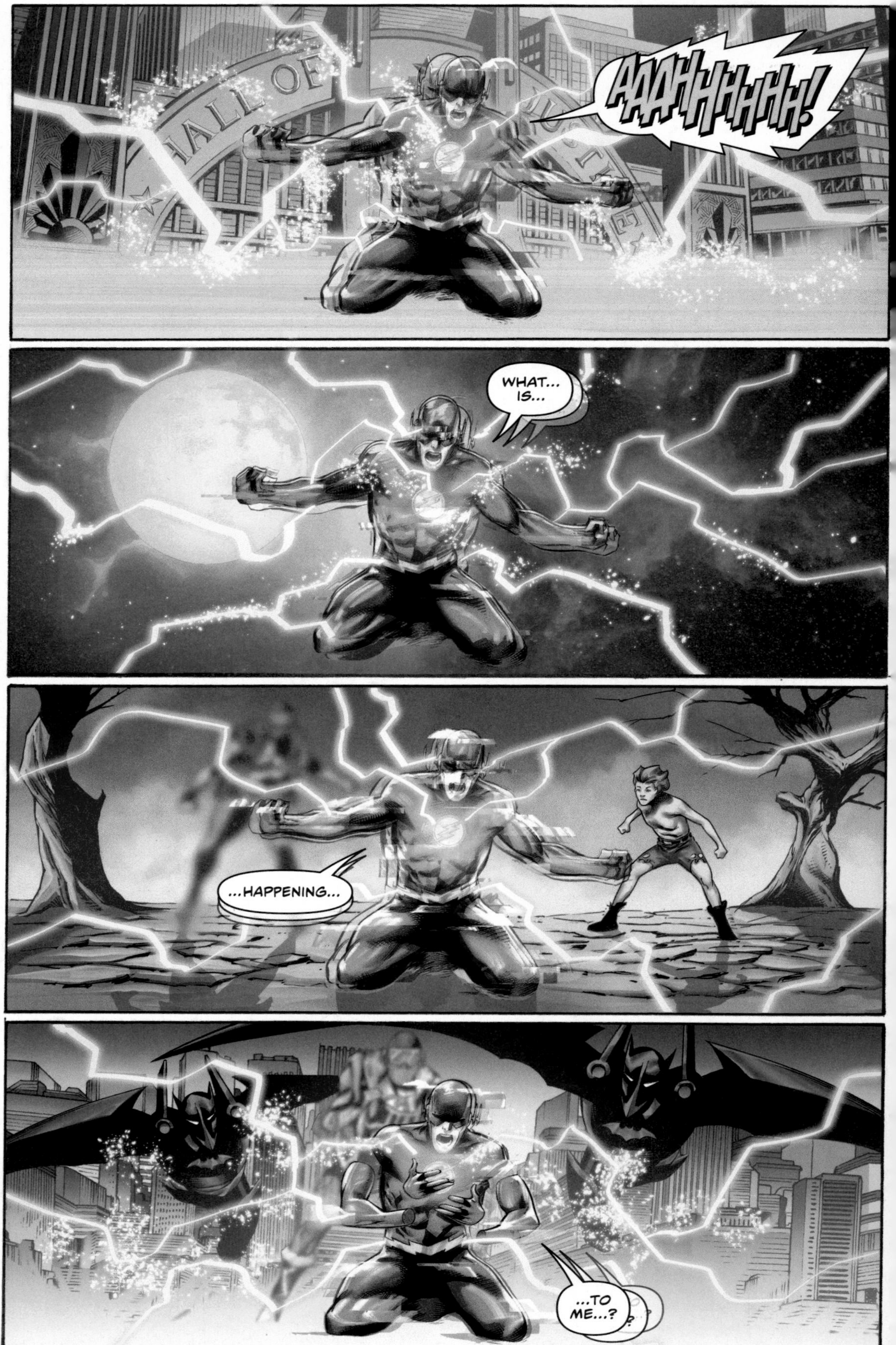
HALL OF
AAAHHHHHH!
WHAT... IS...
...HAPPENING...
...TO ME...?

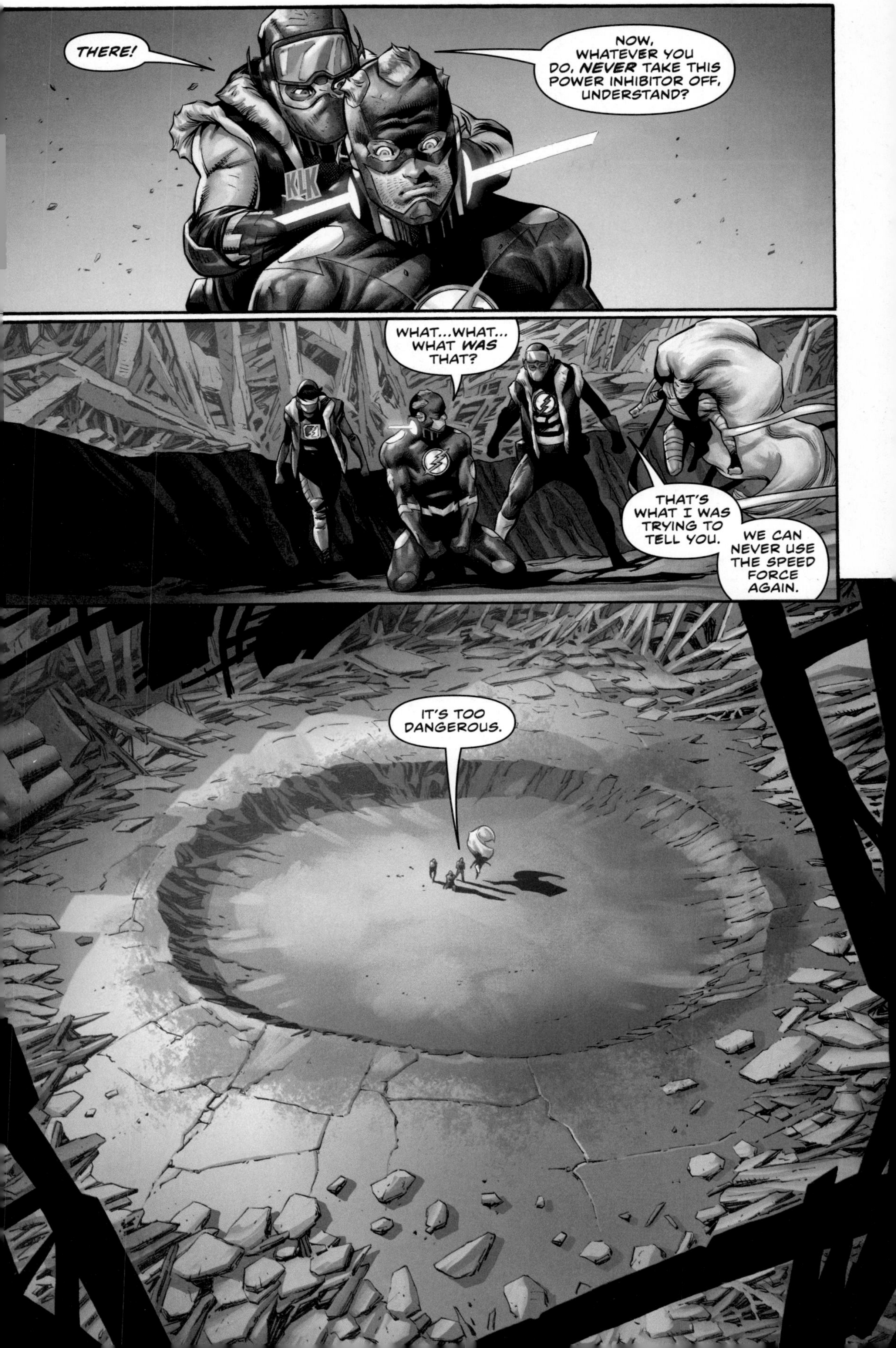
THERE!
NOW, WHATEVER YOU DO, NEVER TAKE THIS POWER INHIBITOR OFF, UNDERSTAND?
KLK
WHAT...WHAT... WHAT WAS THAT?
THAT'S WHAT I WAS TRYING TO TELL YOU.
WE CAN NEVER USE THE SPEED FORCE AGAIN.
IT'S TOO DANGEROUS.

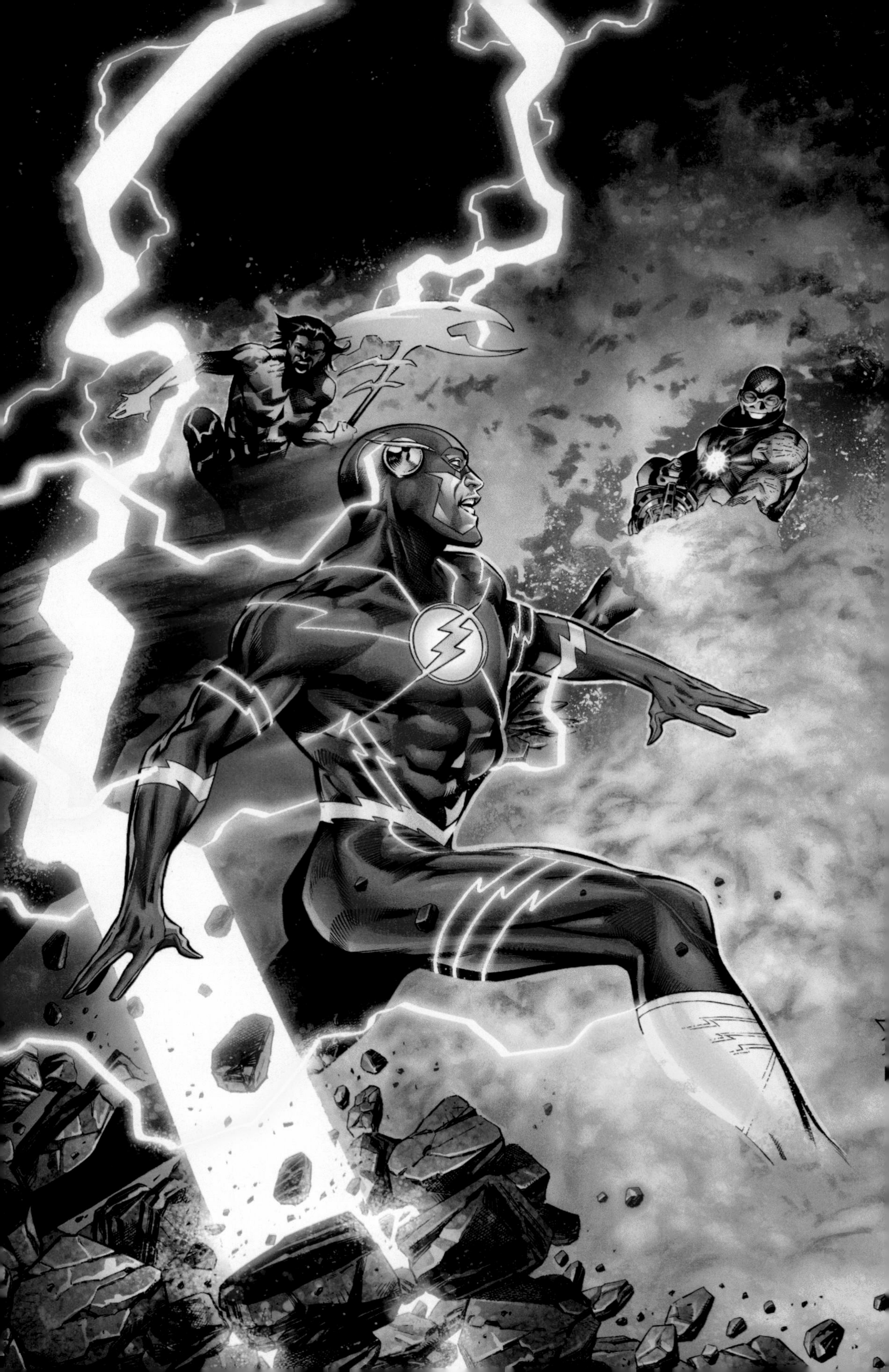

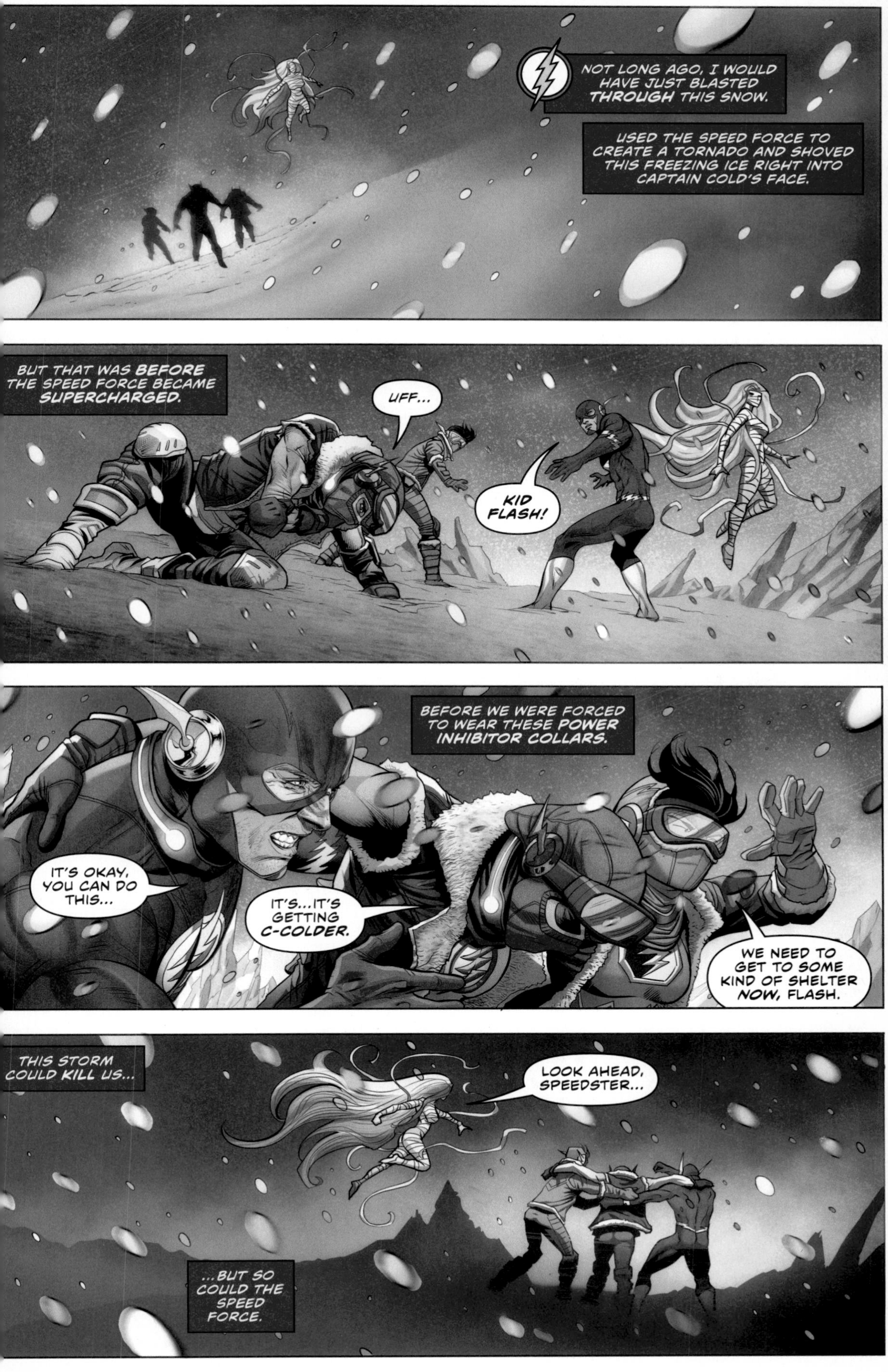
NOT LONG AGO, I WOULD HAVE JUST BLASTED THROUGH THIS SNOW.
USED THE SPEED FORCE TO CREATE A TORNADO AND SHOVED THIS FREEZING ICE RIGHT INTO CAPTAIN COLD'S FACE.
BUT THAT WAS BEFORE THE SPEED FORCE BECAME SUPERCHARGED.
UFF...
KID FLASH!
BEFORE WE WERE FORCED TO WEAR THESE POWER INHIBITOR COLLARS.
IT'S OKAY, YOU CAN DO THIS...
IT'S...IT'S GETTING C-COLDER.
WE NEED TO GET TO SOME KIND OF SHELTER NOW, FLASH.
THIS STORM COULD KILL US...
LOOK AHEAD, SPEEDSTER...
...BUT SO COULD THE SPEED FORCE.

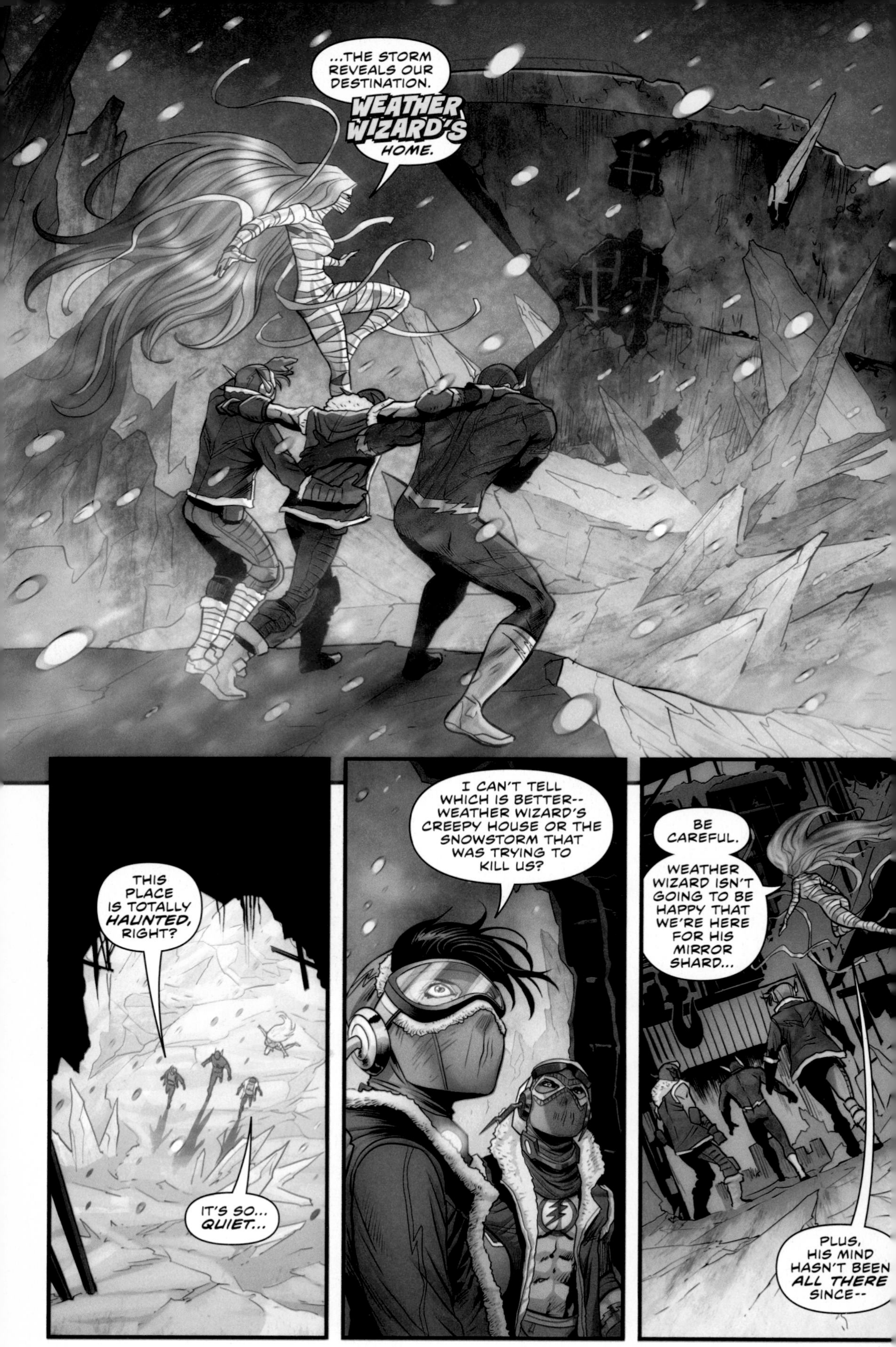
...THE STORM REVEALS OUR DESTINATION.
WEATHER WIZARD'S HOME.
THIS PLACE IS TOTALLY HAUNTED, RIGHT?
IT'S SO... QUIET...
I CAN'T TELL WHICH IS BETTER-- WEATHER WIZARD'S CREEPY HOUSE OR THE SNOWSTORM THAT WAS TRYING TO KILL US?
BE CAREFUL.
WEATHER WIZARD ISN'T GOING TO BE HAPPY THAT WE'RE HERE FOR HIS MIRROR SHARD...
PLUS, HIS MIND HASN'T BEEN ALL THERE SINCE--

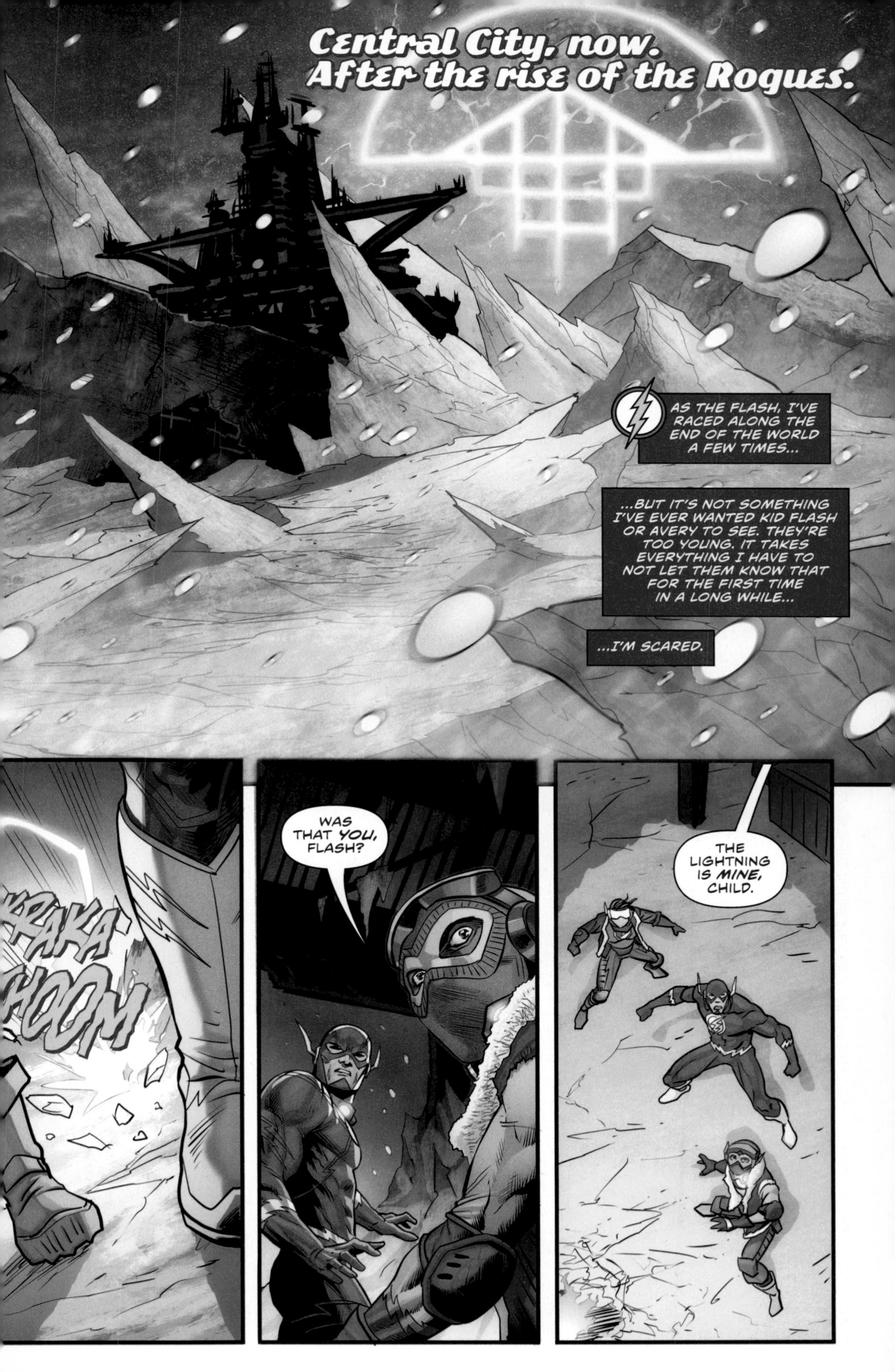
Central City, now.
After the rise of the Rogues.
AS THE FLASH, I'VE RACED ALONG THE END OF THE WORLD A FEW TIMES...
...BUT IT'S NOT SOMETHING I'VE EVER WANTED KID FLASH OR AVERY TO SEE. THEY'RE TOO YOUNG. IT TAKES EVERYTHING I HAVE TO NOT LET THEM KNOW THAT FOR THE FIRST TIME IN A LONG WHILE...
...I'M SCARED.
WAS THAT YOU, FLASH?
THE LIGHTNING IS MINE, CHILD.

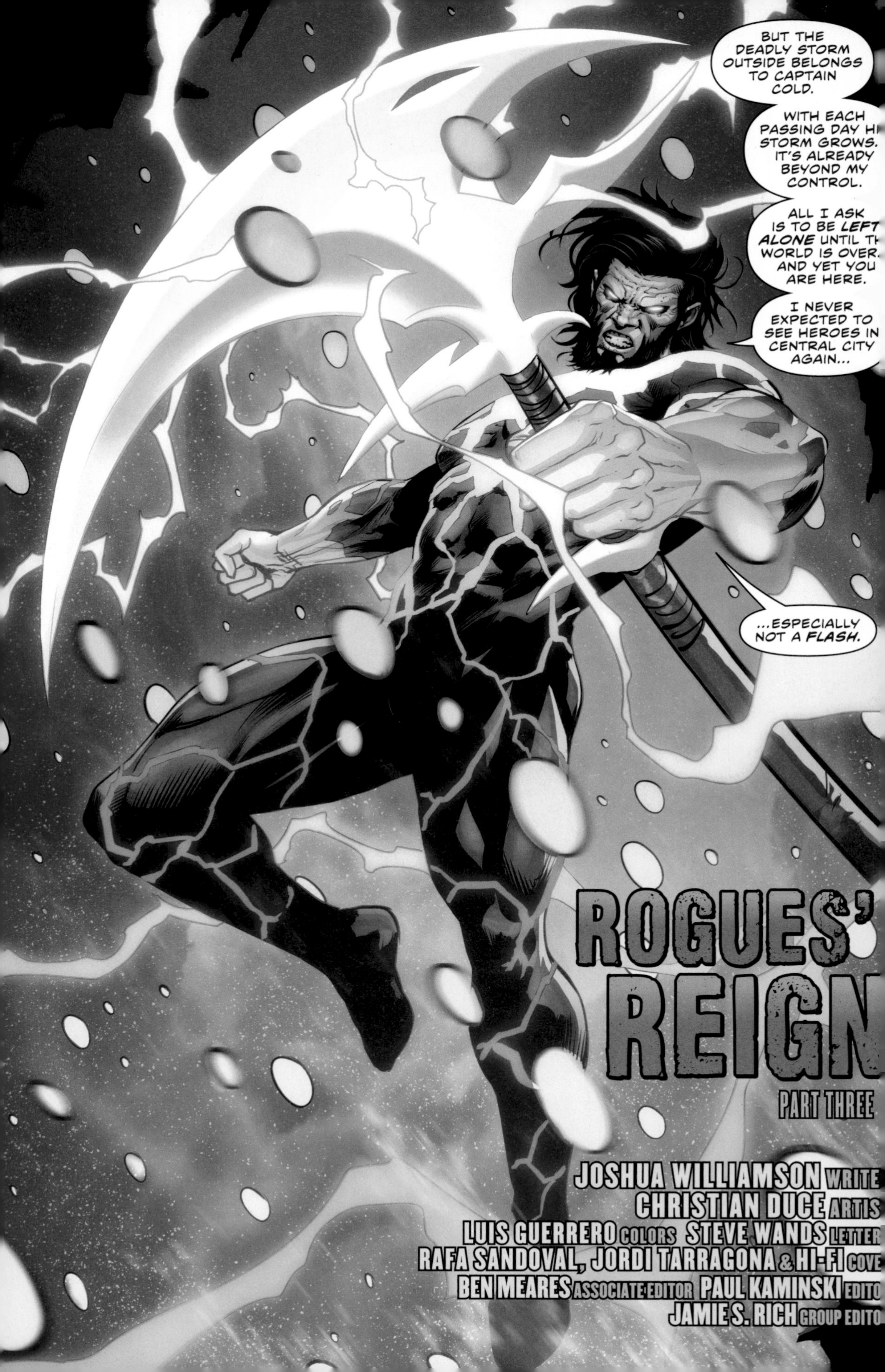
BUT THE DEADLY STORM OUTSIDE BELONGS TO CAPTAIN COLD.
WITH EACH PASSING DAY HI STORM GROWS. IT'S ALREADY BEYOND MY CONTROL.
ALL I ASK IS TO BE LEFT ALONE UNTIL TH WORLD IS OVER. AND YET YOU ARE HERE.
I NEVER EXPECTED TO SEE HEROES IN CENTRAL CITY AGAIN...
...ESPECIALLY NOT A FLASH.
ROGUES' REIGN
PART THREE
JOSHUA WILLIAMSON WRITE
CHRISTIAN DUCE ARTIS
LUIS GUERRERO COLORS STEVE WANDS LETTER
RAFA SANDOVAL, JORDI TARRAGONA & HI-FI COVE
BEN MEARES ASSOCIATE EDITOR PAUL KAMINSKI EDITO
JAMIE S. RICH GROUP EDITO

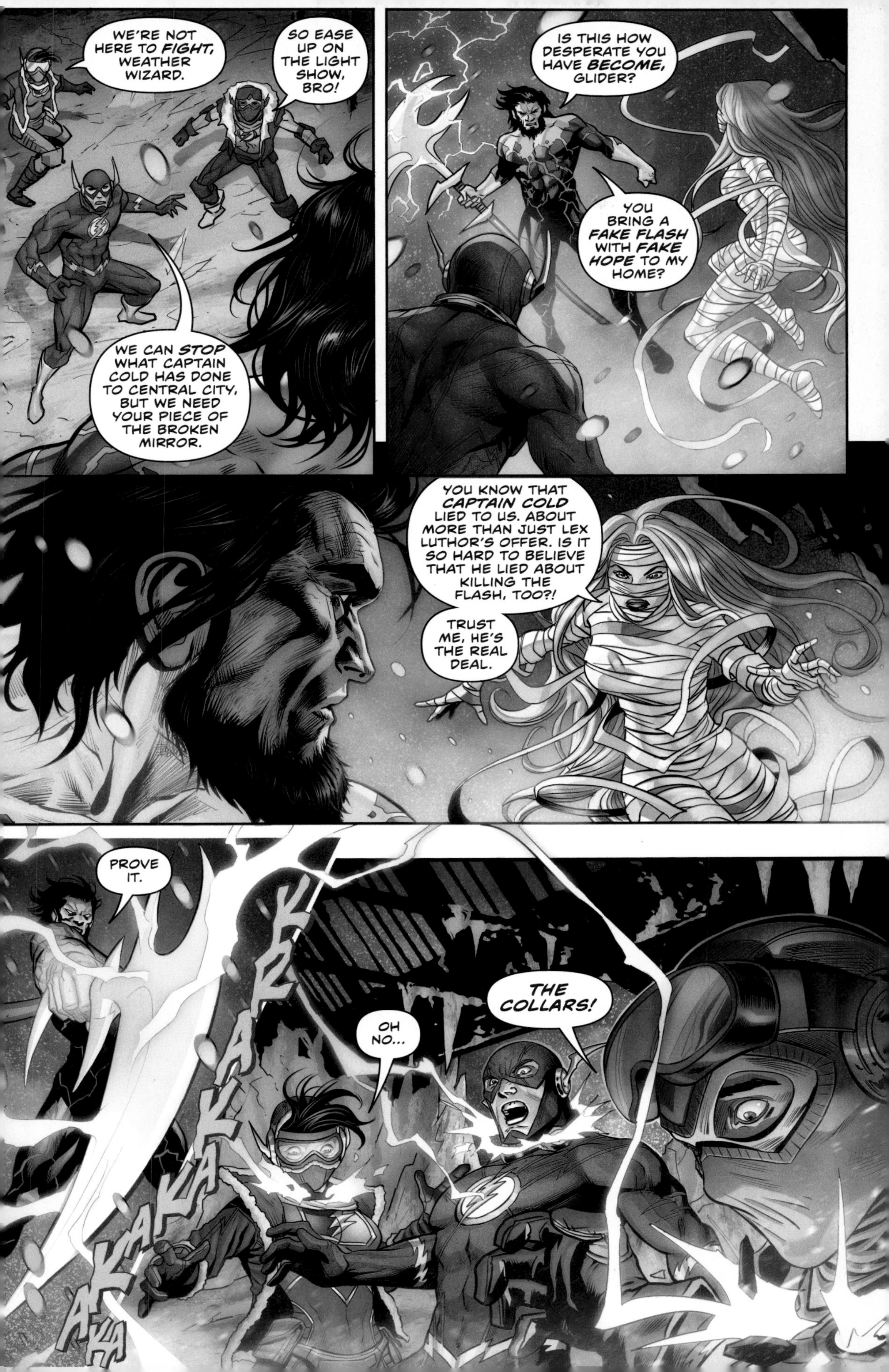
WE'RE NOT HERE TO FIGHT, WEATHER WIZARD.
SO EASE UP ON THE LIGHT SHOW, BRO!
WE CAN STOP WHAT CAPTAIN COLD HAS DONE TO CENTRAL CITY, BUT WE NEED YOUR PIECE OF THE BROKEN MIRROR.
IS THIS HOW DESPERATE YOU HAVE BECOME, GLIDER?
YOU BRING A FAKE FLASH WITH FAKE HOPE TO MY HOME?
YOU KNOW THAT CAPTAIN COLD LIED TO US. ABOUT MORE THAN JUST LEX LUTHOR'S OFFER. IS IT SO HARD TO BELIEVE THAT HE LIED ABOUT KILLING THE FLASH, TOO?!
TRUST ME, HE'S THE REAL DEAL.
PROVE IT.
KRAKAKAKAKA
OH NO...
THE COLLARS!

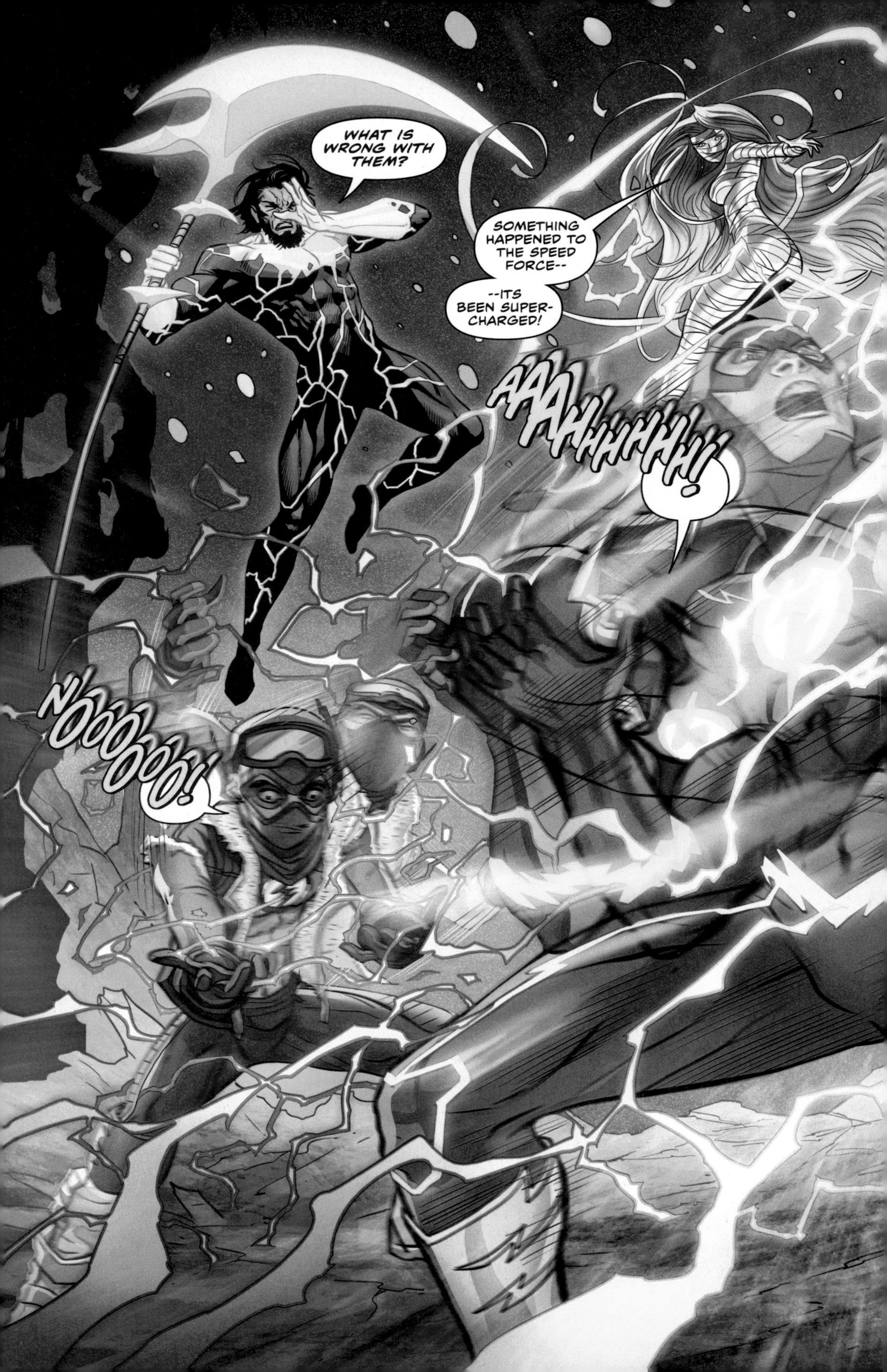
WHAT IS WRONG WITH THEM?
SOMETHING HAPPENED TO THE SPEED FORCE--
--ITS BEEN SUPER-CHARGED!
AAAHHHHHH!
NOOOOOO!

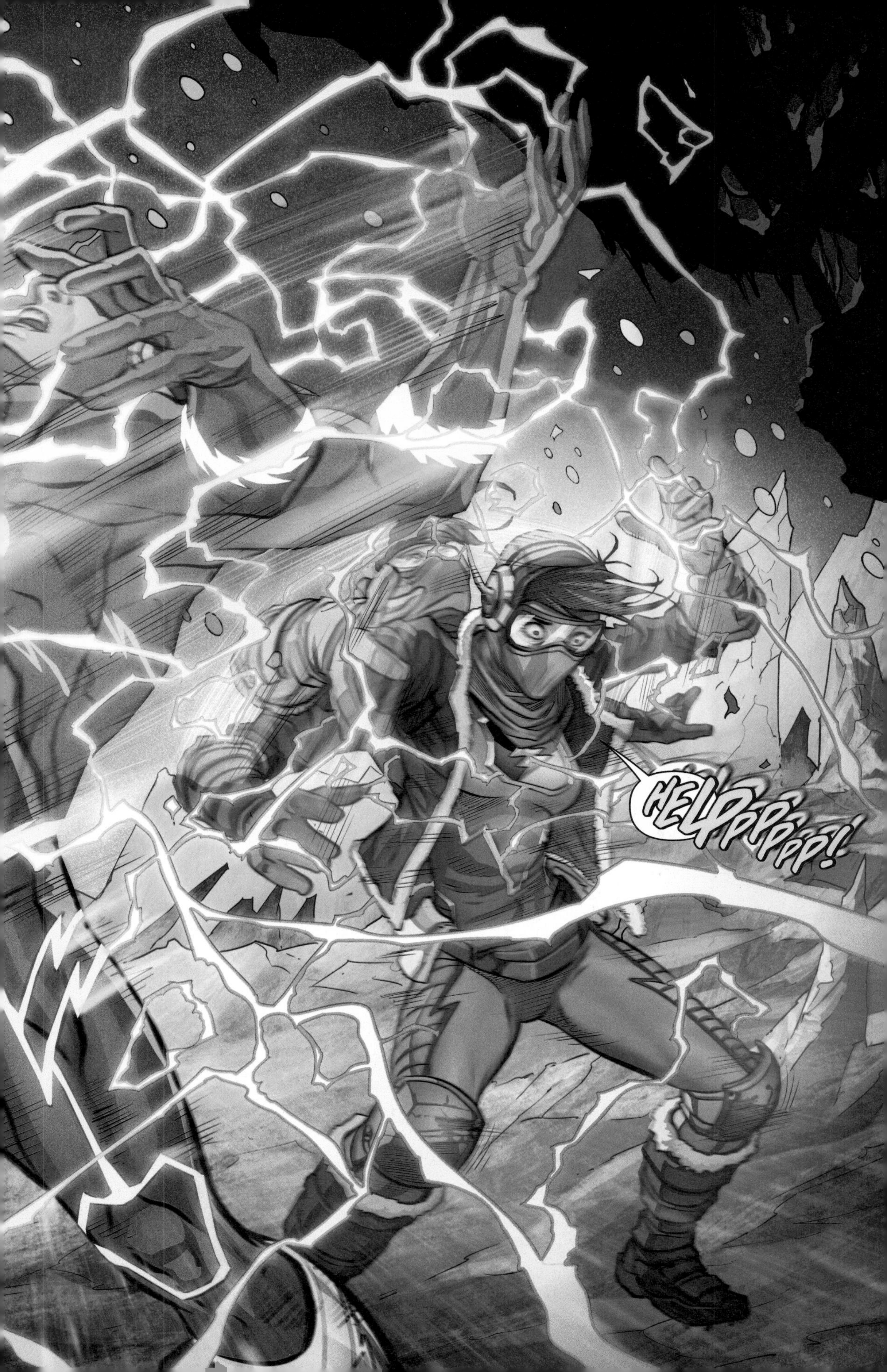
HELPPPPPP!

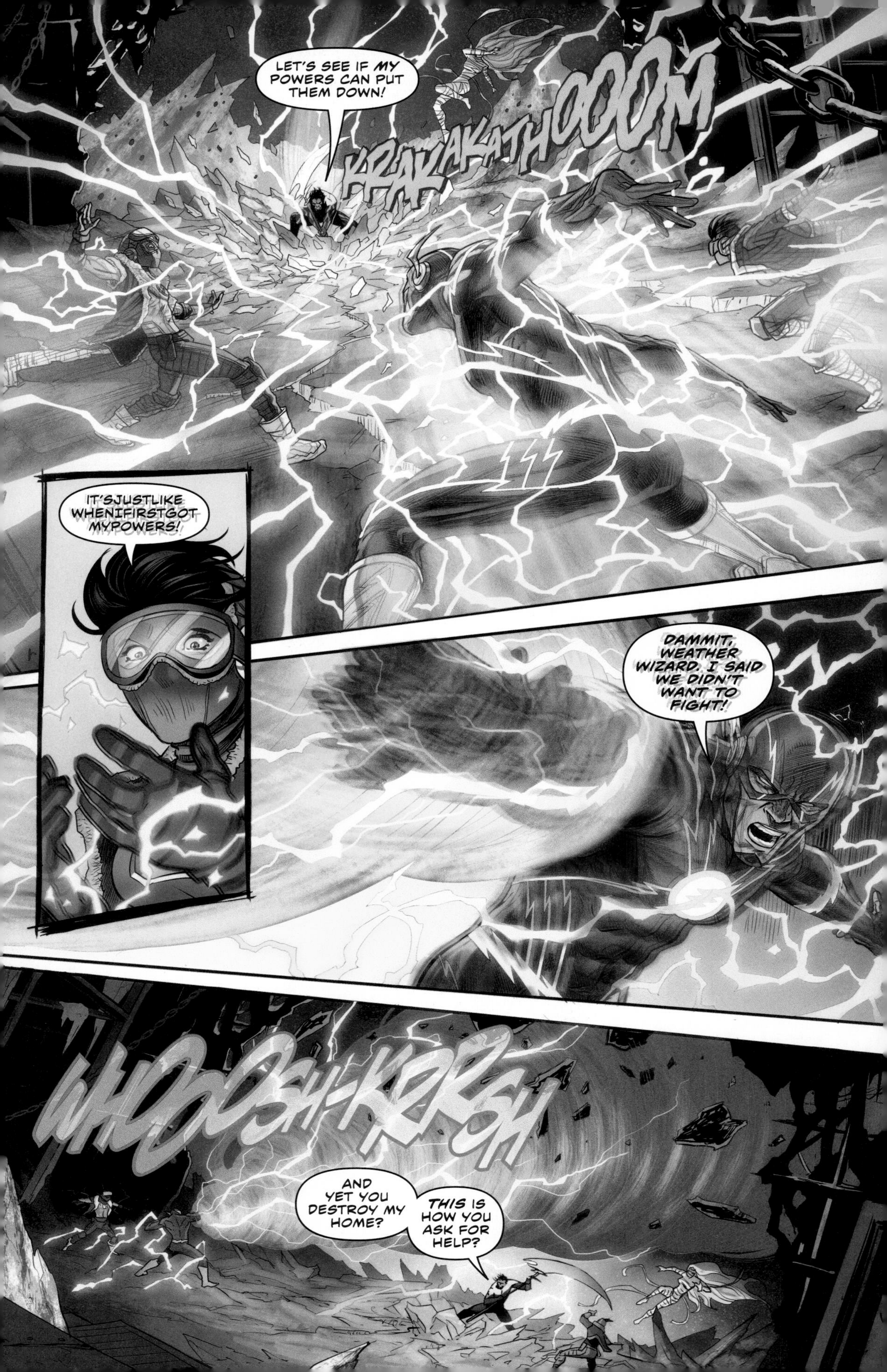

LET'S SEE IF MY POWERS CAN PUT THEM DOWN!
KRAKAKATHOOOOM
IT'SJUSTLIKE WHENIFIRSTGOT MYPOWERS!
DAMMIT, WEATHER WIZARD. I SAID WE DIDN'T WANT TO FIGHT!
WHOOSH-KRRSH
AND YET YOU DESTROY MY HOME?
THIS IS HOW YOU ASK FOR HELP?

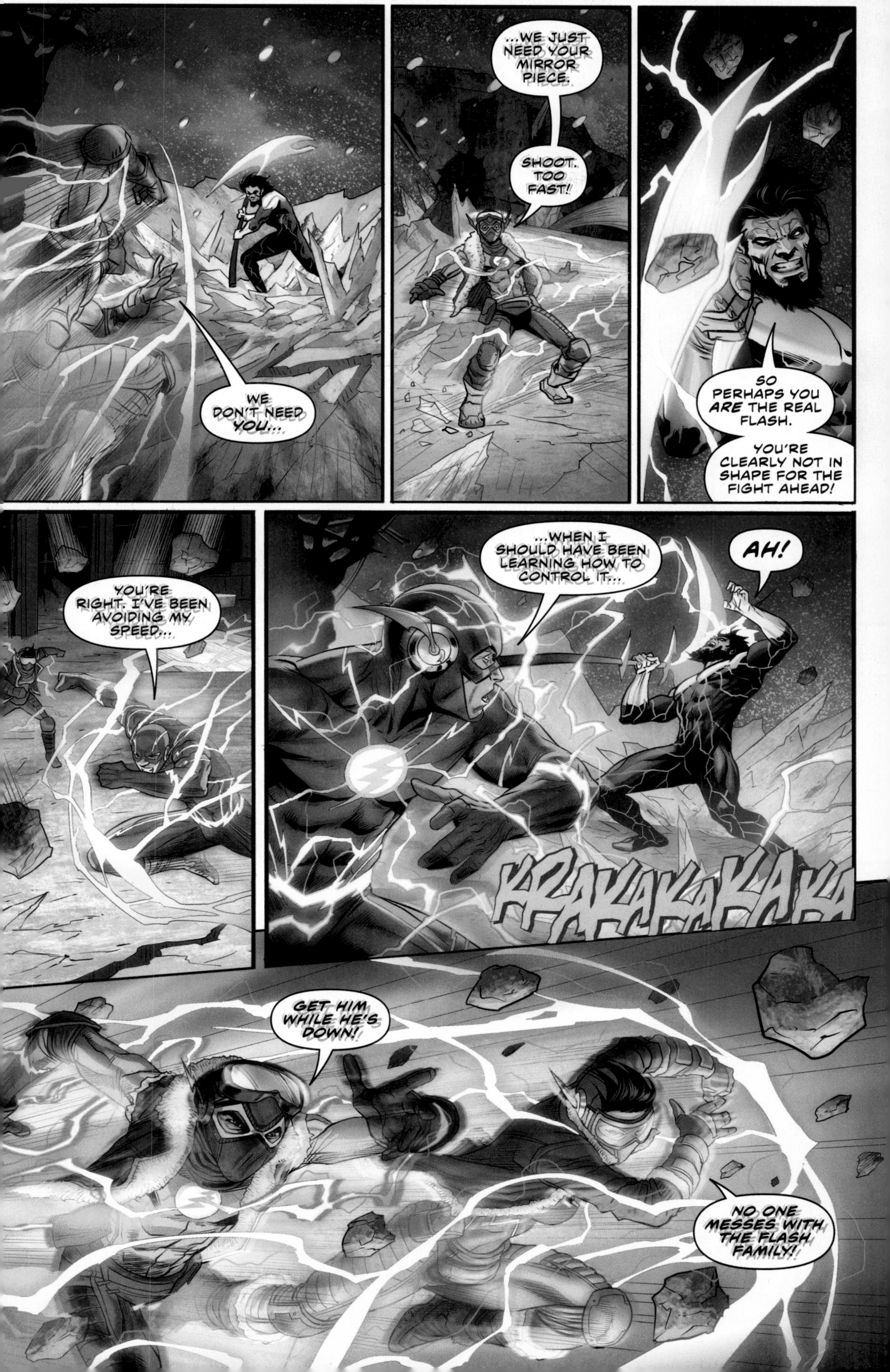
WE DON'T NEED YOU...
...WE JUST NEED YOUR MIRROR PIECE.
SHOOT. TOO FAST!
SO PERHAPS YOU *ARE* THE REAL FLASH.
YOU'RE CLEARLY NOT IN SHAPE FOR THE FIGHT AHEAD!
YOU'RE RIGHT. I'VE BEEN AVOIDING MY SPEED...
...WHEN I SHOULD HAVE BEEN LEARNING HOW TO CONTROL IT...
AH!
KRAKAKAKAKAKA
GET HIM WHILE HE'S DOWN!
NO ONE MESSES WITH THE FLASH FAMILY!

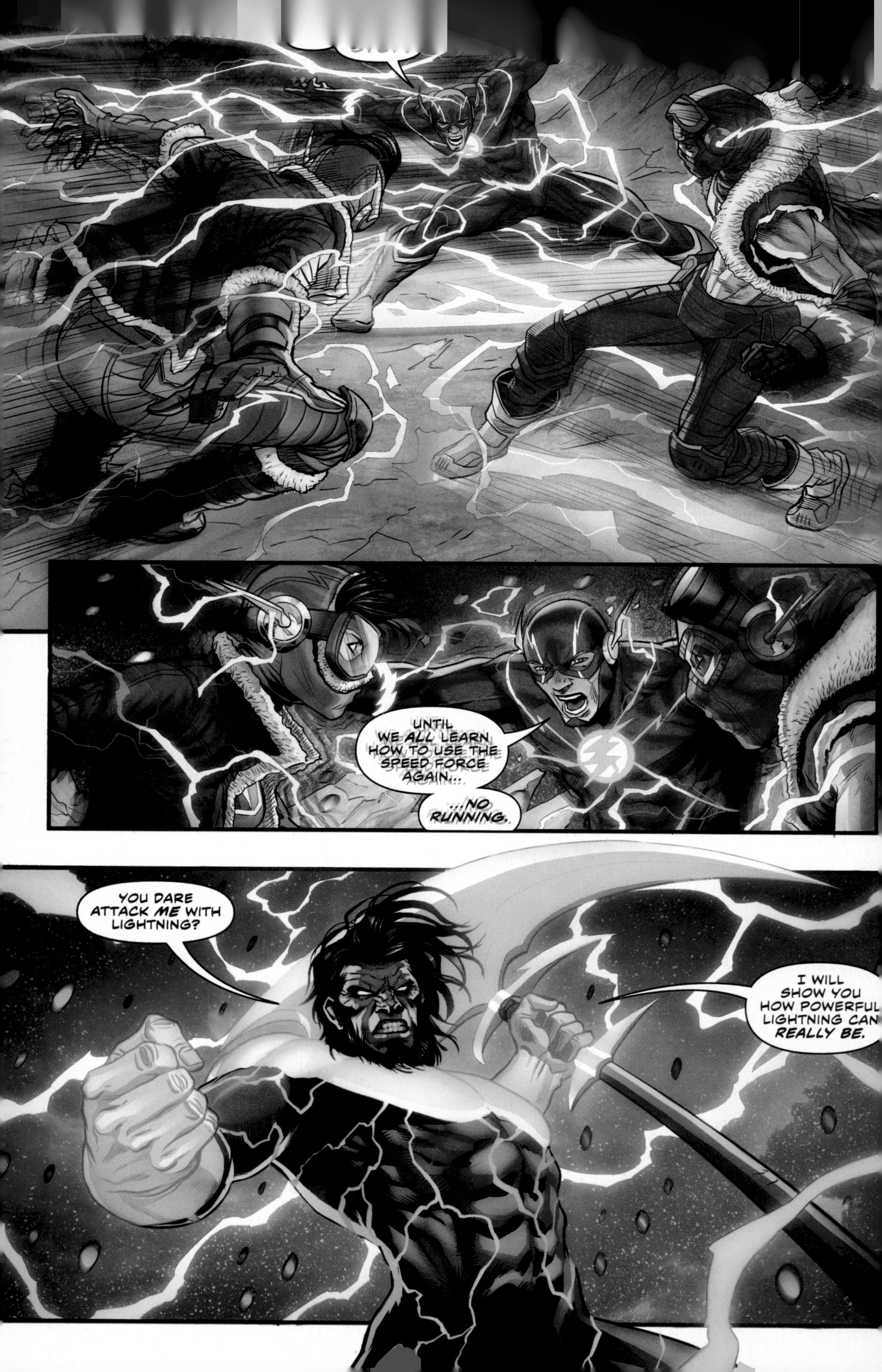
UNTIL WE ALL LEARN HOW TO USE THE SPEED FORCE AGAIN...
...NO RUNNING.
YOU DARE ATTACK ME WITH LIGHTNING?
I WILL SHOW YOU HOW POWERFUL LIGHTNING CAN REALLY BE.

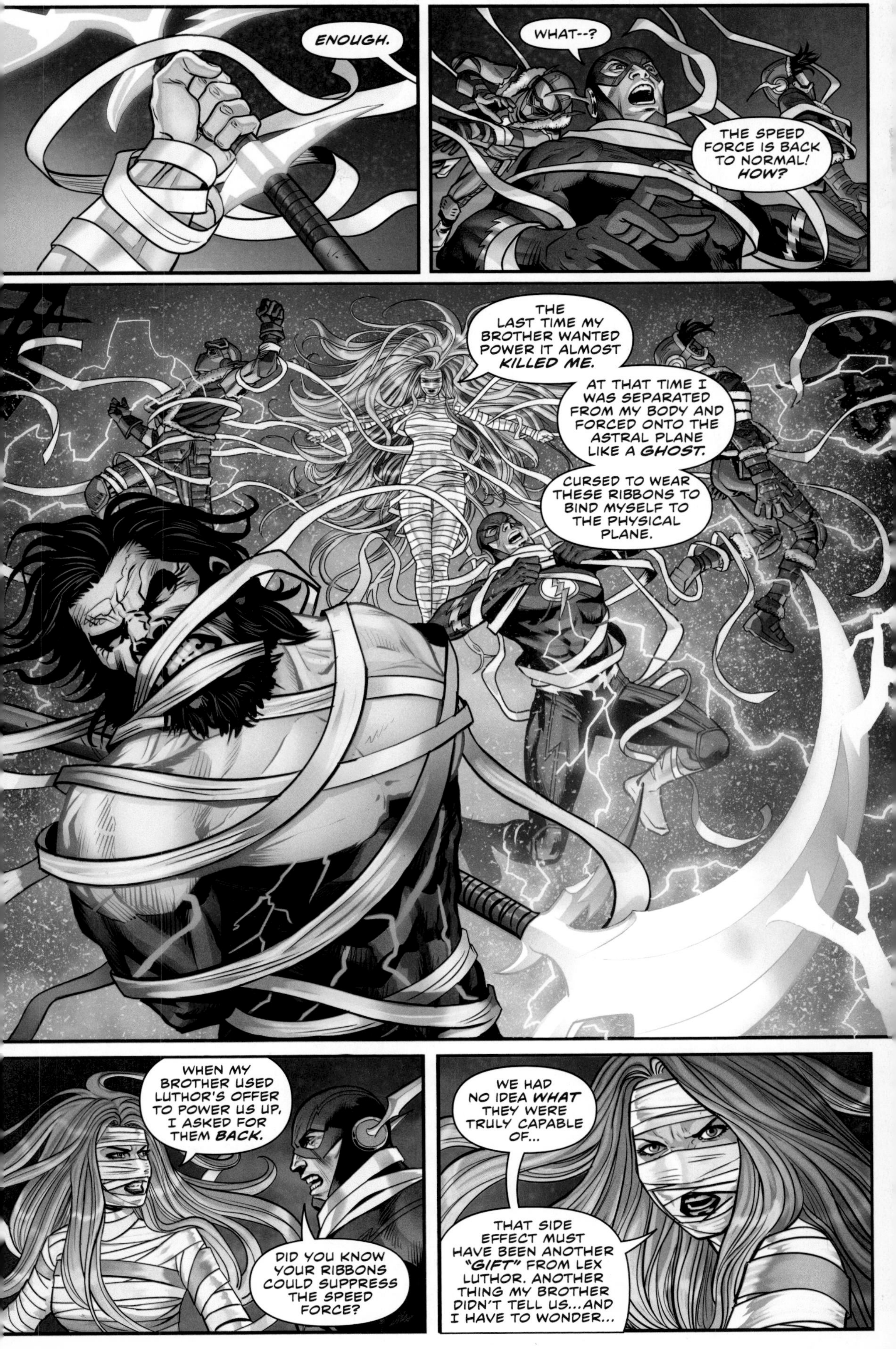
ENOUGH.
WHAT--?
THE SPEED FORCE IS BACK TO NORMAL! HOW?
THE LAST TIME MY BROTHER WANTED POWER IT ALMOST KILLED ME.
AT THAT TIME I WAS SEPARATED FROM MY BODY AND FORCED ONTO THE ASTRAL PLANE LIKE A GHOST.
CURSED TO WEAR THESE RIBBONS TO BIND MYSELF TO THE PHYSICAL PLANE.
WHEN MY BROTHER USED LUTHOR'S OFFER TO POWER US UP, I ASKED FOR THEM BACK.
DID YOU KNOW YOUR RIBBONS COULD SUPPRESS THE SPEED FORCE?
WE HAD NO IDEA WHAT THEY WERE TRULY CAPABLE OF...
THAT SIDE EFFECT MUST HAVE BEEN ANOTHER "GIFT" FROM LEX LUTHOR. ANOTHER THING MY BROTHER DIDN'T TELL US...AND I HAVE TO WONDER...

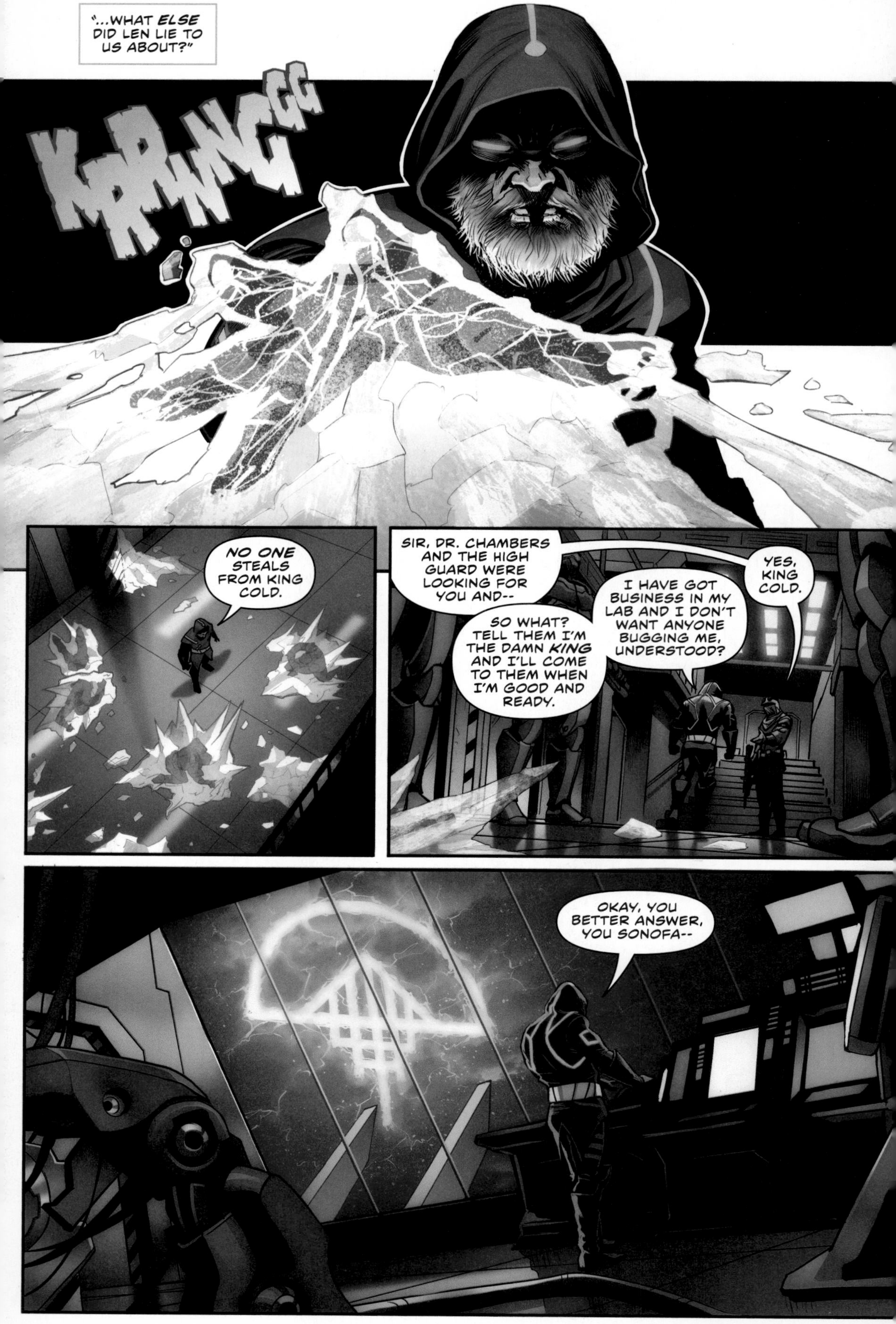
"...WHAT ELSE DID LEN LIE TO US ABOUT?"
KRRANGG
NO ONE STEALS FROM KING COLD.
SIR, DR. CHAMBERS AND THE HIGH GUARD WERE LOOKING FOR YOU AND--
SO WHAT? TELL THEM I'M THE DAMN KING AND I'LL COME TO THEM WHEN I'M GOOD AND READY.
I HAVE GOT BUSINESS IN MY LAB AND I DON'T WANT ANYONE BUGGING ME, UNDERSTOOD?
YES, KING COLD.
OKAY, YOU BETTER ANSWER, YOU SONOFA--

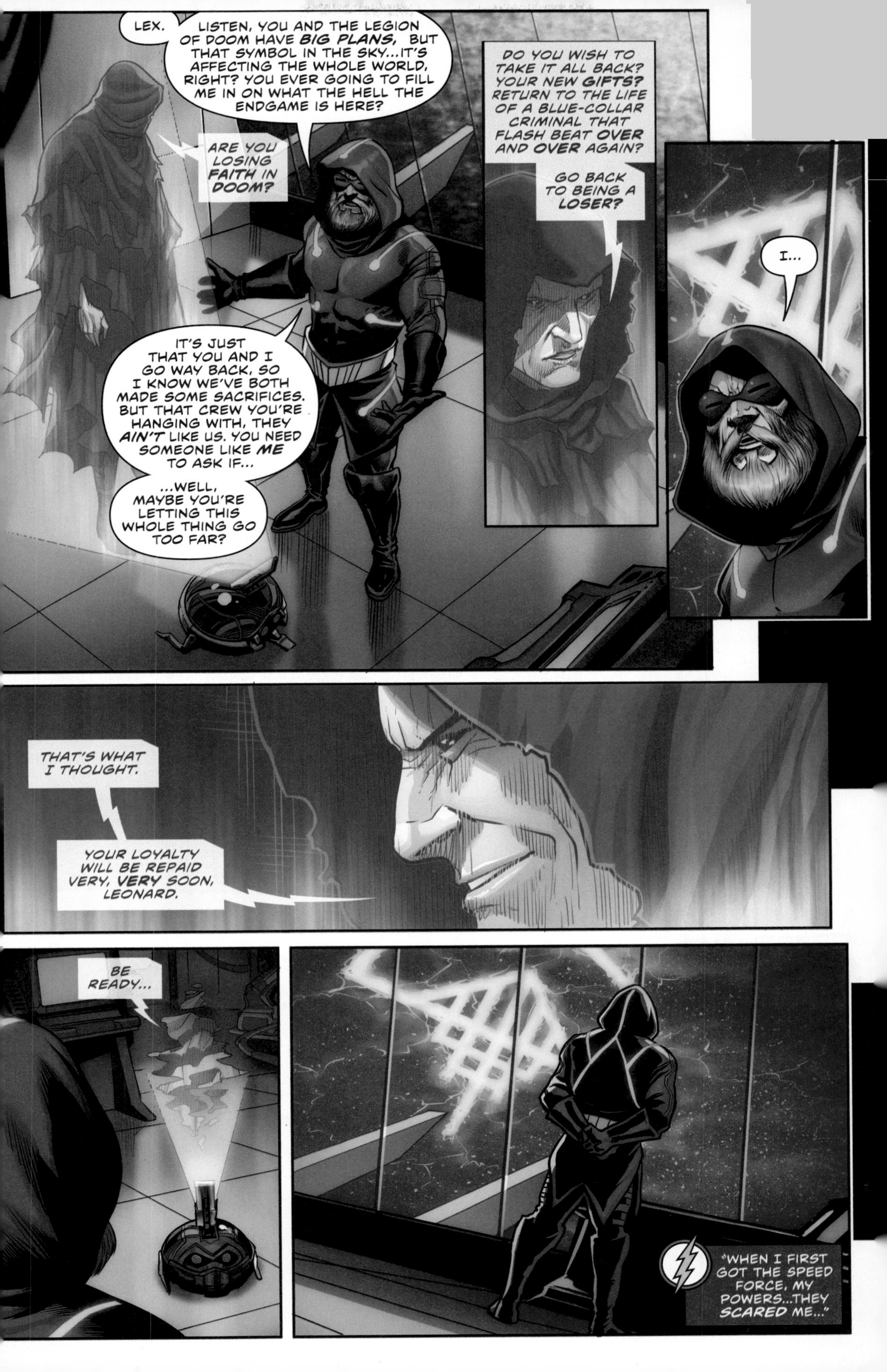

LEX.
LISTEN, YOU AND THE LEGION OF DOOM HAVE BIG PLANS, BUT THAT SYMBOL IN THE SKY...IT'S AFFECTING THE WHOLE WORLD, RIGHT? YOU EVER GOING TO FILL ME IN ON WHAT THE HELL THE ENDGAME IS HERE?
ARE YOU LOSING FAITH IN DOOM?
IT'S JUST THAT YOU AND I GO WAY BACK, SO I KNOW WE'VE BOTH MADE SOME SACRIFICES. BUT THAT CREW YOU'RE HANGING WITH, THEY AIN'T LIKE US. YOU NEED SOMEONE LIKE ME TO ASK IF...
...WELL, MAYBE YOU'RE LETTING THIS WHOLE THING GO TOO FAR?
DO YOU WISH TO TAKE IT ALL BACK? YOUR NEW GIFTS? RETURN TO THE LIFE OF A BLUE-COLLAR CRIMINAL THAT FLASH BEAT OVER AND OVER AGAIN?
GO BACK TO BEING A LOSER?
I...
THAT'S WHAT I THOUGHT.
YOUR LOYALTY WILL BE REPAID VERY, VERY SOON, LEONARD.
BE READY...
"WHEN I FIRST GOT THE SPEED FORCE, MY POWERS...THEY SCARED ME..."

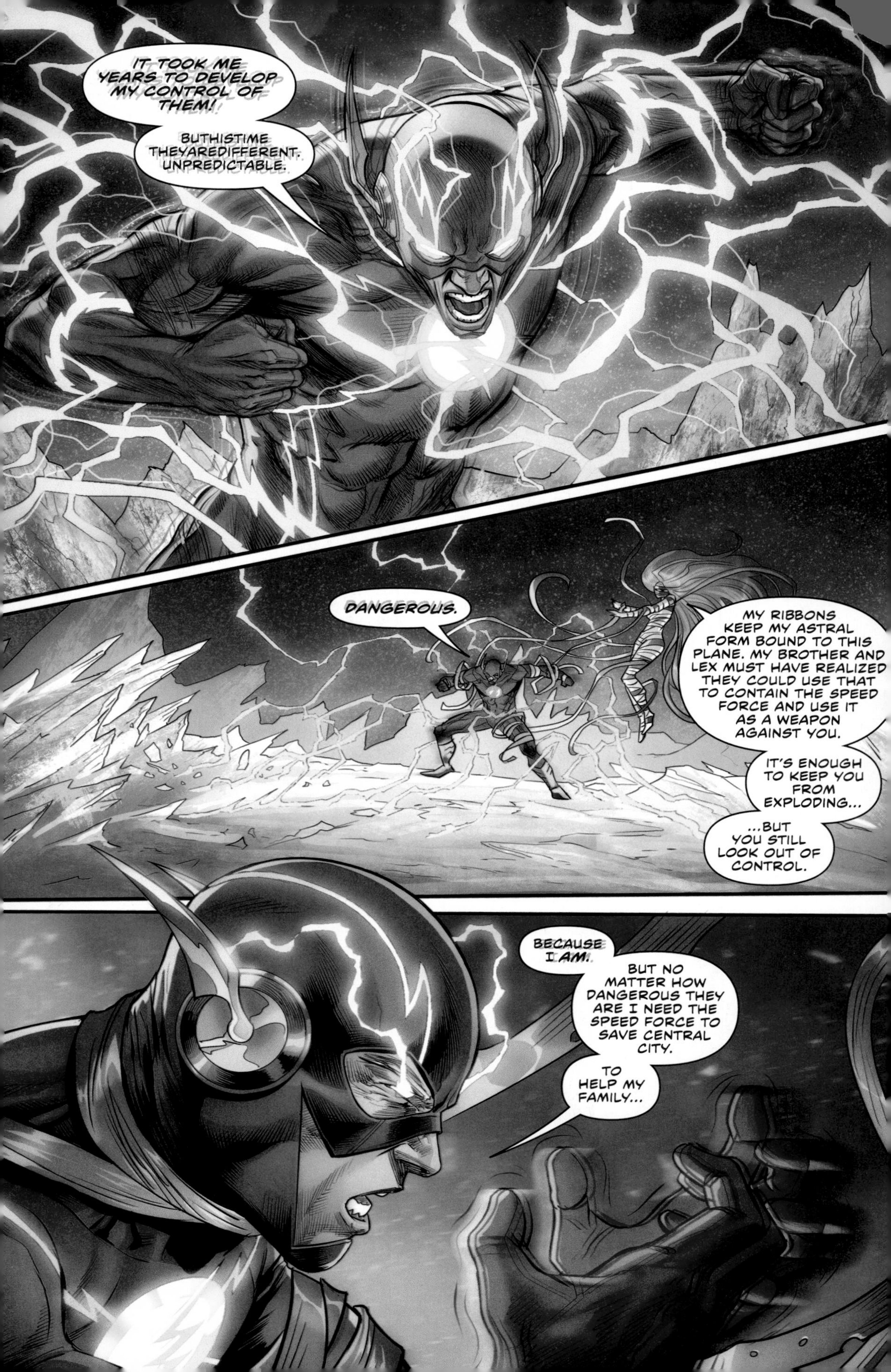
IT TOOK ME YEARS TO DEVELOP MY CONTROL OF THEM!
BUTHISTIME THEYAREDIFFERENT. UNPREDICTABLE.
DANGEROUS.
MY RIBBONS KEEP MY ASTRAL FORM BOUND TO THIS PLANE. MY BROTHER AND LEX MUST HAVE REALIZED THEY COULD USE THAT TO CONTAIN THE SPEED FORCE AND USE IT AS A WEAPON AGAINST YOU.
IT'S ENOUGH TO KEEP YOU FROM EXPLODING...
...BUT YOU STILL LOOK OUT OF CONTROL.
BECAUSE I AM.
BUT NO MATTER HOW DANGEROUS THEY ARE I NEED THE SPEED FORCE TO SAVE CENTRAL CITY.
TO HELP MY FAMILY...

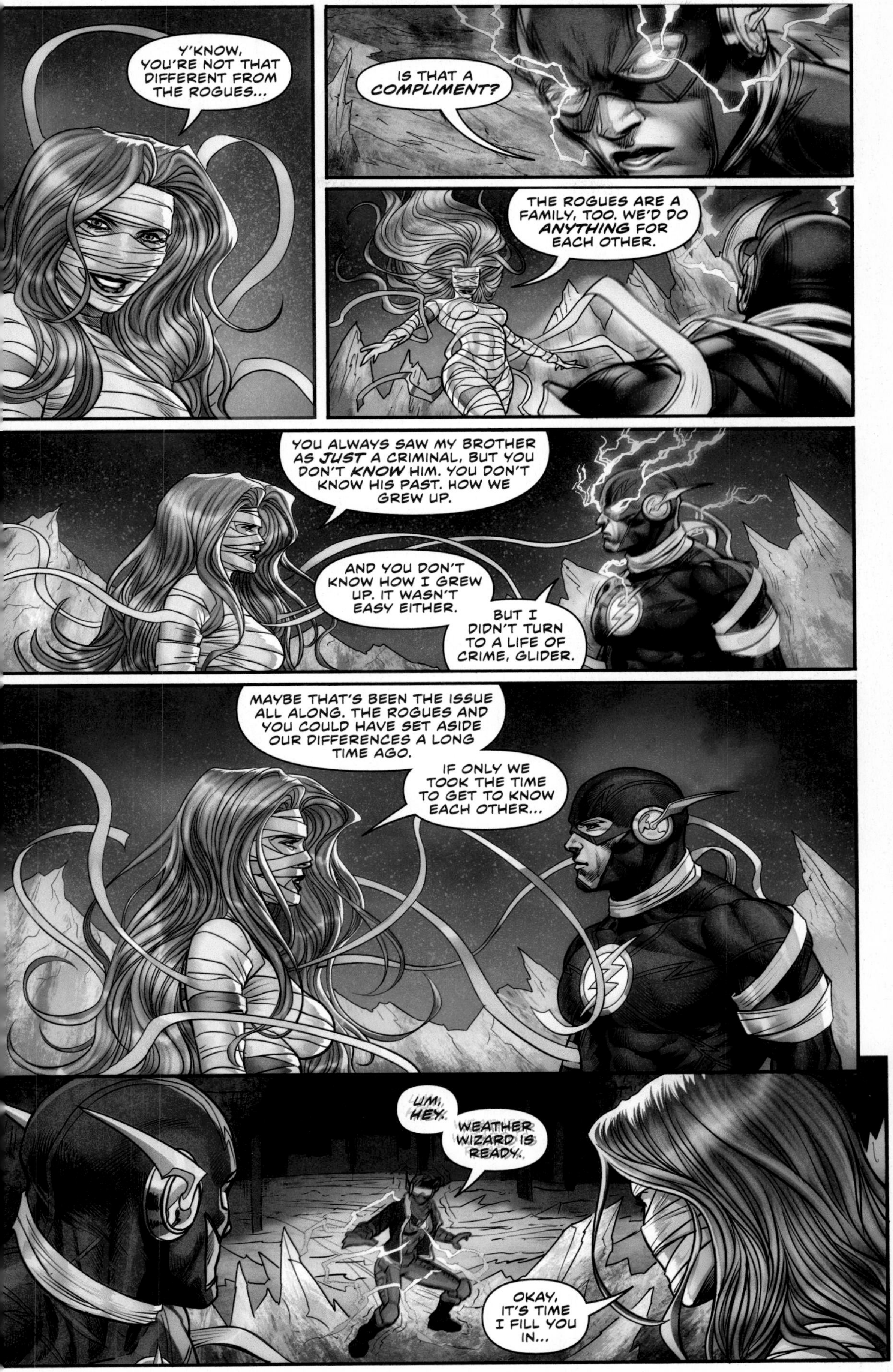
Y'KNOW, YOU'RE NOT THAT DIFFERENT FROM THE ROGUES...
IS THAT A COMPLIMENT?
THE ROGUES ARE A FAMILY, TOO. WE'D DO ANYTHING FOR EACH OTHER.
YOU ALWAYS SAW MY BROTHER AS JUST A CRIMINAL, BUT YOU DON'T KNOW HIM. YOU DON'T KNOW HIS PAST. HOW WE GREW UP.
AND YOU DON'T KNOW HOW I GREW UP. IT WASN'T EASY EITHER.
BUT I DIDN'T TURN TO A LIFE OF CRIME, GLIDER.
MAYBE THAT'S BEEN THE ISSUE ALL ALONG. THE ROGUES AND YOU COULD HAVE SET ASIDE OUR DIFFERENCES A LONG TIME AGO.
IF ONLY WE TOOK THE TIME TO GET TO KNOW EACH OTHER...
UM, HEY.
WEATHER WIZARD IS READY.
OKAY, IT'S TIME I FILL YOU IN...

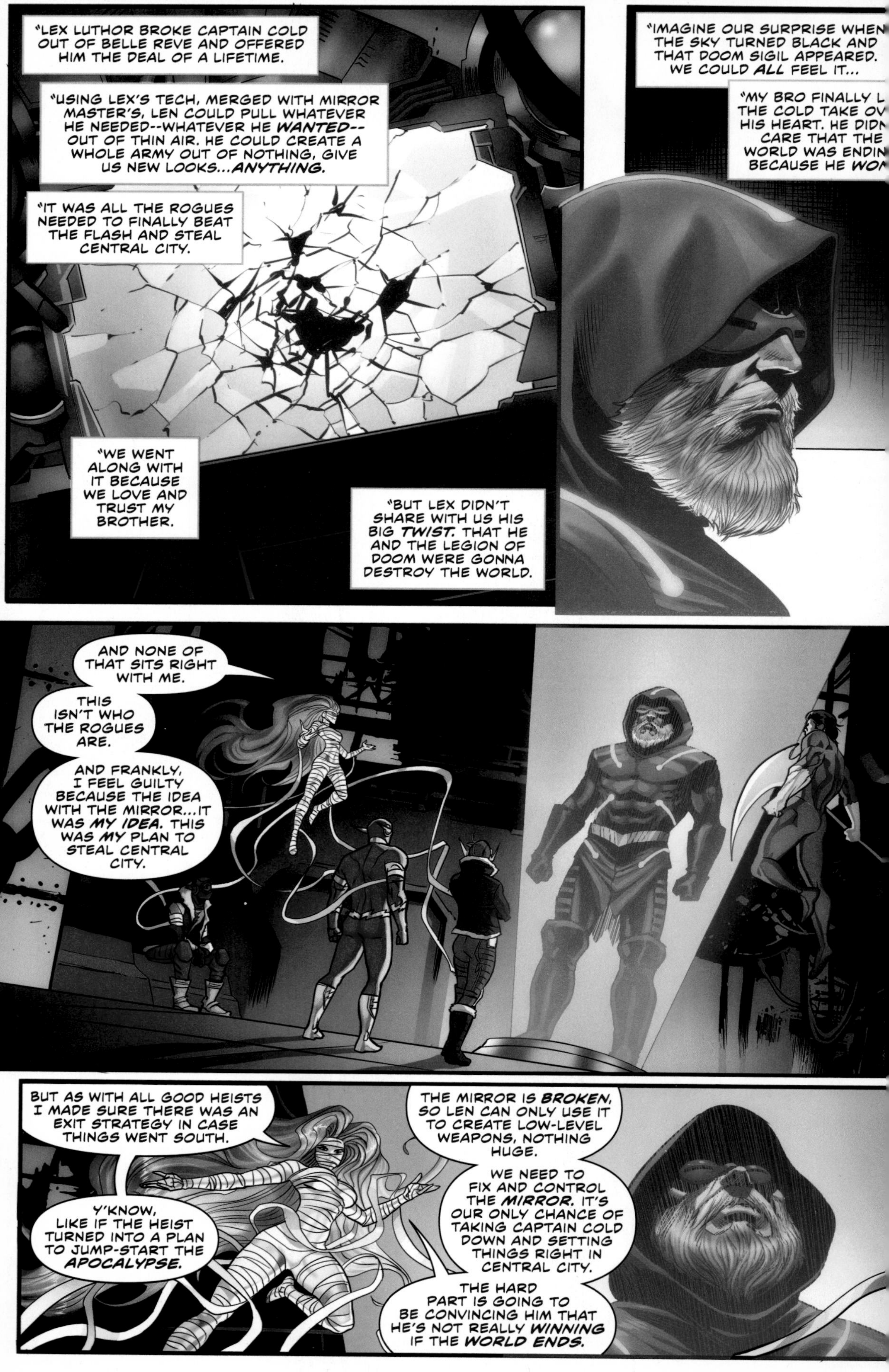
"LEX LUTHOR BROKE CAPTAIN COLD OUT OF BELLE REVE AND OFFERED HIM THE DEAL OF A LIFETIME.
"USING LEX'S TECH, MERGED WITH MIRROR MASTER'S, LEN COULD PULL WHATEVER HE NEEDED--WHATEVER HE WANTED--OUT OF THIN AIR. HE COULD CREATE A WHOLE ARMY OUT OF NOTHING, GIVE US NEW LOOKS...ANYTHING.
"IT WAS ALL THE ROGUES NEEDED TO FINALLY BEAT THE FLASH AND STEAL CENTRAL CITY.
"WE WENT ALONG WITH IT BECAUSE WE LOVE AND TRUST MY BROTHER.
"BUT LEX DIDN'T SHARE WITH US HIS BIG TWIST. THAT HE AND THE LEGION OF DOOM WERE GONNA DESTROY THE WORLD.
"IMAGINE OUR SURPRISE WHEN THE SKY TURNED BLACK AND THAT DOOM SIGIL APPEARED. WE COULD ALL FEEL IT...
"MY BRO FINALLY L THE COLD TAKE OV HIS HEART. HE DIDN CARE THAT THE WORLD WAS ENDIN BECAUSE HE WON
AND NONE OF THAT SITS RIGHT WITH ME.
THIS ISN'T WHO THE ROGUES ARE.
AND FRANKLY, I FEEL GUILTY BECAUSE THE IDEA WITH THE MIRROR...IT WAS MY IDEA. THIS WAS MY PLAN TO STEAL CENTRAL CITY.
BUT AS WITH ALL GOOD HEISTS I MADE SURE THERE WAS AN EXIT STRATEGY IN CASE THINGS WENT SOUTH.
Y'KNOW, LIKE IF THE HEIST TURNED INTO A PLAN TO JUMP-START THE APOCALYPSE.
THE MIRROR IS BROKEN, SO LEN CAN ONLY USE IT TO CREATE LOW-LEVEL WEAPONS, NOTHING HUGE.
WE NEED TO FIX AND CONTROL THE MIRROR. IT'S OUR ONLY CHANCE OF TAKING CAPTAIN COLD DOWN AND SETTING THINGS RIGHT IN CENTRAL CITY.
THE HARD PART IS GOING TO BE CONVINCING HIM THAT HE'S NOT REALLY WINNING IF THE WORLD ENDS.

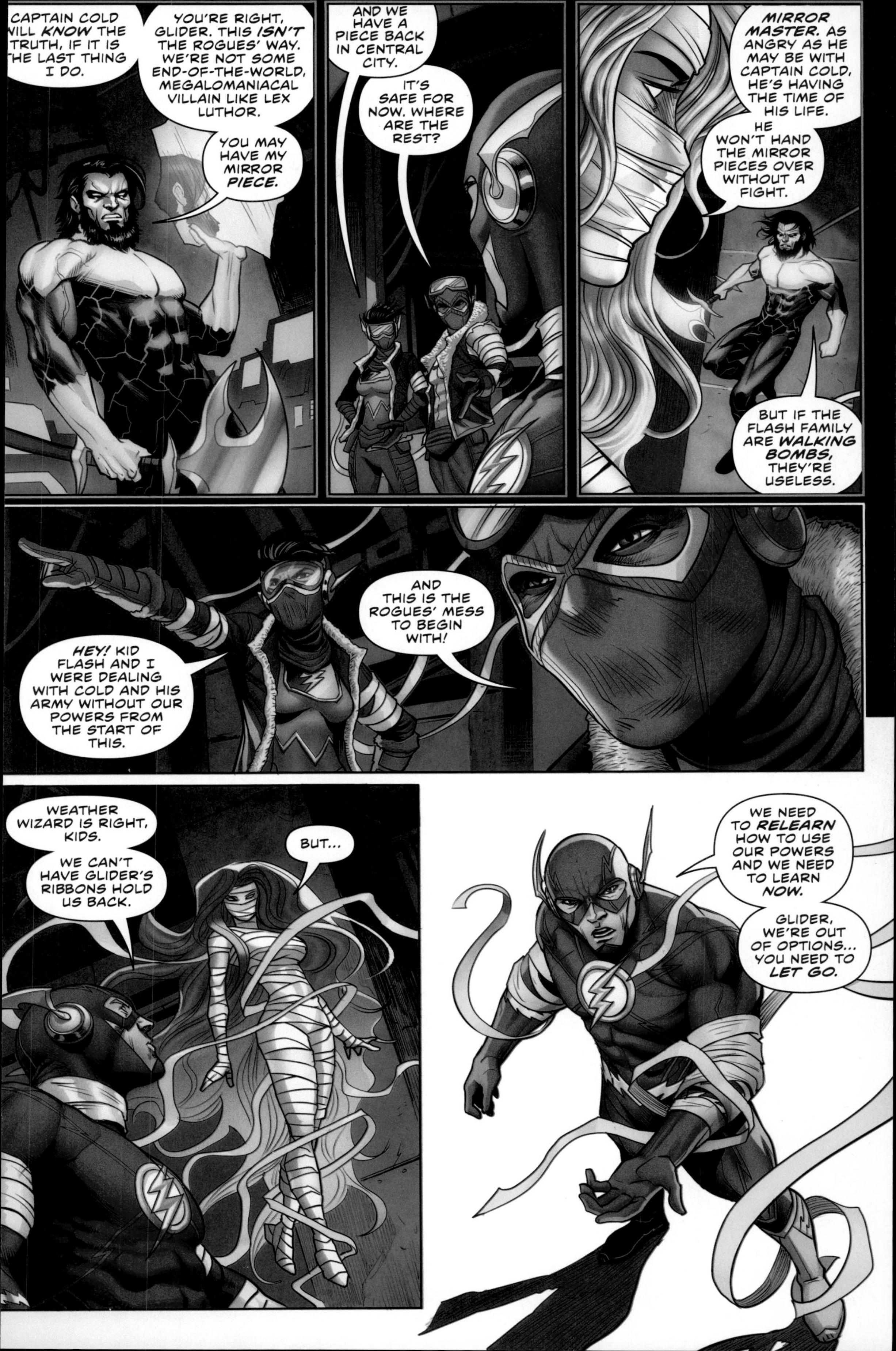

CAPTAIN COLD WILL *KNOW* THE TRUTH, IF IT IS THE LAST THING I DO.
YOU'RE RIGHT, GLIDER. THIS *ISN'T* THE ROGUES' WAY. WE'RE NOT SOME END-OF-THE-WORLD, MEGALOMANIACAL VILLAIN LIKE LEX LUTHOR.
YOU MAY HAVE MY MIRROR *PIECE.*
AND WE HAVE A PIECE BACK IN CENTRAL CITY.
IT'S SAFE FOR NOW. WHERE ARE THE REST?
MIRROR MASTER. AS ANGRY AS HE MAY BE WITH CAPTAIN COLD, HE'S HAVING THE TIME OF HIS LIFE.
HE WON'T HAND THE MIRROR PIECES OVER WITHOUT A FIGHT.
BUT IF THE FLASH FAMILY ARE *WALKING BOMBS,* THEY'RE USELESS.
HEY! KID FLASH AND I WERE DEALING WITH COLD AND HIS ARMY WITHOUT OUR POWERS FROM THE START OF THIS.
AND THIS IS THE ROGUES' MESS TO BEGIN WITH!
WEATHER WIZARD IS RIGHT, KIDS.
WE CAN'T HAVE GLIDER'S RIBBONS HOLD US BACK.
BUT...
WE NEED TO *RELEARN* HOW TO USE OUR POWERS AND WE NEED TO LEARN *NOW.*
GLIDER, WE'RE OUT OF OPTIONS... YOU NEED TO *LET GO.*

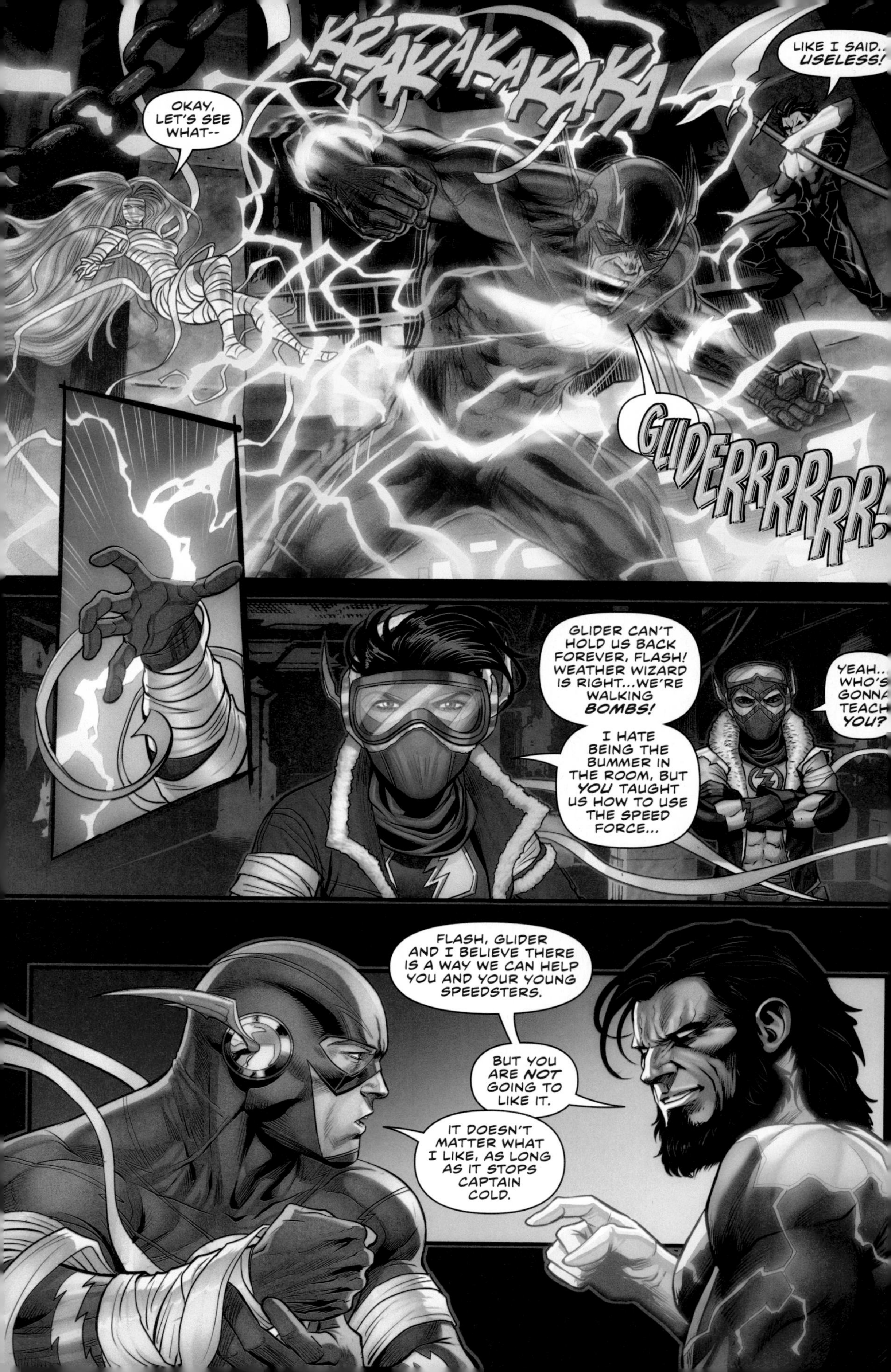
KRAKAKAKAKAKA
OKAY, LET'S SEE WHAT--
LIKE I SAID... USELESS!
GLIDERRRRRRR!
GLIDER CAN'T HOLD US BACK FOREVER, FLASH! WEATHER WIZARD IS RIGHT...WE'RE WALKING BOMBS!
YEAH... WHO'S GONNA TEACH YOU?
I HATE BEING THE BUMMER IN THE ROOM, BUT YOU TAUGHT US HOW TO USE THE SPEED FORCE...
FLASH, GLIDER AND I BELIEVE THERE IS A WAY WE CAN HELP YOU AND YOUR YOUNG SPEEDSTERS.
BUT YOU ARE NOT GOING TO LIKE IT.
IT DOESN'T MATTER WHAT I LIKE, AS LONG AS IT STOPS CAPTAIN COLD.

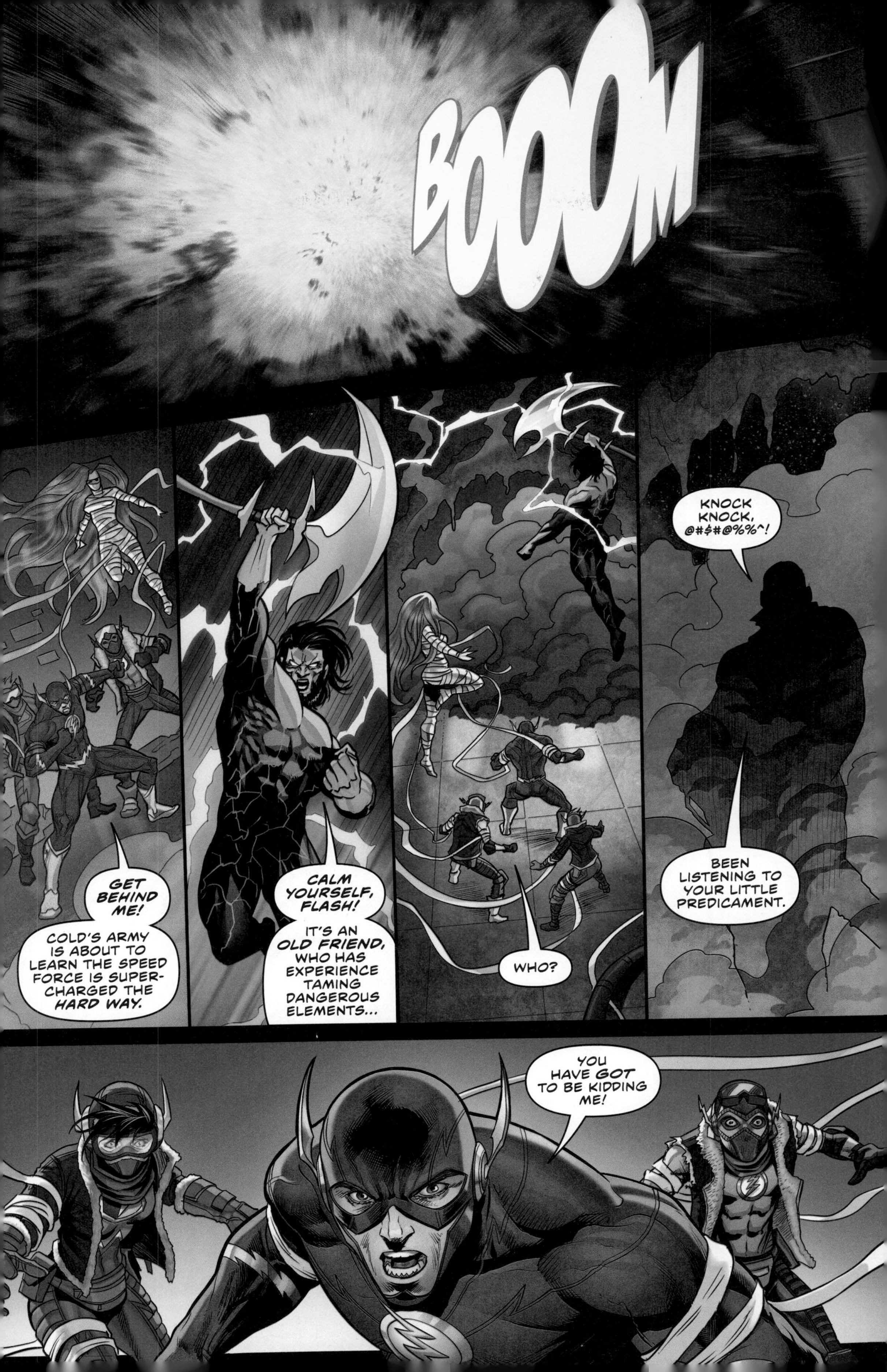
BOOOM
GET BEHIND ME!
COLD'S ARMY IS ABOUT TO LEARN THE SPEED FORCE IS SUPER-CHARGED THE HARD WAY.
CALM YOURSELF, FLASH!
IT'S AN OLD FRIEND, WHO HAS EXPERIENCE TAMING DANGEROUS ELEMENTS...
WHO?
KNOCK KNOCK, @#$#@%%^!
BEEN LISTENING TO YOUR LITTLE PREDICAMENT.
YOU HAVE GOT TO BE KIDDING ME!

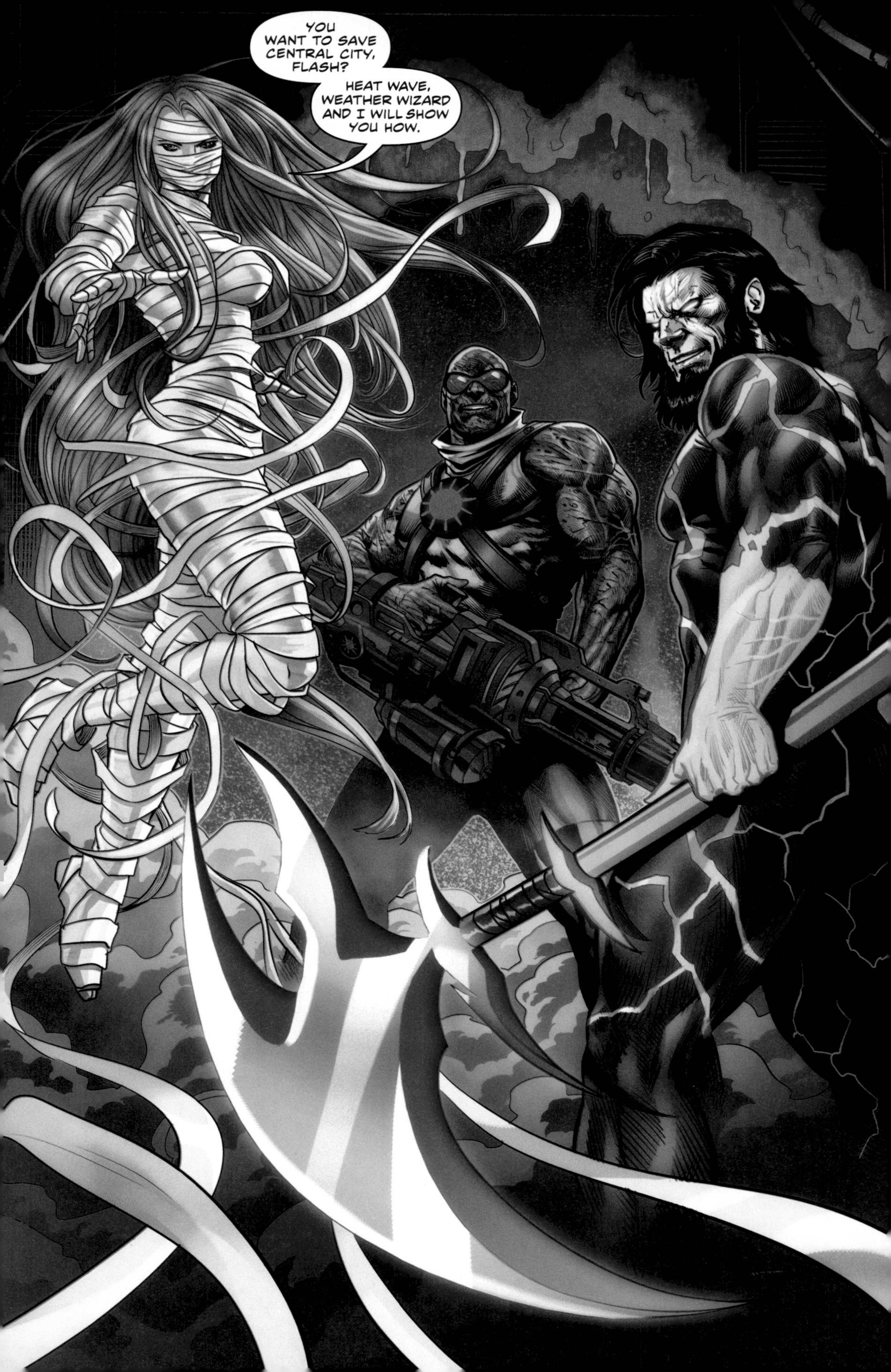
YOU WANT TO SAVE CENTRAL CITY, FLASH?
HEAT WAVE, WEATHER WIZARD AND I WILL SHOW YOU HOW.

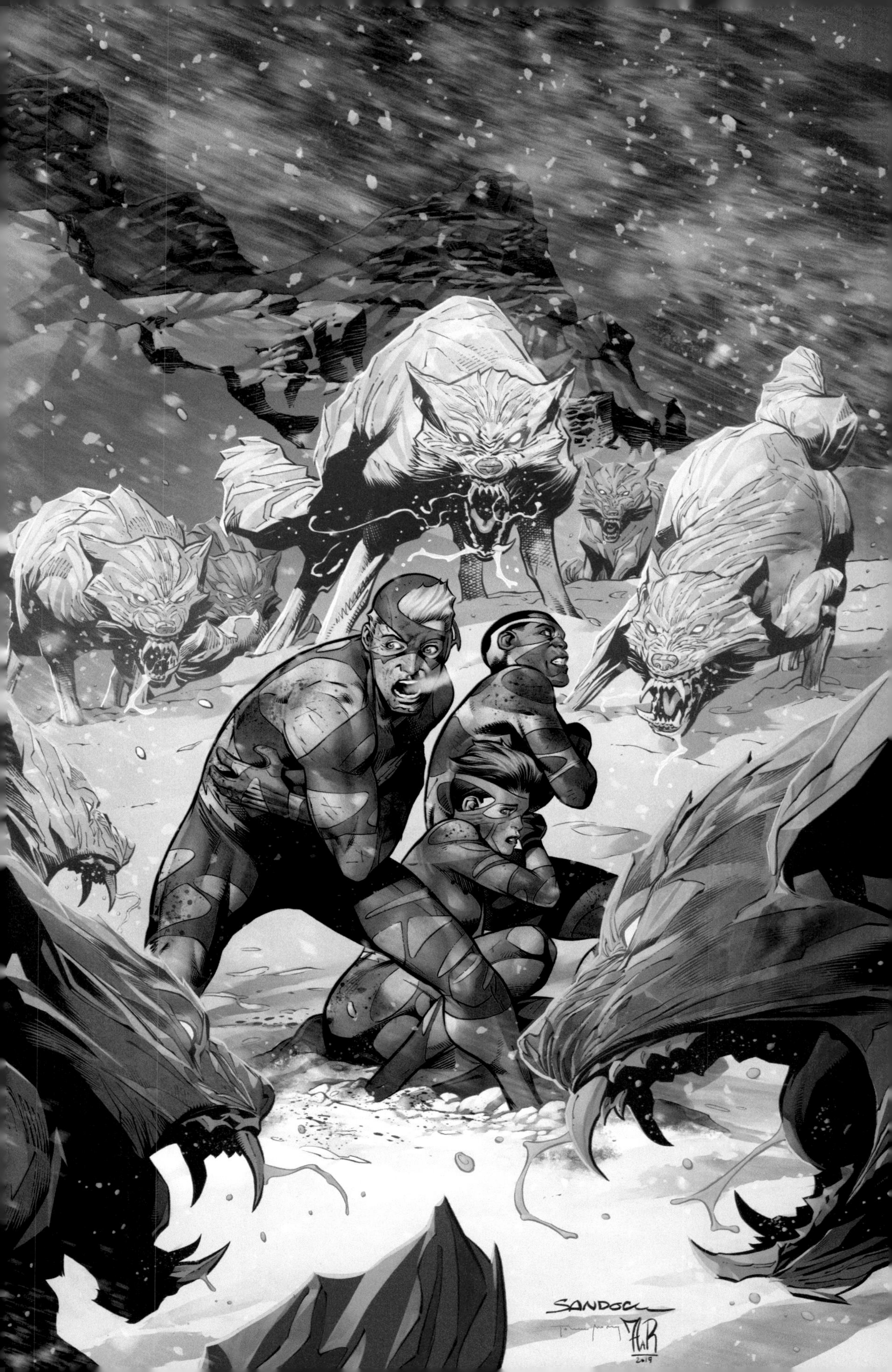

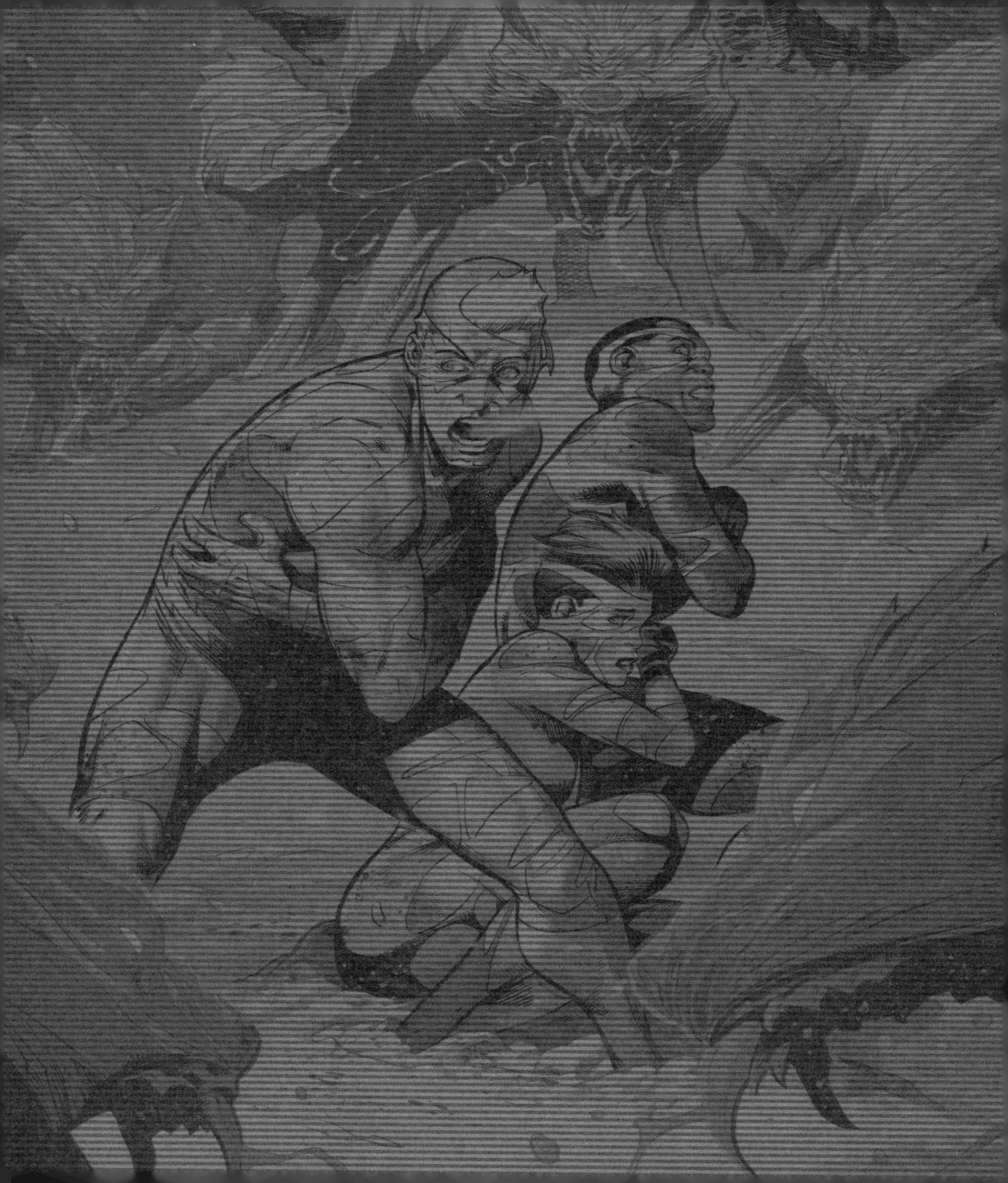

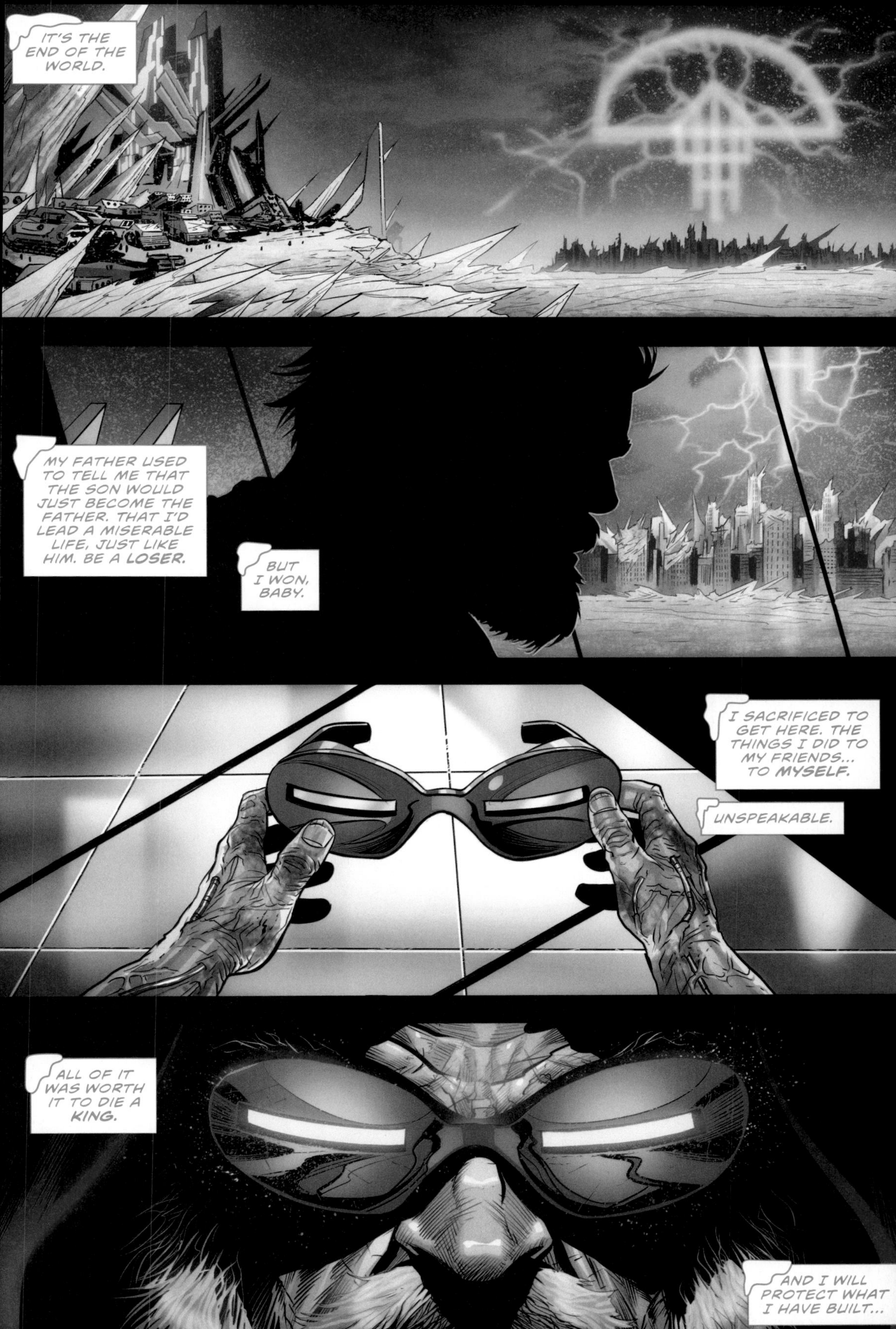
IT'S THE END OF THE WORLD.
MY FATHER USED TO TELL ME THAT THE SON WOULD JUST BECOME THE FATHER. THAT I'D LEAD A MISERABLE LIFE, JUST LIKE HIM. BE A LOSER.
BUT I WON, BABY.
I SACRIFICED TO GET HERE. THE THINGS I DID TO MY FRIENDS... TO MYSELF.
UNSPEAKABLE.
ALL OF IT WAS WORTH IT TO DIE A KING.
AND I WILL PROTECT WHAT I HAVE BUILT...

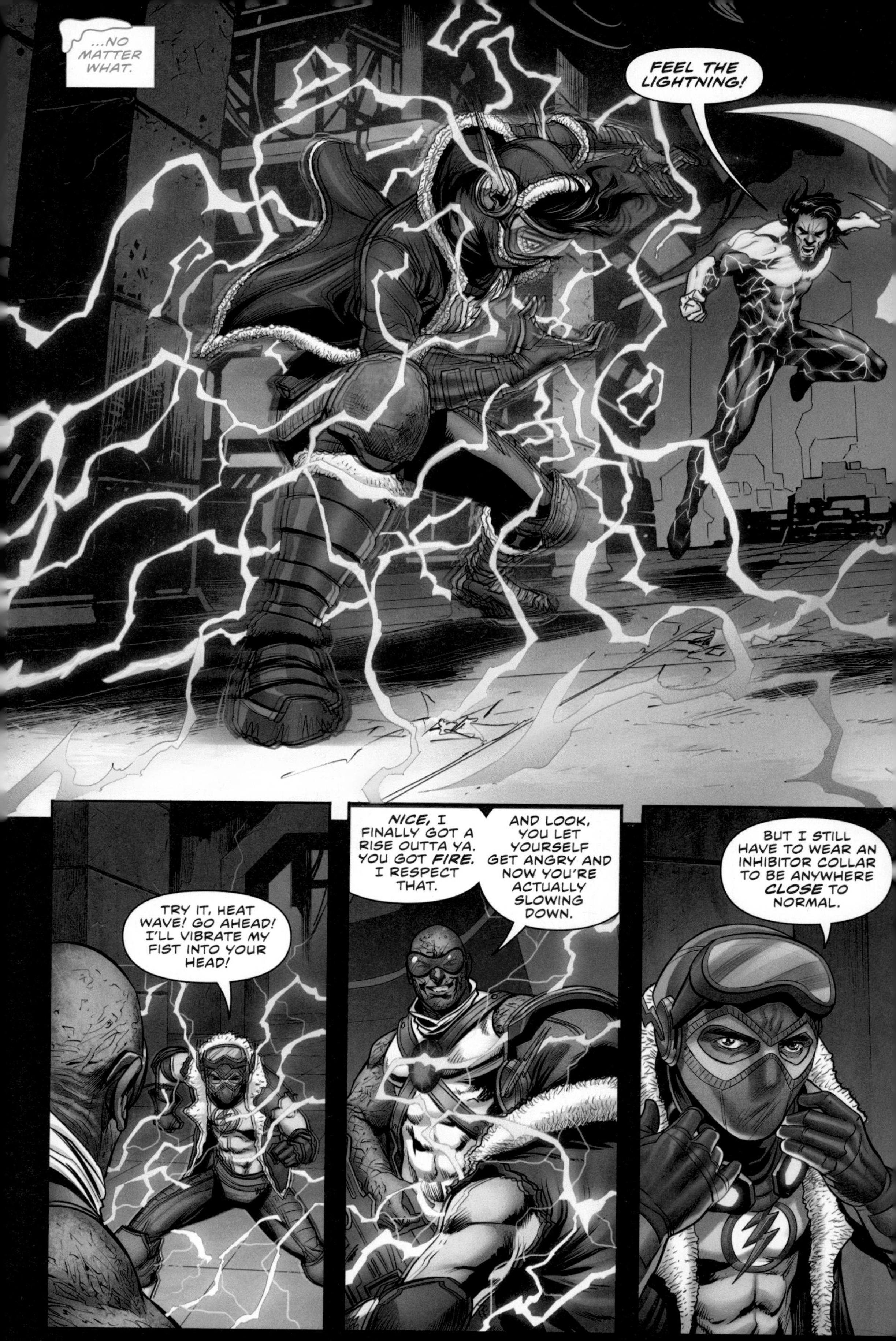
...NO MATTER WHAT.
FEEL THE LIGHTNING!
TRY IT, HEAT WAVE! GO AHEAD! I'LL VIBRATE MY FIST INTO YOUR HEAD!
NICE, I FINALLY GOT A RISE OUTTA YA. YOU GOT FIRE. I RESPECT THAT.
AND LOOK, YOU LET YOURSELF GET ANGRY AND NOW YOU'RE ACTUALLY SLOWING DOWN.
BUT I STILL HAVE TO WEAR AN INHIBITOR COLLAR TO BE ANYWHERE CLOSE TO NORMAL.

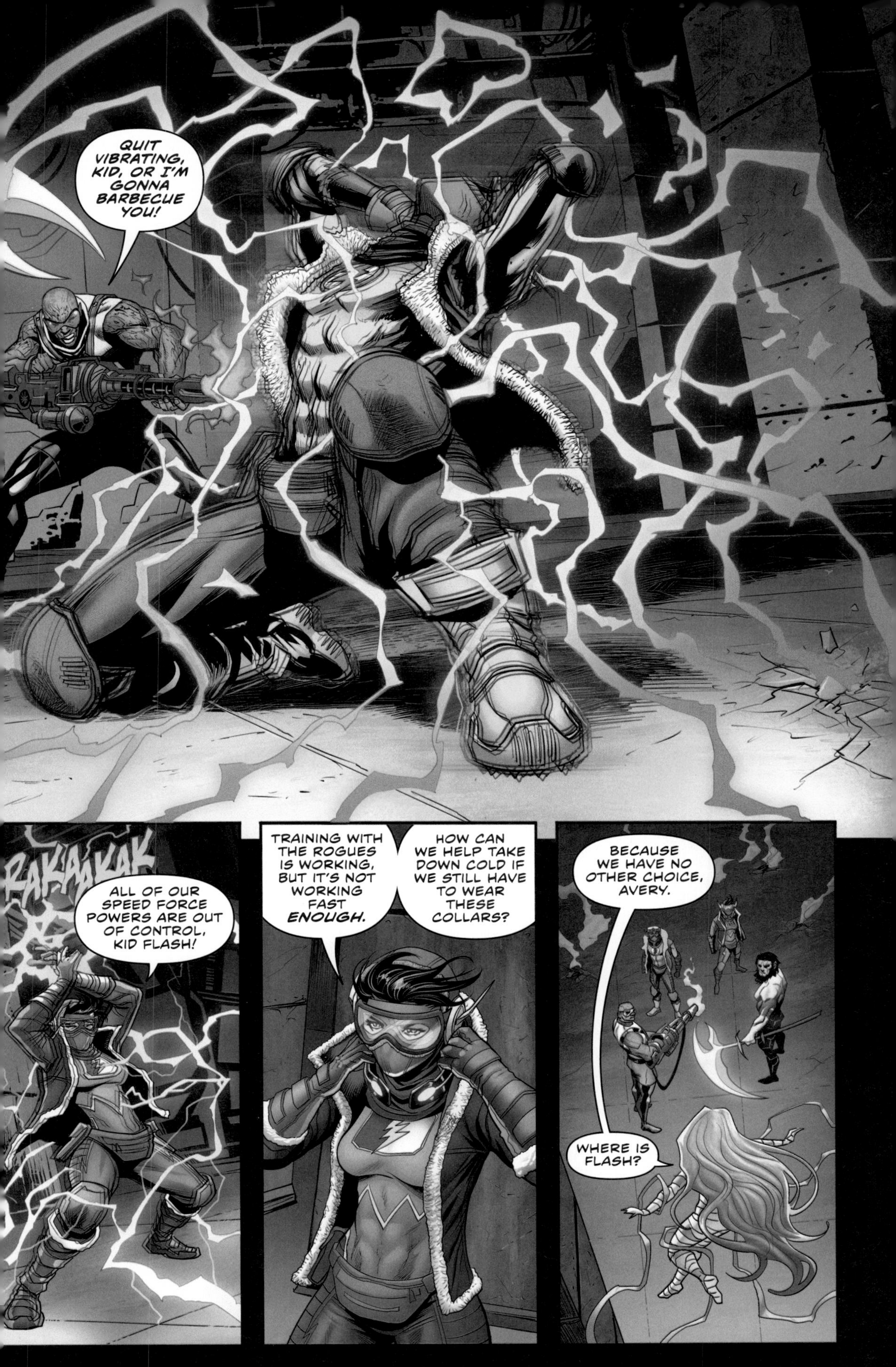
QUIT VIBRATING, KID, OR I'M GONNA BARBECUE YOU!
RAKAKAKAK
ALL OF OUR SPEED FORCE POWERS ARE OUT OF CONTROL, KID FLASH!
TRAINING WITH THE ROGUES IS WORKING, BUT IT'S NOT WORKING FAST ENOUGH.
HOW CAN WE HELP TAKE DOWN COLD IF WE STILL HAVE TO WEAR THESE COLLARS?
BECAUSE WE HAVE NO OTHER CHOICE, AVERY.
WHERE IS FLASH?

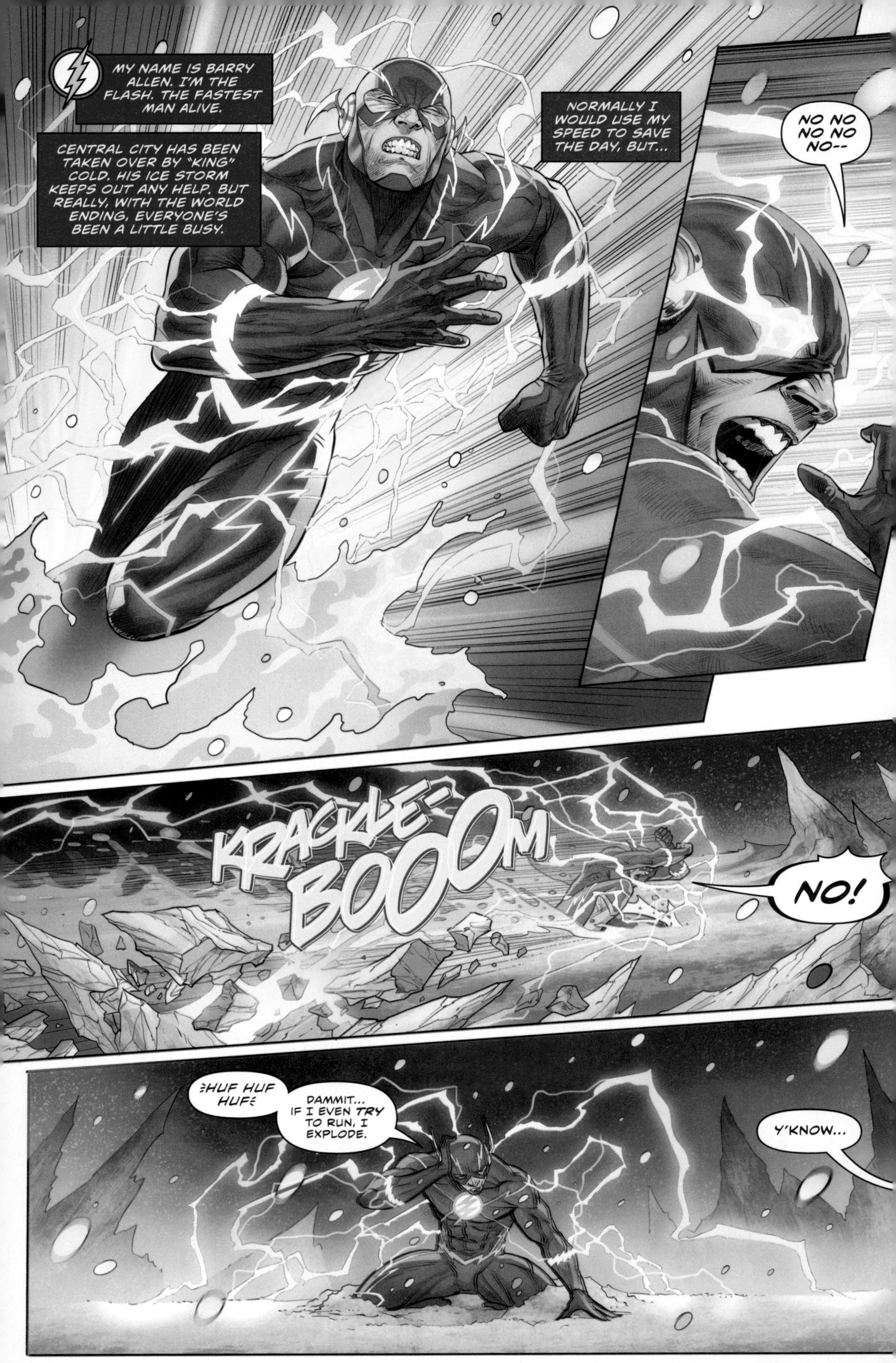
MY NAME IS BARRY ALLEN. I'M THE FLASH. THE FASTEST MAN ALIVE.
CENTRAL CITY HAS BEEN TAKEN OVER BY "KING" COLD. HIS ICE STORM KEEPS OUT ANY HELP. BUT REALLY, WITH THE WORLD ENDING, EVERYONE'S BEEN A LITTLE BUSY.
NORMALLY I WOULD USE MY SPEED TO SAVE THE DAY, BUT...
NO NO NO NO NO--
KRACKLE-BOOOOM
NO!
HUF HUF HUF
DAMMIT... IF I EVEN TRY TO RUN, I EXPLODE.
Y'KNOW...

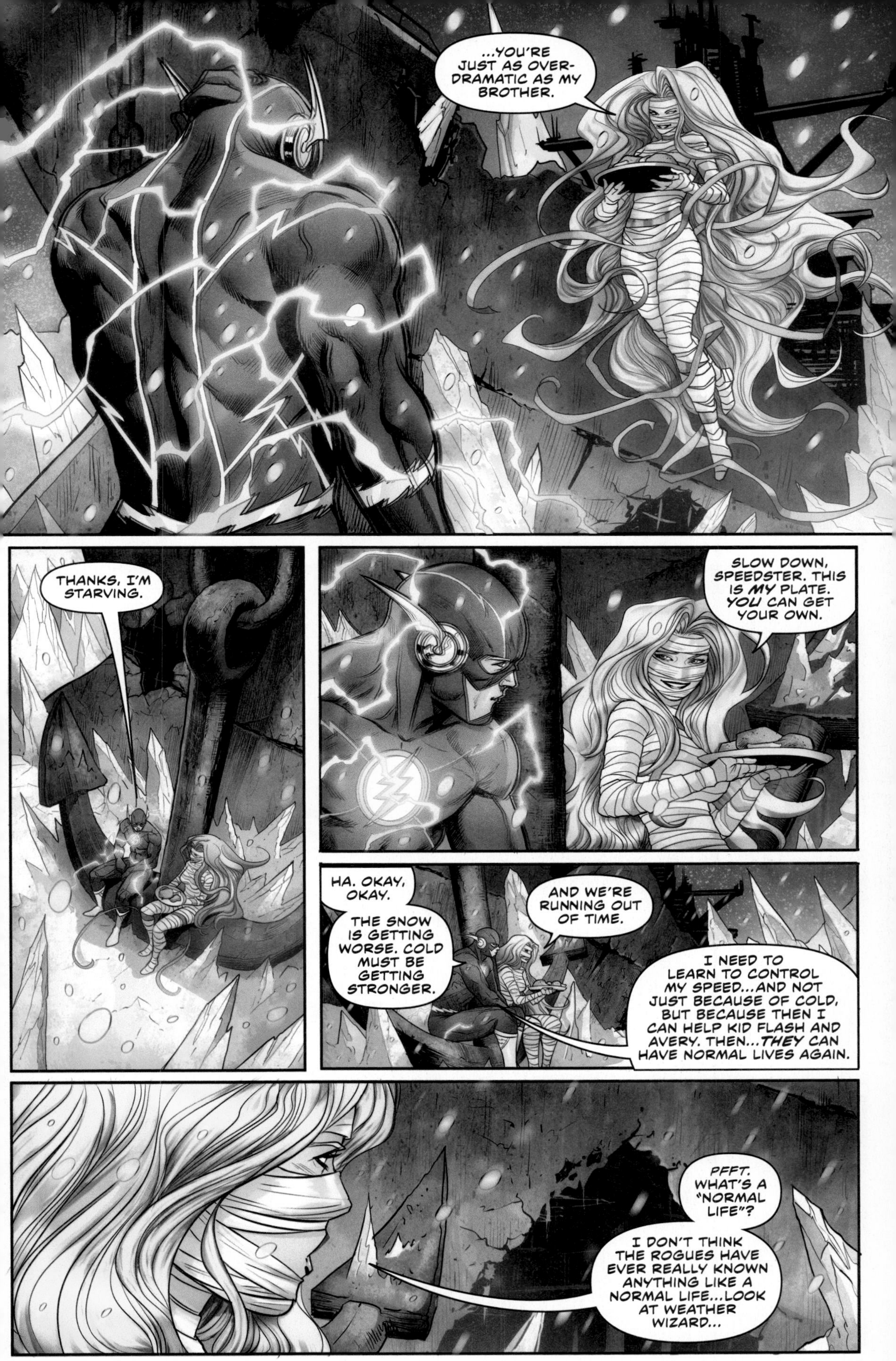
...YOU'RE JUST AS OVER-DRAMATIC AS MY BROTHER.
THANKS, I'M STARVING.
SLOW DOWN, SPEEDSTER. THIS IS MY PLATE. YOU CAN GET YOUR OWN.
HA. OKAY, OKAY.
THE SNOW IS GETTING WORSE. COLD MUST BE GETTING STRONGER.
AND WE'RE RUNNING OUT OF TIME.
I NEED TO LEARN TO CONTROL MY SPEED...AND NOT JUST BECAUSE OF COLD, BUT BECAUSE THEN I CAN HELP KID FLASH AND AVERY. THEN...THEY CAN HAVE NORMAL LIVES AGAIN.
PFFT. WHAT'S A "NORMAL LIFE"?
I DON'T THINK THE ROGUES HAVE EVER REALLY KNOWN ANYTHING LIKE A NORMAL LIFE...LOOK AT WEATHER WIZARD...

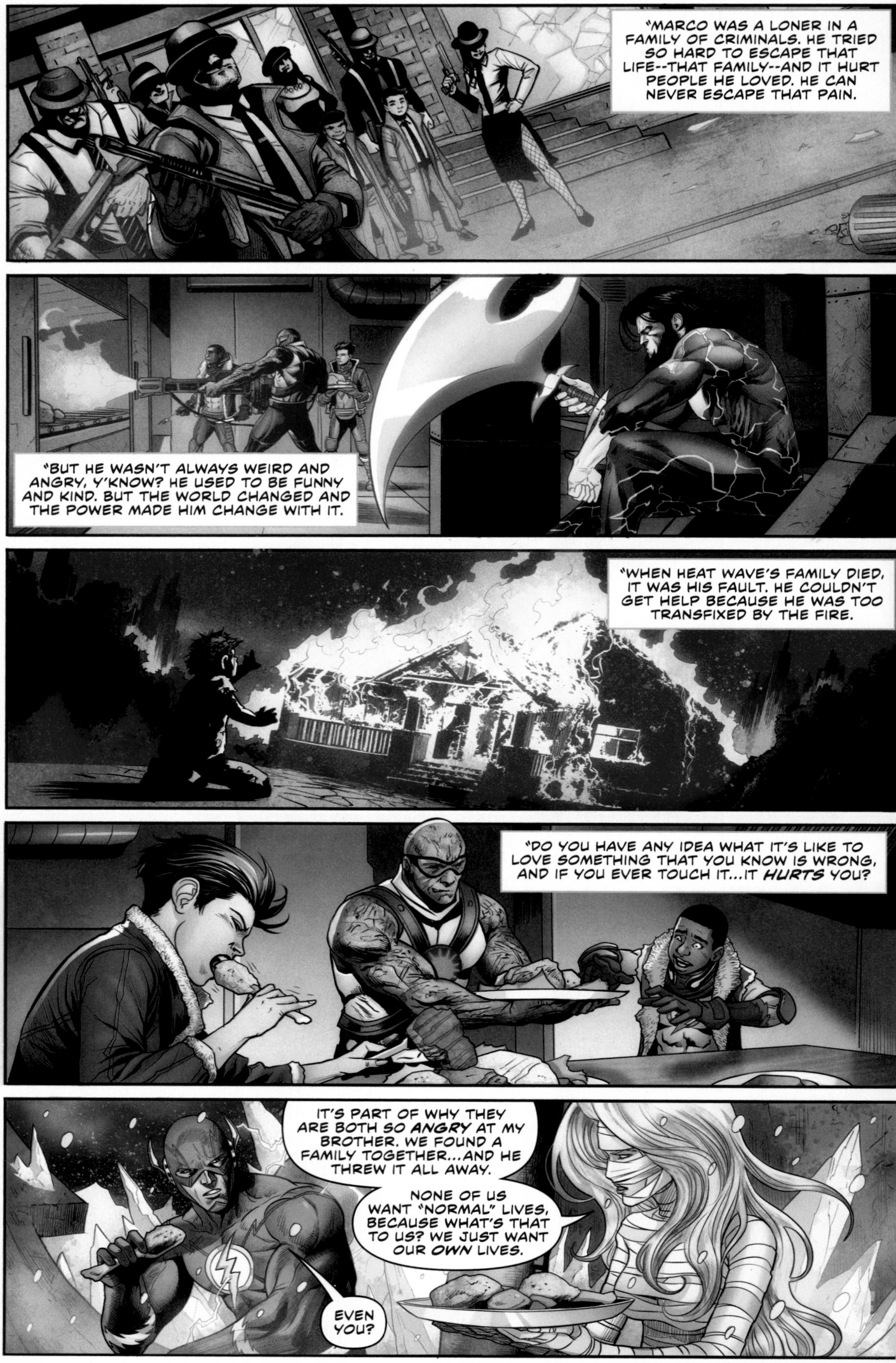
"MARCO WAS A LONER IN A FAMILY OF CRIMINALS. HE TRIED SO HARD TO ESCAPE THAT LIFE--THAT FAMILY--AND IT HURT PEOPLE HE LOVED. HE CAN NEVER ESCAPE THAT PAIN.
"BUT HE WASN'T ALWAYS WEIRD AND ANGRY, Y'KNOW? HE USED TO BE FUNNY AND KIND. BUT THE WORLD CHANGED AND THE POWER MADE HIM CHANGE WITH IT.
"WHEN HEAT WAVE'S FAMILY DIED, IT WAS HIS FAULT. HE COULDN'T GET HELP BECAUSE HE WAS TOO TRANSFIXED BY THE FIRE.
"DO YOU HAVE ANY IDEA WHAT IT'S LIKE TO LOVE SOMETHING THAT YOU KNOW IS WRONG, AND IF YOU EVER TOUCH IT...IT *HURTS* YOU?
IT'S PART OF WHY THEY ARE BOTH SO *ANGRY* AT MY BROTHER. WE FOUND A FAMILY TOGETHER...AND HE THREW IT ALL AWAY.
NONE OF US WANT "NORMAL" LIVES, BECAUSE WHAT'S THAT TO US? WE JUST WANT OUR *OWN* LIVES.
EVEN YOU?

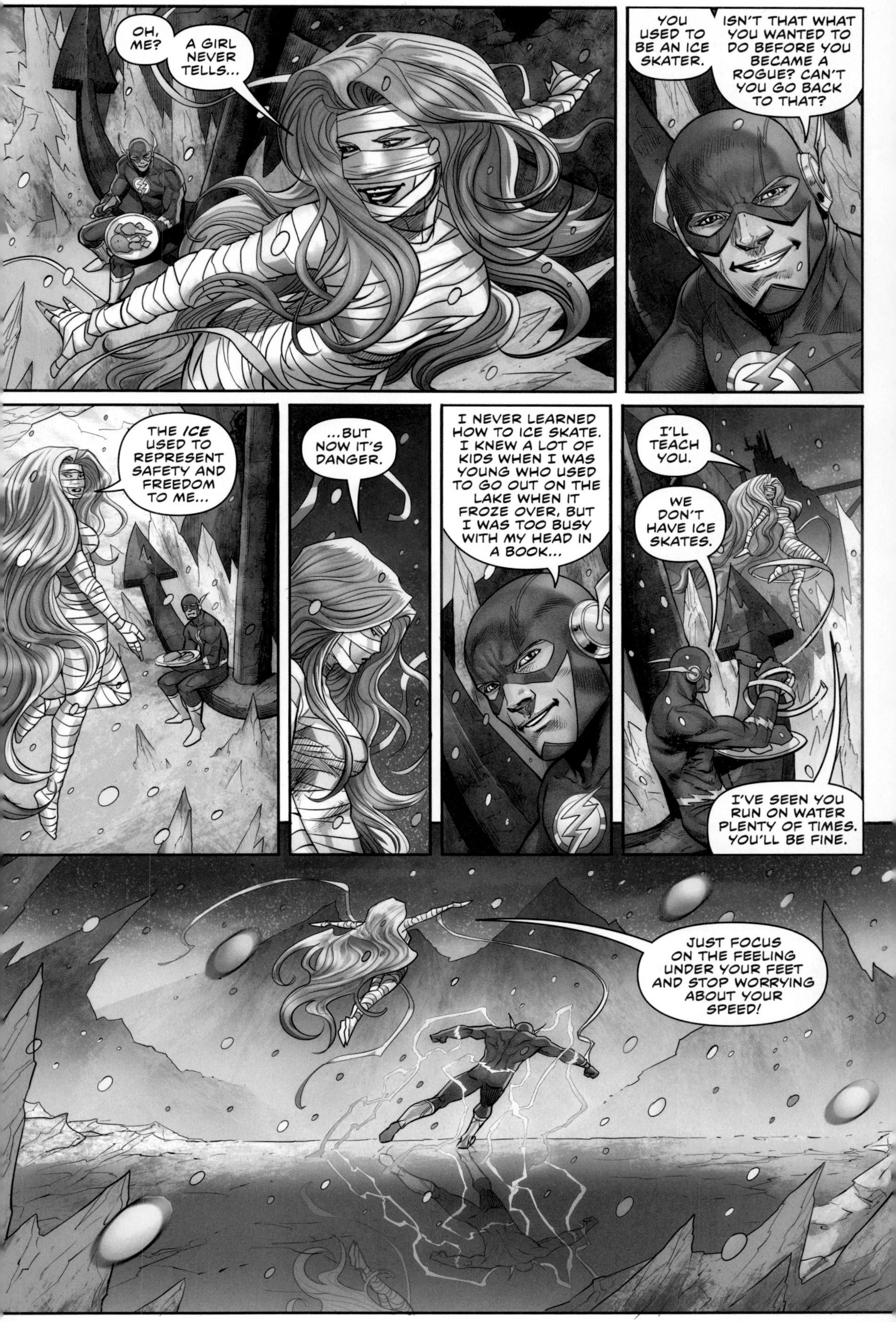
OH, ME?
A GIRL NEVER TELLS...
YOU USED TO BE AN ICE SKATER.
ISN'T THAT WHAT YOU WANTED TO DO BEFORE YOU BECAME A ROGUE? CAN'T YOU GO BACK TO THAT?
THE ICE USED TO REPRESENT SAFETY AND FREEDOM TO ME...
...BUT NOW IT'S DANGER.
I NEVER LEARNED HOW TO ICE SKATE. I KNEW A LOT OF KIDS WHEN I WAS YOUNG WHO USED TO GO OUT ON THE LAKE WHEN IT FROZE OVER, BUT I WAS TOO BUSY WITH MY HEAD IN A BOOK...
I'LL TEACH YOU.
WE DON'T HAVE ICE SKATES.
I'VE SEEN YOU RUN ON WATER PLENTY OF TIMES. YOU'LL BE FINE.
JUST FOCUS ON THE FEELING UNDER YOUR FEET AND STOP WORRYING ABOUT YOUR SPEED!

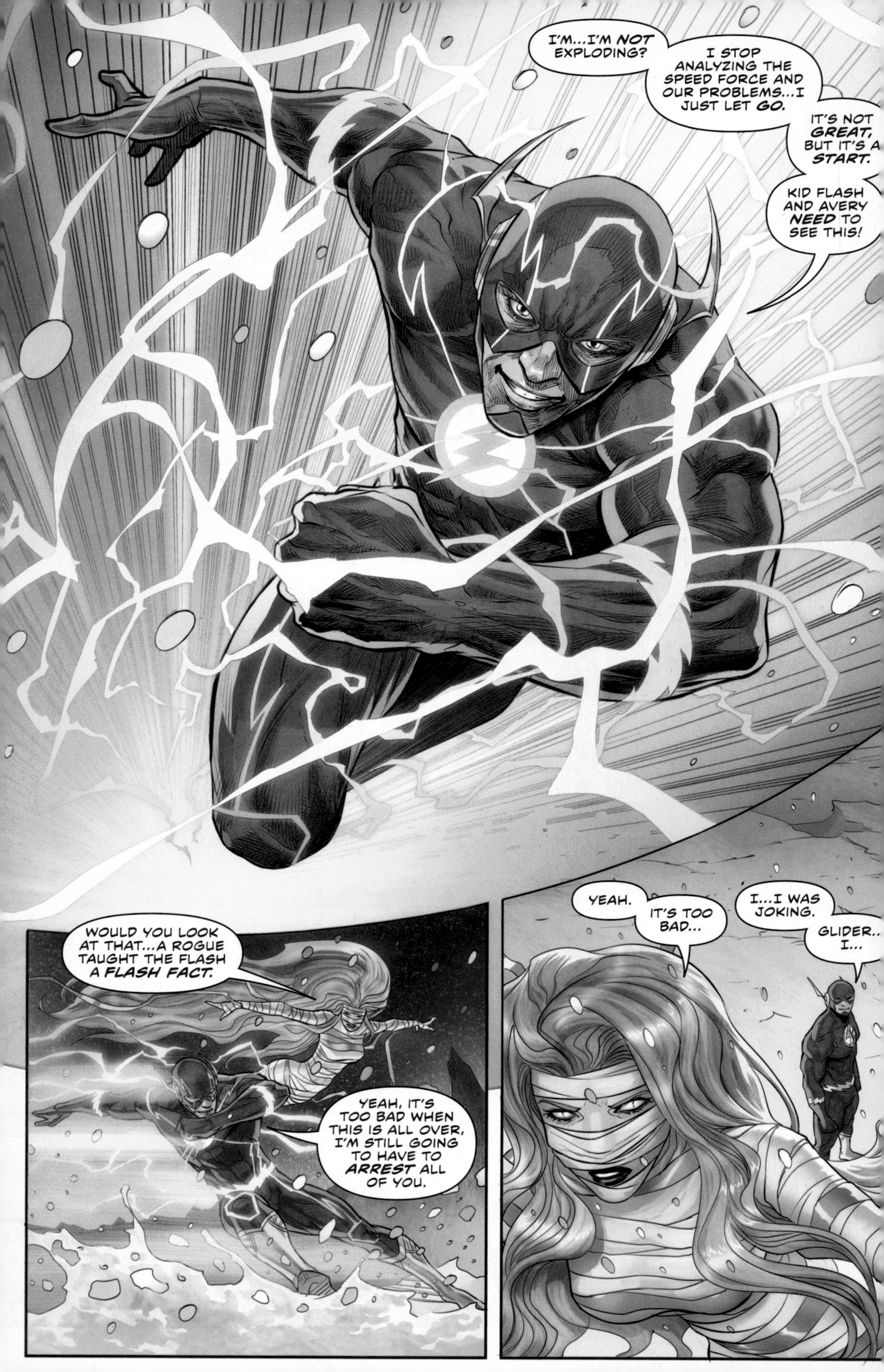
I'M...I'M *NOT* EXPLODING?
I STOP ANALYZING THE SPEED FORCE AND OUR PROBLEMS...I JUST LET *GO.*
IT'S NOT *GREAT,* BUT IT'S A *START.*
KID FLASH AND AVERY *NEED* TO SEE THIS!
WOULD YOU LOOK AT THAT...A ROGUE TAUGHT THE FLASH A *FLASH FACT.*
YEAH, IT'S TOO BAD WHEN THIS IS ALL OVER, I'M STILL GOING TO HAVE TO *ARREST* ALL OF YOU.
YEAH.
IT'S TOO BAD...
I...I WAS JOKING.
GLIDER... I...

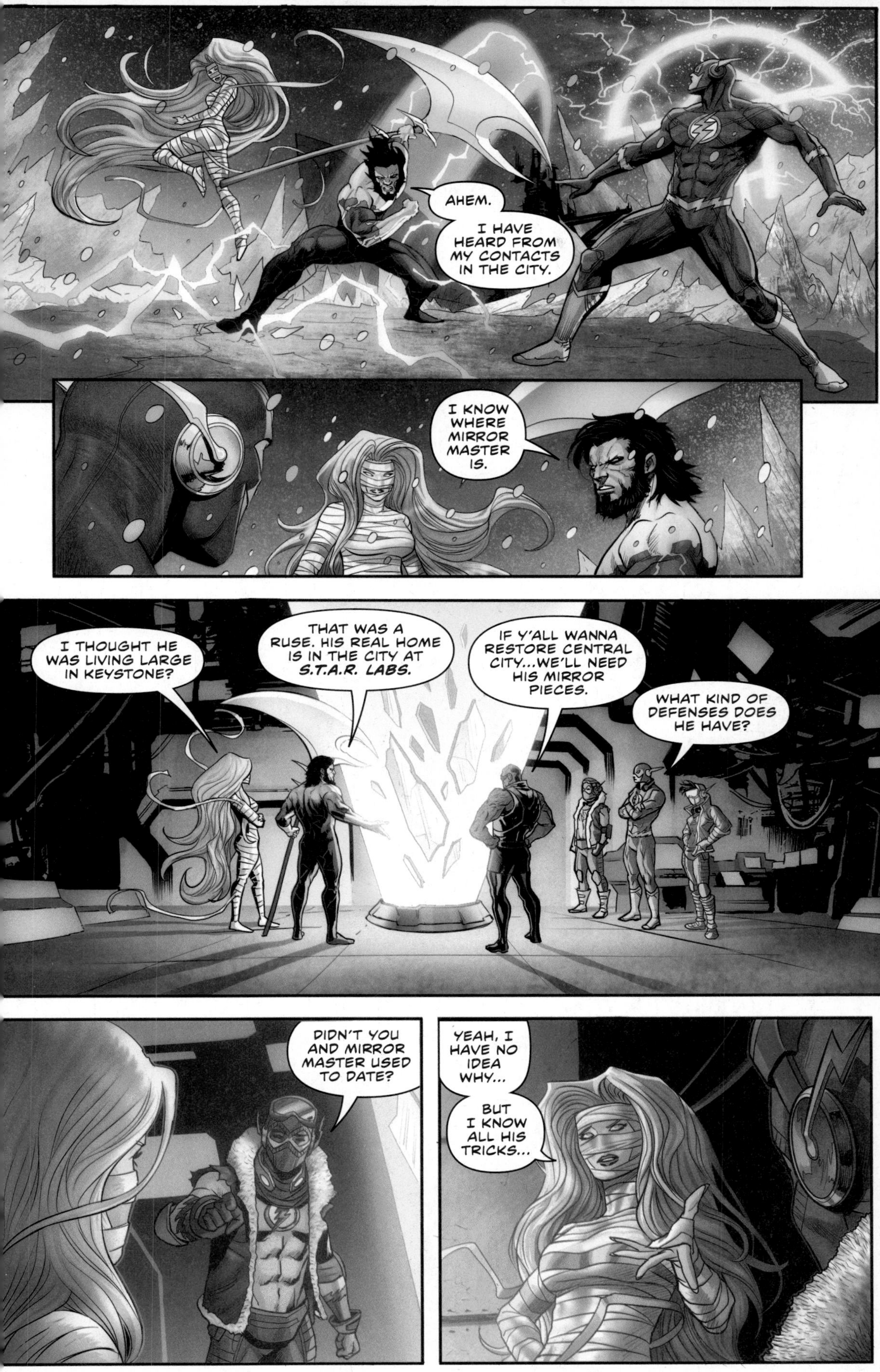
AHEM.
I HAVE HEARD FROM MY CONTACTS IN THE CITY.
I KNOW WHERE MIRROR MASTER IS.
I THOUGHT HE WAS LIVING LARGE IN KEYSTONE?
THAT WAS A RUSE. HIS REAL HOME IS IN THE CITY AT S.T.A.R. LABS.
IF Y'ALL WANNA RESTORE CENTRAL CITY...WE'LL NEED HIS MIRROR PIECES.
WHAT KIND OF DEFENSES DOES HE HAVE?
DIDN'T YOU AND MIRROR MASTER USED TO DATE?
YEAH, I HAVE NO IDEA WHY...
BUT I KNOW ALL HIS TRICKS...

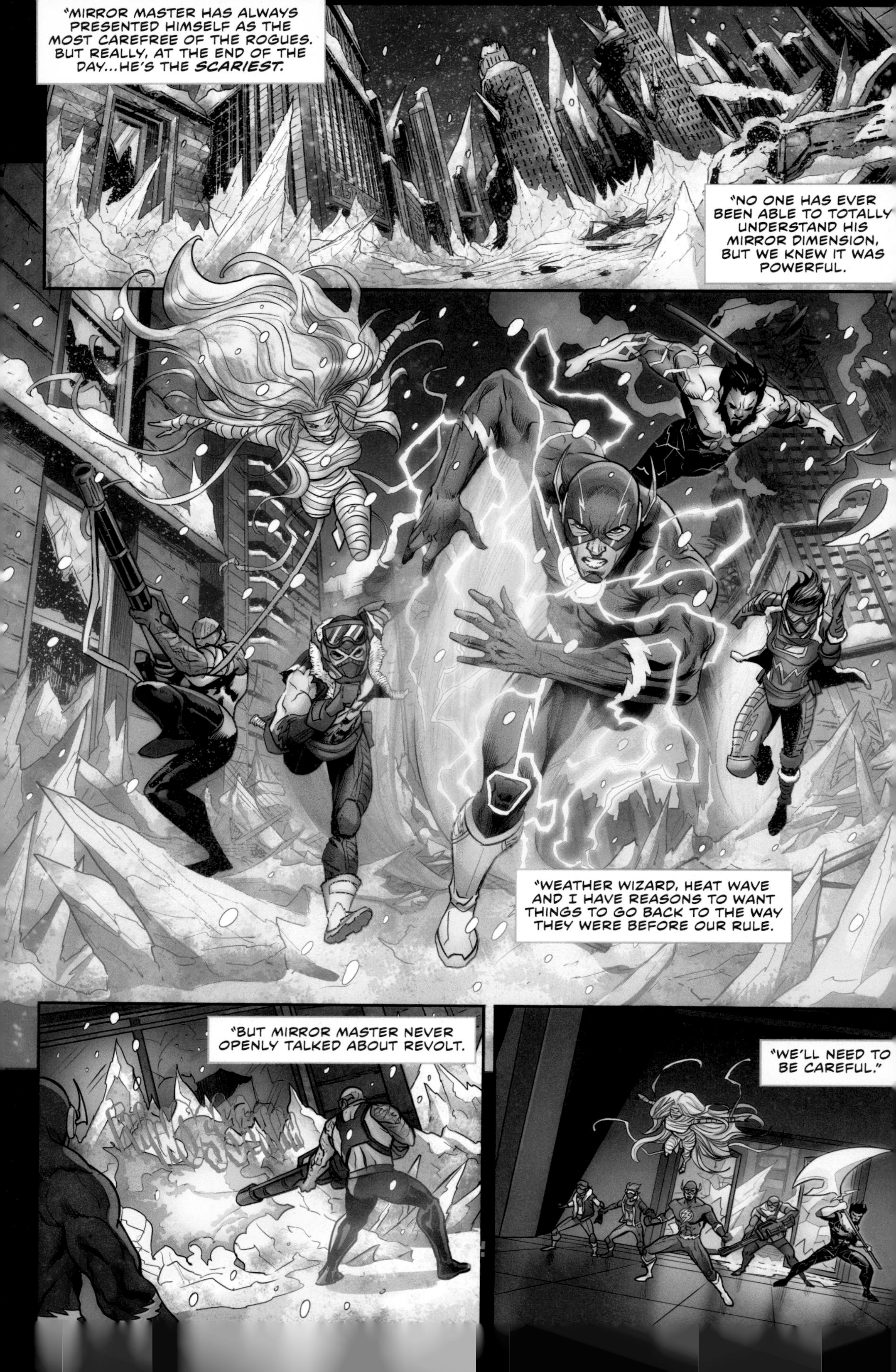
"MIRROR MASTER HAS ALWAYS PRESENTED HIMSELF AS THE MOST CAREFREE OF THE ROGUES. BUT REALLY, AT THE END OF THE DAY...HE'S THE *SCARIEST.*
"NO ONE HAS EVER BEEN ABLE TO TOTALLY UNDERSTAND HIS MIRROR DIMENSION, BUT WE KNEW IT WAS POWERFUL.
"WEATHER WIZARD, HEAT WAVE AND I HAVE REASONS TO WANT THINGS TO GO BACK TO THE WAY THEY WERE BEFORE OUR RULE.
"BUT MIRROR MASTER NEVER OPENLY TALKED ABOUT REVOLT.
"WE'LL NEED TO BE CAREFUL."

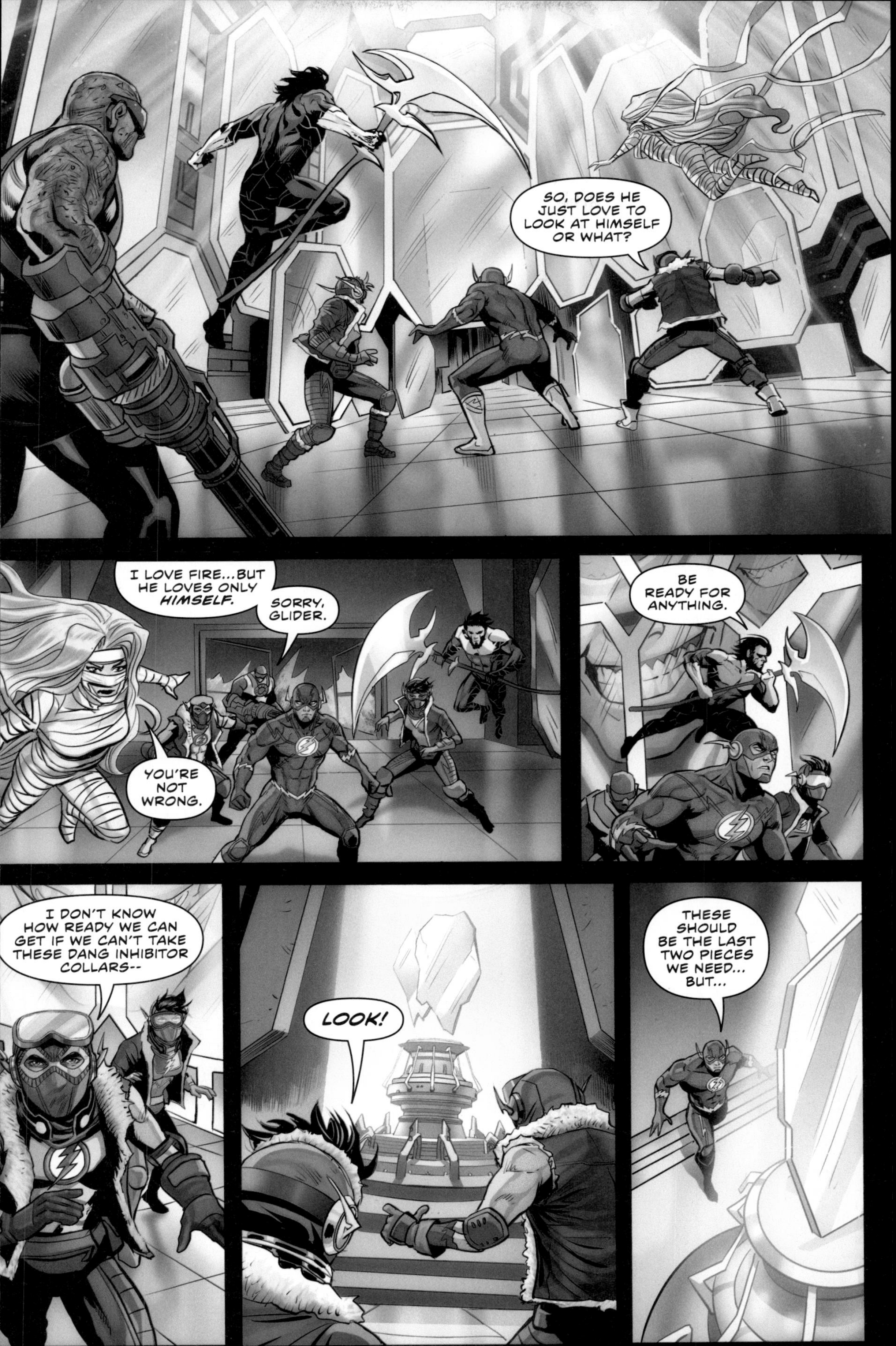
SO, DOES HE JUST LOVE TO LOOK AT HIMSELF OR WHAT?
I LOVE FIRE...BUT HE LOVES ONLY *HIMSELF*.
SORRY, GLIDER.
YOU'RE NOT WRONG.
BE READY FOR ANYTHING.
I DON'T KNOW HOW READY WE CAN GET IF WE CAN'T TAKE THESE DANG INHIBITOR COLLARS--
LOOK!
THESE SHOULD BE THE LAST TWO PIECES WE NEED... BUT...

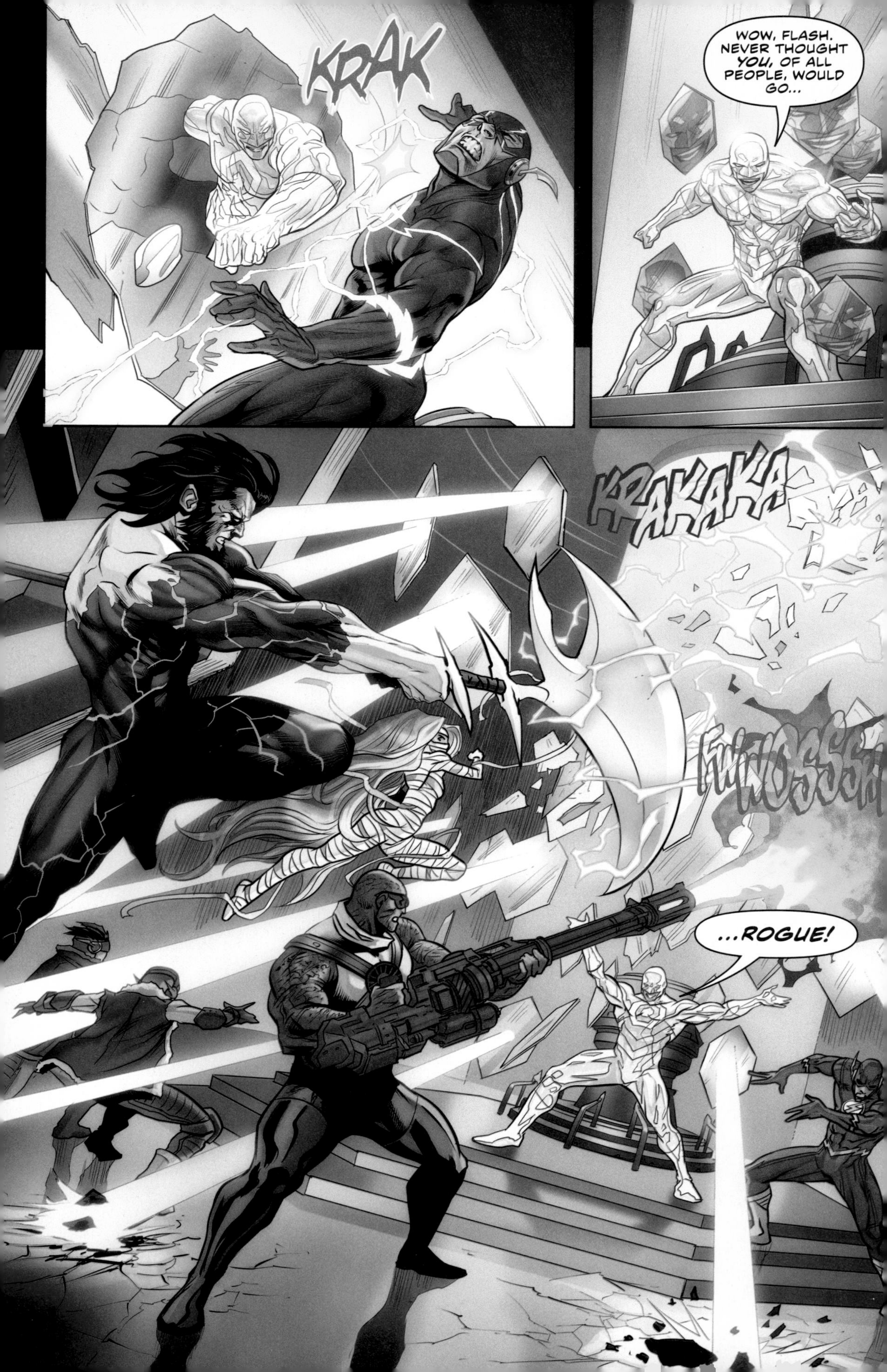
KRAK
WOW, FLASH. NEVER THOUGHT YOU, OF ALL PEOPLE, WOULD GO...
KRAKAKA
...ROGUE!

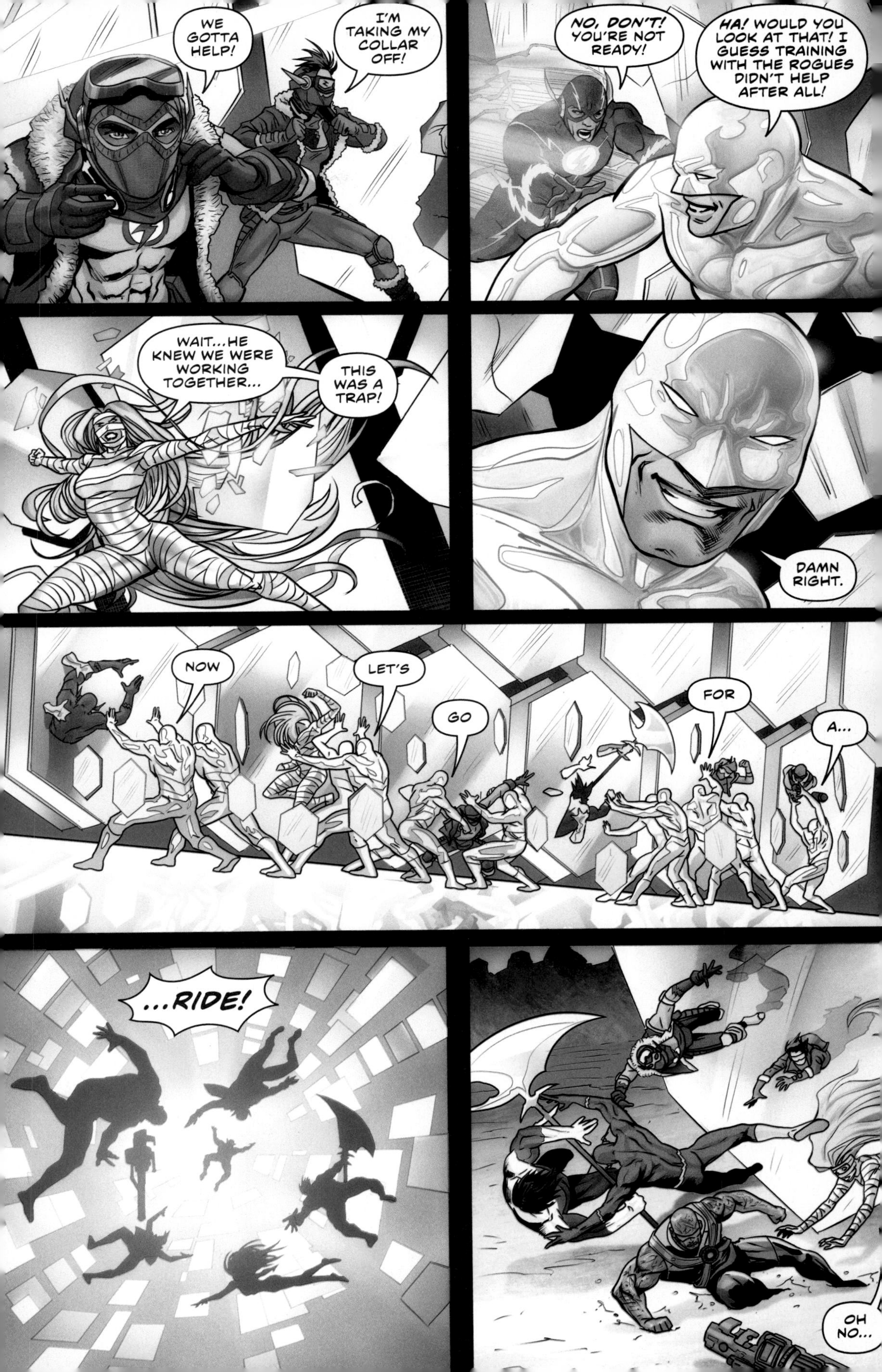
WE GOTTA HELP!
I'M TAKING MY COLLAR OFF!
NO, DON'T! YOU'RE NOT READY!
HA! WOULD YOU LOOK AT THAT! I GUESS TRAINING WITH THE ROGUES DIDN'T HELP AFTER ALL!
WAIT...HE KNEW WE WERE WORKING TOGETHER...
THIS WAS A TRAP!
DAMN RIGHT.
NOW
LET'S
GO
FOR
A...
...RIDE!
OH NO...

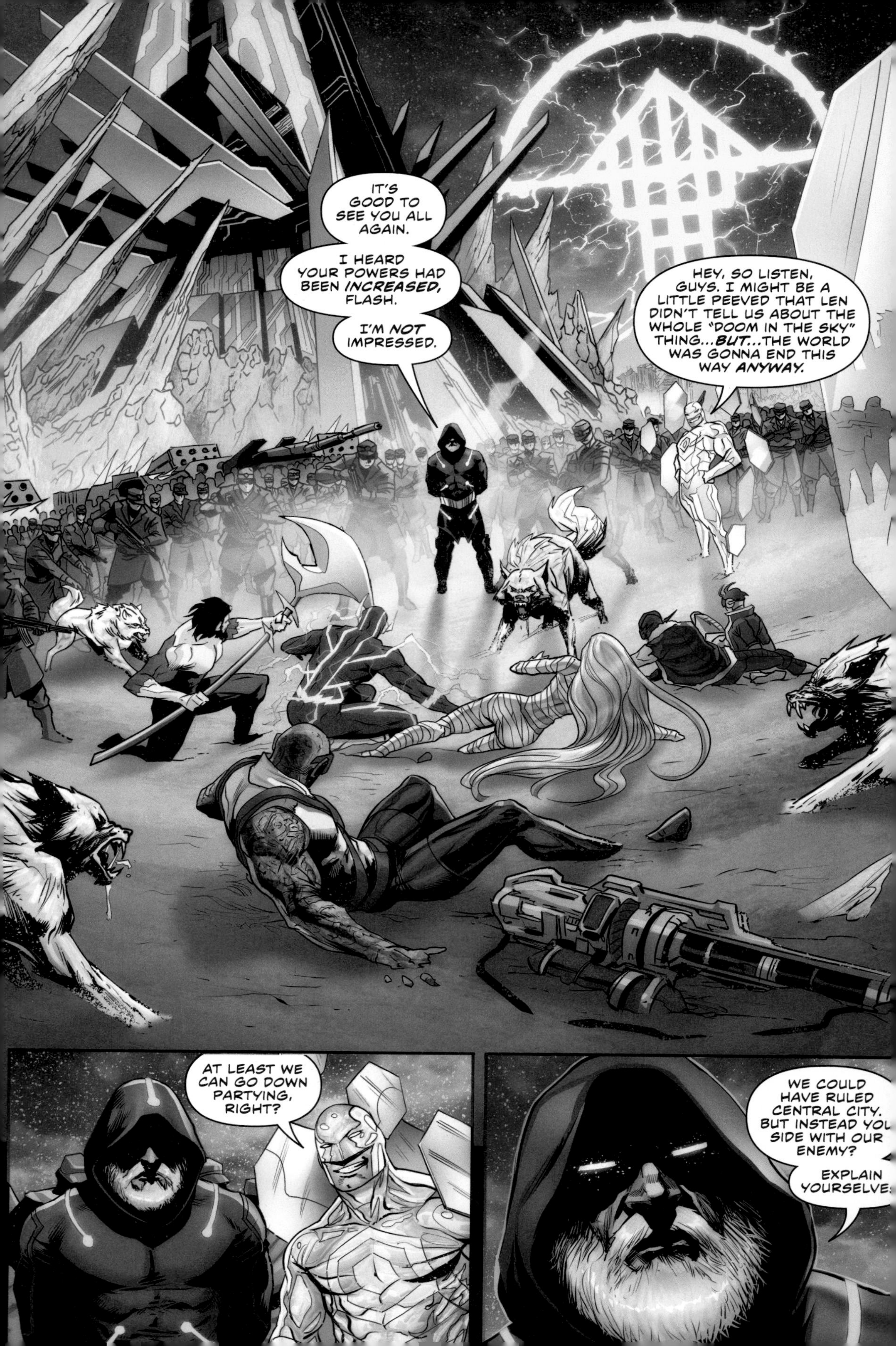
IT'S GOOD TO SEE YOU ALL AGAIN.
I HEARD YOUR POWERS HAD BEEN INCREASED, FLASH.
I'M NOT IMPRESSED.
HEY, SO LISTEN, GUYS. I MIGHT BE A LITTLE PEEVED THAT LEN DIDN'T TELL US ABOUT THE WHOLE "DOOM IN THE SKY" THING...BUT...THE WORLD WAS GONNA END THIS WAY ANYWAY.
AT LEAST WE CAN GO DOWN PARTYING, RIGHT?
WE COULD HAVE RULED CENTRAL CITY. BUT INSTEAD YOU SIDE WITH OUR ENEMY?
EXPLAIN YOURSELVES

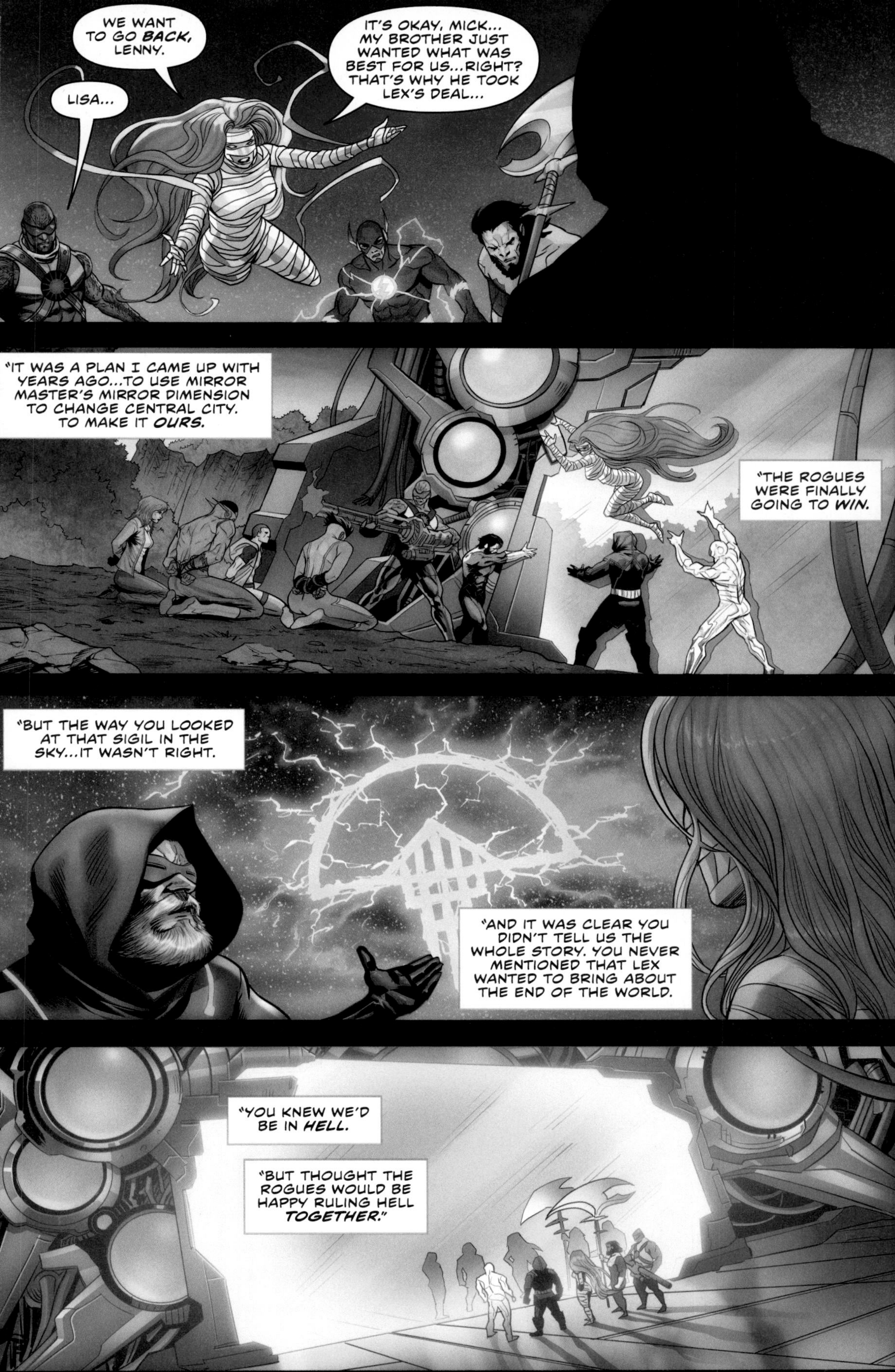
WE WANT TO GO BACK, LENNY.
LISA...
IT'S OKAY, MICK... MY BROTHER JUST WANTED WHAT WAS BEST FOR US...RIGHT? THAT'S WHY HE TOOK LEX'S DEAL...
"IT WAS A PLAN I CAME UP WITH YEARS AGO...TO USE MIRROR MASTER'S MIRROR DIMENSION TO CHANGE CENTRAL CITY. TO MAKE IT OURS.
"THE ROGUES WERE FINALLY GOING TO WIN.
"BUT THE WAY YOU LOOKED AT THAT SIGIL IN THE SKY...IT WASN'T RIGHT.
"AND IT WAS CLEAR YOU DIDN'T TELL US THE WHOLE STORY. YOU NEVER MENTIONED THAT LEX WANTED TO BRING ABOUT THE END OF THE WORLD.
"YOU KNEW WE'D BE IN HELL.
"BUT THOUGHT THE ROGUES WOULD BE HAPPY RULING HELL TOGETHER."

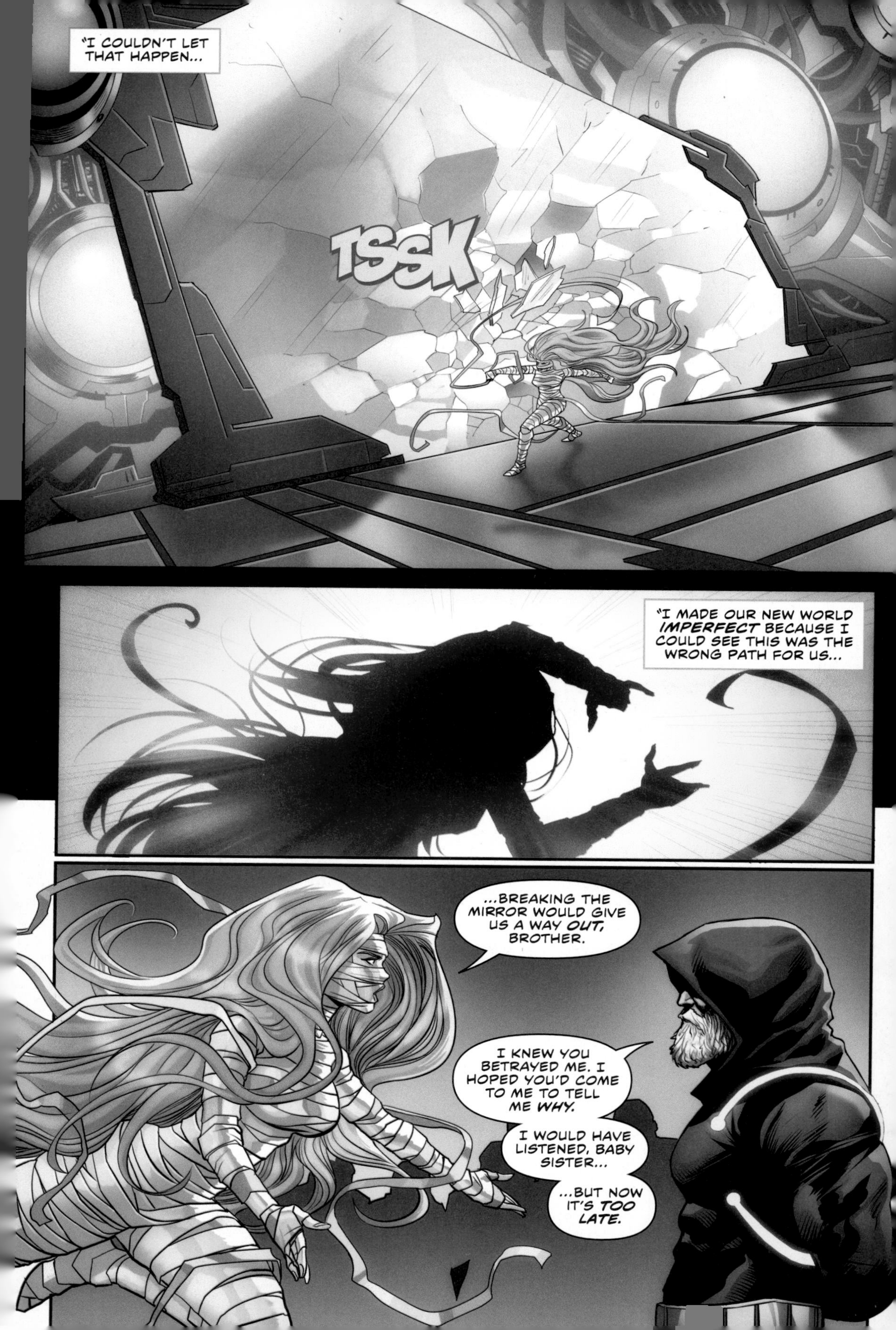
"I COULDN'T LET THAT HAPPEN...
TSSK
"I MADE OUR NEW WORLD *IMPERFECT* BECAUSE I COULD SEE THIS WAS THE WRONG PATH FOR US...
...BREAKING THE MIRROR WOULD GIVE US A WAY *OUT,* BROTHER.
I KNEW YOU BETRAYED ME. I HOPED YOU'D COME TO ME TO TELL ME *WHY.*
I WOULD HAVE LISTENED, BABY SISTER...
...BUT NOW IT'S *TOO LATE.*

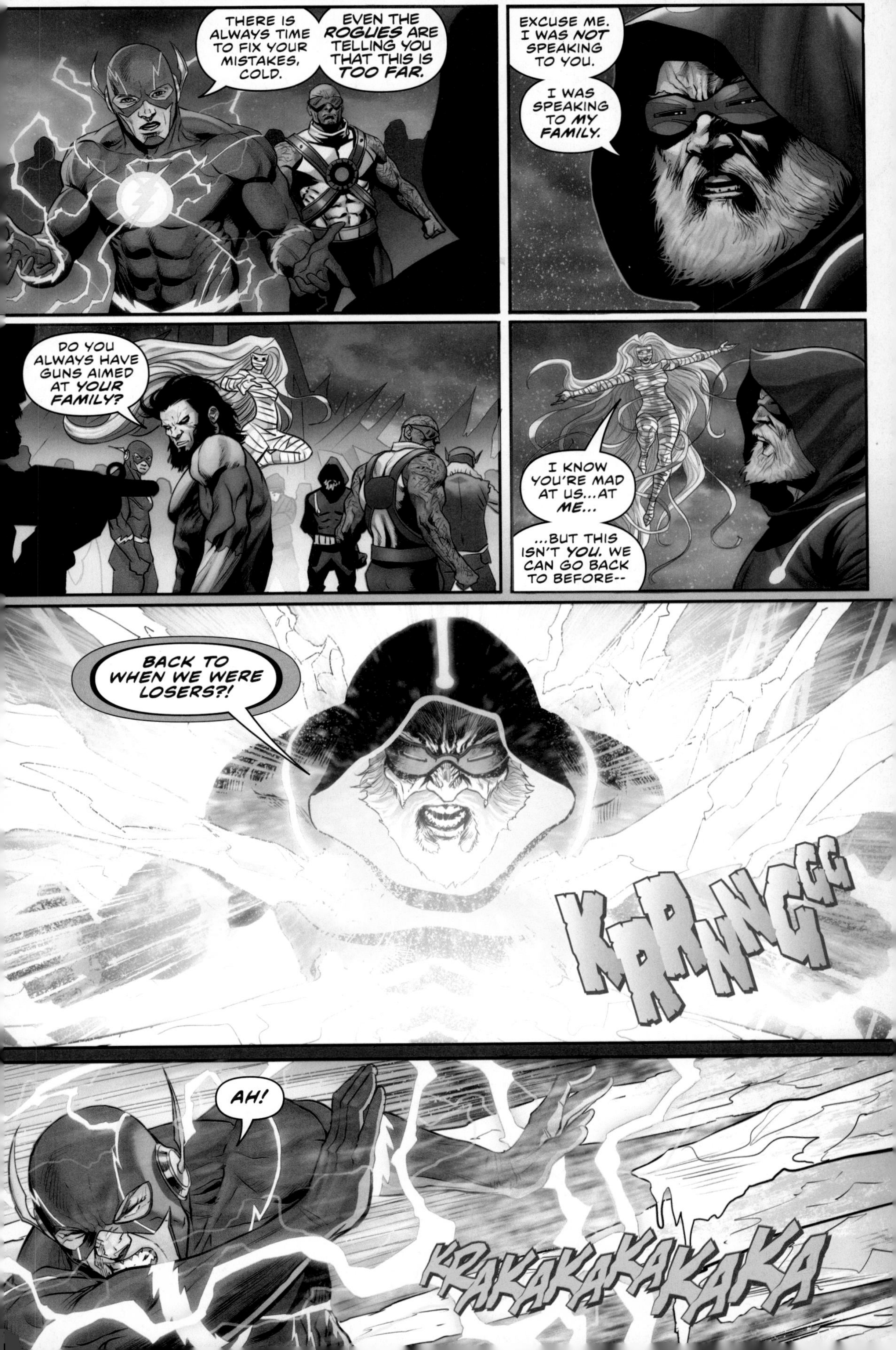

THERE IS ALWAYS TIME TO FIX YOUR MISTAKES, COLD.
EVEN THE ROGUES ARE TELLING YOU THAT THIS IS TOO FAR.
EXCUSE ME. I WAS NOT SPEAKING TO YOU.
I WAS SPEAKING TO MY FAMILY.
DO YOU ALWAYS HAVE GUNS AIMED AT YOUR FAMILY?
I KNOW YOU'RE MAD AT US...AT ME...
...BUT THIS ISN'T YOU. WE CAN GO BACK TO BEFORE--
BACK TO WHEN WE WERE LOSERS?!
KRRNNGGG
AH!
KRAKAKAKAKAKAKA

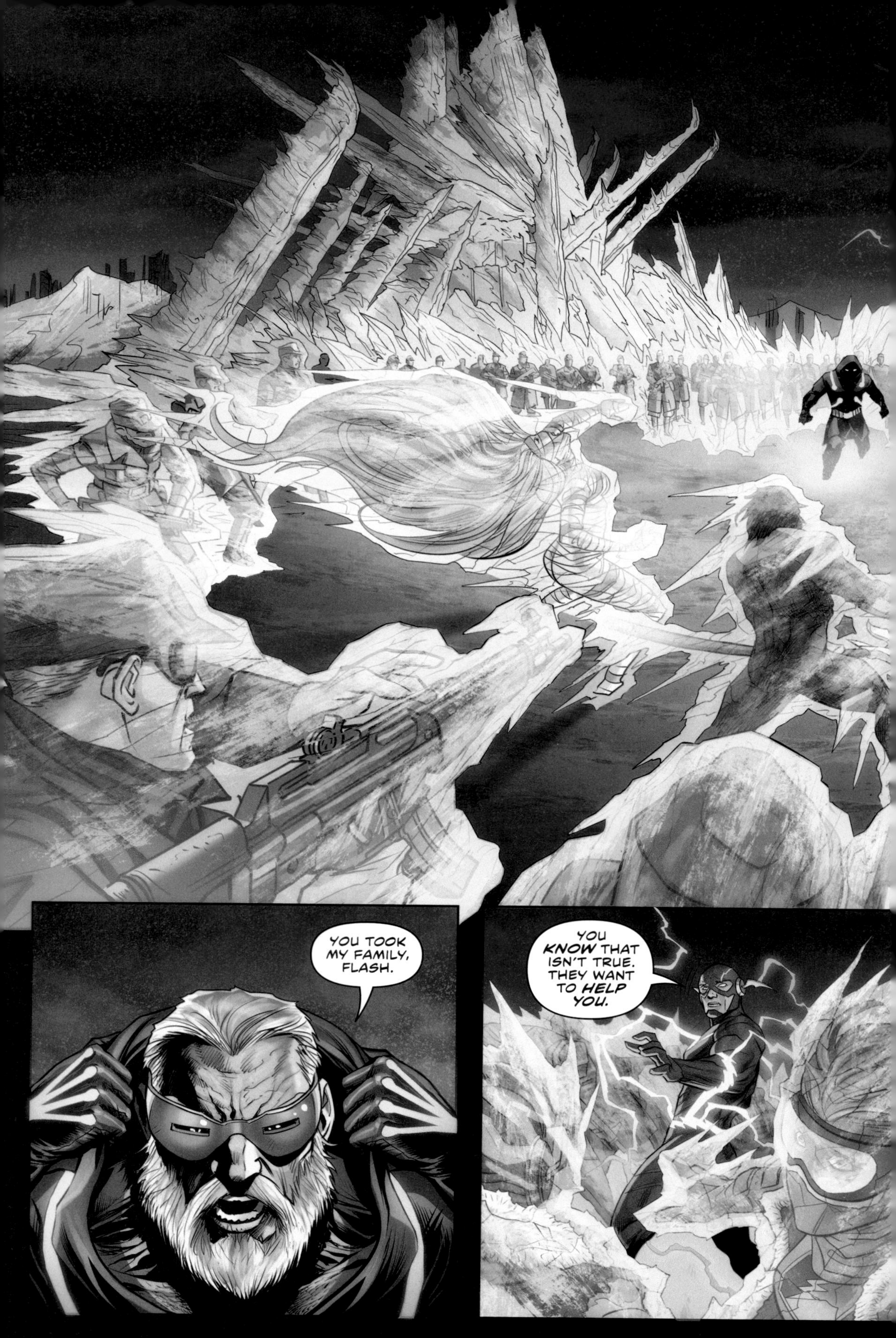
YOU TOOK MY FAMILY, FLASH.
YOU KNOW THAT ISN'T TRUE. THEY WANT TO HELP YOU.

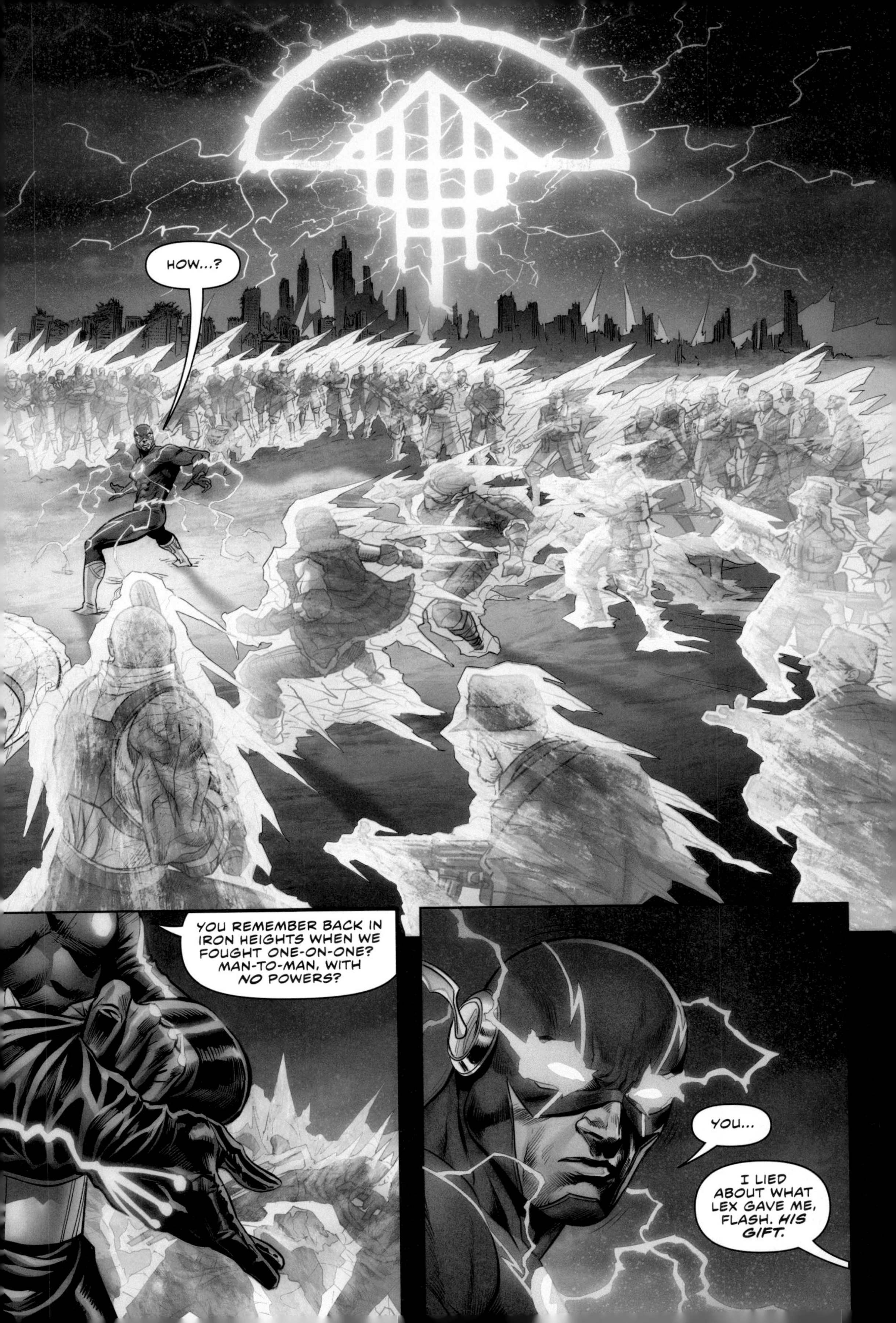
HOW...?
YOU REMEMBER BACK IN IRON HEIGHTS WHEN WE FOUGHT ONE-ON-ONE? MAN-TO-MAN, WITH *NO* POWERS?
YOU...
I LIED ABOUT WHAT LEX GAVE ME, FLASH. *HIS GIFT.*

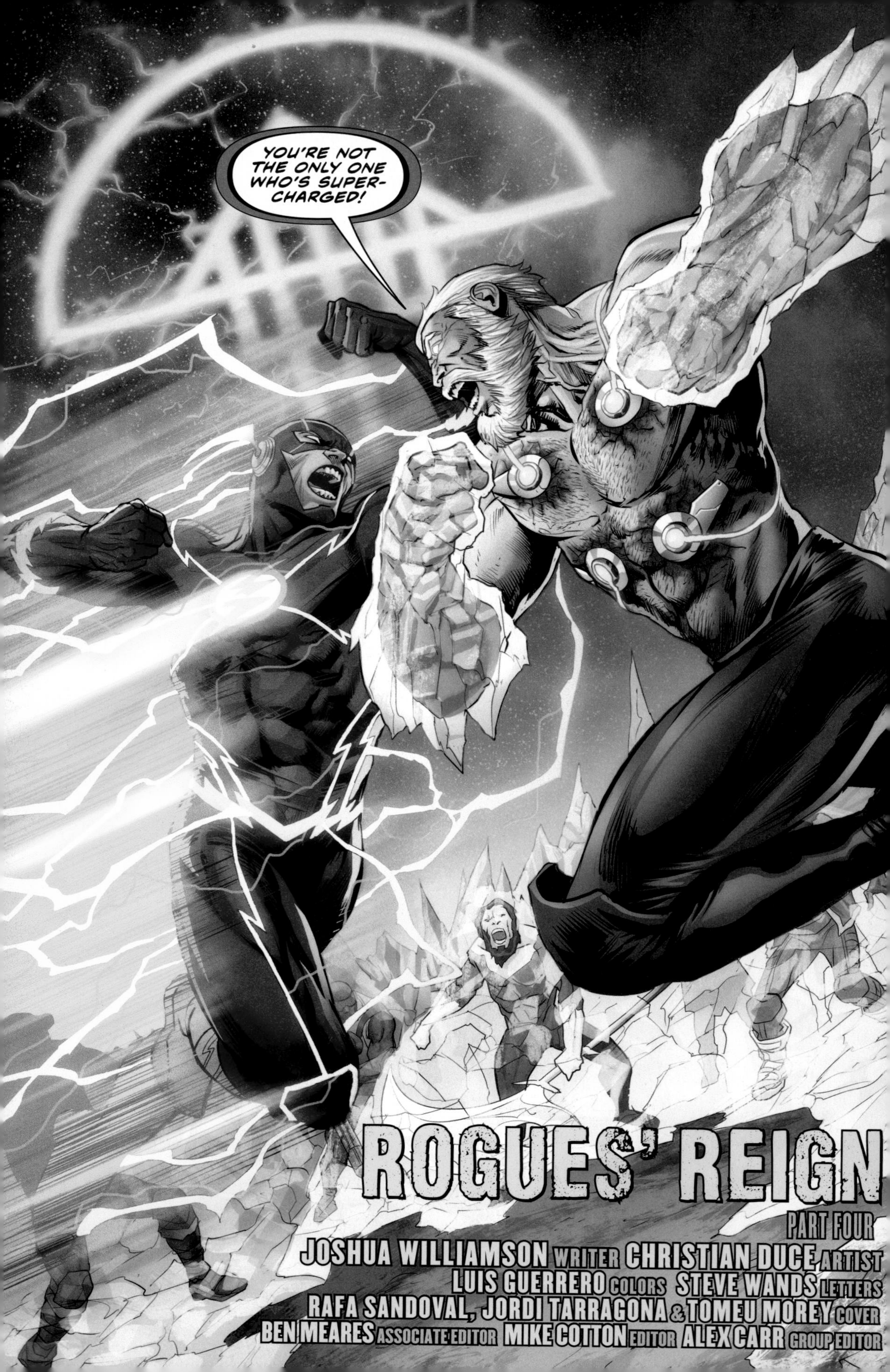
YOU'RE NOT THE ONLY ONE WHO'S SUPER-CHARGED!
ROGUES' REIGN
PART FOUR
JOSHUA WILLIAMSON WRITER CHRISTIAN DUCE ARTIST
LUIS GUERRERO COLORS STEVE WANDS LETTERS
RAFA SANDOVAL, JORDI TARRAGONA & TOMEU MOREY COVER
BEN MEARES ASSOCIATE EDITOR MIKE COTTON EDITOR ALEX CARR GROUP EDITOR

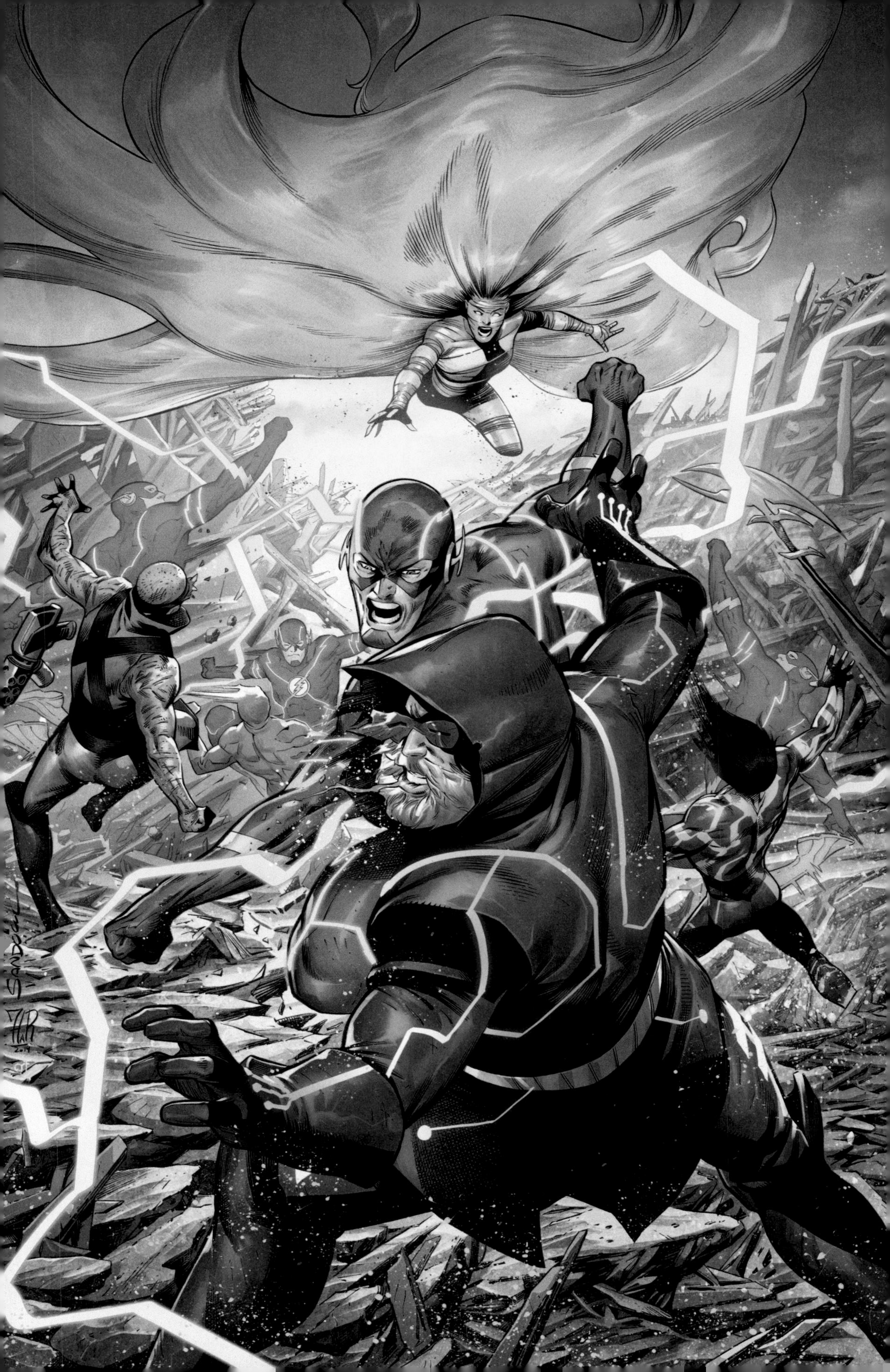

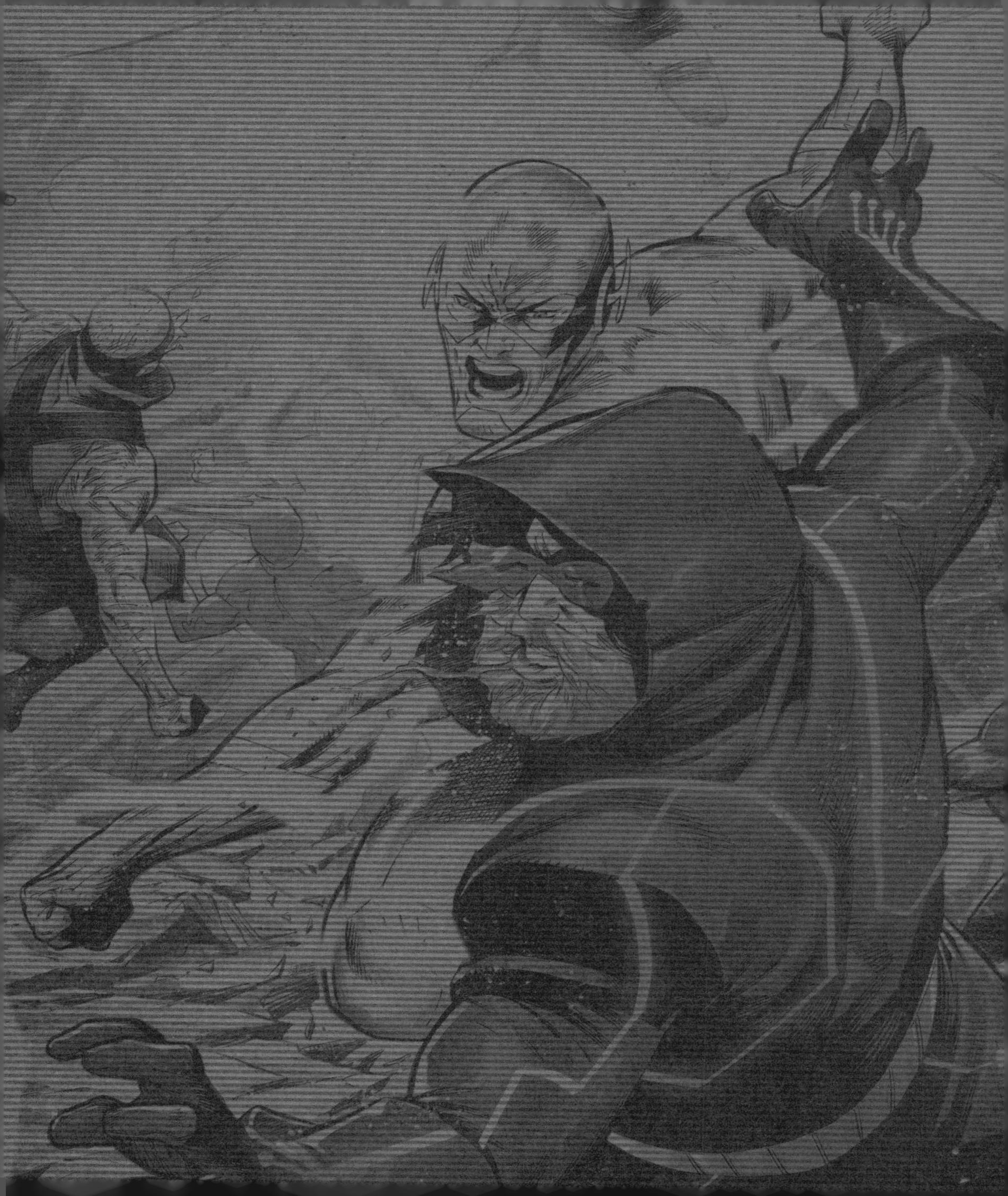

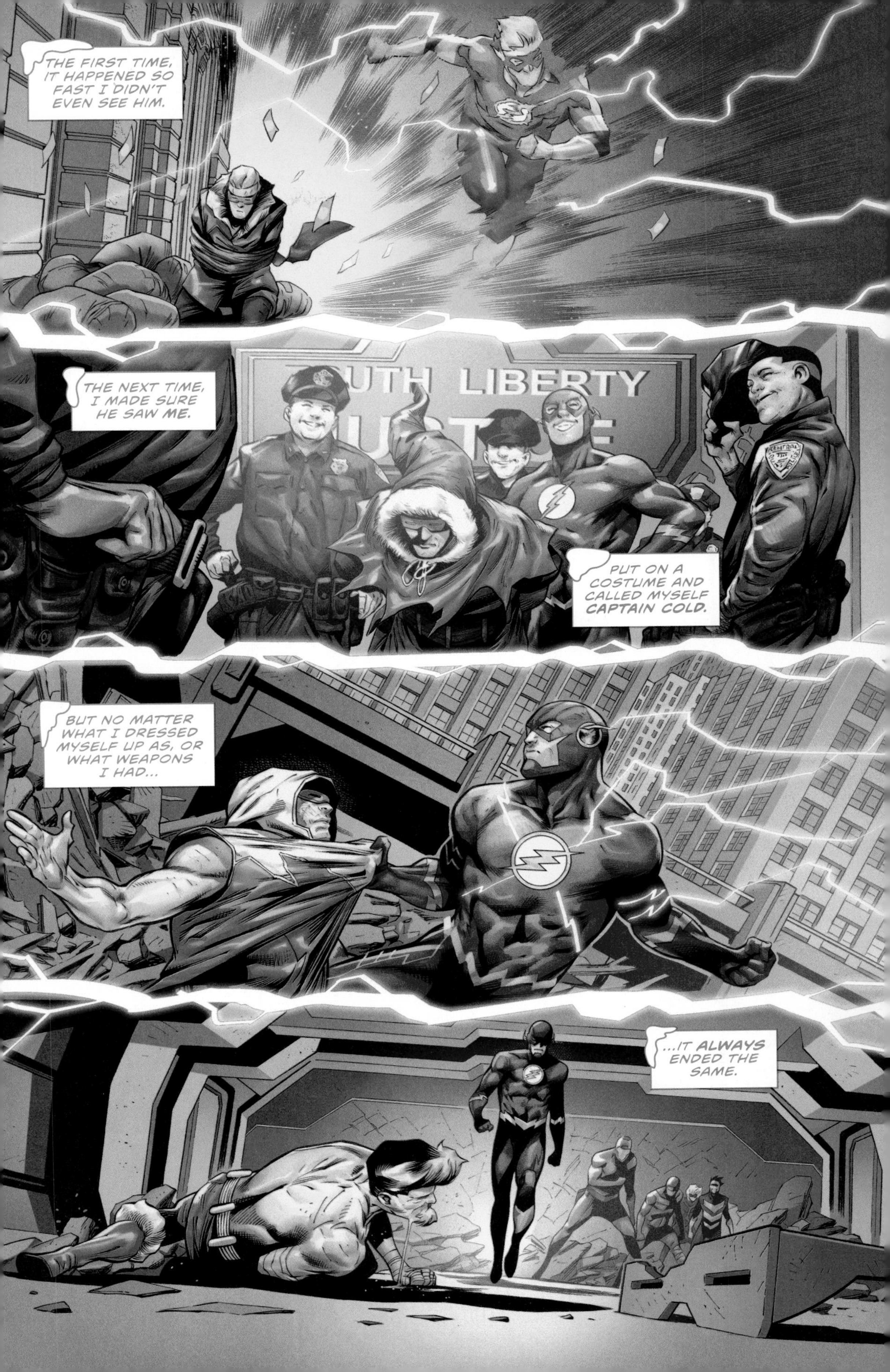
THE FIRST TIME, IT HAPPENED SO FAST I DIDN'T EVEN SEE HIM.
THE NEXT TIME, I MADE SURE HE SAW ME.
SOUTH LIBERTY
PUT ON A COSTUME AND CALLED MYSELF CAPTAIN COLD.
BUT NO MATTER WHAT I DRESSED MYSELF UP AS, OR WHAT WEAPONS I HAD...
...IT ALWAYS ENDED THE SAME.

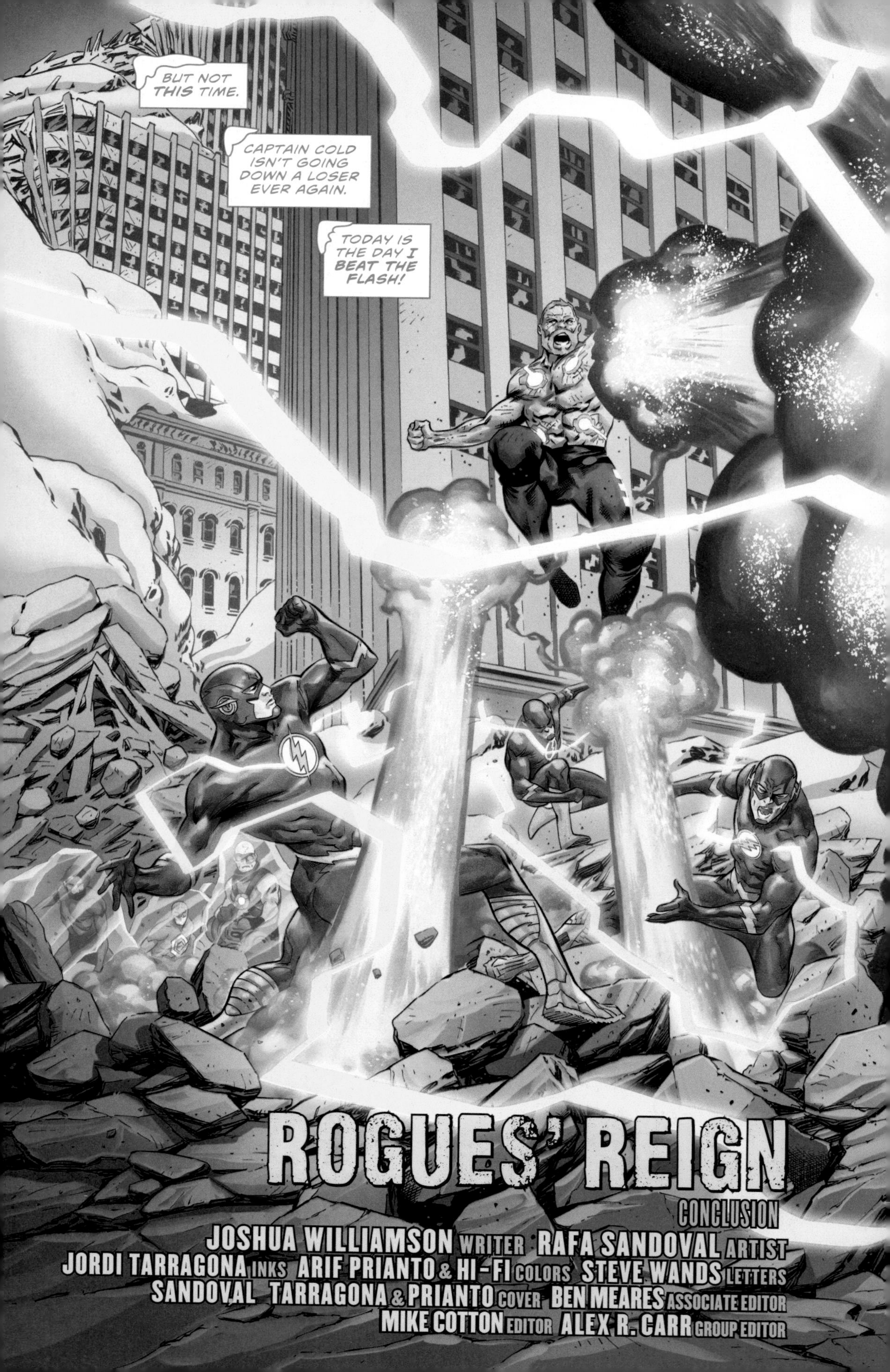
BUT NOT THIS TIME.
CAPTAIN COLD ISN'T GOING DOWN A LOSER EVER AGAIN.
TODAY IS THE DAY I BEAT THE FLASH!
ROGUES' REIGN
CONCLUSION
JOSHUA WILLIAMSON WRITER RAFA SANDOVAL ARTIST
JORDI TARRAGONA INKS ARIF PRIANTO & HI-FI COLORS STEVE WANDS LETTERS
SANDOVAL TARRAGONA & PRIANTO COVER BEN MEARES ASSOCIATE EDITOR
MIKE COTTON EDITOR ALEX R. CARR GROUP EDITOR

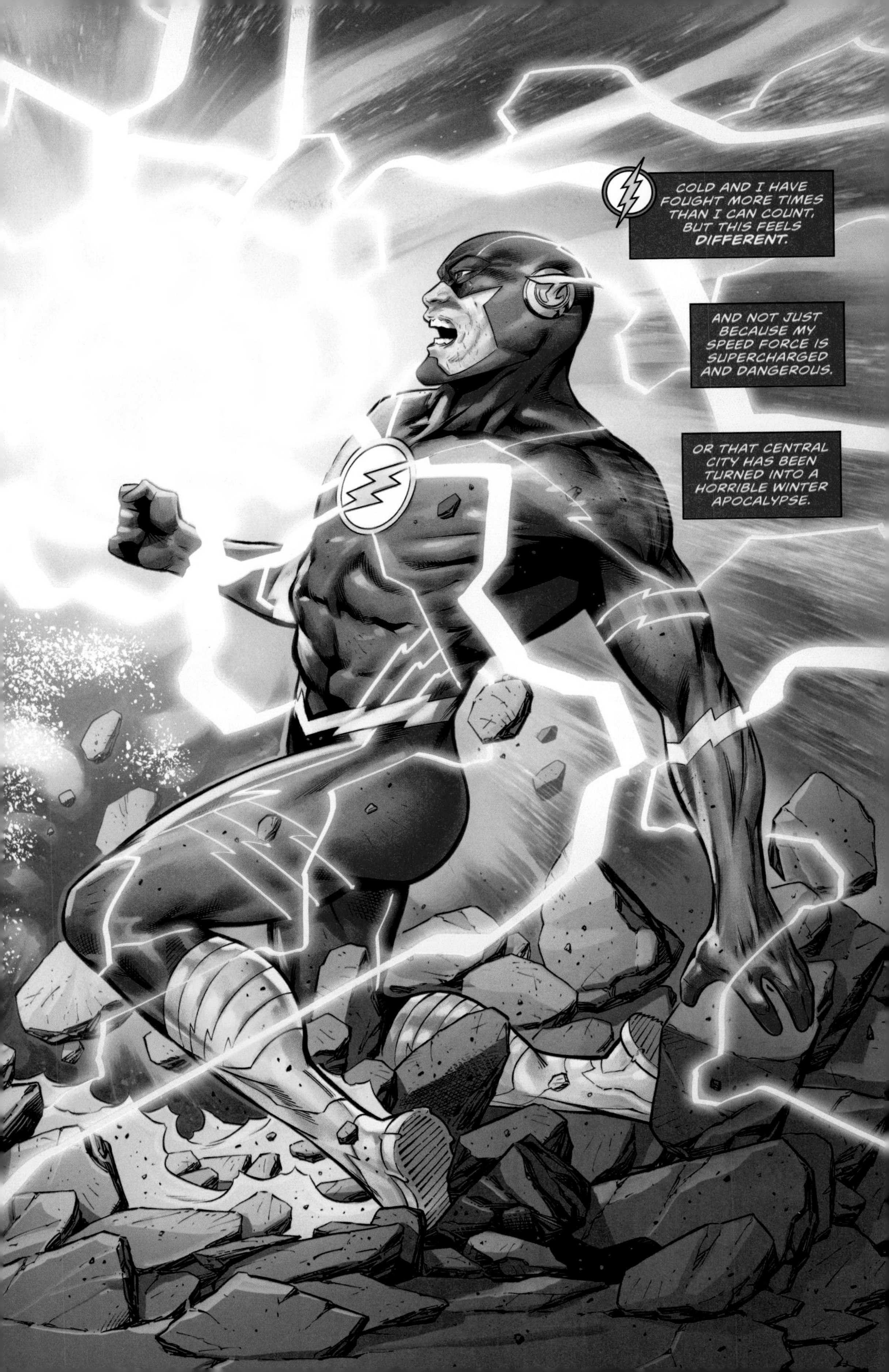
COLD AND I HAVE FOUGHT MORE TIMES THAN I CAN COUNT, BUT THIS FEELS **DIFFERENT.**
AND NOT JUST BECAUSE MY SPEED FORCE IS SUPERCHARGED AND DANGEROUS.
OR THAT CENTRAL CITY HAS BEEN TURNED INTO A HORRIBLE WINTER APOCALYPSE.

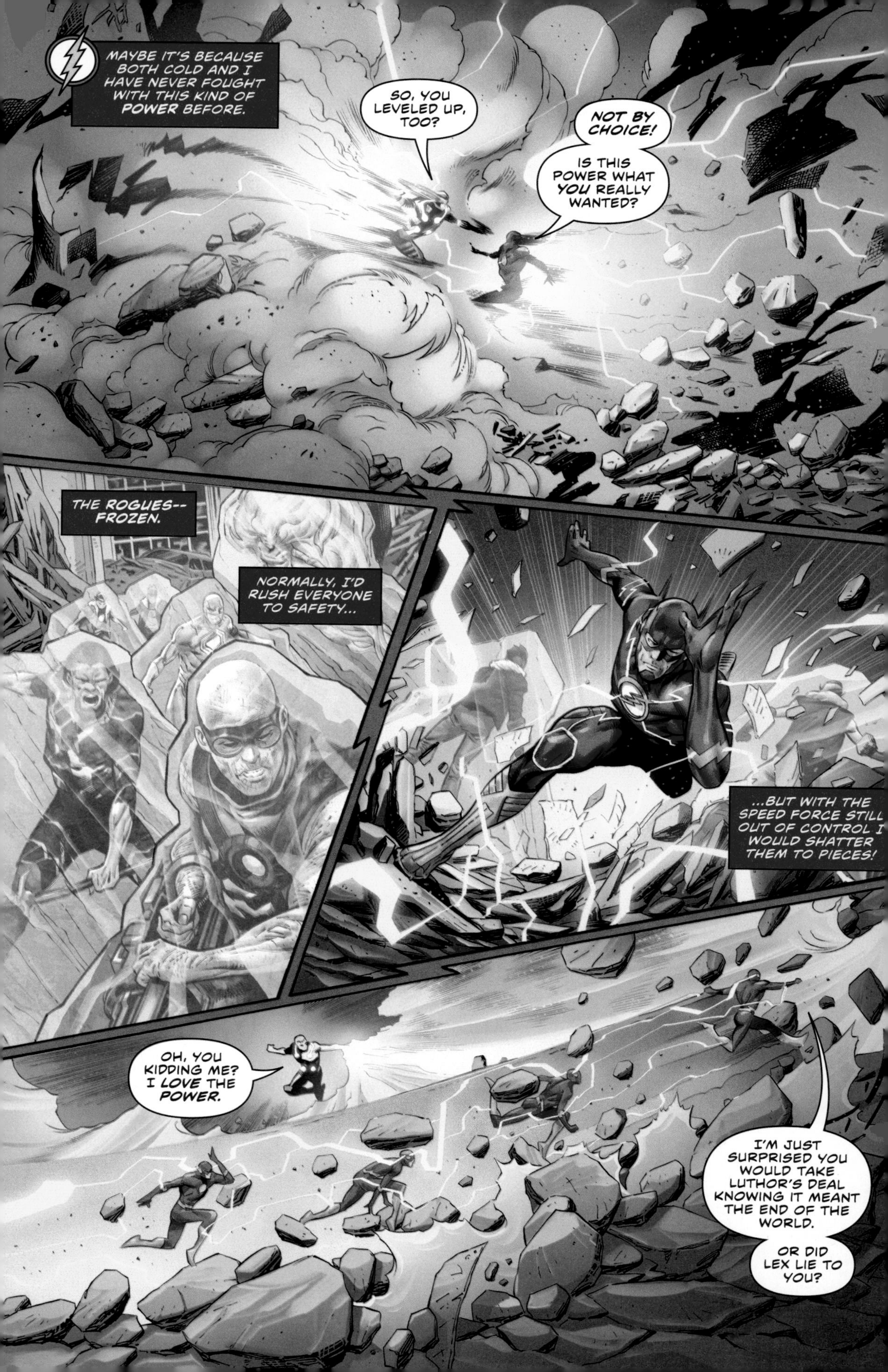
MAYBE IT'S BECAUSE BOTH COLD AND I HAVE NEVER FOUGHT WITH THIS KIND OF POWER BEFORE.
SO, YOU LEVELED UP, TOO?
NOT BY CHOICE!
IS THIS POWER WHAT YOU REALLY WANTED?
THE ROGUES--FROZEN.
NORMALLY, I'D RUSH EVERYONE TO SAFETY...
...BUT WITH THE SPEED FORCE STILL OUT OF CONTROL I WOULD SHATTER THEM TO PIECES!
OH, YOU KIDDING ME? I LOVE THE POWER.
I'M JUST SURPRISED YOU WOULD TAKE LUTHOR'S DEAL KNOWING IT MEANT THE END OF THE WORLD.
OR DID LEX LIE TO YOU?

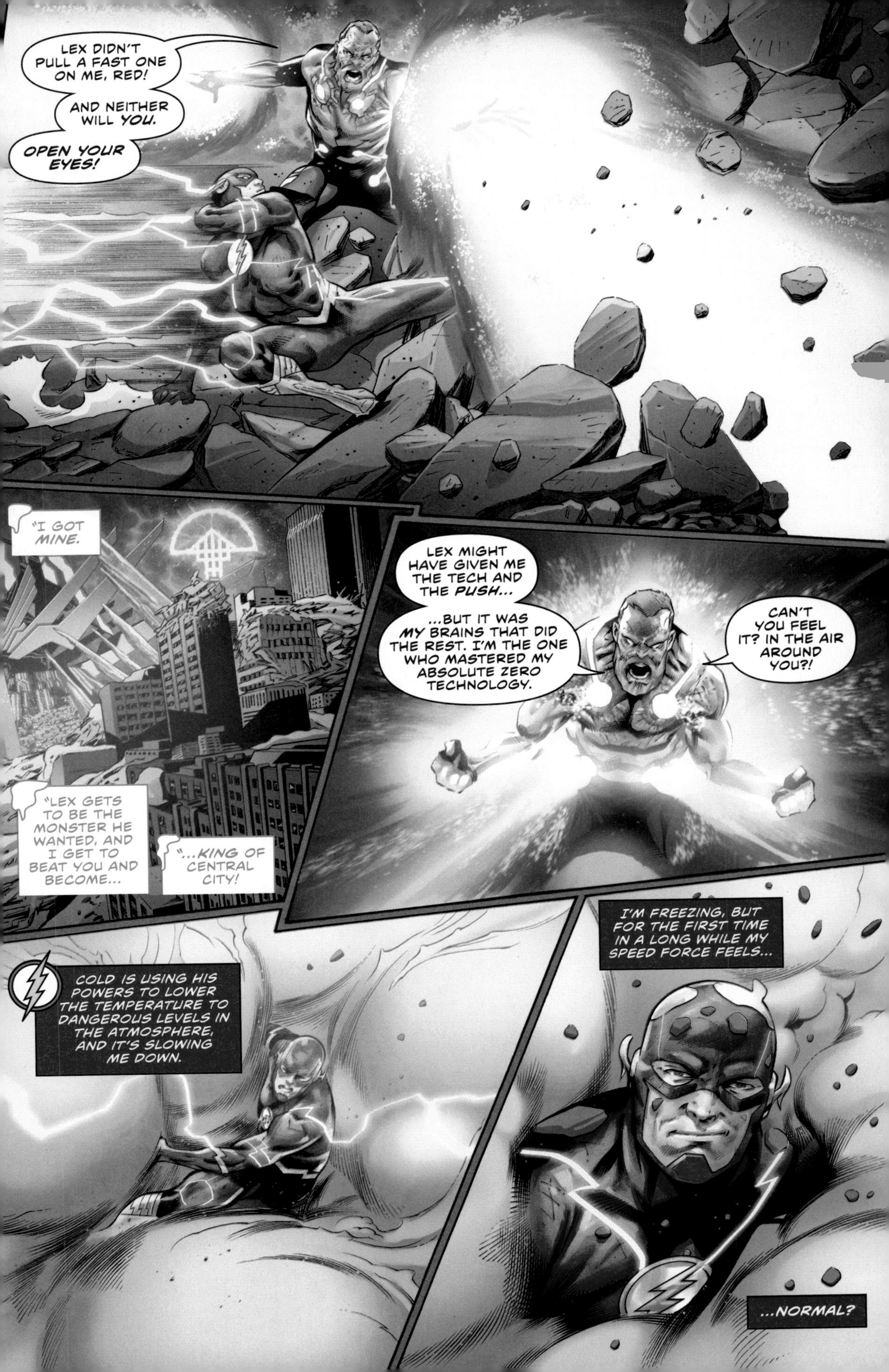
LEX DIDN'T PULL A FAST ONE ON ME, RED!
AND NEITHER WILL YOU.
OPEN YOUR EYES!
"I GOT MINE.
LEX MIGHT HAVE GIVEN ME THE TECH AND THE PUSH...
...BUT IT WAS MY BRAINS THAT DID THE REST. I'M THE ONE WHO MASTERED MY ABSOLUTE ZERO TECHNOLOGY.
CAN'T YOU FEEL IT? IN THE AIR AROUND YOU?!
"LEX GETS TO BE THE MONSTER HE WANTED, AND I GET TO BEAT YOU AND BECOME...
"...KING OF CENTRAL CITY!
COLD IS USING HIS POWERS TO LOWER THE TEMPERATURE TO DANGEROUS LEVELS IN THE ATMOSPHERE, AND IT'S SLOWING ME DOWN.
I'M FREEZING, BUT FOR THE FIRST TIME IN A LONG WHILE MY SPEED FORCE FEELS...
...NORMAL?

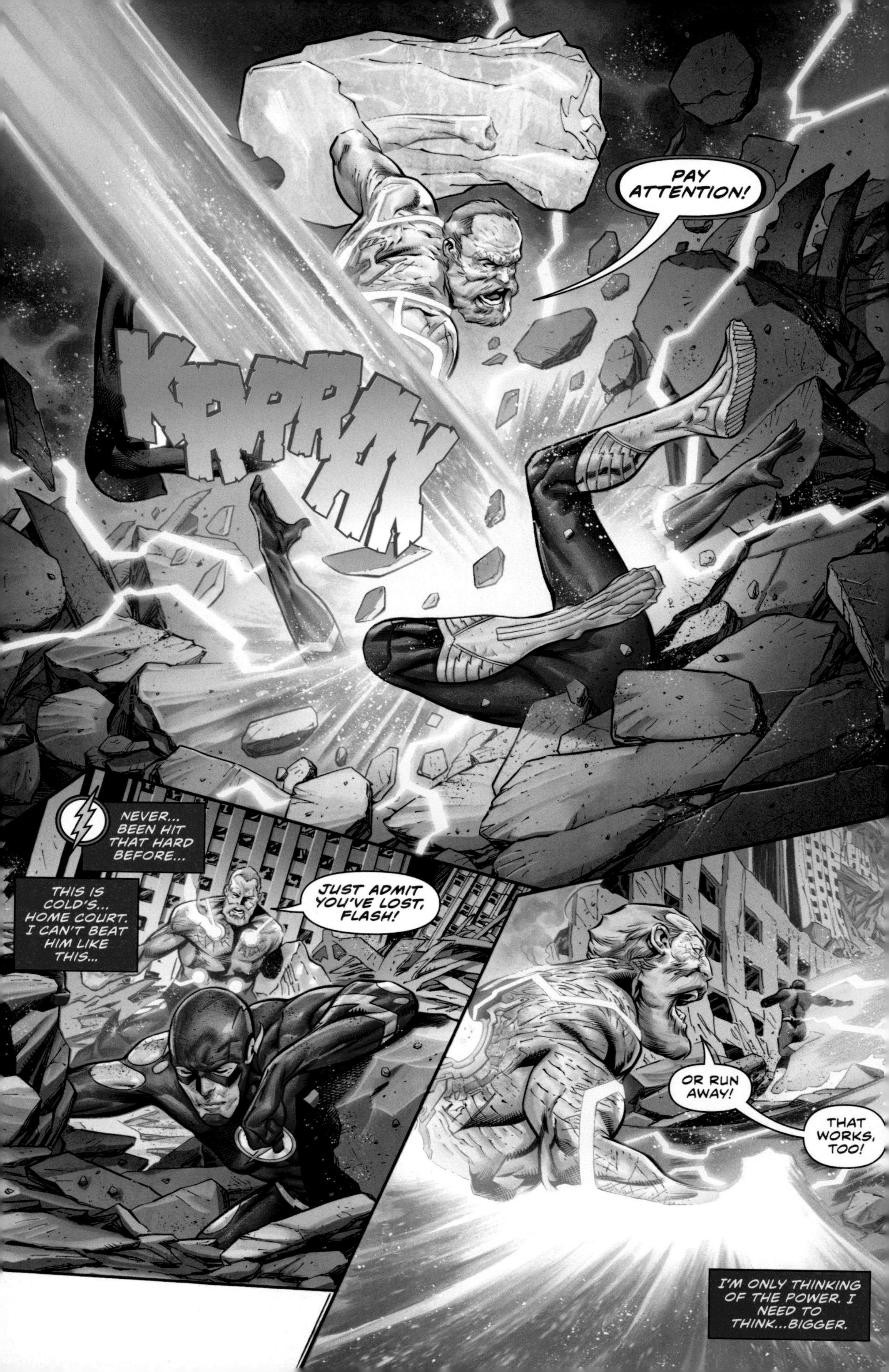
PAY ATTENTION!
KRRRAK
NEVER... BEEN HIT THAT HARD BEFORE...
THIS IS COLD'S... HOME COURT. I CAN'T BEAT HIM LIKE THIS...
JUST ADMIT YOU'VE LOST, FLASH!
OR RUN AWAY!
THAT WORKS, TOO!
I'M ONLY THINKING OF THE POWER. I NEED TO THINK...BIGGER.

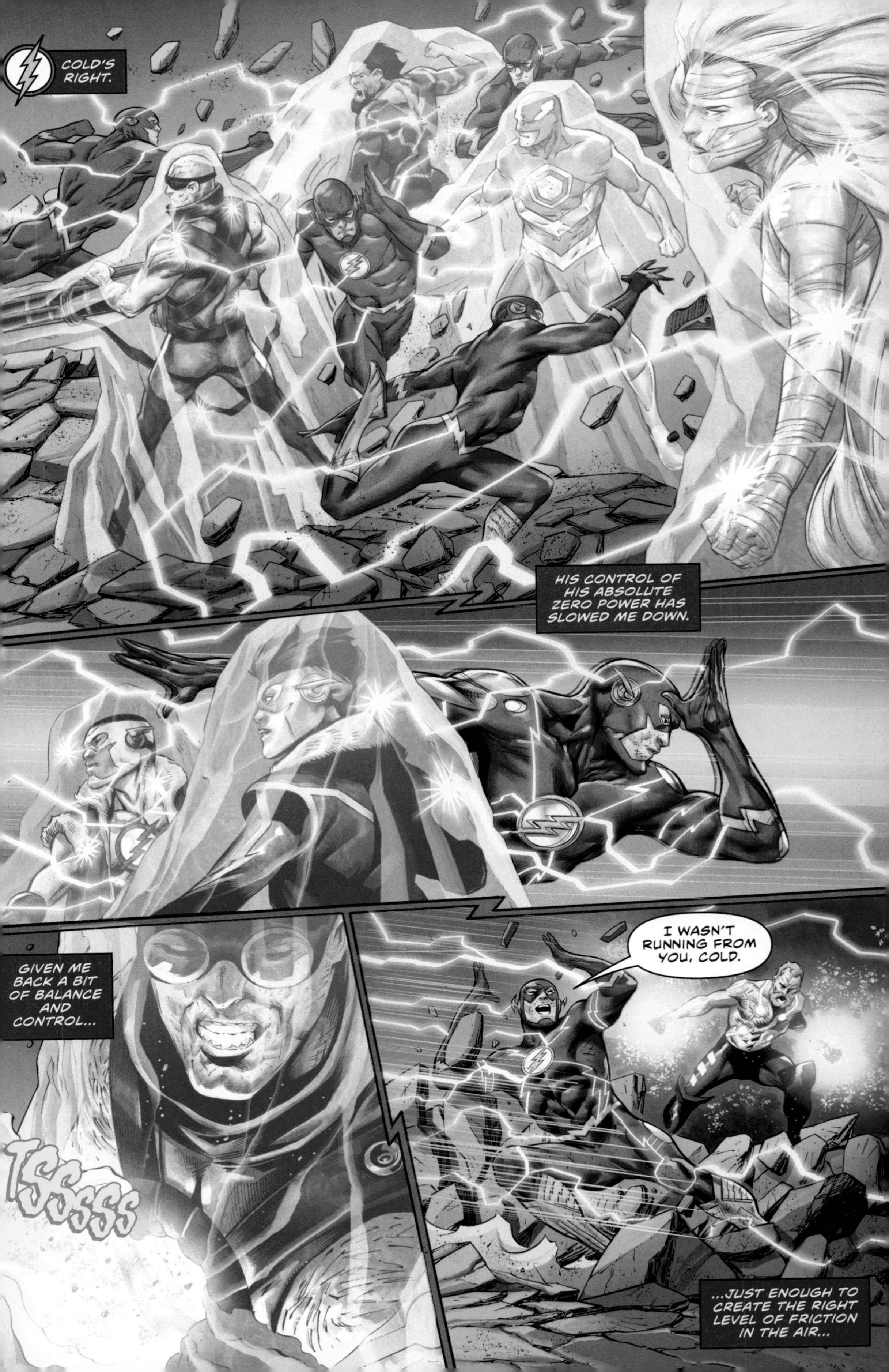
COLD'S RIGHT.
HIS CONTROL OF HIS ABSOLUTE ZERO POWER HAS SLOWED ME DOWN.
GIVEN ME BACK A BIT OF BALANCE AND CONTROL...
TSSSSSS
I WASN'T RUNNING FROM YOU, COLD.
...JUST ENOUGH TO CREATE THE RIGHT LEVEL OF FRICTION IN THE AIR...

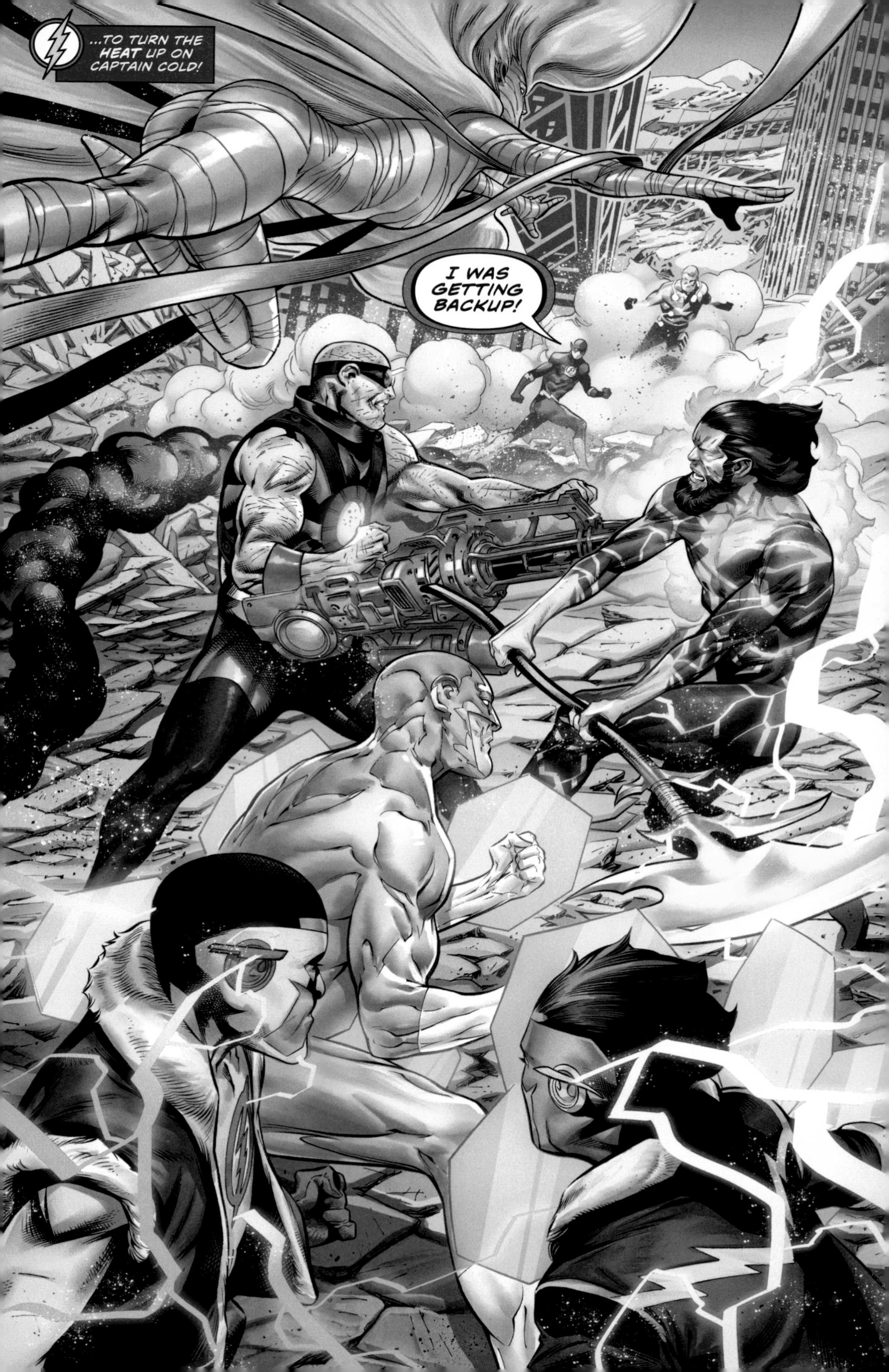
...TO TURN THE HEAT UP ON CAPTAIN COLD!
I WAS GETTING BACKUP!

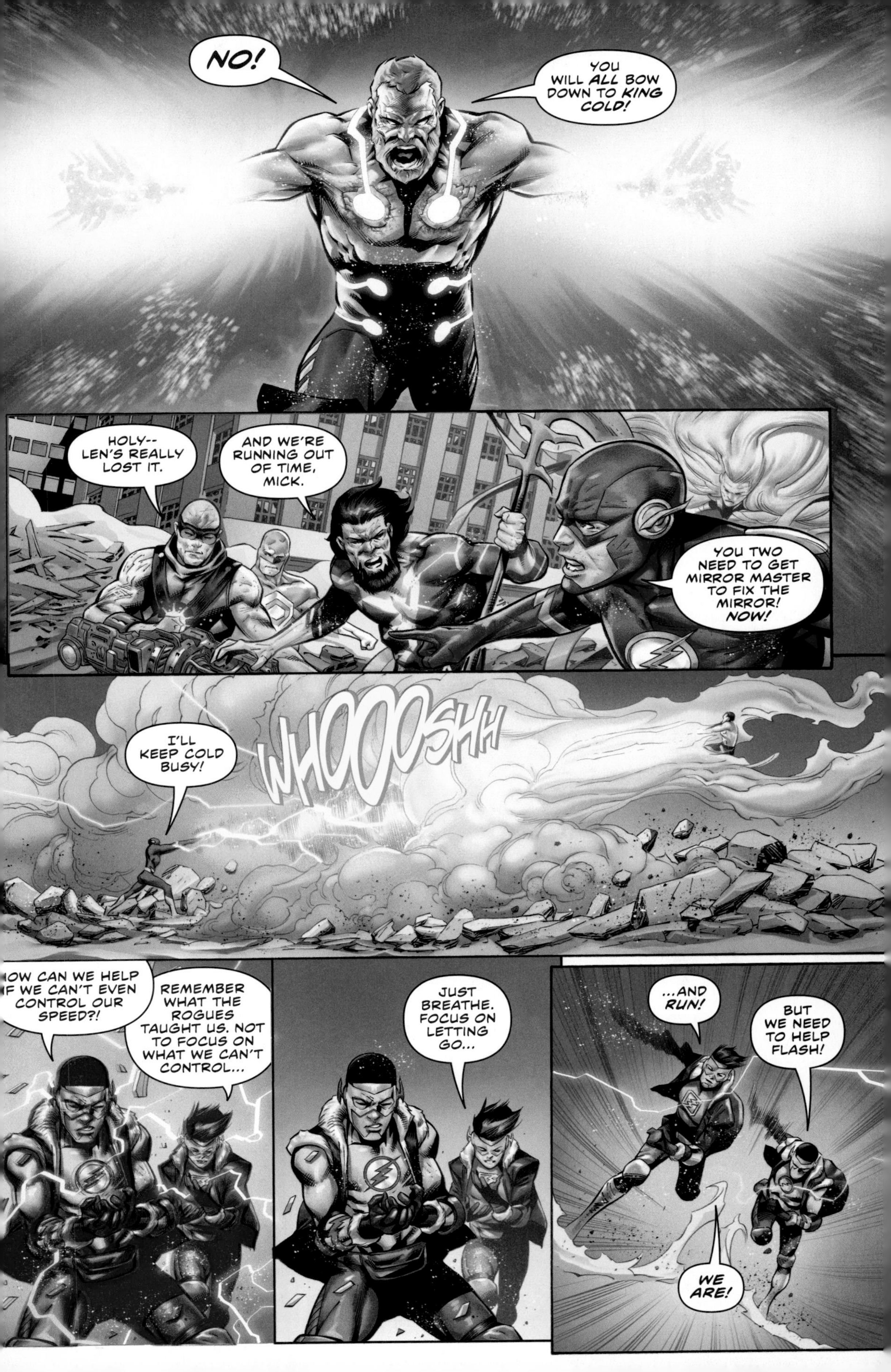
NO!
YOU WILL ALL BOW DOWN TO KING COLD!
HOLY-- LEN'S REALLY LOST IT.
AND WE'RE RUNNING OUT OF TIME, MICK.
YOU TWO NEED TO GET MIRROR MASTER TO FIX THE MIRROR! NOW!
WHOOOSHH
I'LL KEEP COLD BUSY!
OW CAN WE HELP F WE CAN'T EVEN CONTROL OUR SPEED?!
REMEMBER WHAT THE ROGUES TAUGHT US. NOT TO FOCUS ON WHAT WE CAN'T CONTROL...
JUST BREATHE. FOCUS ON LETTING GO...
...AND RUN!
BUT WE NEED TO HELP FLASH!
WE ARE!

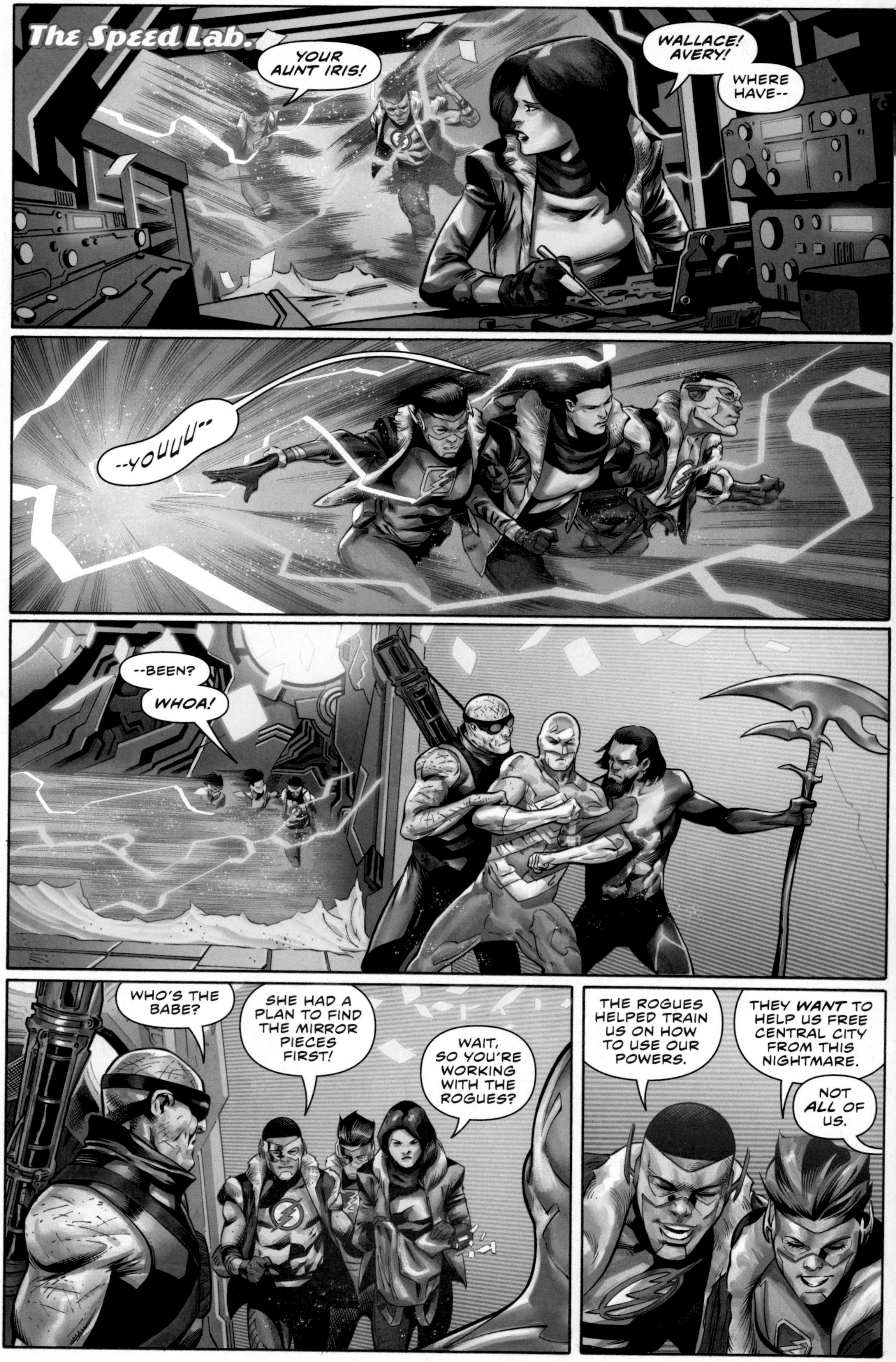
The Speed Lab.
YOUR AUNT IRIS!
WALLACE! AVERY!
WHERE HAVE--
--YOUUU--
--BEEN?
WHOA!
WHO'S THE BABE?
SHE HAD A PLAN TO FIND THE MIRROR PIECES FIRST!
WAIT, SO YOU'RE WORKING WITH THE ROGUES?
THE ROGUES HELPED TRAIN US ON HOW TO USE OUR POWERS.
THEY WANT TO HELP US FREE CENTRAL CITY FROM THIS NIGHTMARE.
NOT ALL OF US.

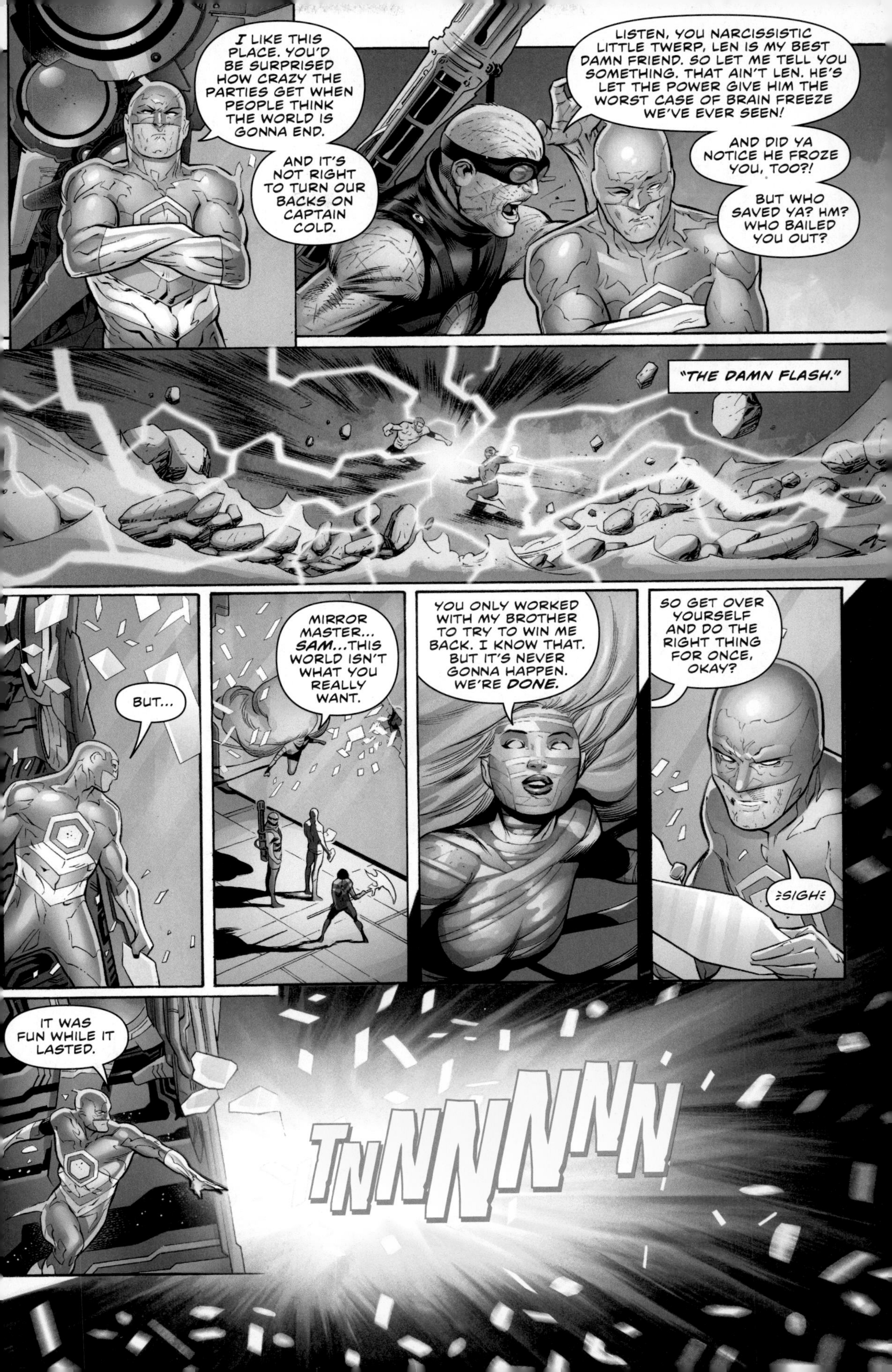
I LIKE THIS PLACE. YOU'D BE SURPRISED HOW CRAZY THE PARTIES GET WHEN PEOPLE THINK THE WORLD IS GONNA END.
AND IT'S NOT RIGHT TO TURN OUR BACKS ON CAPTAIN COLD.
LISTEN, YOU NARCISSISTIC LITTLE TWERP, LEN IS MY BEST DAMN FRIEND. SO LET ME TELL YOU SOMETHING. THAT AIN'T LEN. HE'S LET THE POWER GIVE HIM THE WORST CASE OF BRAIN FREEZE WE'VE EVER SEEN!
AND DID YA NOTICE HE FROZE YOU, TOO?!
BUT WHO SAVED YA? HM? WHO BAILED YOU OUT?
"THE DAMN FLASH."
BUT...
MIRROR MASTER... SAM...THIS WORLD ISN'T WHAT YOU REALLY WANT.
YOU ONLY WORKED WITH MY BROTHER TO TRY TO WIN ME BACK. I KNOW THAT. BUT IT'S NEVER GONNA HAPPEN. WE'RE DONE.
SO GET OVER YOURSELF AND DO THE RIGHT THING FOR ONCE, OKAY?
SIGH
IT WAS FUN WHILE IT LASTED.
TNNNNNNN

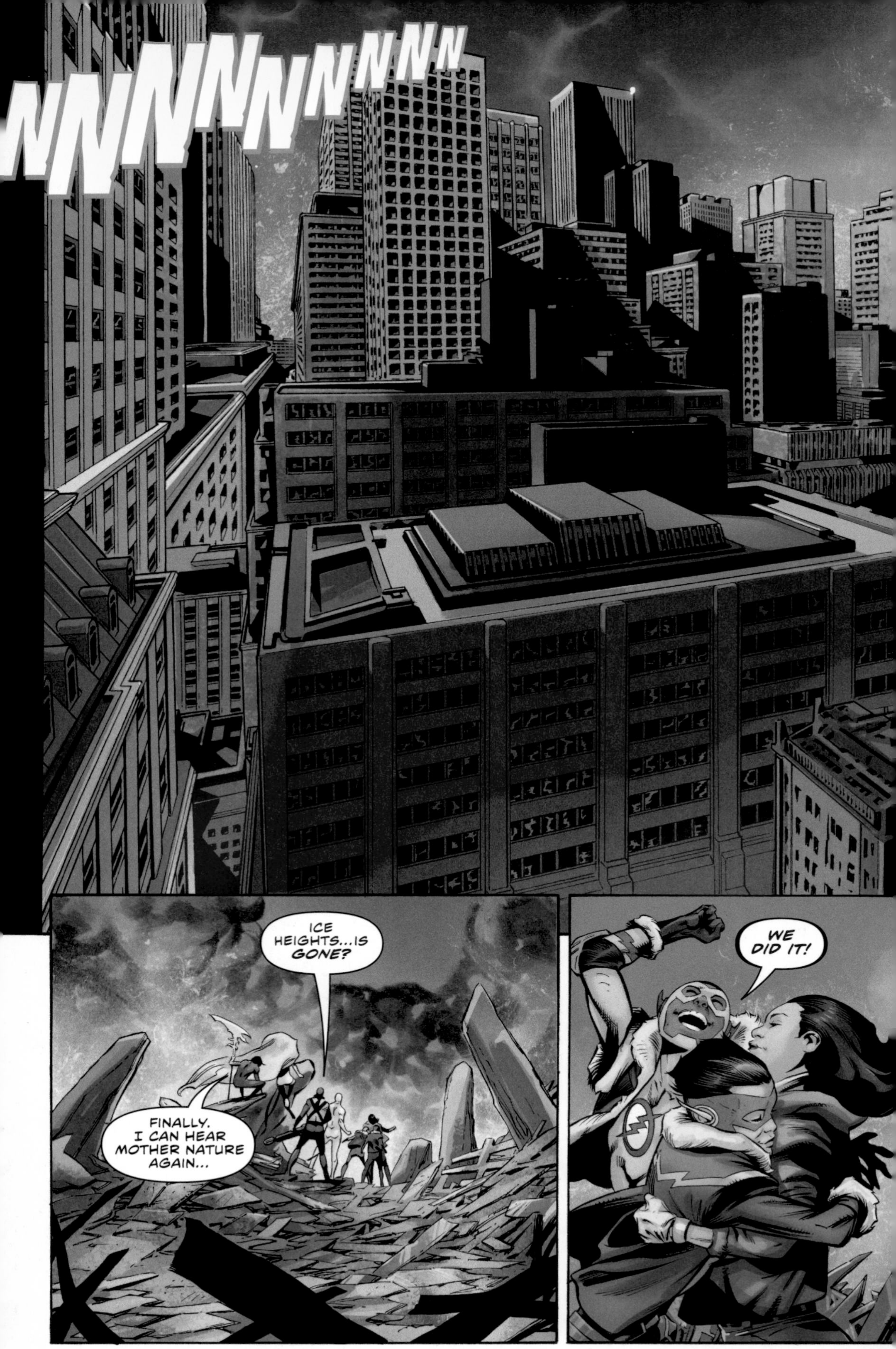
NNNNNNNNNNN
ICE HEIGHTS...IS GONE?
FINALLY. I CAN HEAR MOTHER NATURE AGAIN...
WE DID IT!

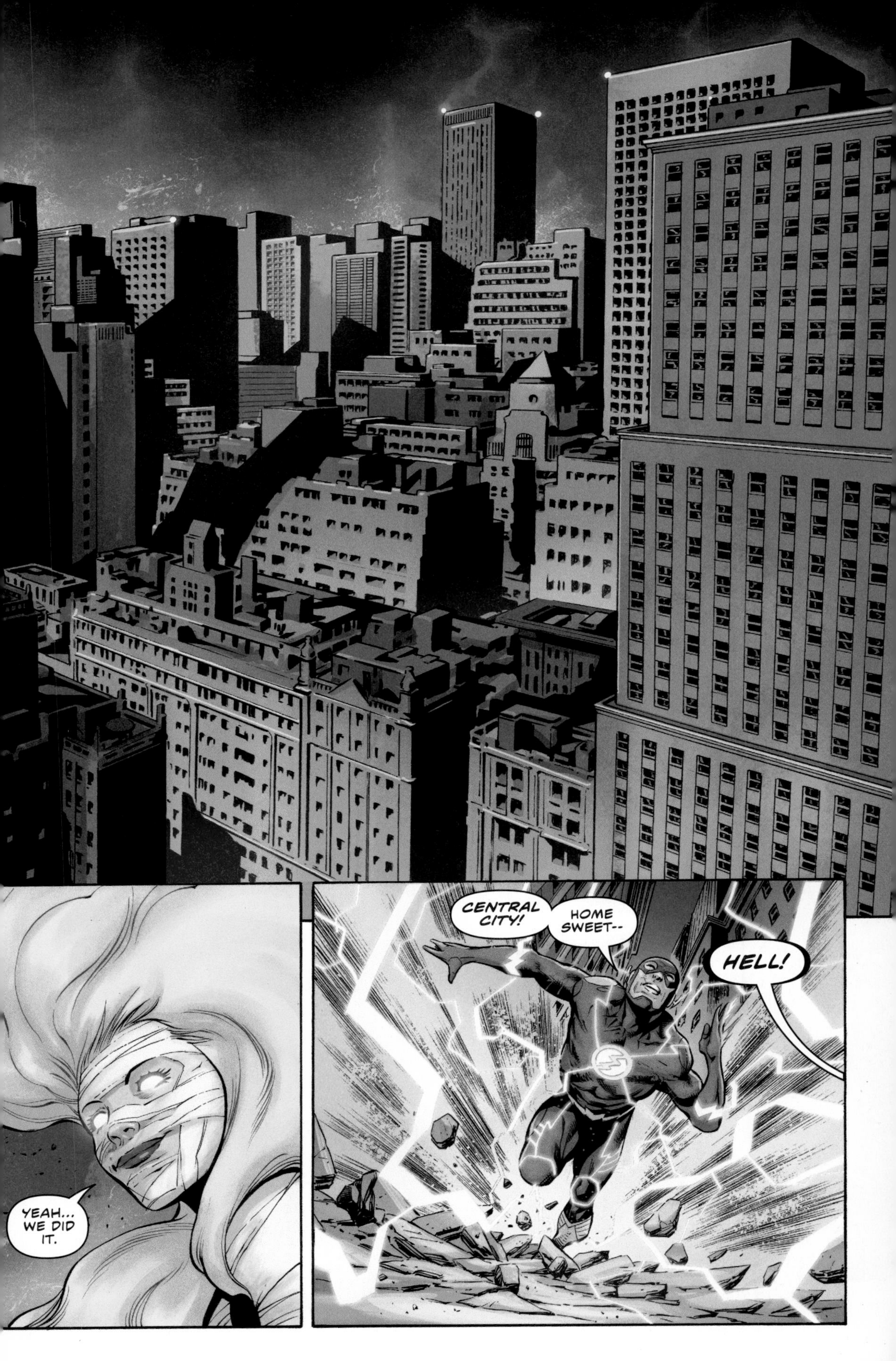
YEAH... WE DID IT.
CENTRAL CITY!
HOME SWEET--
HELL!

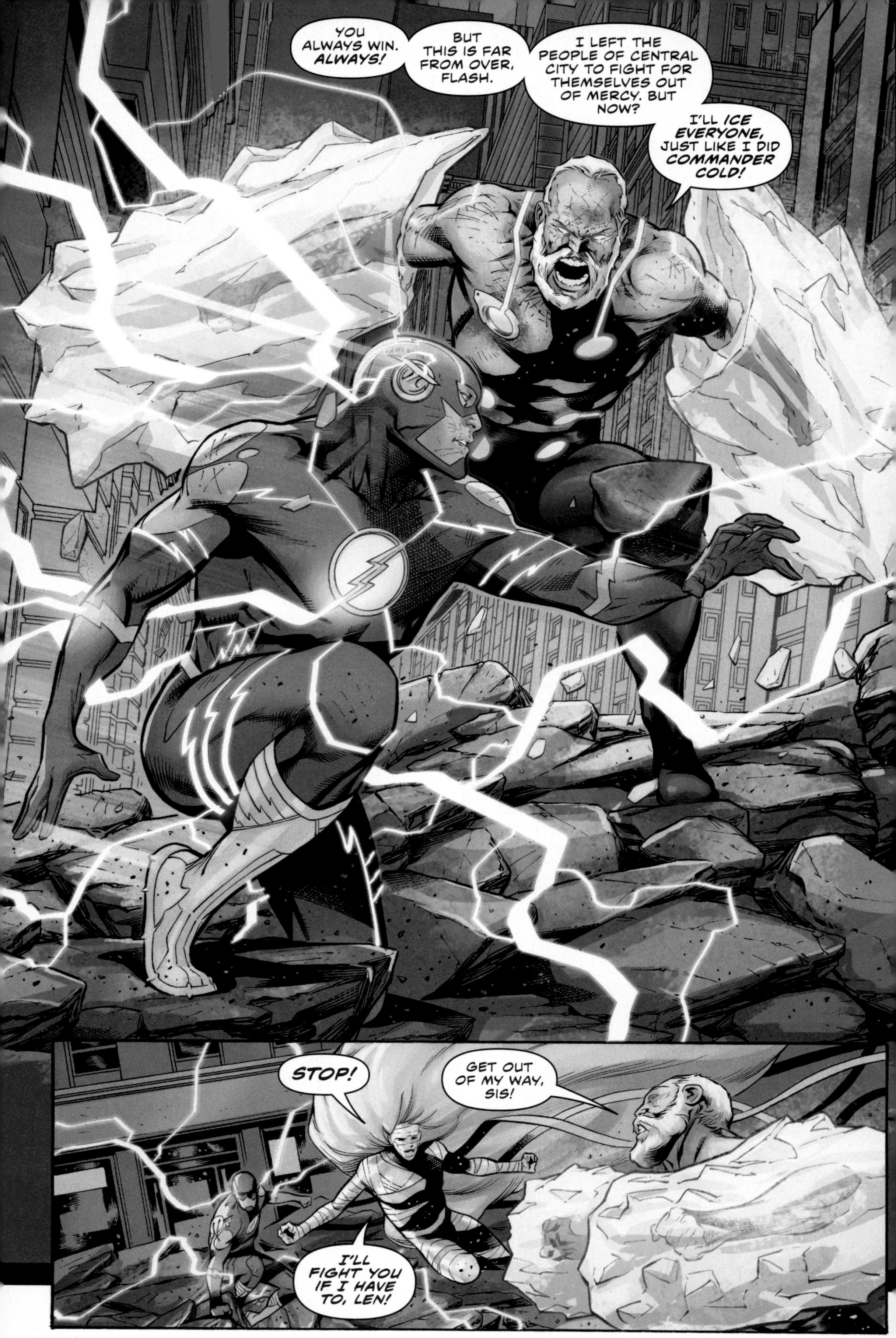
YOU ALWAYS WIN. ALWAYS!
BUT THIS IS FAR FROM OVER, FLASH.
I LEFT THE PEOPLE OF CENTRAL CITY TO FIGHT FOR THEMSELVES OUT OF MERCY. BUT NOW?
I'LL ICE EVERYONE, JUST LIKE I DID COMMANDER COLD!
STOP!
GET OUT OF MY WAY, SIS!
I'LL FIGHT YOU IF I HAVE TO, LEN!

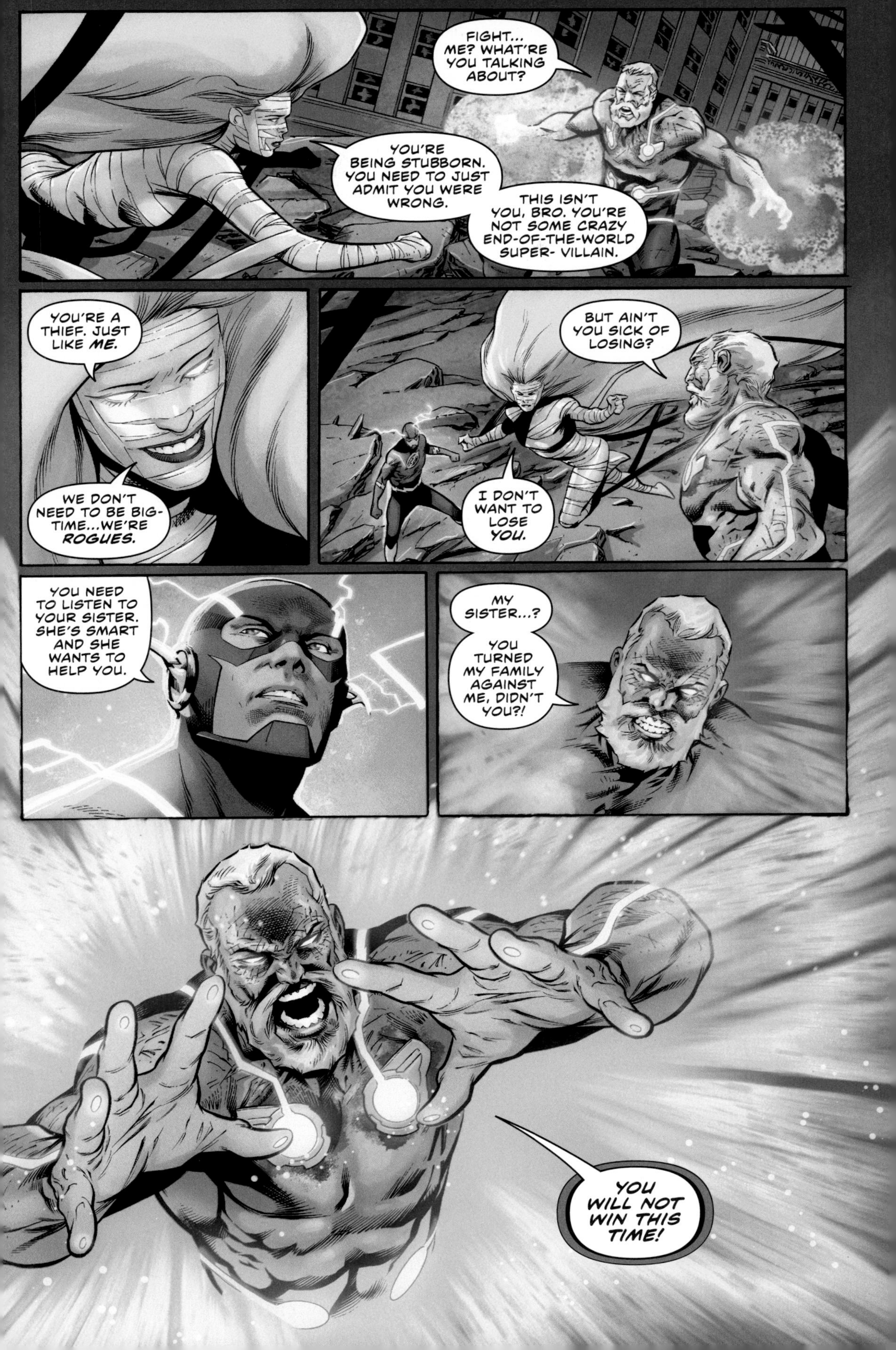
FIGHT... ME? WHAT'RE YOU TALKING ABOUT?
YOU'RE BEING STUBBORN. YOU NEED TO JUST ADMIT YOU WERE WRONG.
THIS ISN'T YOU, BRO. YOU'RE NOT SOME CRAZY END-OF-THE-WORLD SUPER- VILLAIN.
YOU'RE A THIEF. JUST LIKE ME.
WE DON'T NEED TO BE BIG-TIME...WE'RE ROGUES.
BUT AIN'T YOU SICK OF LOSING?
I DON'T WANT TO LOSE YOU.
YOU NEED TO LISTEN TO YOUR SISTER. SHE'S SMART AND SHE WANTS TO HELP YOU.
MY SISTER...?
YOU TURNED MY FAMILY AGAINST ME, DIDN'T YOU?!
YOU WILL NOT WIN THIS TIME!

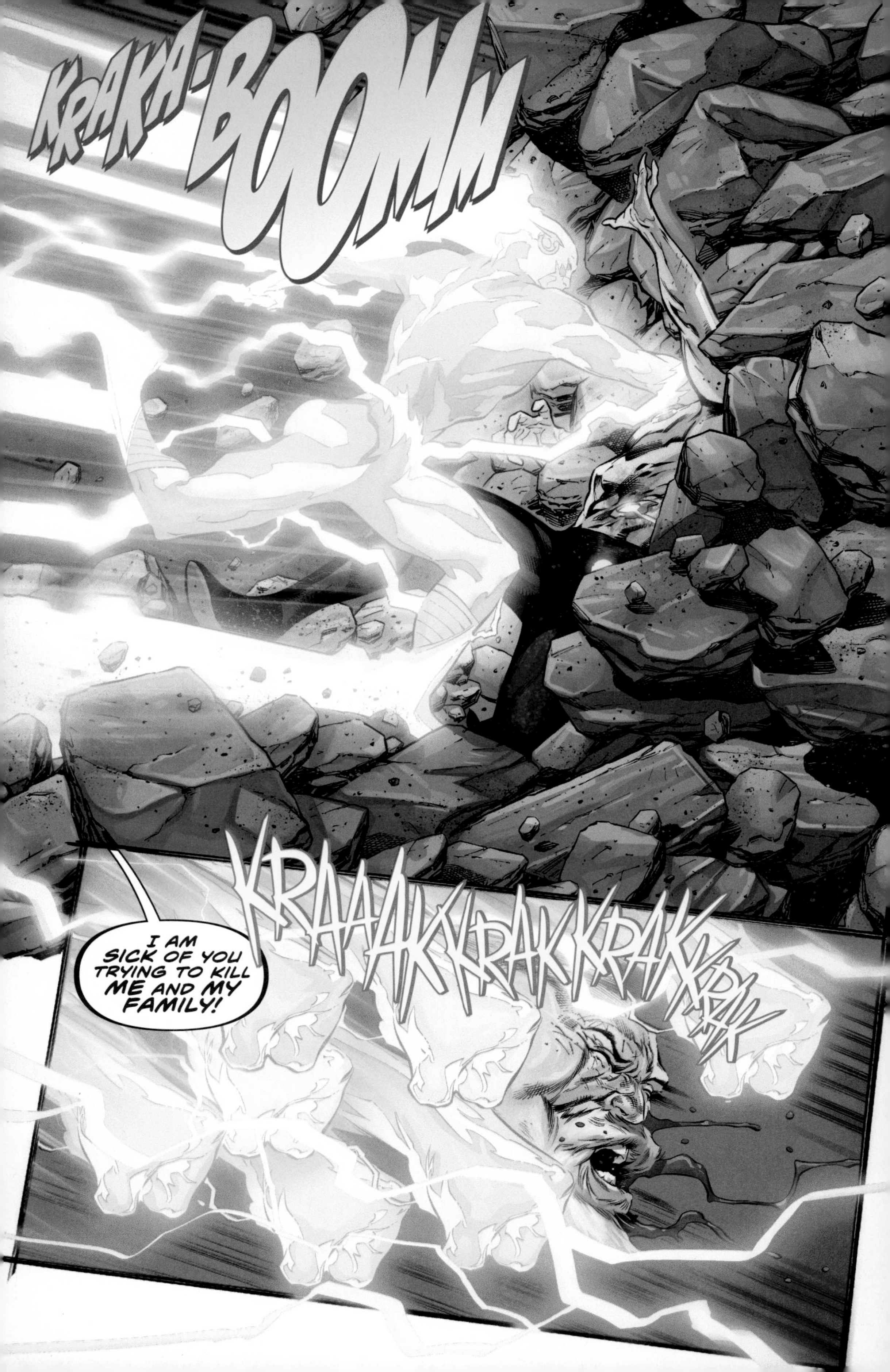
KRAKA-BOOMM
KRAAAK KRAK KRAK KRAK KRAK
I AM SICK OF YOU TRYING TO KILL ME AND MY FAMILY!

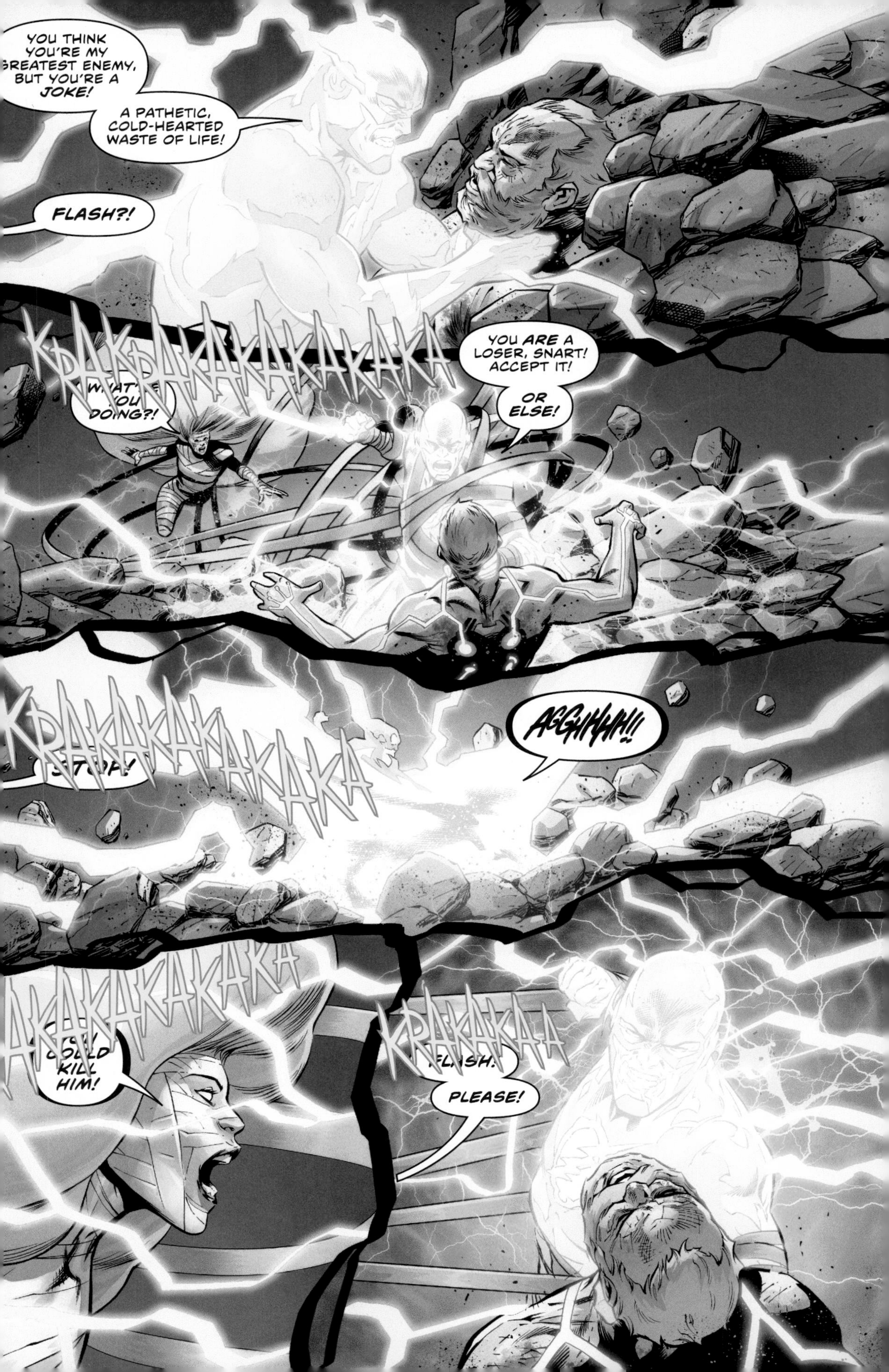
YOU THINK YOU'RE MY GREATEST ENEMY, BUT YOU'RE A JOKE!
A PATHETIC, COLD-HEARTED WASTE OF LIFE!
FLASH?!
YOU ARE A LOSER, SNART! ACCEPT IT!
OR ELSE!
DOING?!
AGGHHHH!!
KILL HIM!
KRAKAKAA
FLASH.
PLEASE!

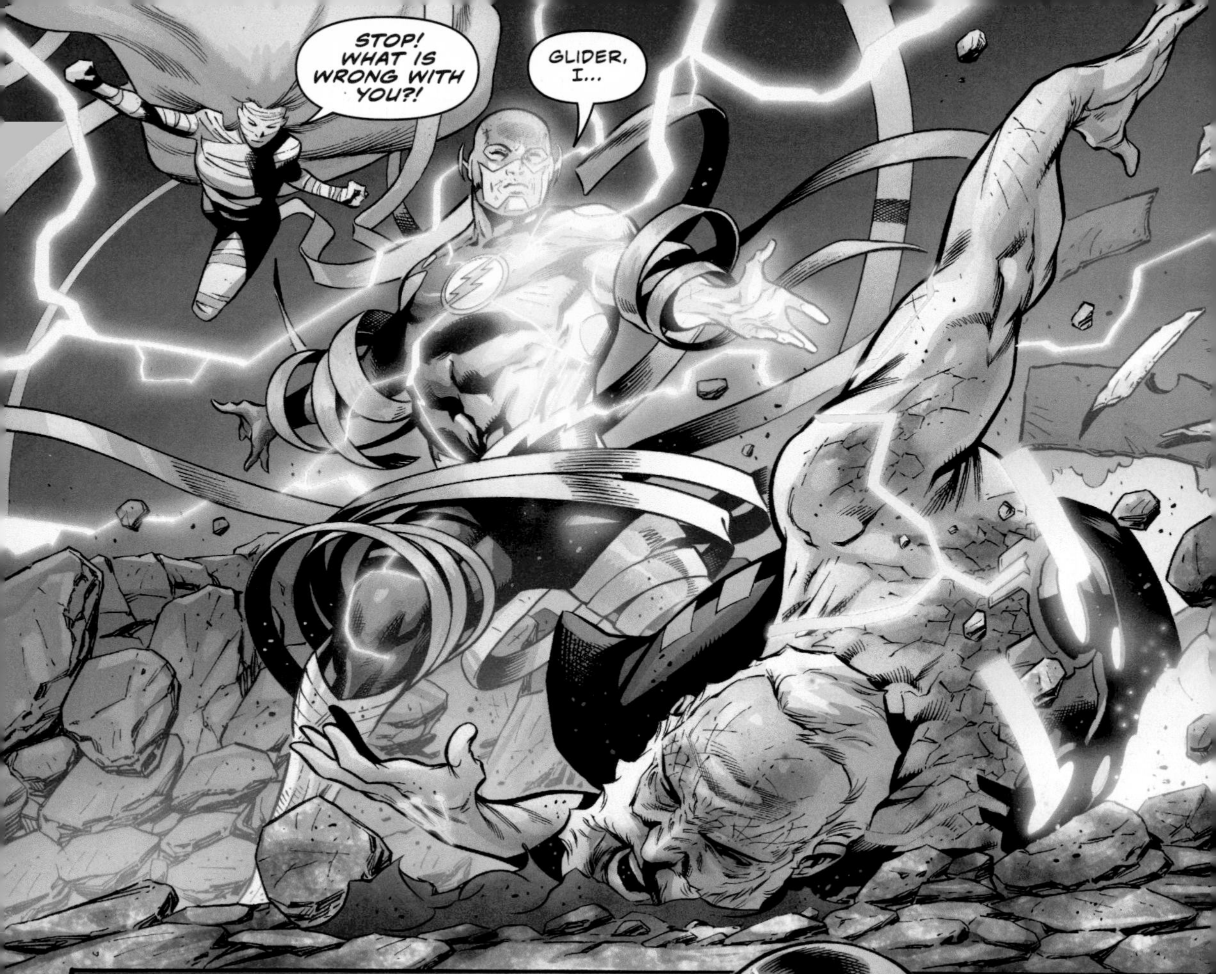
STOP! WHAT IS WRONG WITH YOU?!
GLIDER, I...

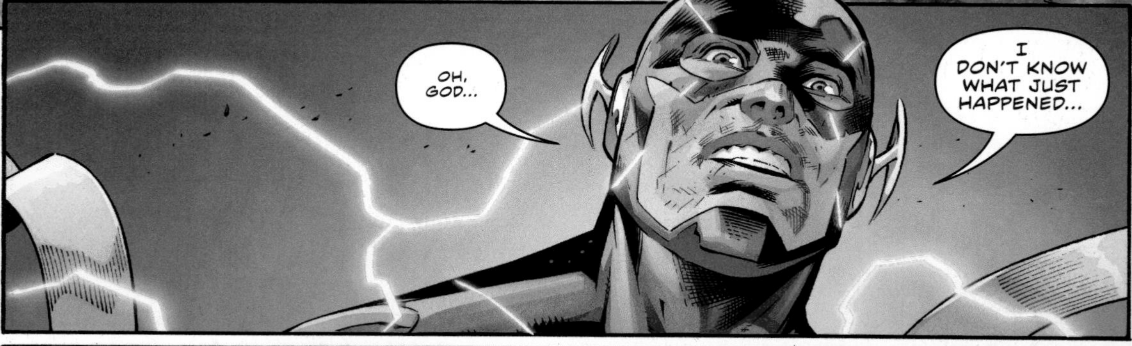
OH, GOD...
I DON'T KNOW WHAT JUST HAPPENED...

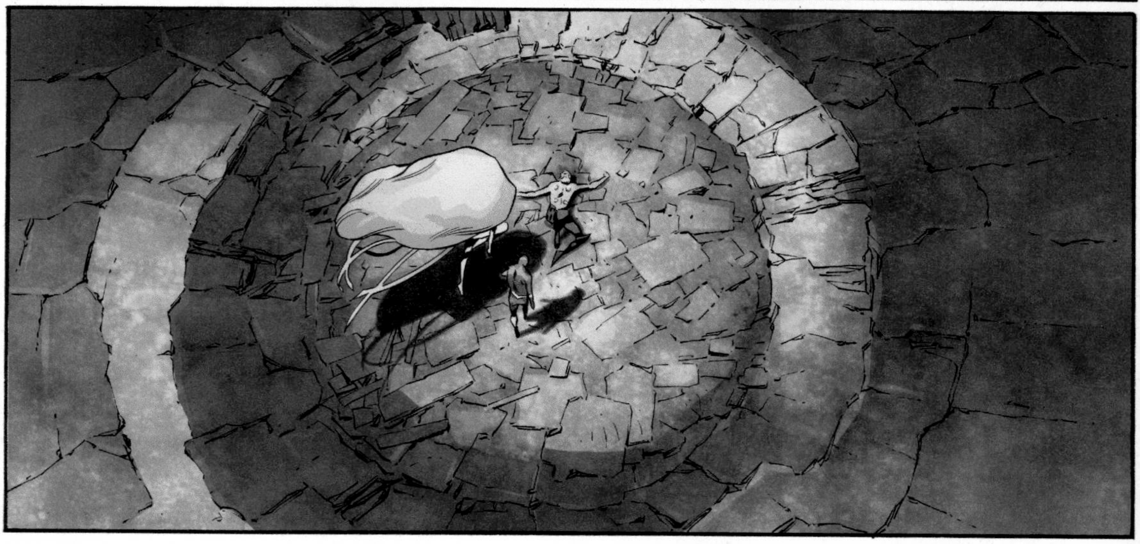

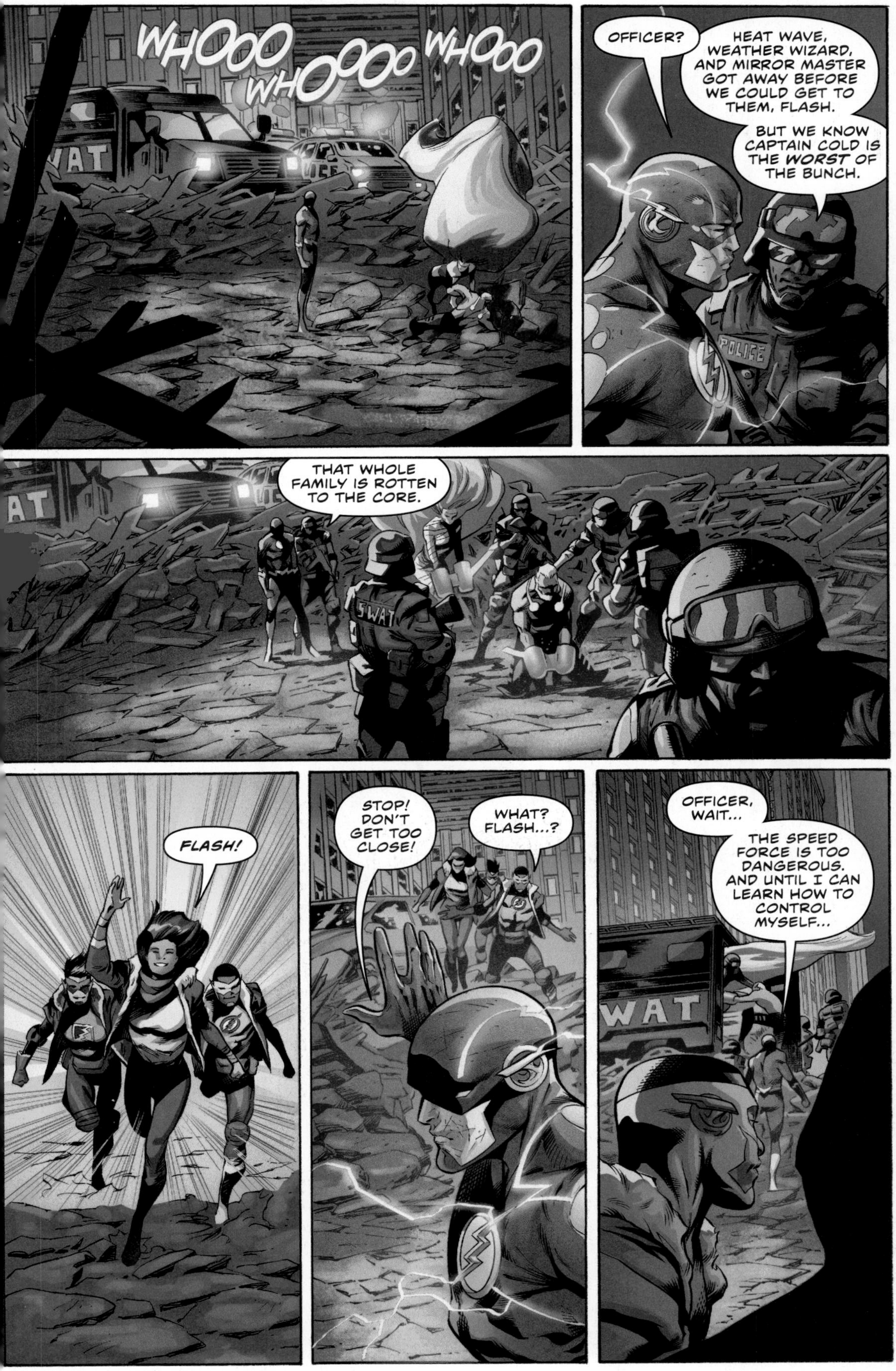
WHOOO WHOOOOO WHOOO
OFFICER?
HEAT WAVE, WEATHER WIZARD, AND MIRROR MASTER GOT AWAY BEFORE WE COULD GET TO THEM, FLASH.
BUT WE KNOW CAPTAIN COLD IS THE WORST OF THE BUNCH.
SWAT
POLICE
THAT WHOLE FAMILY IS ROTTEN TO THE CORE.
SWAT
FLASH!
STOP! DON'T GET TOO CLOSE!
WHAT? FLASH...?
OFFICER, WAIT...
THE SPEED FORCE IS TOO DANGEROUS. AND UNTIL I CAN LEARN HOW TO CONTROL MYSELF...
WAT

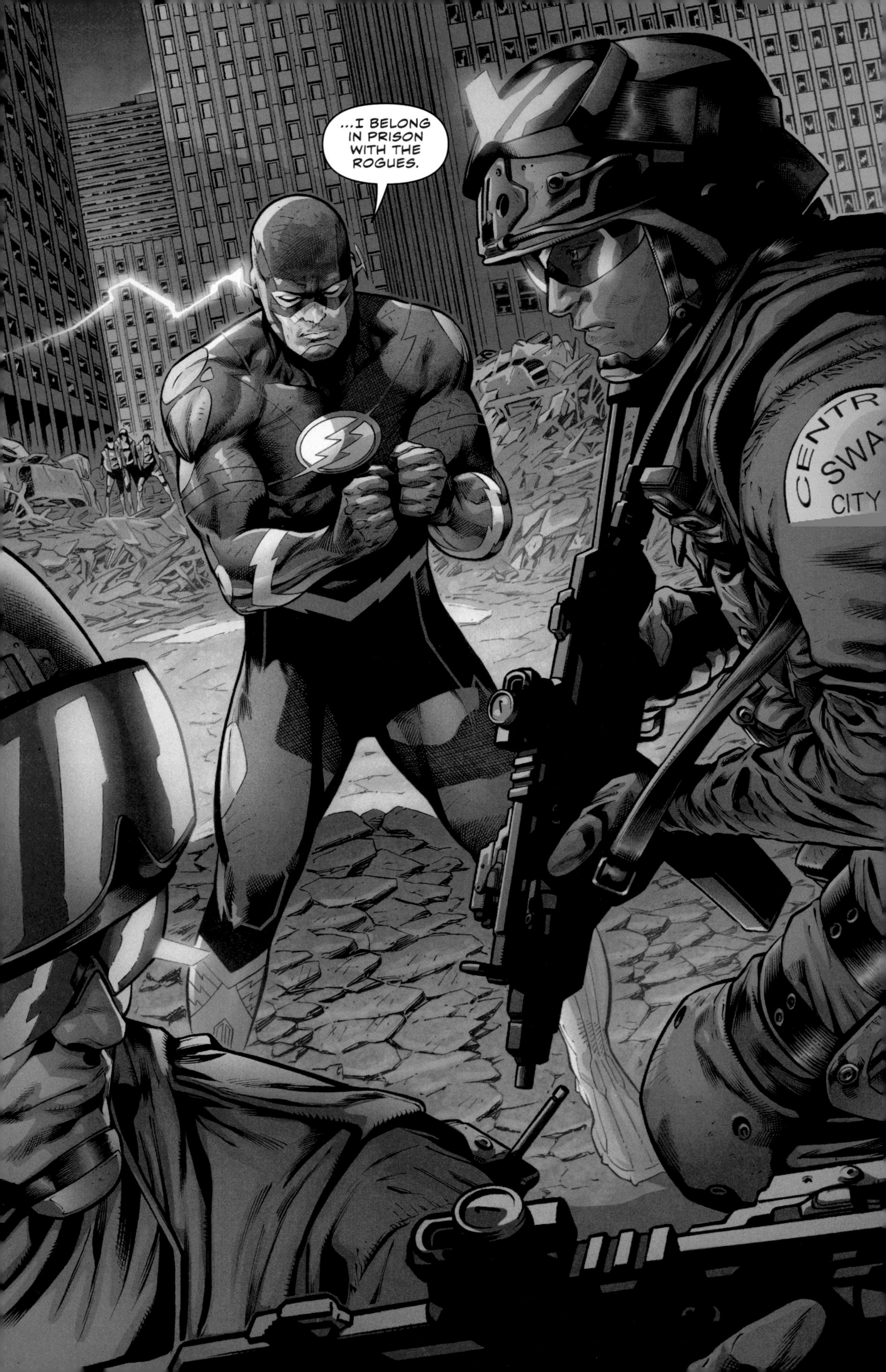
...I BELONG IN PRISON WITH THE ROGUES.
CENTR
SWA
CITY

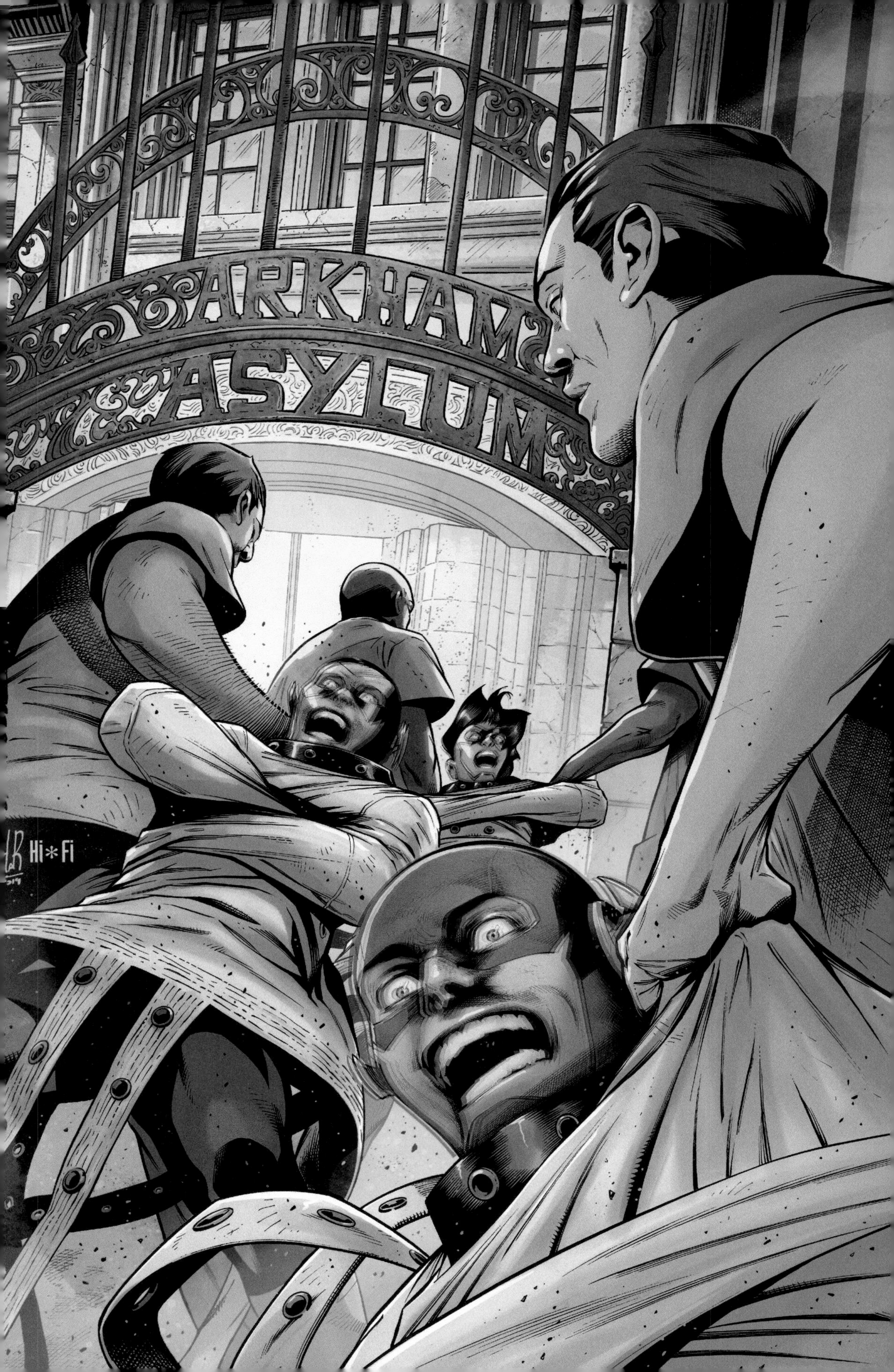
ARKHAM
ASYLUM
Hi*Fi

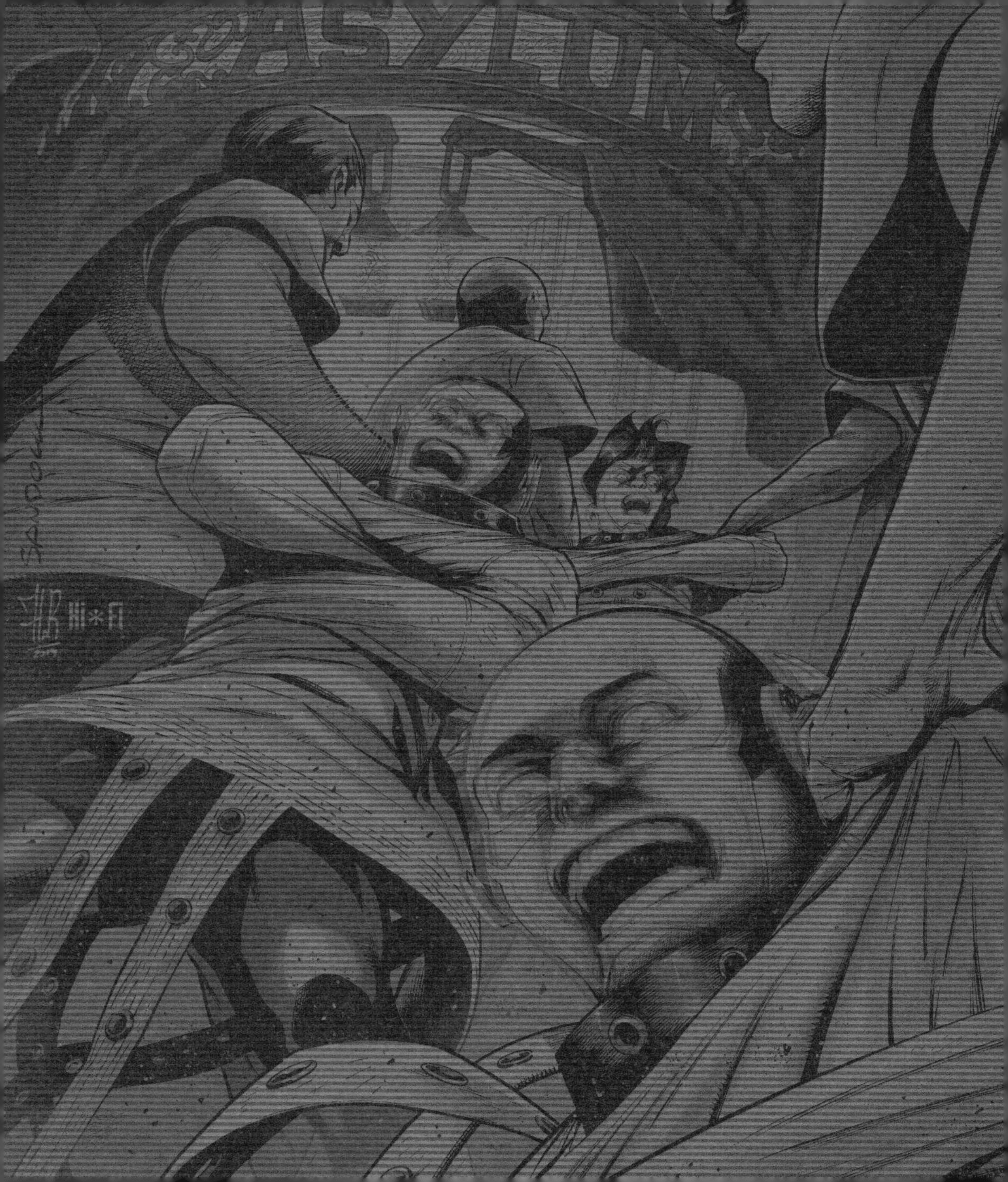
ASYLUM
HI*FI

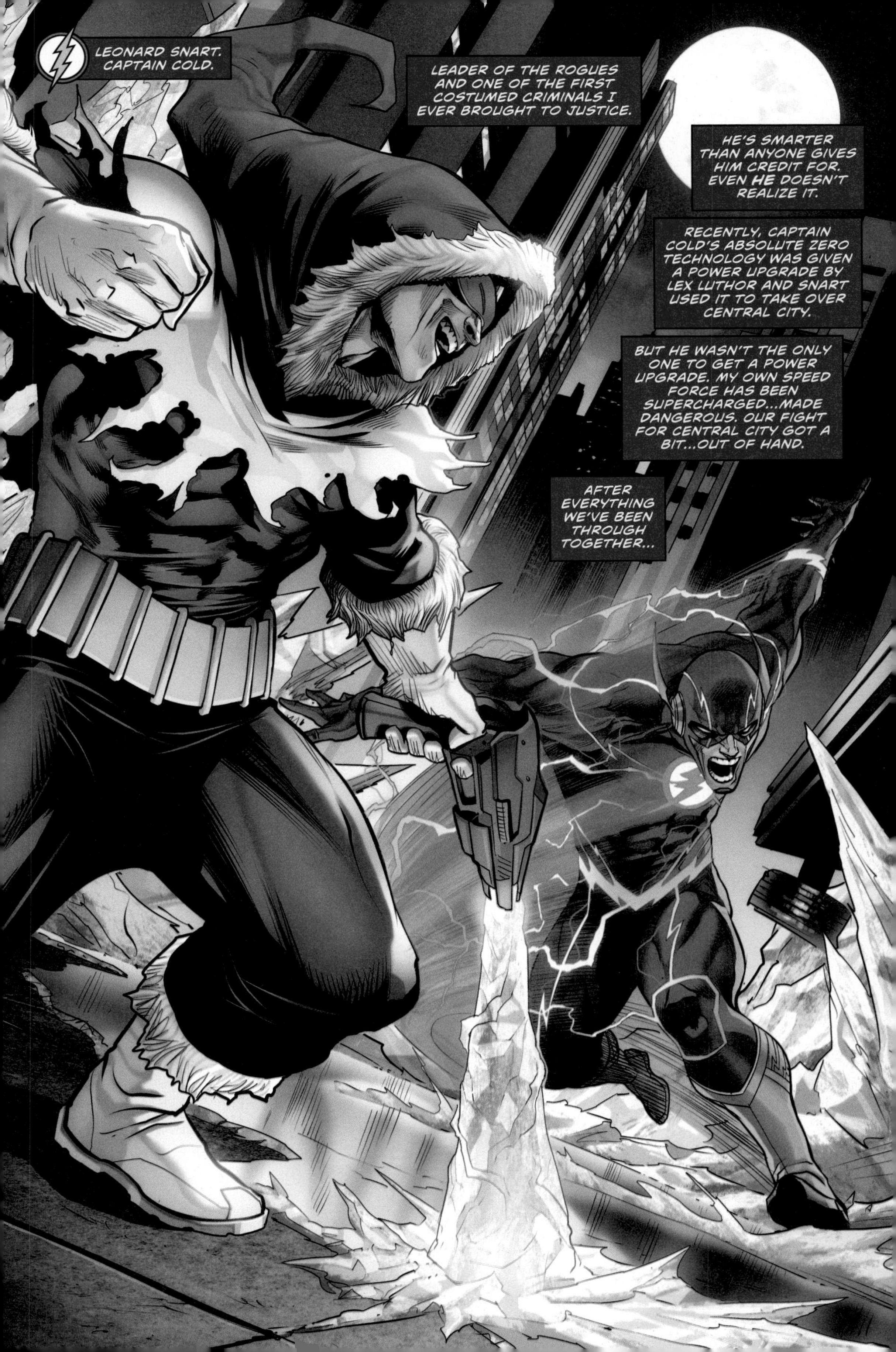
LEONARD SNART. CAPTAIN COLD.
LEADER OF THE ROGUES AND ONE OF THE FIRST COSTUMED CRIMINALS I EVER BROUGHT TO JUSTICE.
HE'S SMARTER THAN ANYONE GIVES HIM CREDIT FOR. EVEN **HE** DOESN'T REALIZE IT.
RECENTLY, CAPTAIN COLD'S ABSOLUTE ZERO TECHNOLOGY WAS GIVEN A POWER UPGRADE BY LEX LUTHOR AND SNART USED IT TO TAKE OVER CENTRAL CITY.
BUT HE WASN'T THE ONLY ONE TO GET A POWER UPGRADE. MY OWN SPEED FORCE HAS BEEN SUPERCHARGED...MADE DANGEROUS. OUR FIGHT FOR CENTRAL CITY GOT A BIT...OUT OF HAND.
AFTER EVERYTHING WE'VE BEEN THROUGH TOGETHER...

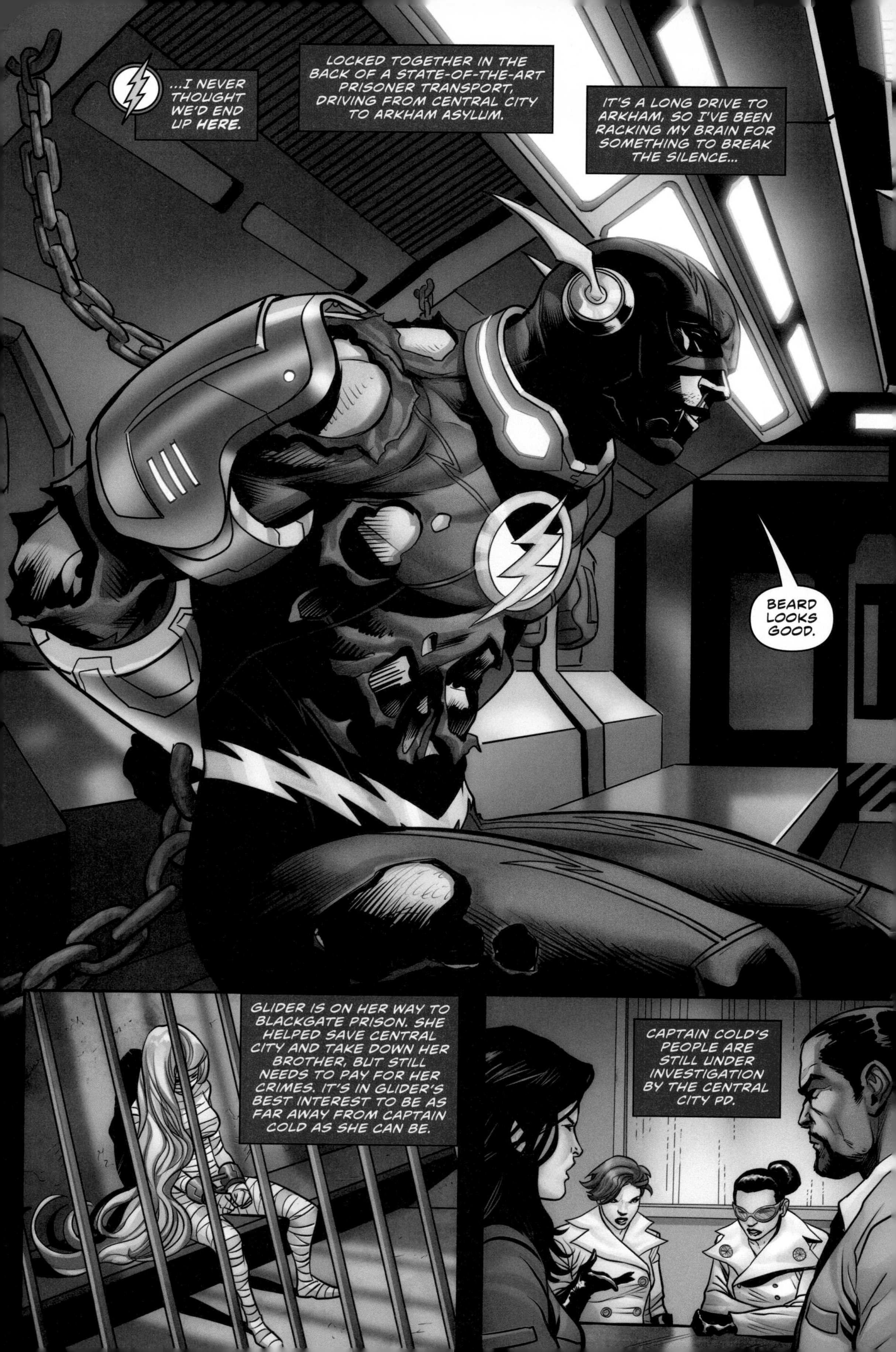
...I NEVER THOUGHT WE'D END UP HERE.
LOCKED TOGETHER IN THE BACK OF A STATE-OF-THE-ART PRISONER TRANSPORT, DRIVING FROM CENTRAL CITY TO ARKHAM ASYLUM.
IT'S A LONG DRIVE TO ARKHAM, SO I'VE BEEN RACKING MY BRAIN FOR SOMETHING TO BREAK THE SILENCE...
BEARD LOOKS GOOD.
GLIDER IS ON HER WAY TO BLACKGATE PRISON. SHE HELPED SAVE CENTRAL CITY AND TAKE DOWN HER BROTHER, BUT STILL NEEDS TO PAY FOR HER CRIMES. IT'S IN GLIDER'S BEST INTEREST TO BE AS FAR AWAY FROM CAPTAIN COLD AS SHE CAN BE.
CAPTAIN COLD'S PEOPLE ARE STILL UNDER INVESTIGATION BY THE CENTRAL CITY PD.

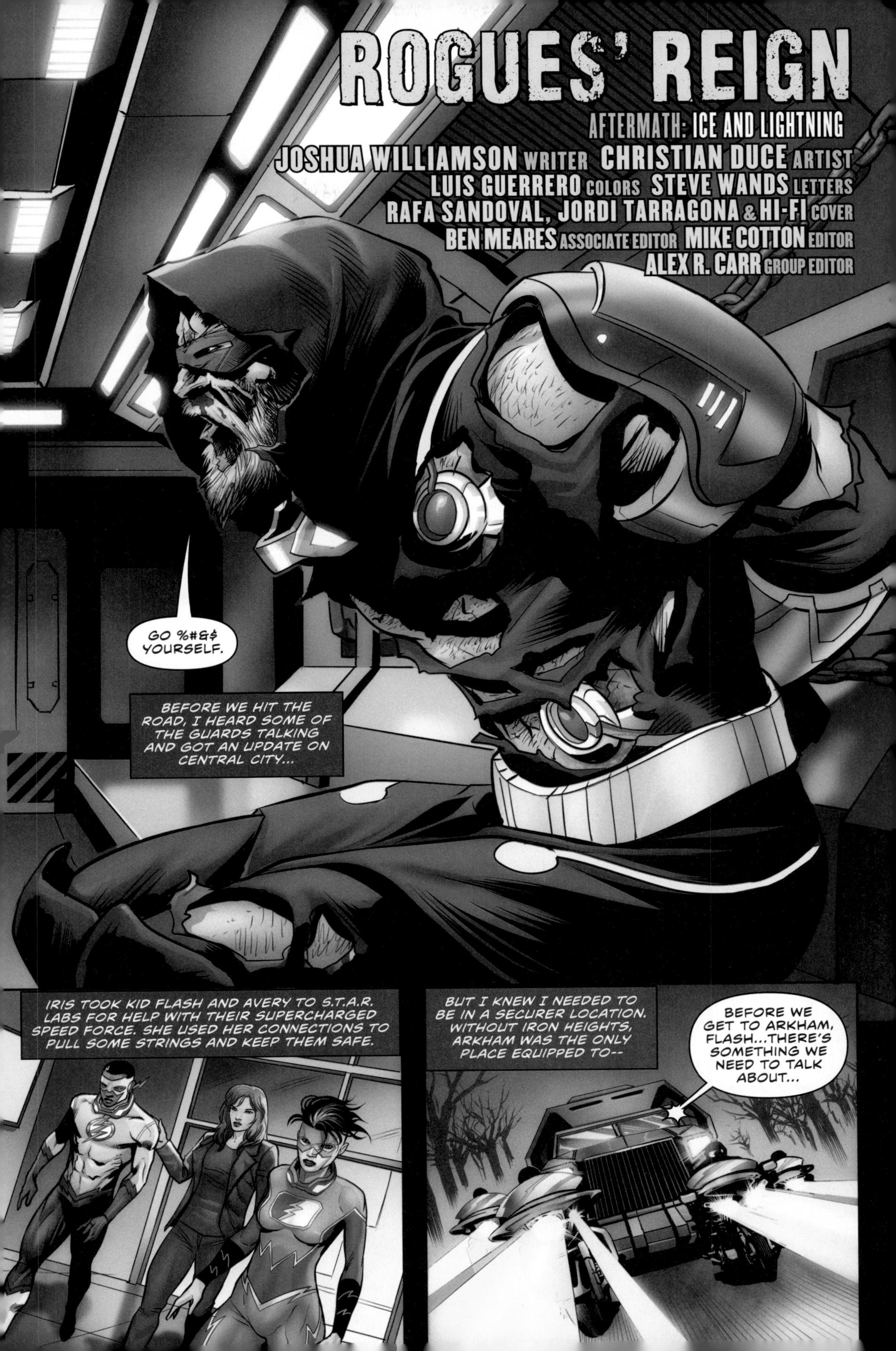
ROGUES' REIGN
AFTERMATH: ICE AND LIGHTNING
JOSHUA WILLIAMSON WRITER CHRISTIAN DUCE ARTIST
LUIS GUERRERO COLORS STEVE WANDS LETTERS
RAFA SANDOVAL, JORDI TARRAGONA & HI-FI COVER
BEN MEARES ASSOCIATE EDITOR MIKE COTTON EDITOR
ALEX R. CARR GROUP EDITOR
GO %#&$ YOURSELF.
BEFORE WE HIT THE ROAD, I HEARD SOME OF THE GUARDS TALKING AND GOT AN UPDATE ON CENTRAL CITY...
IRIS TOOK KID FLASH AND AVERY TO S.T.A.R. LABS FOR HELP WITH THEIR SUPERCHARGED SPEED FORCE. SHE USED HER CONNECTIONS TO PULL SOME STRINGS AND KEEP THEM SAFE.
BUT I KNEW I NEEDED TO BE IN A SECURER LOCATION. WITHOUT IRON HEIGHTS, ARKHAM WAS THE ONLY PLACE EQUIPPED TO--
BEFORE WE GET TO ARKHAM, FLASH...THERE'S SOMETHING WE NEED TO TALK ABOUT...

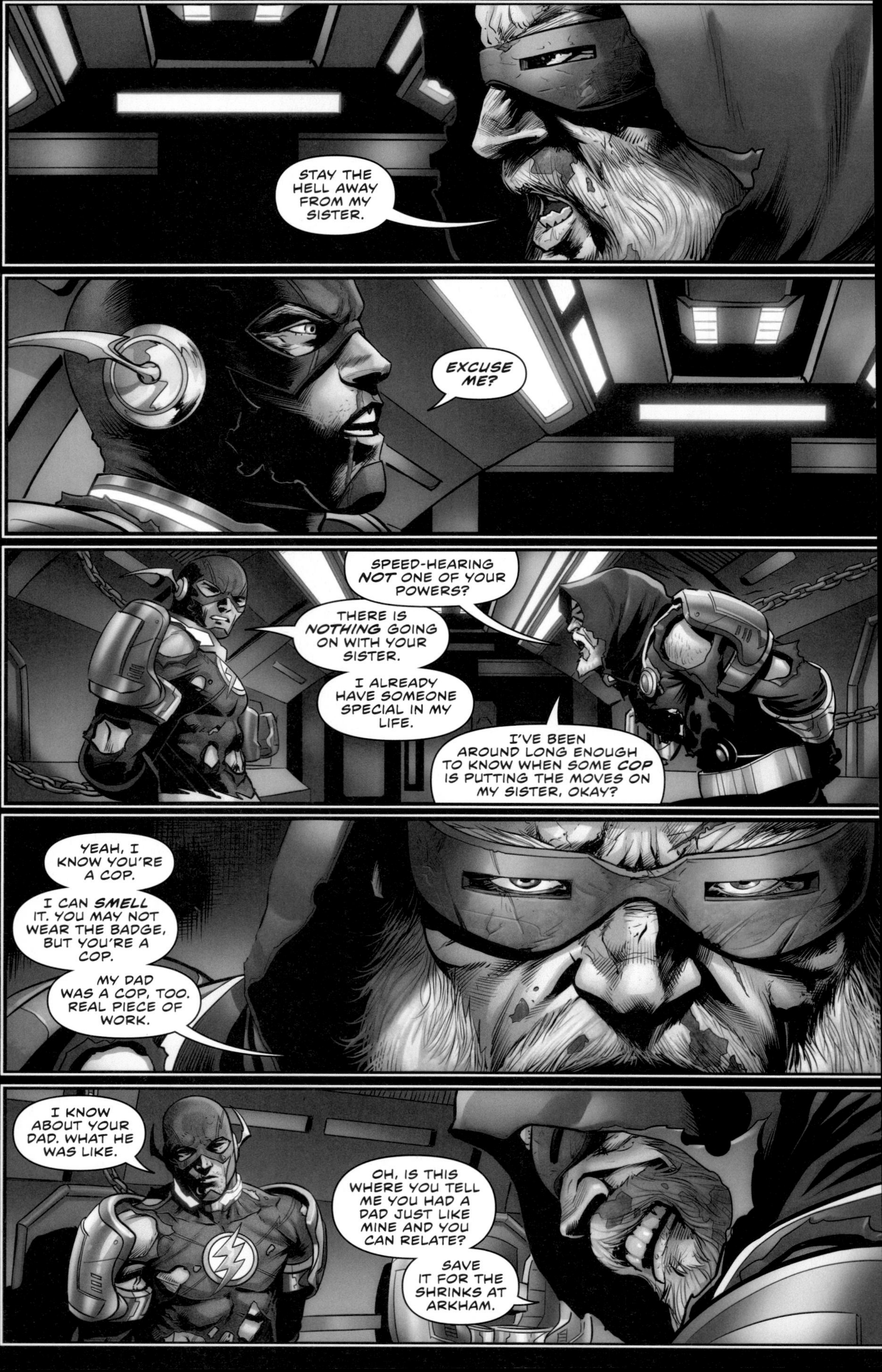
STAY THE HELL AWAY FROM MY SISTER.
EXCUSE ME?
SPEED-HEARING NOT ONE OF YOUR POWERS?
THERE IS NOTHING GOING ON WITH YOUR SISTER.
I ALREADY HAVE SOMEONE SPECIAL IN MY LIFE.
I'VE BEEN AROUND LONG ENOUGH TO KNOW WHEN SOME COP IS PUTTING THE MOVES ON MY SISTER, OKAY?
YEAH, I KNOW YOU'RE A COP.
I CAN SMELL IT. YOU MAY NOT WEAR THE BADGE, BUT YOU'RE A COP.
MY DAD WAS A COP, TOO. REAL PIECE OF WORK.
I KNOW ABOUT YOUR DAD. WHAT HE WAS LIKE.
OH, IS THIS WHERE YOU TELL ME YOU HAD A DAD JUST LIKE MINE AND YOU CAN RELATE?
SAVE IT FOR THE SHRINKS AT ARKHAM.

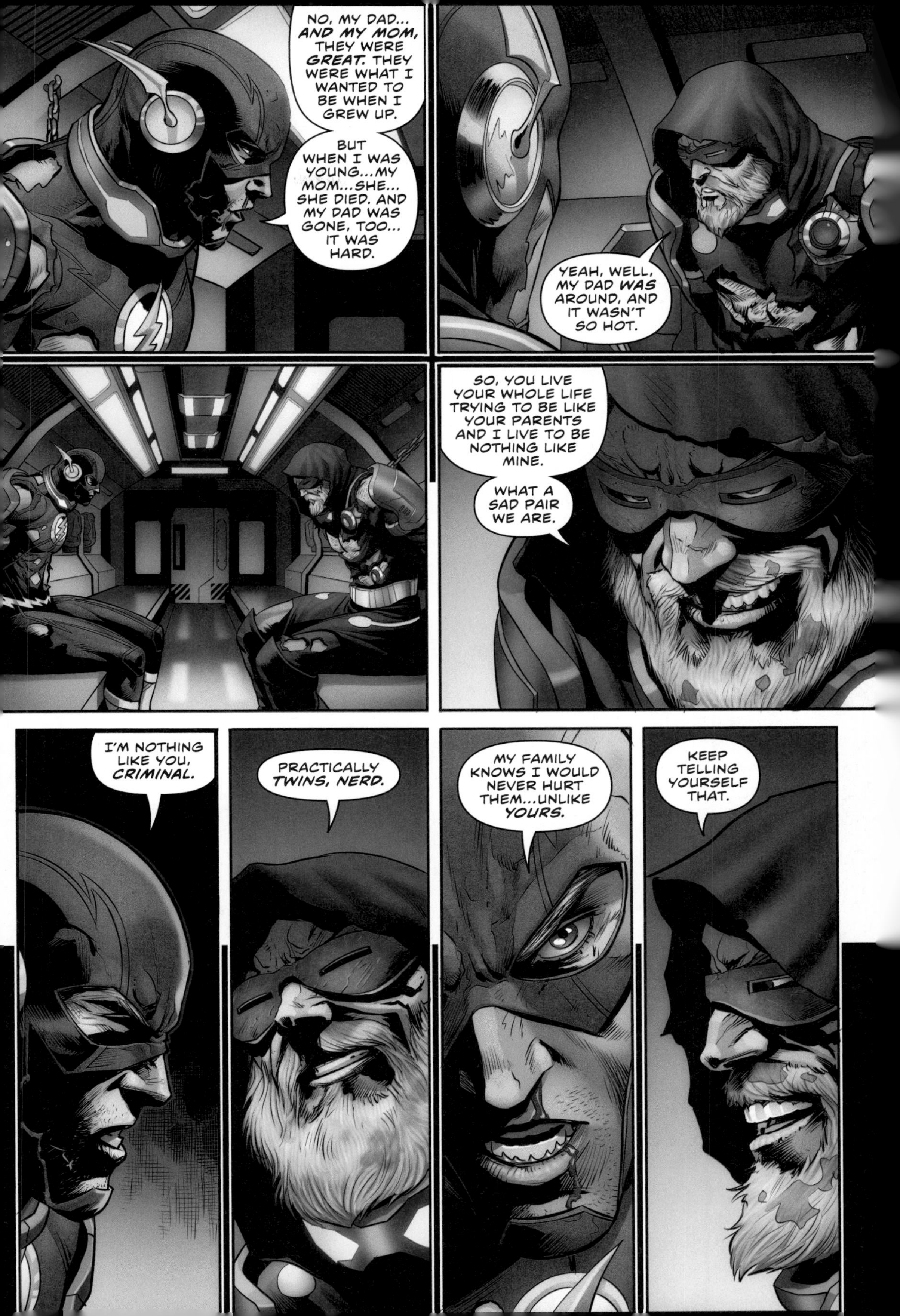

NO, MY DAD... AND MY MOM, THEY WERE GREAT. THEY WERE WHAT I WANTED TO BE WHEN I GREW UP.
BUT WHEN I WAS YOUNG...MY MOM...SHE... SHE DIED. AND MY DAD WAS GONE, TOO... IT WAS HARD.
YEAH, WELL, MY DAD WAS AROUND, AND IT WASN'T SO HOT.
SO, YOU LIVE YOUR WHOLE LIFE TRYING TO BE LIKE YOUR PARENTS AND I LIVE TO BE NOTHING LIKE MINE.
WHAT A SAD PAIR WE ARE.
I'M NOTHING LIKE YOU, CRIMINAL.
PRACTICALLY TWINS, NERD.
MY FAMILY KNOWS I WOULD NEVER HURT THEM...UNLIKE YOURS.
KEEP TELLING YOURSELF THAT.

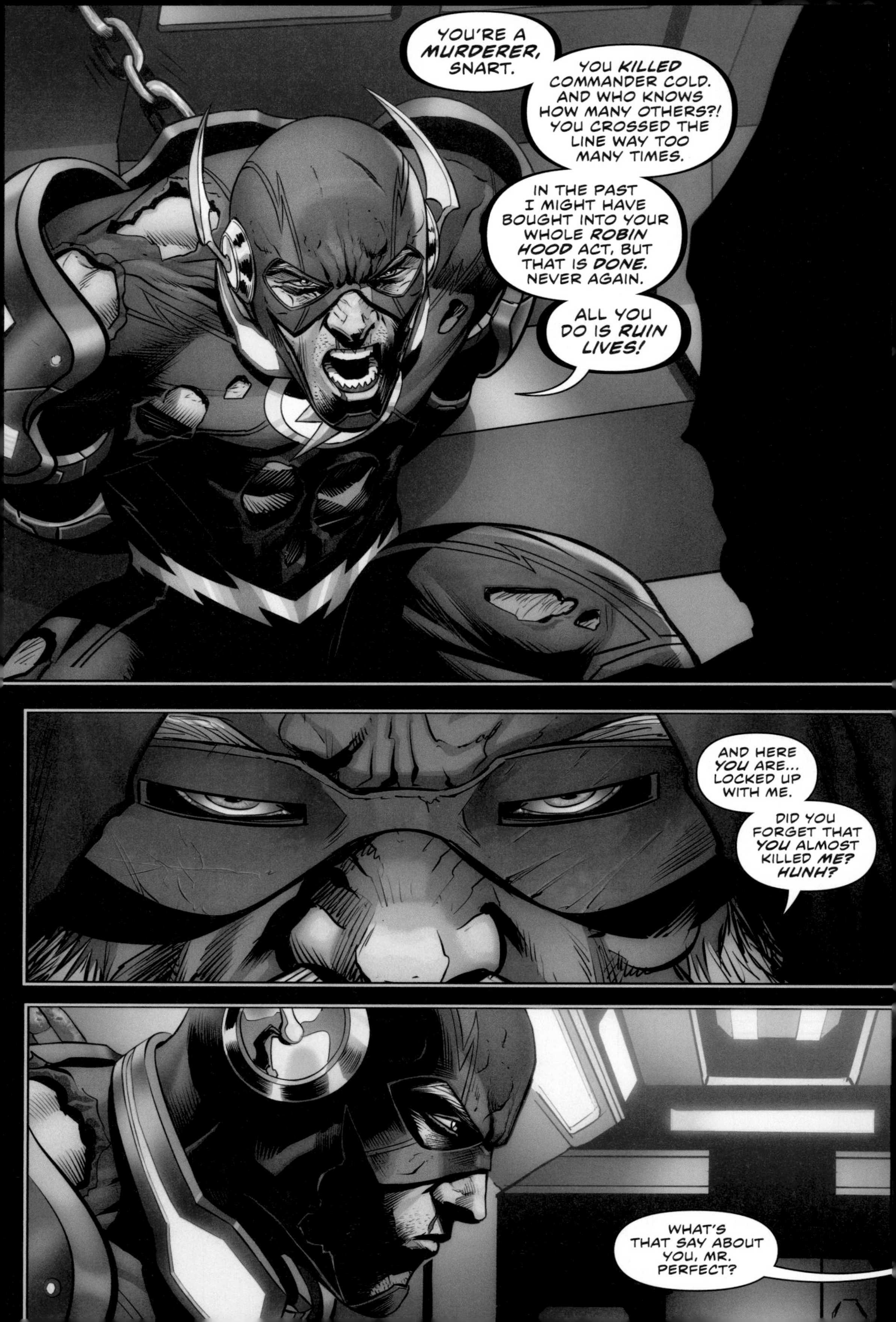
YOU'RE A MURDERER, SNART.
YOU KILLED COMMANDER COLD. AND WHO KNOWS HOW MANY OTHERS?! YOU CROSSED THE LINE WAY TOO MANY TIMES.
IN THE PAST I MIGHT HAVE BOUGHT INTO YOUR WHOLE ROBIN HOOD ACT, BUT THAT IS DONE. NEVER AGAIN.
ALL YOU DO IS RUIN LIVES!
AND HERE YOU ARE... LOCKED UP WITH ME.
DID YOU FORGET THAT YOU ALMOST KILLED ME? HUNH?
WHAT'S THAT SAY ABOUT YOU, MR. PERFECT?

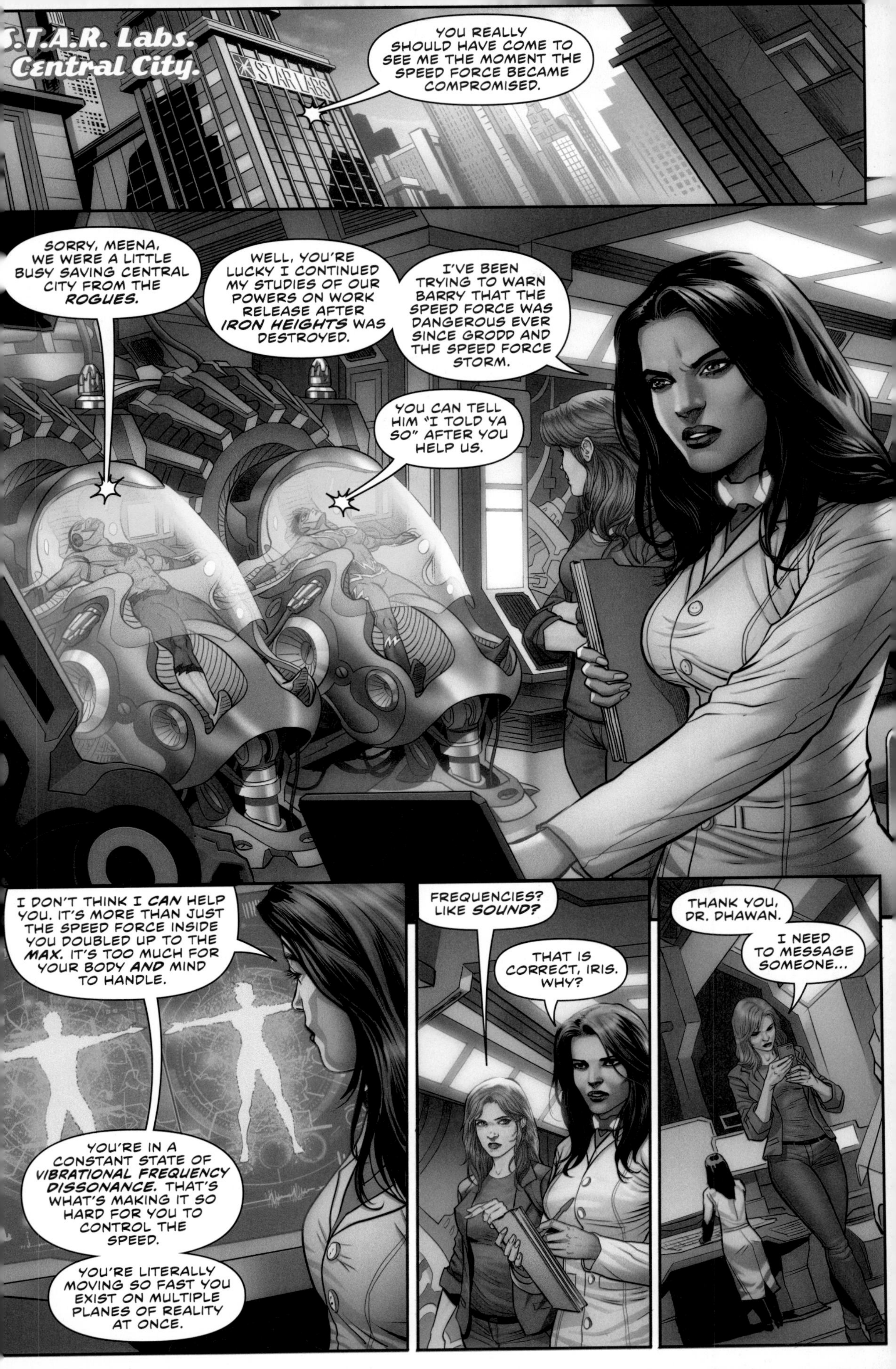
S.T.A.R. Labs. Central City.
STAR LABS
YOU REALLY SHOULD HAVE COME TO SEE ME THE MOMENT THE SPEED FORCE BECAME COMPROMISED.
SORRY, MEENA, WE WERE A LITTLE BUSY SAVING CENTRAL CITY FROM THE ROGUES.
WELL, YOU'RE LUCKY I CONTINUED MY STUDIES OF OUR POWERS ON WORK RELEASE AFTER IRON HEIGHTS WAS DESTROYED.
I'VE BEEN TRYING TO WARN BARRY THAT THE SPEED FORCE WAS DANGEROUS EVER SINCE GRODD AND THE SPEED FORCE STORM.
YOU CAN TELL HIM "I TOLD YA SO" AFTER YOU HELP US.
I DON'T THINK I CAN HELP YOU. IT'S MORE THAN JUST THE SPEED FORCE INSIDE YOU DOUBLED UP TO THE MAX. IT'S TOO MUCH FOR YOUR BODY AND MIND TO HANDLE.
YOU'RE IN A CONSTANT STATE OF VIBRATIONAL FREQUENCY DISSONANCE. THAT'S WHAT'S MAKING IT SO HARD FOR YOU TO CONTROL THE SPEED.
YOU'RE LITERALLY MOVING SO FAST YOU EXIST ON MULTIPLE PLANES OF REALITY AT ONCE.
FREQUENCIES? LIKE SOUND?
THAT IS CORRECT, IRIS. WHY?
THANK YOU, DR. DHAWAN.
I NEED TO MESSAGE SOMEONE...

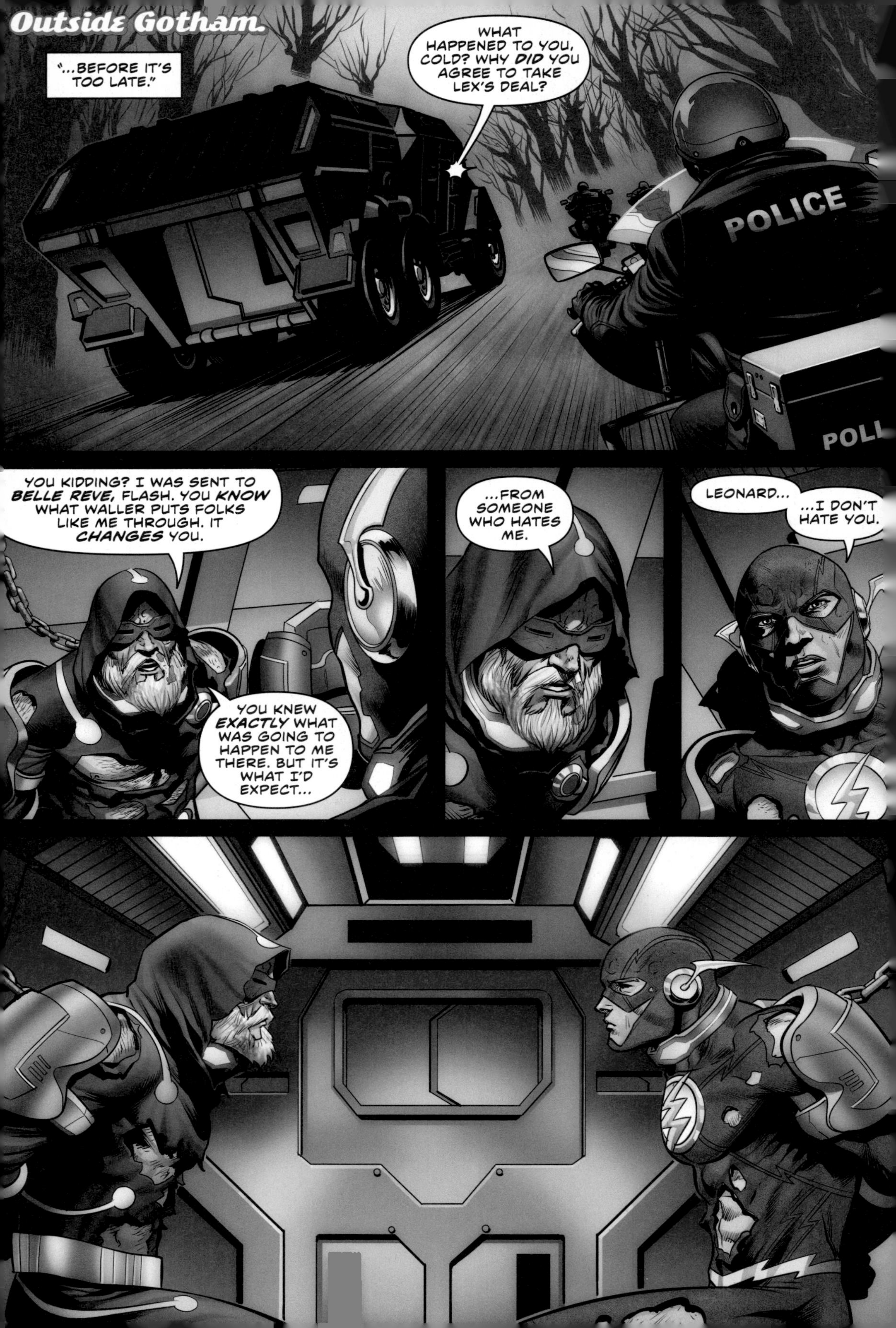

Outside Gotham.
"...BEFORE IT'S TOO LATE."
WHAT HAPPENED TO YOU, COLD? WHY DID YOU AGREE TO TAKE LEX'S DEAL?
POLICE
POLI
YOU KIDDING? I WAS SENT TO BELLE REVE, FLASH. YOU KNOW WHAT WALLER PUTS FOLKS LIKE ME THROUGH. IT CHANGES YOU.
YOU KNEW EXACTLY WHAT WAS GOING TO HAPPEN TO ME THERE. BUT IT'S WHAT I'D EXPECT...
...FROM SOMEONE WHO HATES ME.
LEONARD...
...I DON'T HATE YOU.

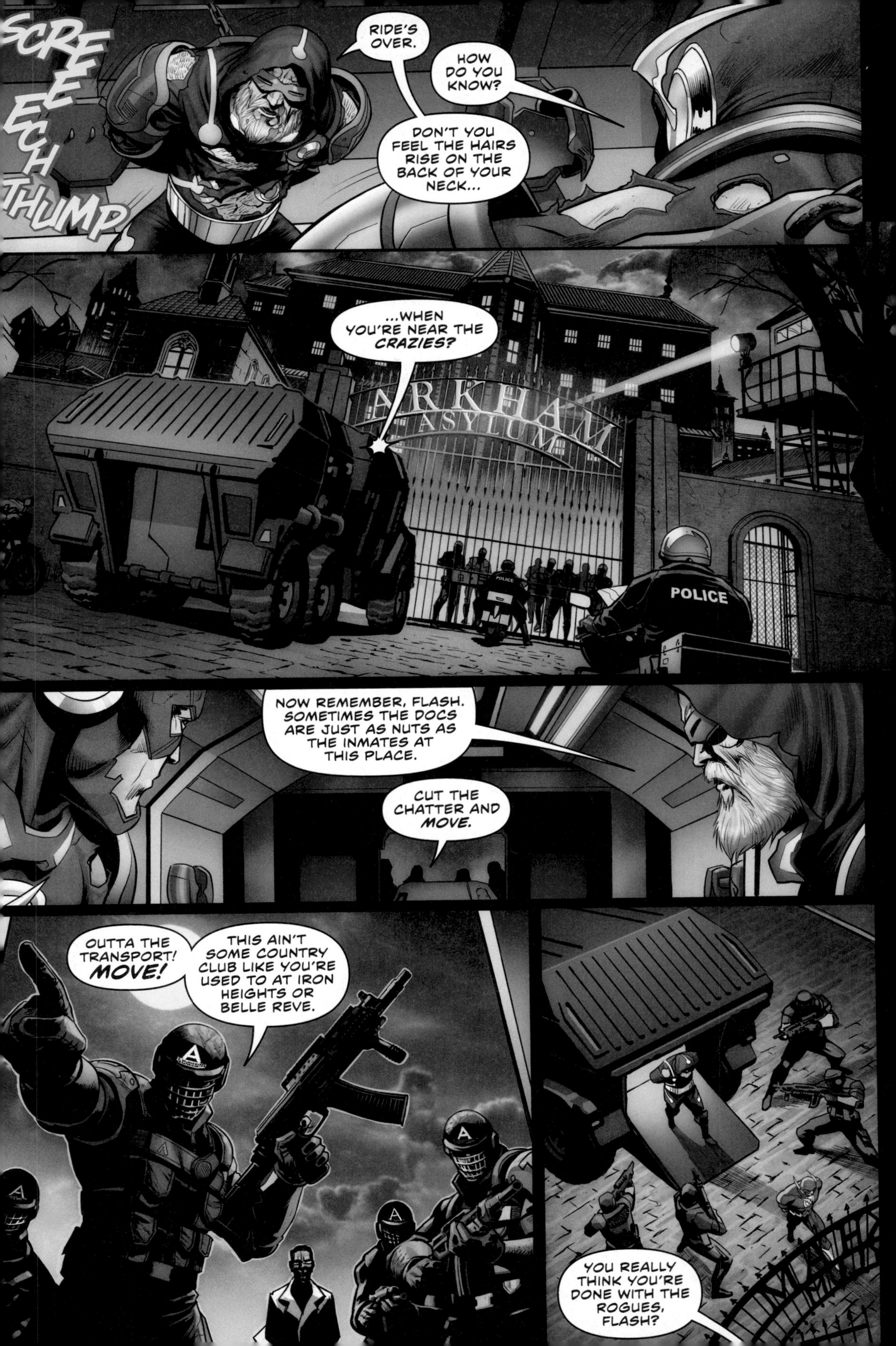
SCREEECH
THUMP
RIDE'S OVER.
HOW DO YOU KNOW?
DON'T YOU FEEL THE HAIRS RISE ON THE BACK OF YOUR NECK...
...WHEN YOU'RE NEAR THE *CRAZIES?*
ARKHAM ASYLUM
POLICE
POLICE
NOW REMEMBER, FLASH. SOMETIMES THE DOCS ARE JUST AS NUTS AS THE INMATES AT THIS PLACE.
CUT THE CHATTER AND *MOVE.*
OUTTA THE TRANSPORT! ***MOVE!***
THIS AIN'T SOME COUNTRY CLUB LIKE YOU'RE USED TO AT IRON HEIGHTS OR BELLE REVE.
YOU REALLY THINK YOU'RE DONE WITH THE ROGUES, FLASH?

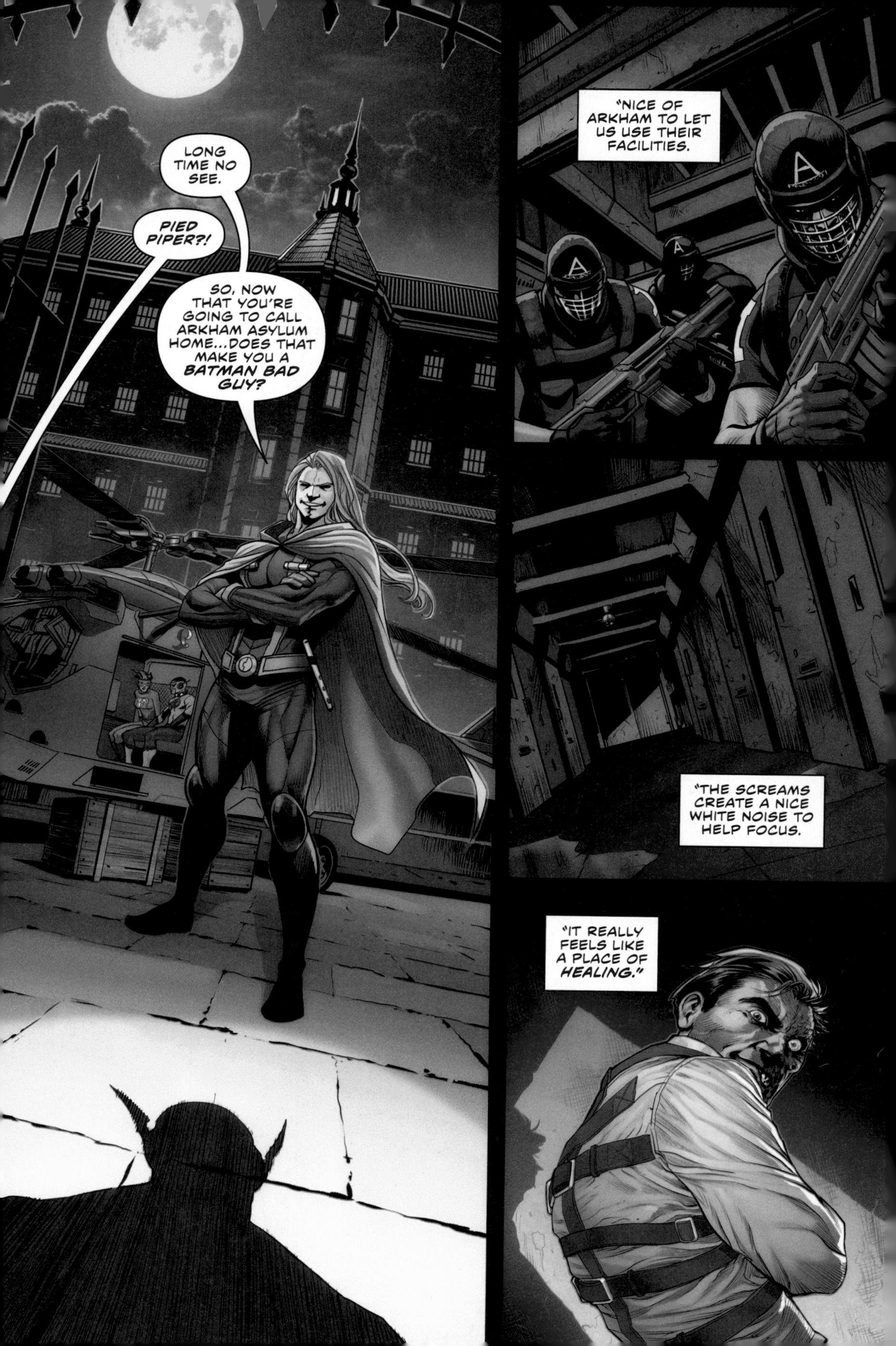
LONG TIME NO SEE.
PIED PIPER?!
SO, NOW THAT YOU'RE GOING TO CALL ARKHAM ASYLUM HOME...DOES THAT MAKE YOU A *BATMAN BAD GUY?*
"NICE OF ARKHAM TO LET US USE THEIR FACILITIES.
"THE SCREAMS CREATE A NICE WHITE NOISE TO HELP FOCUS.
"IT REALLY FEELS LIKE A PLACE OF *HEALING.*"

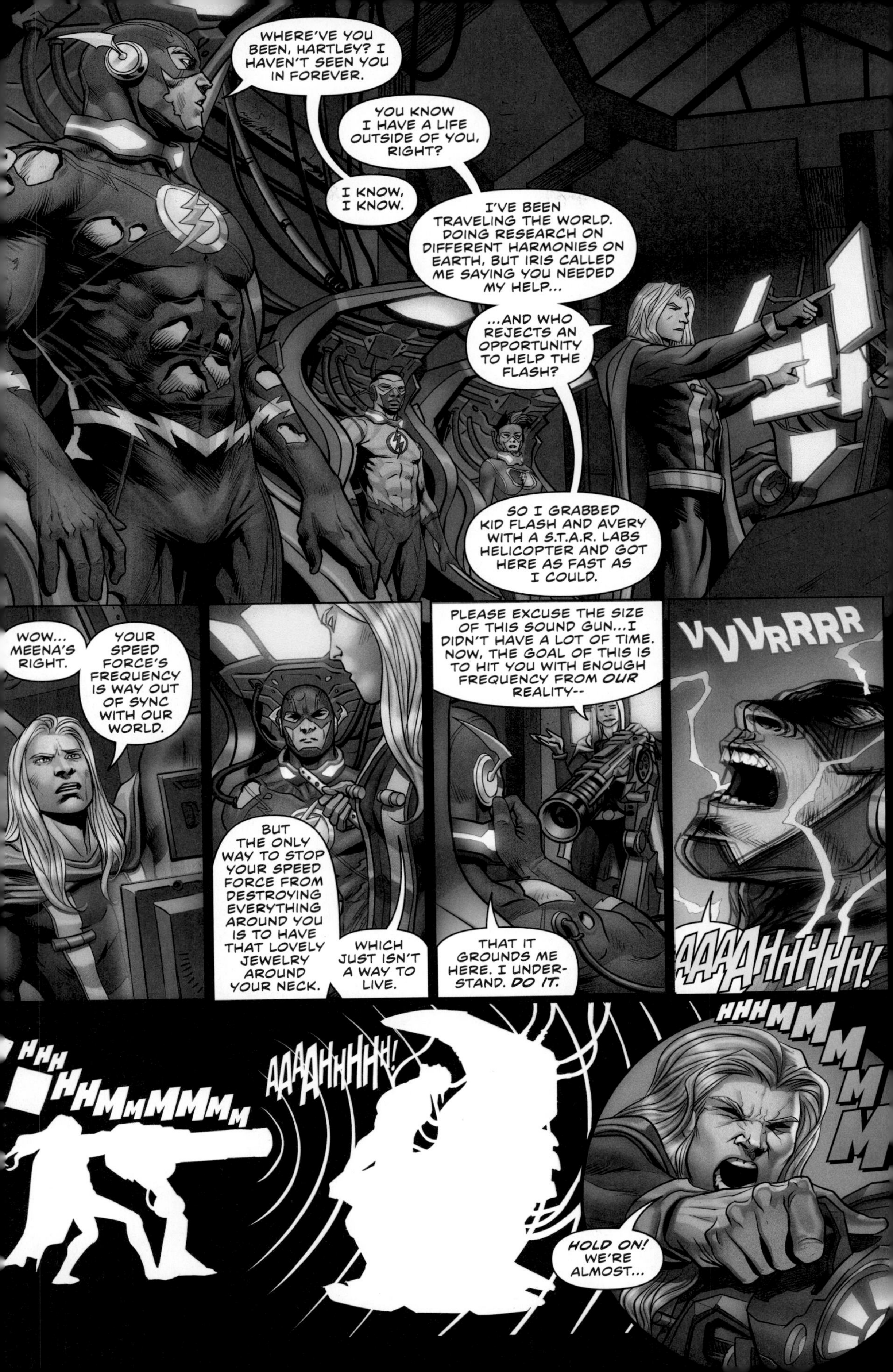
WHERE'VE YOU BEEN, HARTLEY? I HAVEN'T SEEN YOU IN FOREVER.
YOU KNOW I HAVE A LIFE OUTSIDE OF YOU, RIGHT?
I KNOW, I KNOW.
I'VE BEEN TRAVELING THE WORLD. DOING RESEARCH ON DIFFERENT HARMONIES ON EARTH, BUT IRIS CALLED ME SAYING YOU NEEDED MY HELP...
...AND WHO REJECTS AN OPPORTUNITY TO HELP THE FLASH?
SO I GRABBED KID FLASH AND AVERY WITH A S.T.A.R. LABS HELICOPTER AND GOT HERE AS FAST AS I COULD.
WOW... MEENA'S RIGHT.
YOUR SPEED FORCE'S FREQUENCY IS WAY OUT OF SYNC WITH OUR WORLD.
BUT THE ONLY WAY TO STOP YOUR SPEED FORCE FROM DESTROYING EVERYTHING AROUND YOU IS TO HAVE THAT LOVELY JEWELRY AROUND YOUR NECK.
WHICH JUST ISN'T A WAY TO LIVE.
PLEASE EXCUSE THE SIZE OF THIS SOUND GUN...I DIDN'T HAVE A LOT OF TIME. NOW, THE GOAL OF THIS IS TO HIT YOU WITH ENOUGH FREQUENCY FROM *OUR* REALITY--
THAT IT GROUNDS ME HERE. I UNDERSTAND. *DO IT.*
VVVRRRR
AAAAHHHHH!
HHHHMMMMMMM
AAAAHHHH!
HHHMMMMMMM
HOLD ON! WE'RE ALMOST...

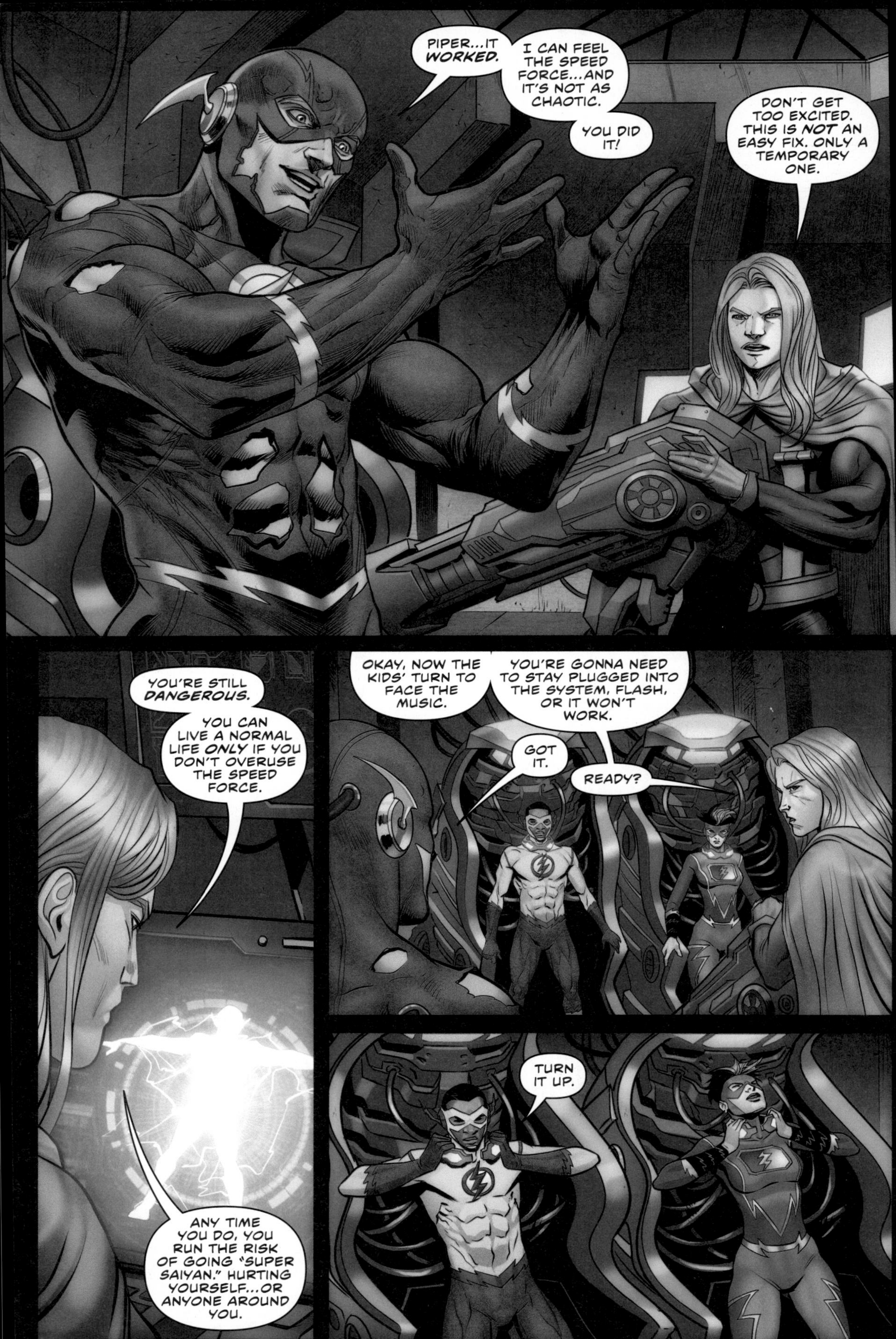
PIPER...IT WORKED.
I CAN FEEL THE SPEED FORCE...AND IT'S NOT AS CHAOTIC.
YOU DID IT!
DON'T GET TOO EXCITED. THIS IS NOT AN EASY FIX. ONLY A TEMPORARY ONE.
YOU'RE STILL DANGEROUS.
YOU CAN LIVE A NORMAL LIFE ONLY IF YOU DON'T OVERUSE THE SPEED FORCE.
ANY TIME YOU DO, YOU RUN THE RISK OF GOING "SUPER SAIYAN." HURTING YOURSELF...OR ANYONE AROUND YOU.
OKAY, NOW THE KIDS' TURN TO FACE THE MUSIC.
YOU'RE GONNA NEED TO STAY PLUGGED INTO THE SYSTEM, FLASH, OR IT WON'T WORK.
GOT IT.
READY?
TURN IT UP.

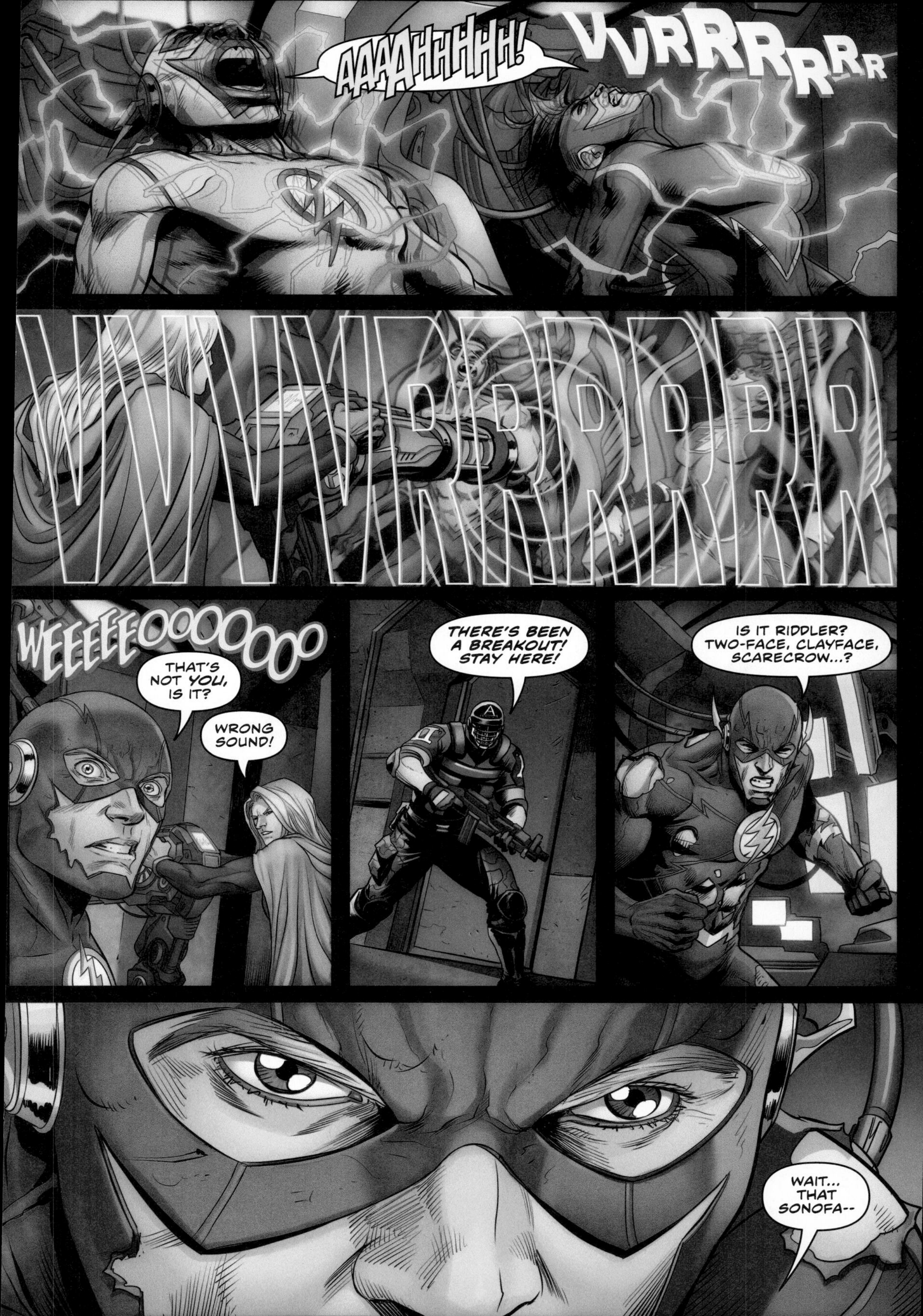
AAAAHHHHH!
VVRRRRRR
VVVVRRRRRR
WEEEEEOOOOOOOO
THAT'S NOT YOU, IS IT?
WRONG SOUND!
THERE'S BEEN A BREAKOUT! STAY HERE!
IS IT RIDDLER? TWO-FACE, CLAYFACE, SCARECROW...?
WAIT... THAT SONOFA--

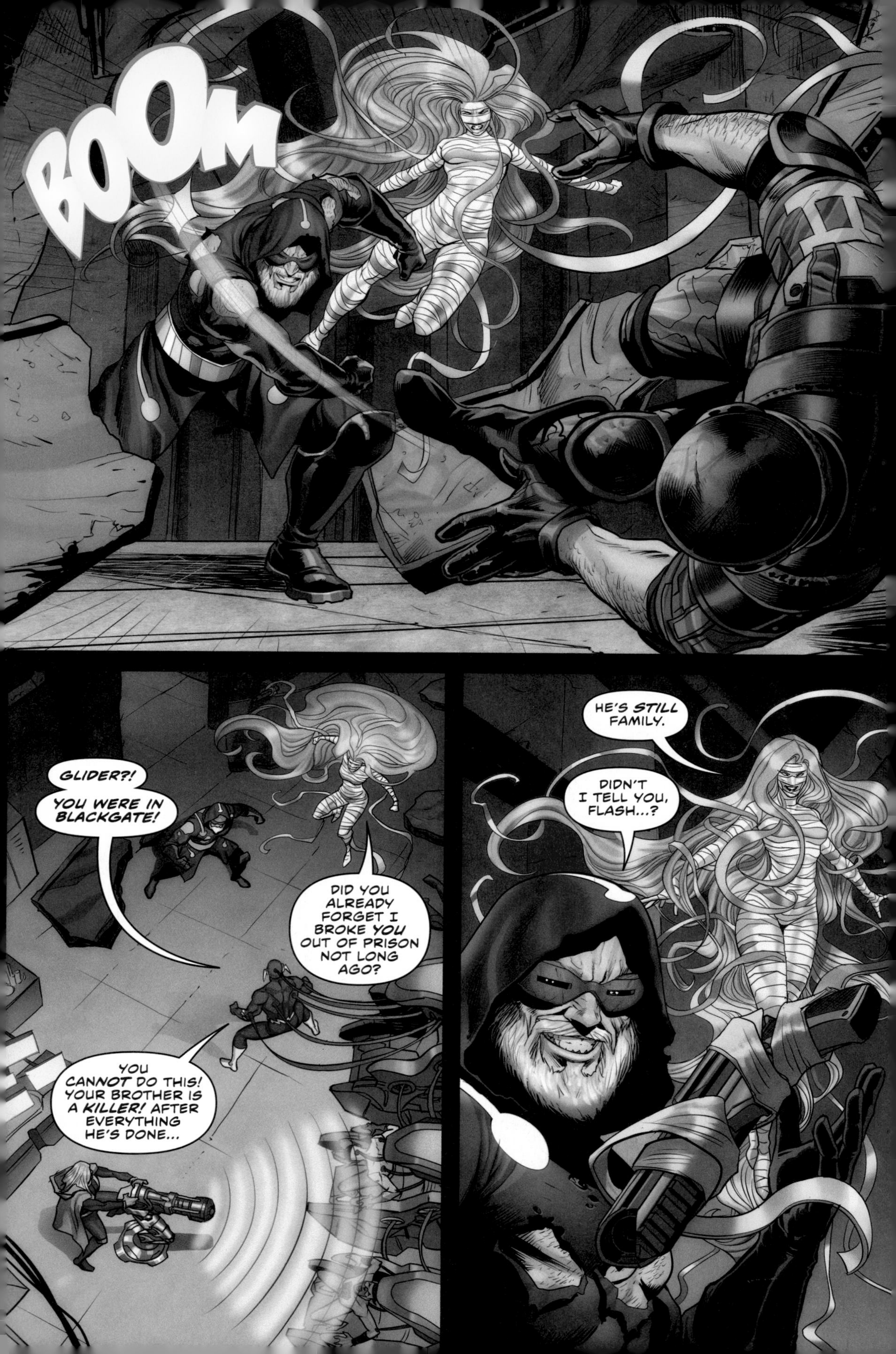
BOOM
GLIDER?!
YOU WERE IN BLACKGATE!
DID YOU ALREADY FORGET I BROKE YOU OUT OF PRISON NOT LONG AGO?
YOU CANNOT DO THIS! YOUR BROTHER IS A KILLER! AFTER EVERYTHING HE'S DONE...
HE'S STILL FAMILY.
DIDN'T I TELL YOU, FLASH...?

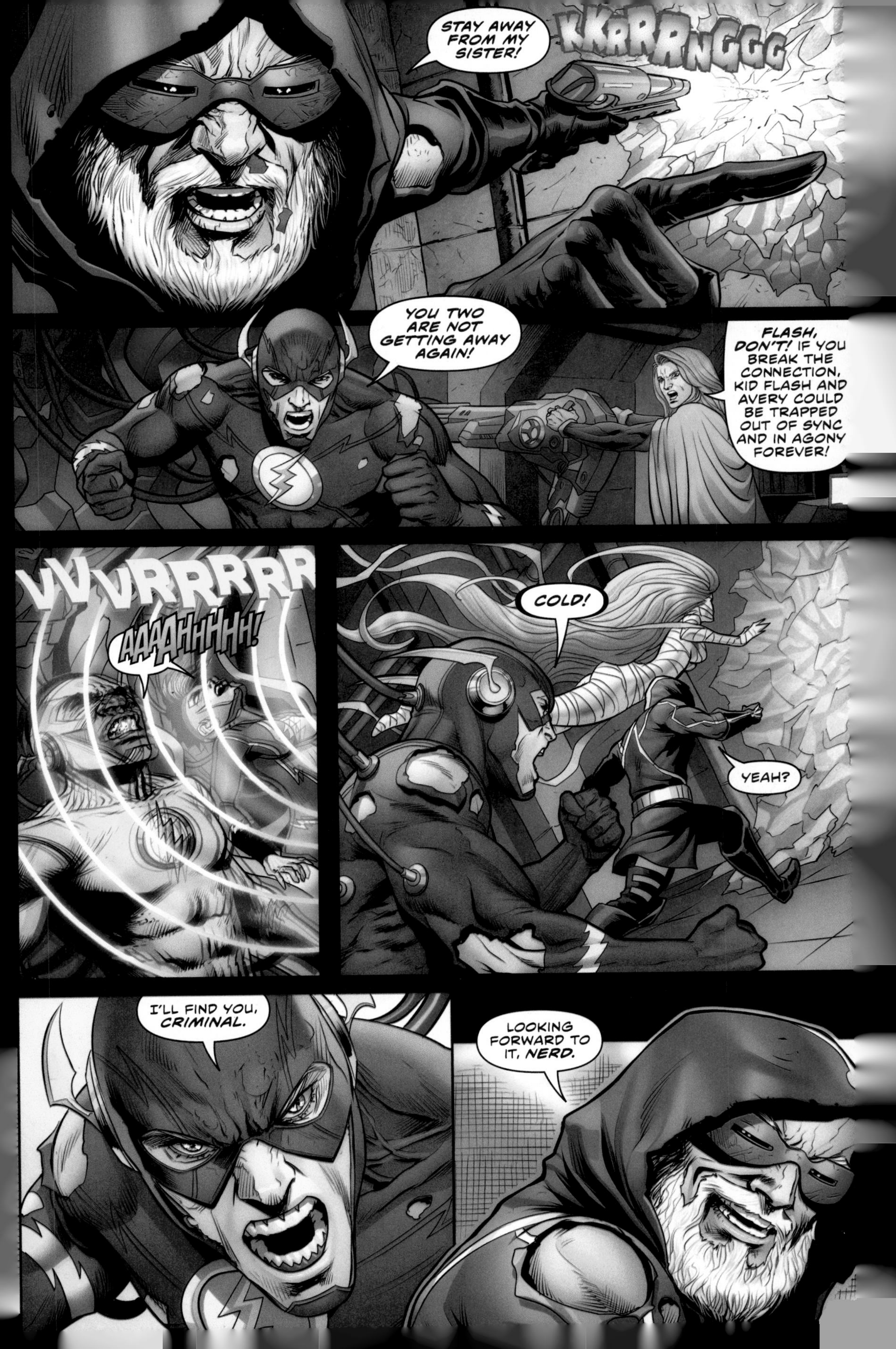
STAY AWAY FROM MY SISTER!
KKRRRNGGG
YOU TWO ARE NOT GETTING AWAY AGAIN!
FLASH, DON'T! IF YOU BREAK THE CONNECTION, KID FLASH AND AVERY COULD BE TRAPPED OUT OF SYNC AND IN AGONY FOREVER!
VVVRRRRR
AAAAHHHH!
COLD!
YEAH?
I'LL FIND YOU, CRIMINAL.
LOOKING FORWARD TO IT, NERD.

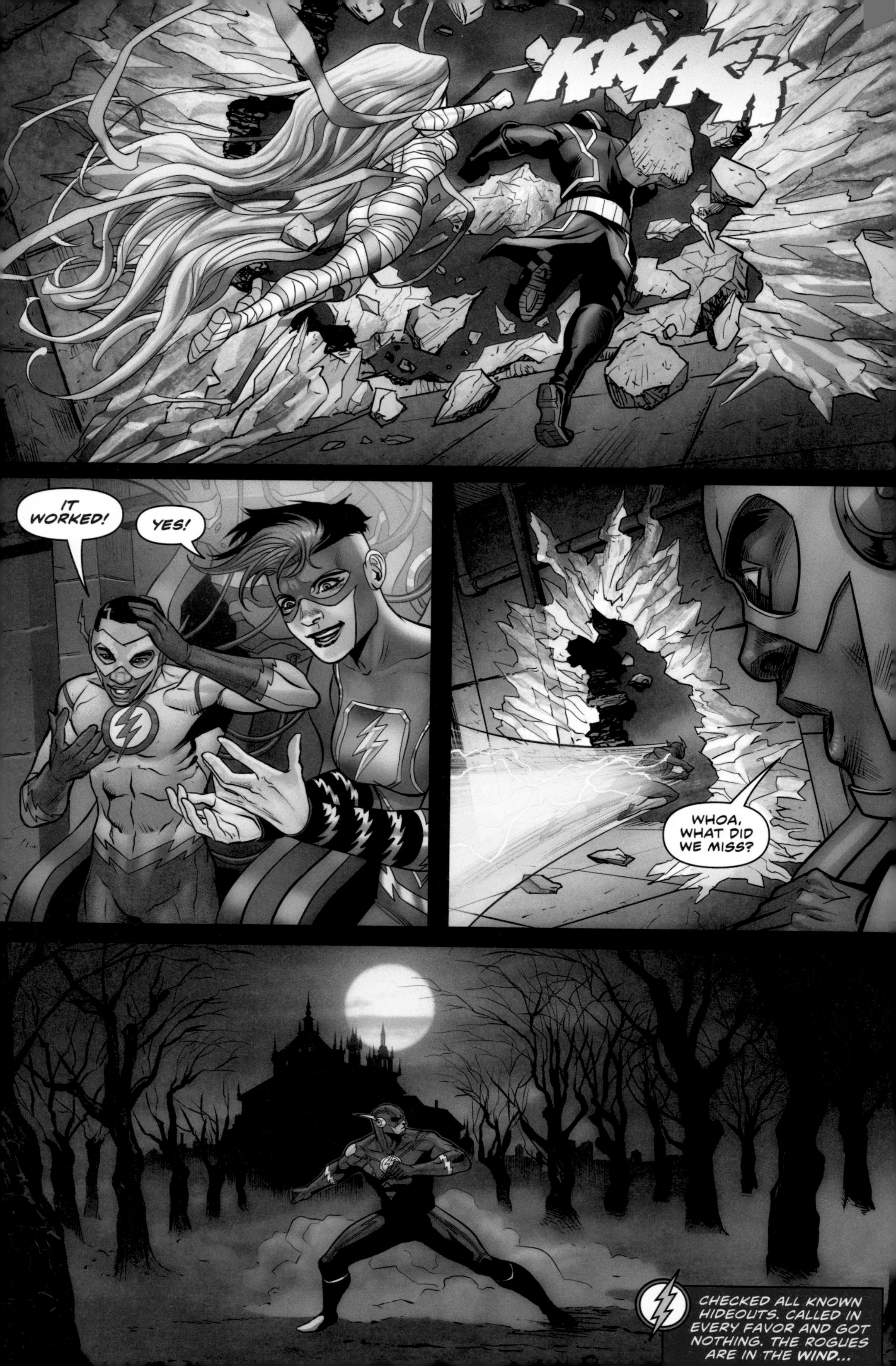
KRAK
IT WORKED!
YES!
WHOA, WHAT DID WE MISS?
CHECKED ALL KNOWN HIDEOUTS. CALLED IN EVERY FAVOR AND GOT NOTHING. THE ROGUES ARE IN THE WIND...

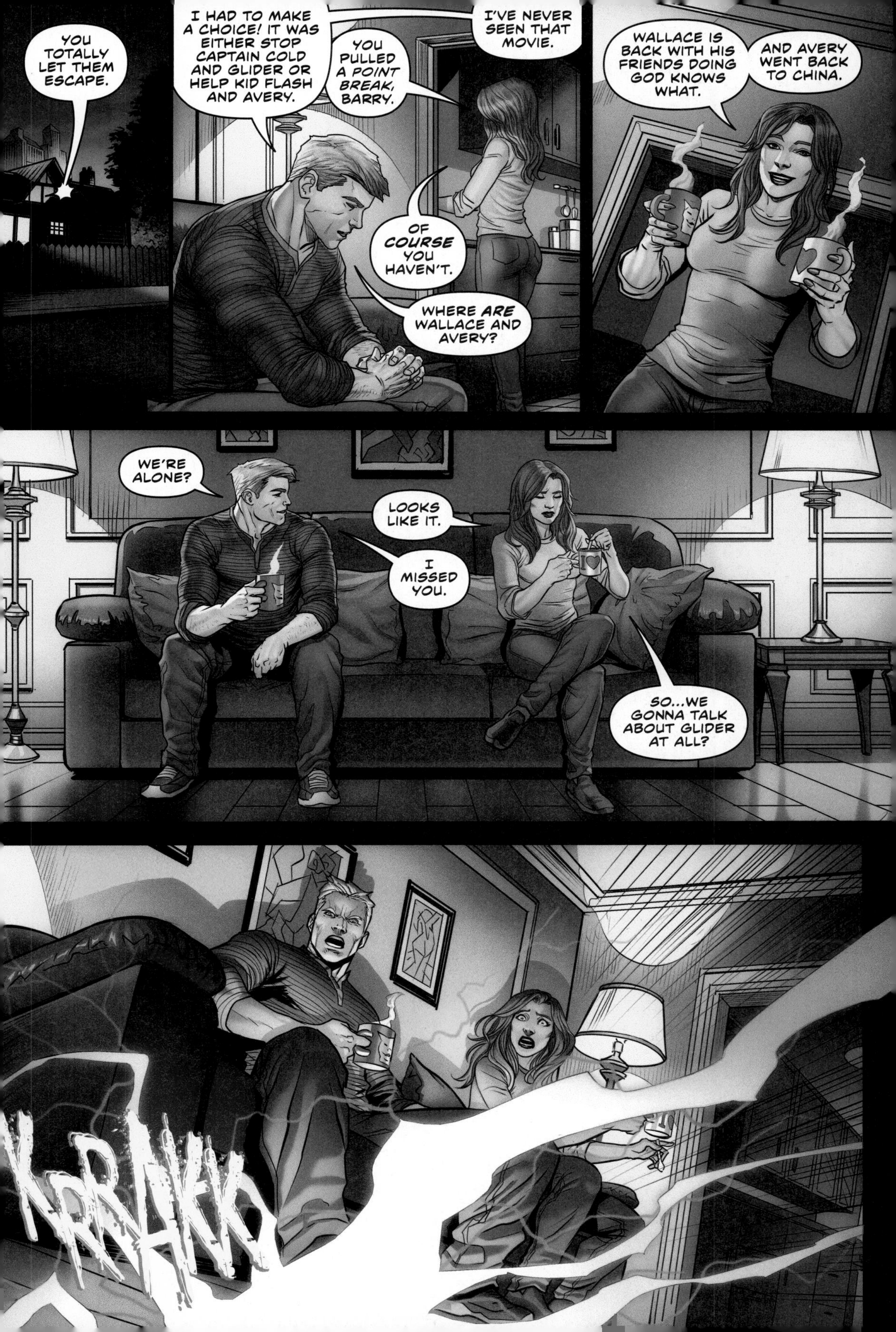
YOU TOTALLY LET THEM ESCAPE.
I HAD TO MAKE A CHOICE! IT WAS EITHER STOP CAPTAIN COLD AND GLIDER OR HELP KID FLASH AND AVERY.
YOU PULLED A *POINT BREAK*, BARRY.
I'VE NEVER SEEN THAT MOVIE.
OF *COURSE* YOU HAVEN'T.
WHERE *ARE* WALLACE AND AVERY?
WALLACE IS BACK WITH HIS FRIENDS DOING GOD KNOWS WHAT.
AND AVERY WENT BACK TO CHINA.
WE'RE ALONE?
LOOKS LIKE IT.
I MISSED YOU.
SO...WE GONNA TALK ABOUT GLIDER AT ALL?
KRAKK

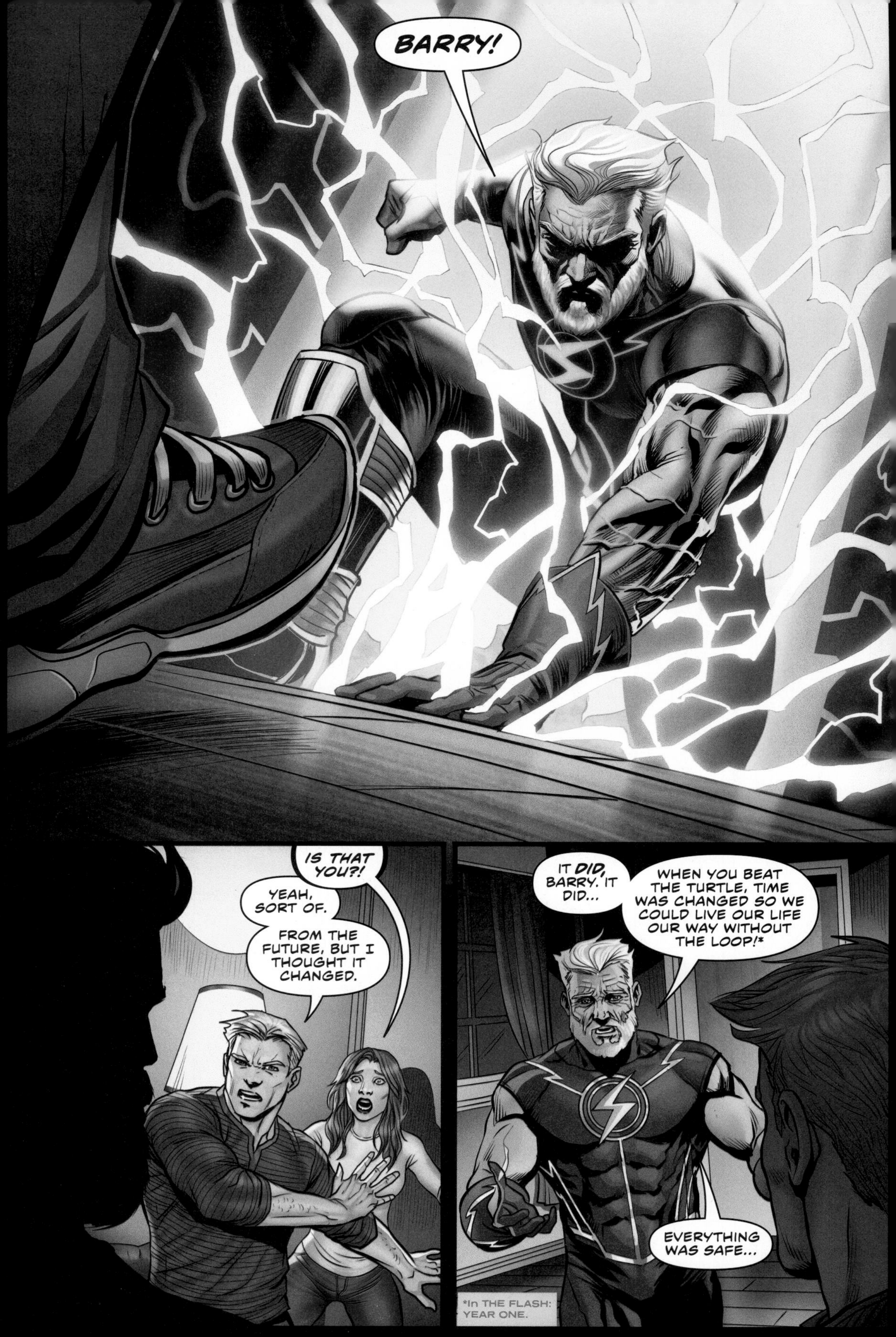
BARRY!
IS THAT YOU?!
YEAH, SORT OF.
FROM THE FUTURE, BUT I THOUGHT IT CHANGED.
IT *DID*, BARRY. IT DID...
WHEN YOU BEAT THE TURTLE, TIME WAS CHANGED SO WE COULD LIVE OUR LIFE OUR WAY WITHOUT THE LOOP!*
EVERYTHING WAS SAFE...
*In THE FLASH: YEAR ONE.

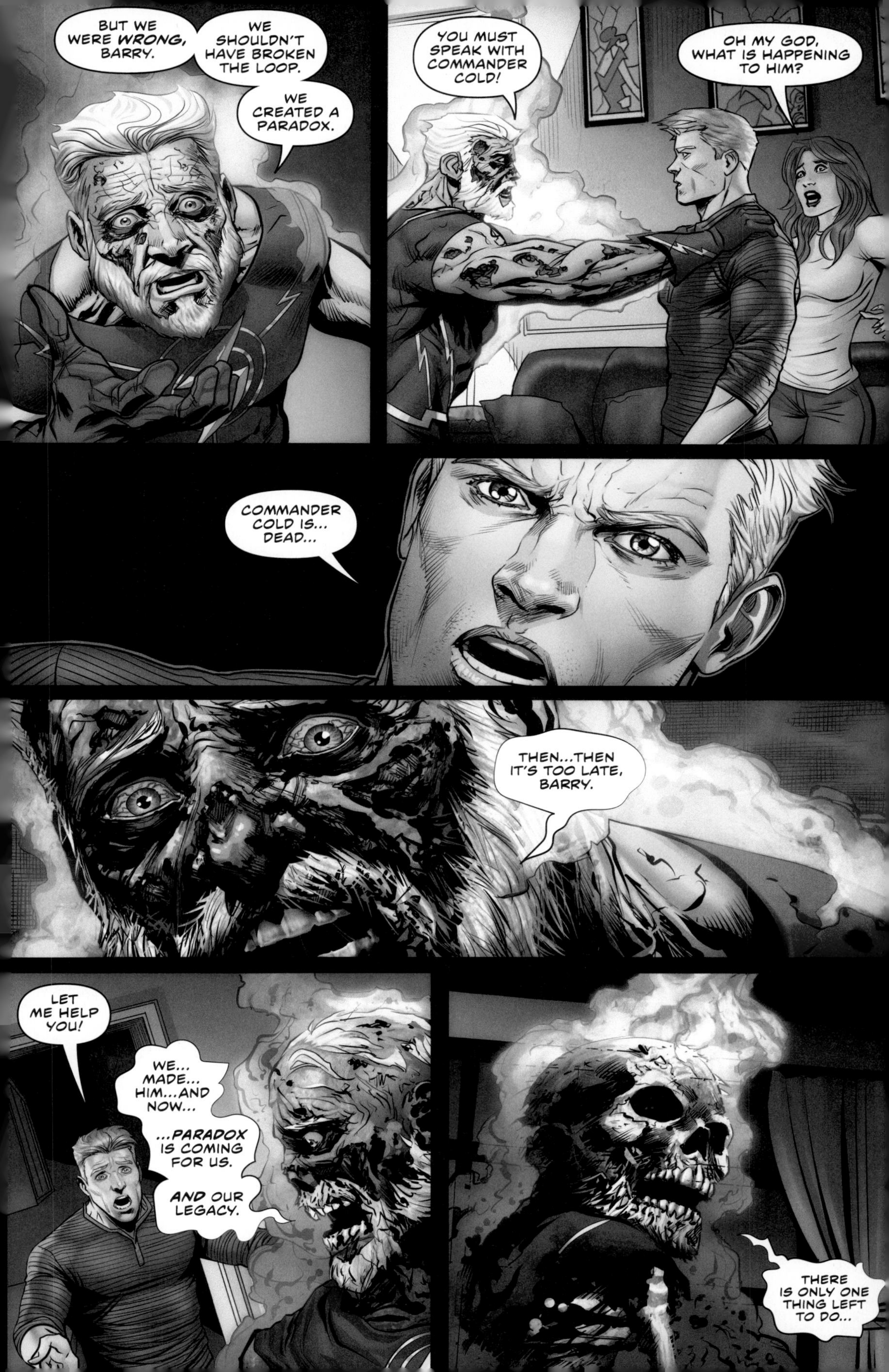
BUT WE WERE *WRONG*, BARRY.
WE SHOULDN'T HAVE BROKEN THE LOOP.
WE CREATED A PARADOX.
YOU MUST SPEAK WITH COMMANDER COLD!
OH MY GOD, WHAT IS HAPPENING TO HIM?
COMMANDER COLD IS... DEAD...
THEN...THEN IT'S TOO LATE, BARRY.
LET ME HELP YOU!
WE... MADE... HIM...AND NOW...
...*PARADOX* IS COMING FOR US.
AND OUR LEGACY.
THERE IS ONLY ONE THING LEFT TO DO...

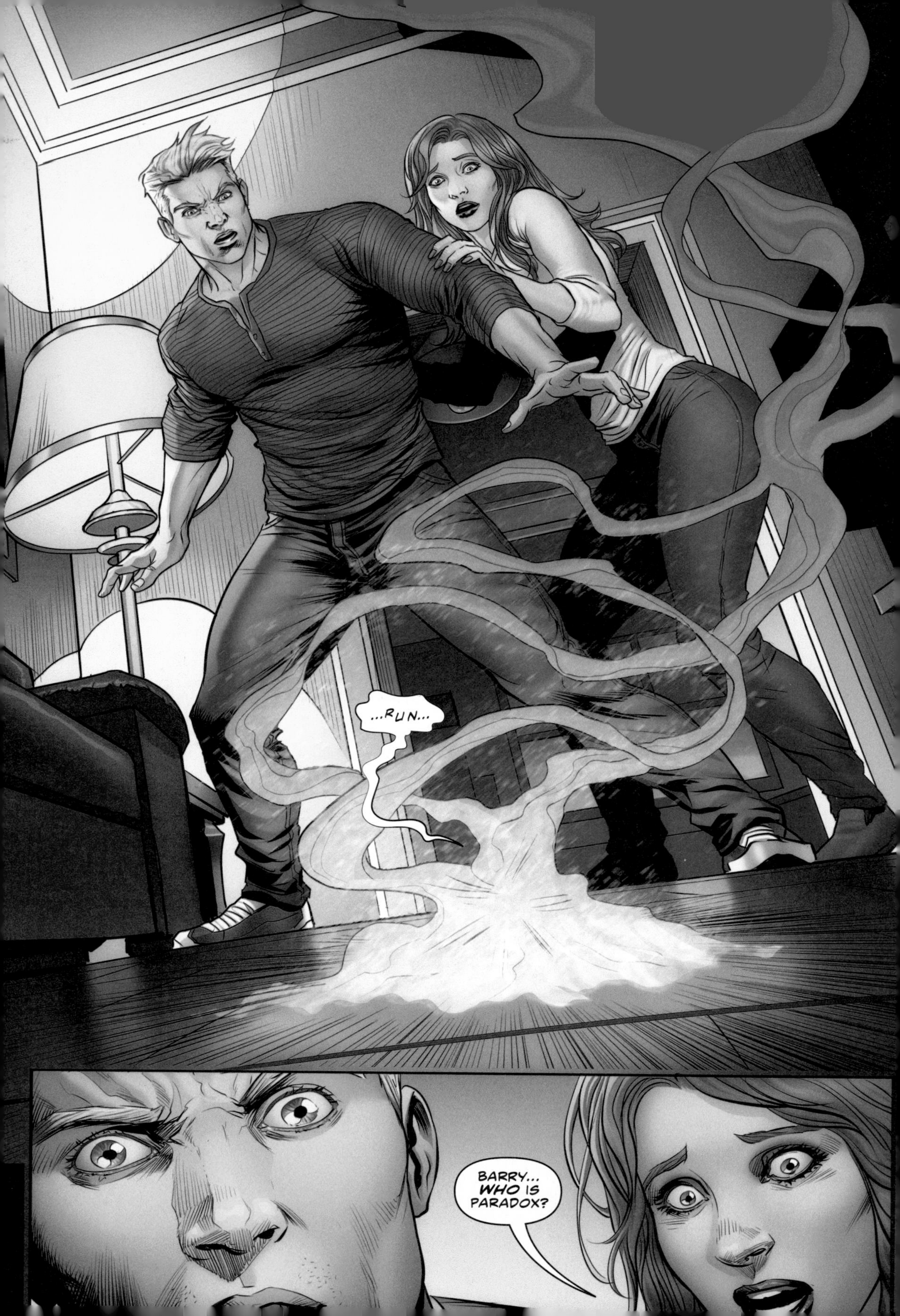
...RUN...
BARRY... WHO IS PARADOX?

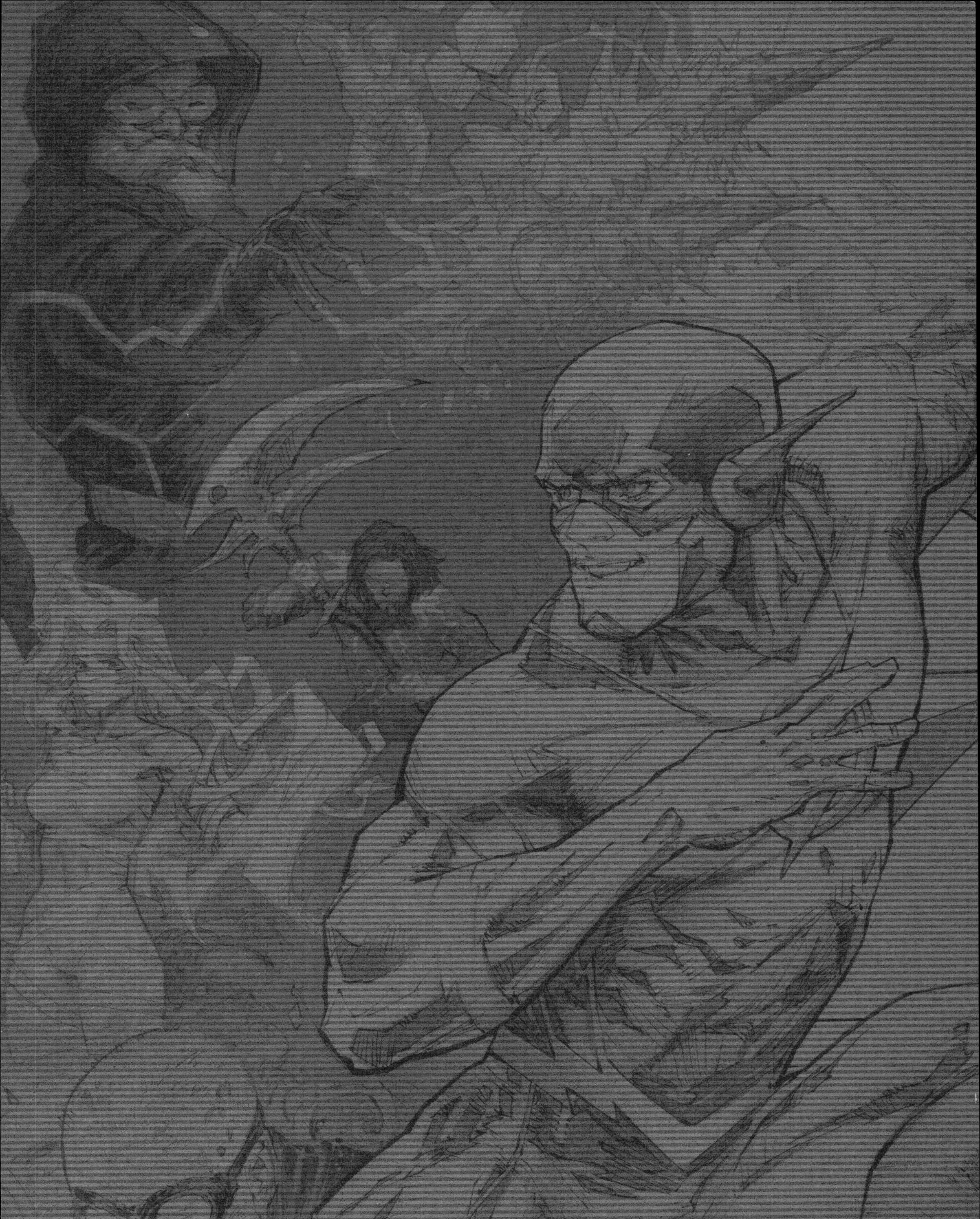

VARIANT COVER GALLERY

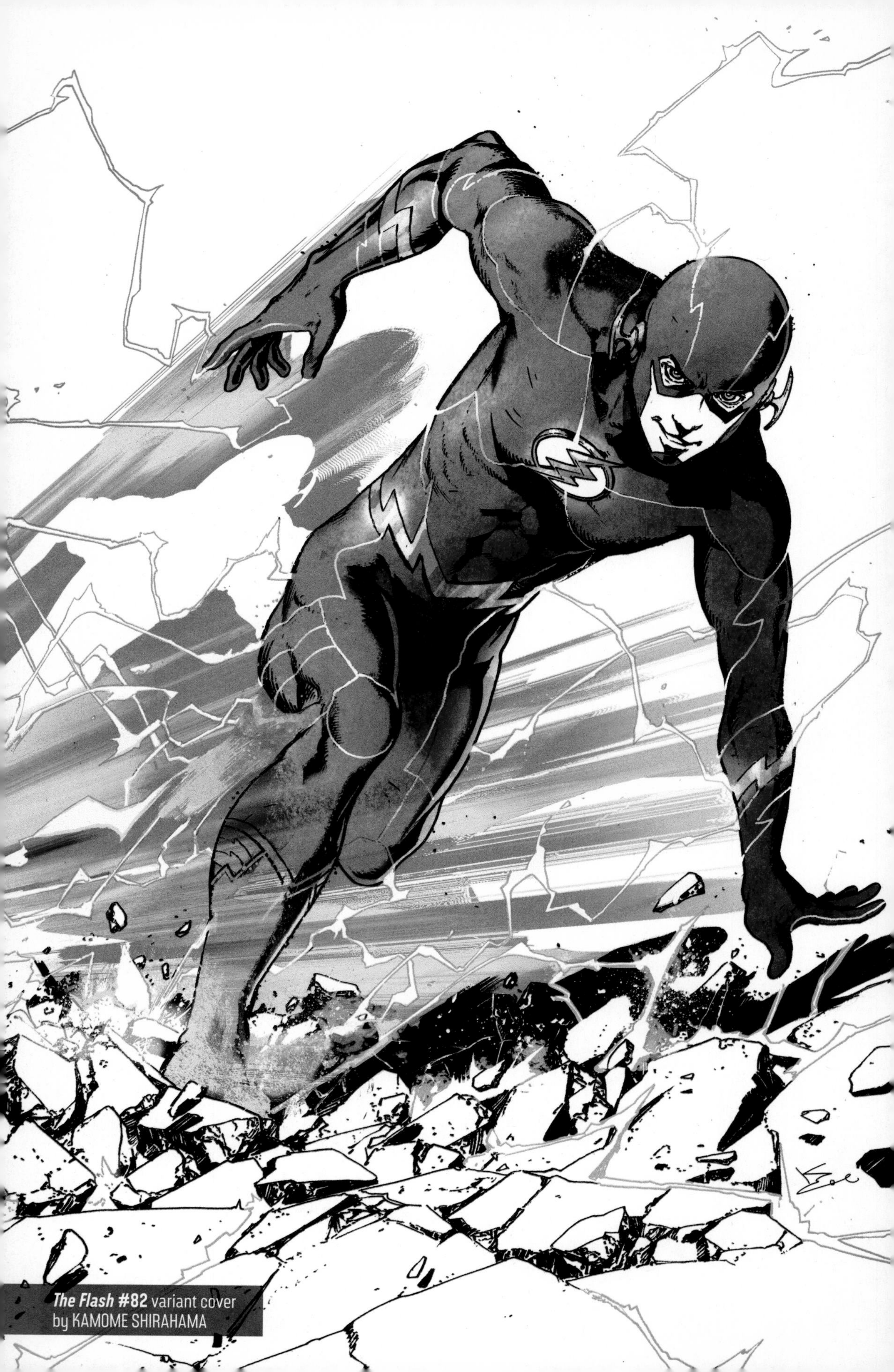

The Flash **#82** variant cover
by KAMOME SHIRAHAMA

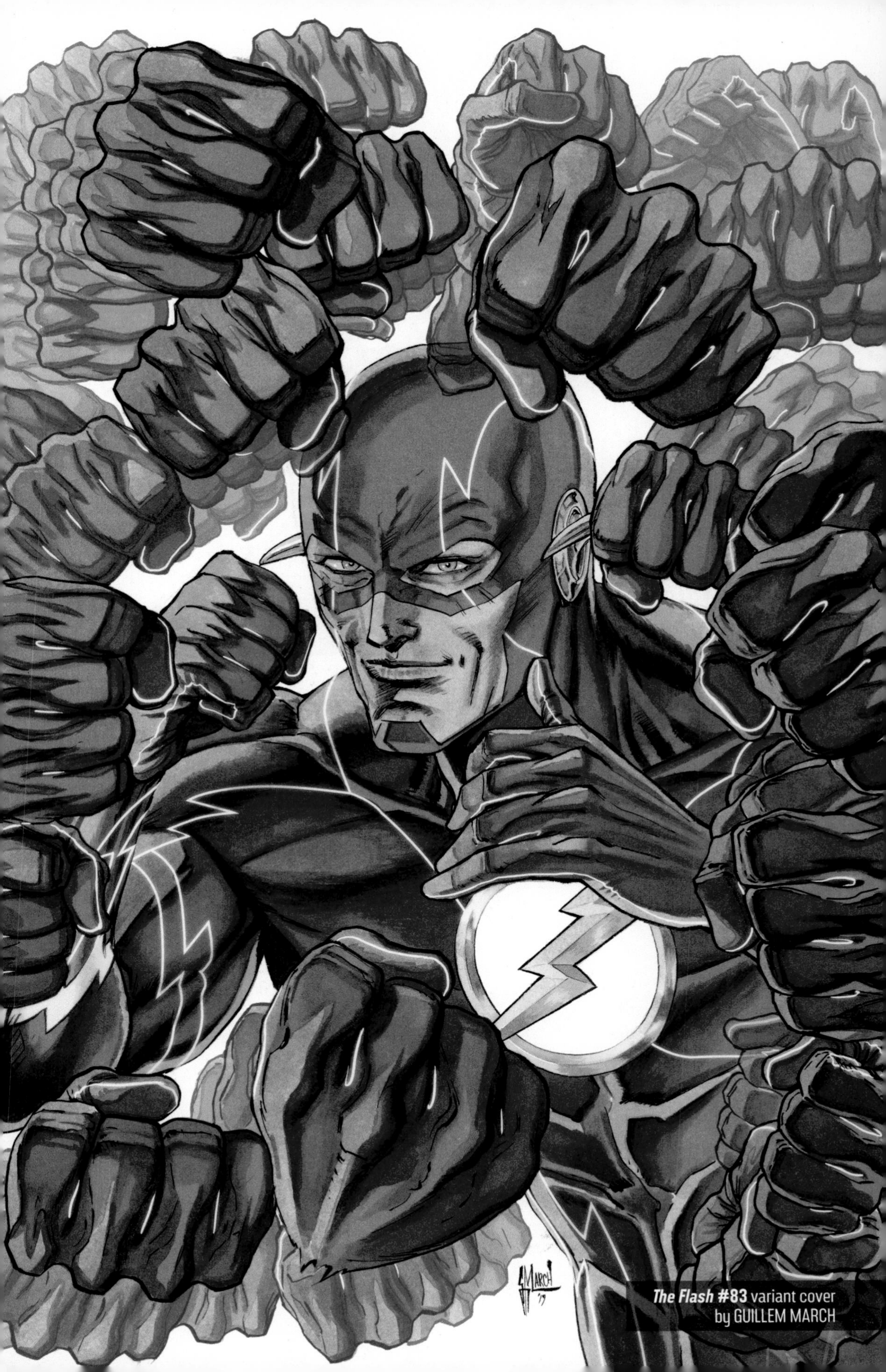
MARCH '19

The Flash **#83** variant cover
by GUILLEM MARCH

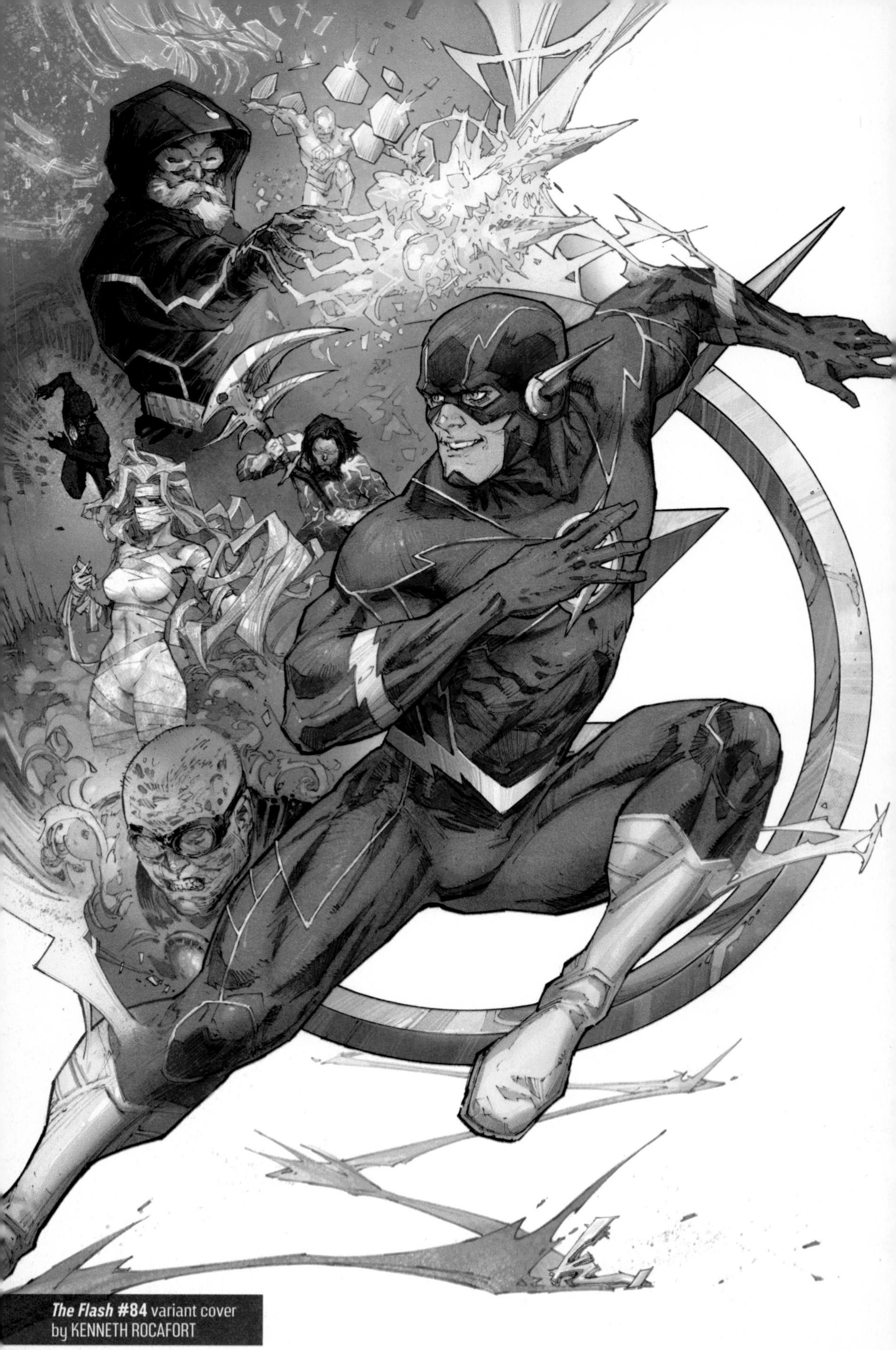

***The Flash* #84** variant cover
by KENNETH ROCAFORT

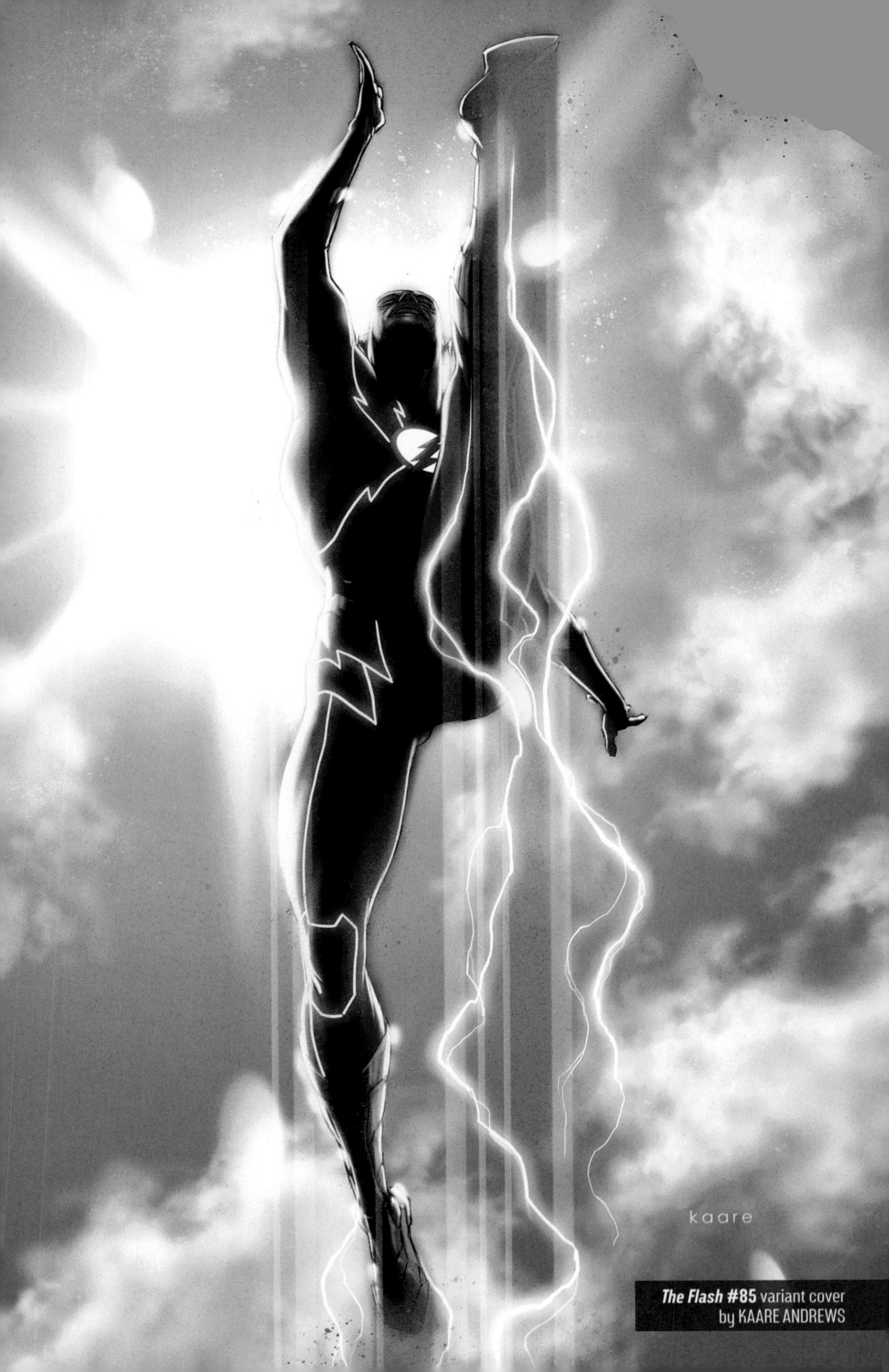
kaare

***The Flash* #85** variant cover
by KAARE ANDREWS

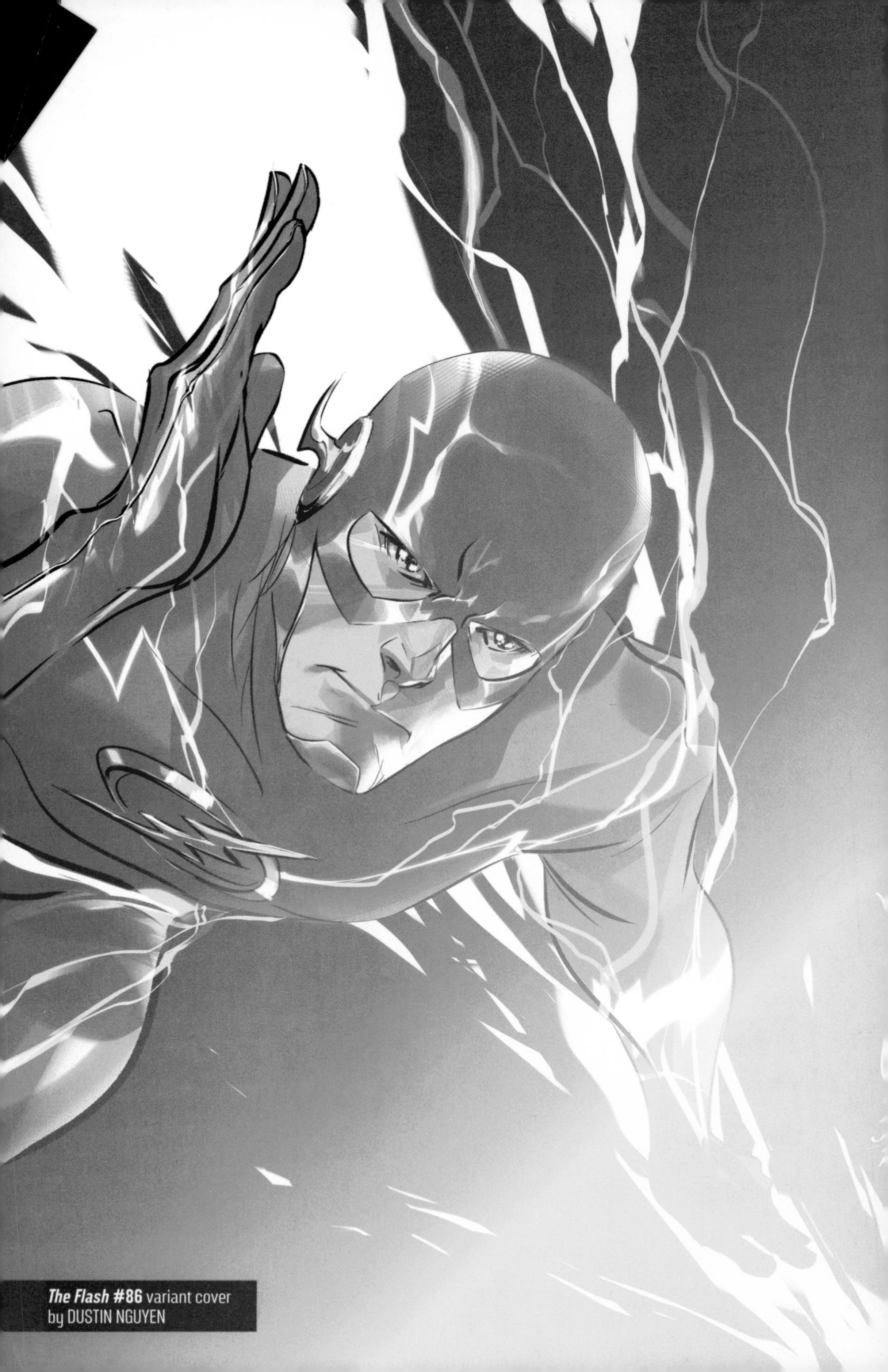

The Flash **#86** variant cover
by DUSTIN NGUYEN

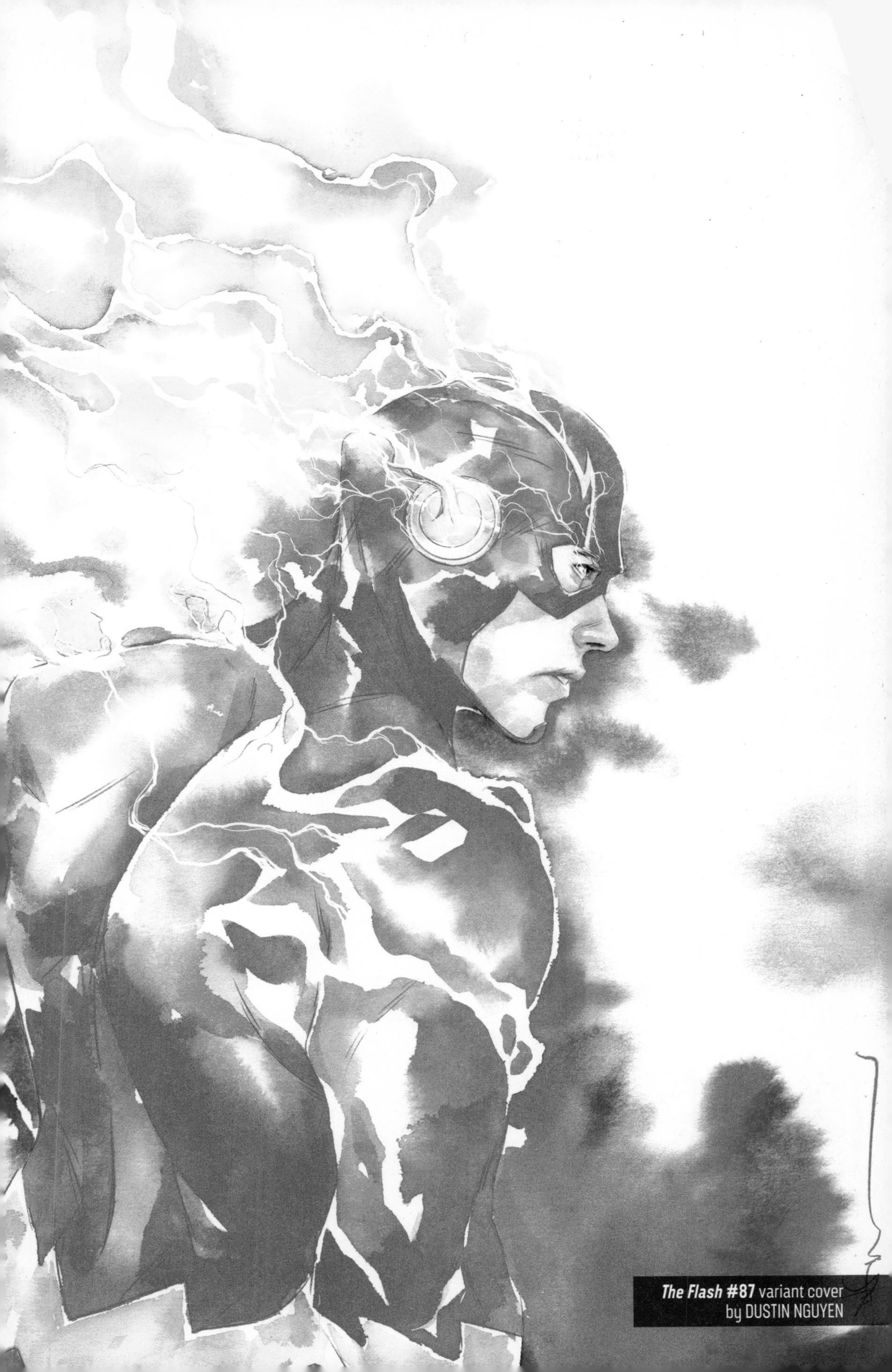

***The Flash* #87** variant cover
by DUSTIN NGUYEN

FLASHPOINT

GEOFF JOHNS
with ANDY KUBERT

FLASHPOINT: THE WORLD OF FLASHPOINT FEATURING BATMAN

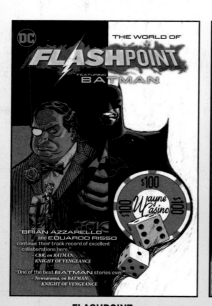

**FLASHPOINT:
THE WORLD OF FLASHPOINT
FEATURING BATMAN**

**FLASHPOINT:
THE WORLD OF FLASHPOINT
FEATURING GREEN LANTERN**